Social History of Canada

Allan Greer and Craig Heron, general editors

Sweatshop Strife:
Class, Ethnicity, and Gender in the Jewish Labour Movement
of Toronto, 1900–1939

In the first half of the twentieth century, many of Toronto's immigrant Jews eked out a living in the needle-trade sweatshops of Spadina Avenue. In response to their exploitation on the shop floor, immigrant Jewish garment workers built one of the most advanced sections of the Canadian and American labour movements. Much more than a collective bargaining agency, Toronto's Jewish labour movement had a distinctly socialist orientation and grew out of a vibrant Jewish working-class culture.

Ruth Frager examines the development of this unique movement, its sources of strength, and its limitations, focusing particularly on the complex interplay of class, ethnic, and gender interests and identities in the history of the movement. She examines the relationships between Jewish workers and Jewish manufacturers as well as relations between Jewish and non-Jewish workers and male and female workers in the city's clothing industry.

In its prime, Toronto's Jewish labour movement struggled not only to improve harsh sweatshop conditions but also to bring about a fundamental socialist transformation. It was an uphill battle. Drastic economic downturns, harsh employer offensives, and state repression all worked against unionists' workplace demands. Ethnic, gender, and ideological divisions weakened the movement and were manipulated by employers and their allies.

Drawing on her knowledge of Yiddish, Frager has been able to gain access to original records that shed new light on an important chapter in Canadian ethnic, labour, and women's history.

RUTH A. FRAGER is a member of the Department of History, McMaster University.

RUTH A. FRAGER

Sweatshop Strife

Class, Ethnicity, and Gender
in the Jewish Labour
Movement of Toronto
1900–1939

UNIVERSITY OF TORONTO PRESS
Toronto Buffalo London

© University of Toronto Press Incorporated 1992
Toronto Buffalo London

Printed in Canada

ISBN 0-8020-5968-6 (cloth)
ISBN 0-8020-6895-2 (paper)

Printed on acid-free paper

Canadian Cataloguing in Publication Data

Frager, Ruth A., 1950–
  Sweatshop strife: class, ethnicity, and gender
  in the Jewish labour movement in Toronto, 1900–1939

  (The Social history of Canada ; 47)
  Includes bibliographical references and index.
  ISBN 0-8020-5968-6 (bound) ISBN 0-8020-6895-2 (pbk.)

  1. Jewish trade-unions – Ontario – Toronto.
  2. Labor movements – Ontario – Toronto – History.
  3. Women in the labor movement – Ontario – Toronto.
  4. Jews – Ontario – Toronto. I. Title. II. Series.

  HD8108.5.J4F73 1993   331.6'39240713541   C92-094700-X

Social History of Canada 47

This book has been published with the help of a grant from the Social Science Federation of Canada, using funds provided by the Social Sciences and Humanities Research Council of Canada.

For my parents, Anna and Sam Frager

Contents

APPENDIX / 219

Part A: Statistical Information on the Jewish Population of
Toronto / 219

Part B: Statistical Information on the Garment Workers of
Toronto / 220

Part C: The Garment Unions in Toronto / 223

Part D: Key Strikes in Toronto's Needle Trades / 225

NOTES / 229
SELECT BIBLIOGRAPHY / 273
INDEX / 287
PICTURE CREDITS / 299

Illustrations following pages 66 and 162

Acknowledgments

I am grateful to Labour Canada, the Memorial Foundation for Jewish Culture, and the Social Sciences and Humanities Research Council of Canada for financial support while working on this project. In addition, the publication of this book has been assisted by a grant from the Arts Research Board of McMaster University.

I am indebted to Christopher Armstrong, Michael Bodemann, Susan Houston, Leo Panitch, Norman Penner, and Gerald Tulchinsky for their helpful suggestions on earlier drafts of this manuscript. I am grateful to Irving Abella in particular for all his help. His knowledge of the sources in this area was of special benefit to me in the early stages of this project, and I have also benefited from his many further suggestions as the project progressed.

I am also grateful to my Yiddish teacher, Isaac Shoichet. In teaching me the first language of my grandparents, he not only facilitated my research but he also helped add a whole new dimension to my own experience of Jewish culture. He enthusiastically answered my hundreds of questions about Yiddish vocabulary and syntax and enriched my understanding of Yiddish literature.

The people I have interviewed have made an invaluable contribution to this study. They welcomed me into their homes and generously shared important aspects of their lives with me. They spoke to me about the difficult times they have lived through and the difficult decisions they have had to make. Although they will not agree with everything I have to say in this book, I hope they will understand that I have listened to them carefully and have tried to understand what it meant for them to undergo these experiences. I am aware that it is easier to try to analyse these issues decades later than to make hard and often courageous choices in the midst of turbulent times. I have learned a lot from these people, and not just about the specific issues I set out to learn. I am sorry I cannot thank them by name, for, in many cases, I have used pseudonyms to protect their identity.

I also wish to thank the two anonymous referees for the University of Toronto Press for their constructive comments on an earlier version of this manuscript. I am grateful, as well, to Allan Greer for the suggestions and encouragement he has provided while editor of the Social History of Canada. I also thank Laura Macleod and Gerry Hallowell of the press for all their help, and I am indebted to Rosemary Shipton for her skilful editing of the text.

I thank, as well, the editors of *Studies in Political Economy* for permission to reprint material that appeared in my article in volume 30 of this journal.

In addition, I have benefited from the interest and encouragement of many of my colleagues in the history department of McMaster University, especially Bernice Kaczynski, Richard Rempel, and John Weaver. I have also profited from the stimulating discussions undertaken by the students of my Canadian women's history seminar.

I am grateful to members of the Labour Studies Research Group, who provided the opportunity for me to clarify my ideas in discussion. In particular, I thank Pat Baker, Charlene Gannagé, Craig Heron, Chris Huxley, Franca Iacovetta, Lynne Marks, Pat McDermott, Jim Naylor, Carmela Patrias, Ian Radforth, Ester Reiter, Mark Rosenfeld, and Robert Storey for their many useful comments on my work. I am grateful, too, to members of the Women's Studies Research Group – Kathy Arnup, Karen Dubinsky, Margaret Hobbs, Franca Iacovetta, Lynne Marks, Janice Newton, Joan Sangster, Carolyn Strange, Mariana Valverde, and Cynthia Wright – for their many helpful and insightful suggestions.

I am indebted to several other friends as well. Daphne Read's supportiveness and intellectual companionship have meant a lot to me. Gail van Varseveld has helped me in so many ways, while hearing more about Jewish garment workers than she ever needed to know. I am also grateful to Janet Patterson, whose friendship and insights have been of great assistance. In addition, I have benefited from friendships with Lynne Marks and Carmela Patrias, who, beyond being members of our study groups, have taken a keen interest in my topic and provided special encouragement. Donald Wells helped me at every stage of this endeavour.

At times he served as my research assistant during out-of-town trips, and through countless discussions over the years he has enhanced my understanding of many key issues. He has enriched my work and my life more than I can say.

My grandmother, Gert Solomon, helped me explore the world of first-generation Jewish immigrants by sharing her early experiences with me, as well as teaching me so much else over the years. My brother and sister-in-law, Steve and Camilla Frager, provided encouragement and state-of-the-art office supplies. In addition, I am deeply indebted to my parents, Anna and Sam Frager. My mother assisted me expertly with the research at Harvard's library, and both of my parents have helped me in countless ways. I cannot thank them enough. This book is dedicated to them.

Abbreviations Used in the Text

ACCL   All-Canadian Congress of Labour
ACW   Amalgamated Clothing Workers
AFL   American Federation of Labor
AR   Arbeiter Ring
CCF   Co-operative Commonwealth Federation
CIO   Congress of Industrial Organizations
CP   Communist party
CPC   Communist Party of Canada
GEB   general executive board
IFWU   International Fur Workers' Union
ILGWU   International Ladies' Garment Workers' Union
IUNTW   Industrial Union of Needle Trades Workers
JTUA   Journeymen Tailors' Union of America
NCWC   National Clothing Workers of Canada
NWTUL   National Women's Trade Union League
TLC   Trades and Labour Congress
TUEL   Trade Union Educational League
UGW   United Garment Workers
WUL   Workers' Unity League
YCL   Young Communist League

A Note on the Use of Yiddish

Throughout this book, all translations from the Yiddish language are my own unless otherwise specified. Where transcriptions have been used, I have followed the transcription system of the YIVO Institute for Jewish Research, except for cases where I am quoting someone else's transcription or where a word (like 'arbeiter') is already commonly known under a different English spelling. The YIVO system has three notable features:

- the use of 'ay' to represent the sound of 'i' in the English word 'fire';
- the use of 'ey' to represent the sound of 'ay' in the English word 'way'; and
- the use of 'kh' to represent the sound of 'ch' in the name 'Bach.'

GLOSSARY OF YIDDISH TERMS

Arbeiter (plural *Arbeiters*) worker
Landsman (plural *Landslayt*) person who came from the same town or region in Eastern Europe
Landsmanshaft (plural *Landsmanshaftn*) fraternal association of Jews who came from the same town or region in Eastern Europe
Shtetl (Anglicized plural *Shtetls*) Jewish town in Eastern Europe

SWEATSHOP STRIFE

Introduction

Toronto cloakmakers and dressmakers applauded wildly and flung their hats into the air as the strains of 'The Internationale' filled their meeting hall. It was late June 1919 and these union men and women had just endorsed a comprehensive set of demands in a bold action that was to lead two thousand of them out on strike a week later. The majority were East European Jewish immigrants, and as they girded themselves for the sacrifices ahead the Yiddish version of 'The Internationale' rang in their ears, inspiring them with its prophecy that 'the working man will create a Garden of Eden of freedom and equality.'[1]

What was this vision? Would this Garden of Eden abolish more than class domination? Would it encompass freedom and equality for persecuted ethnic groups? For women? As Toronto's Jewish garment workers struggled to build the Jewish labour movement, how were their shop-floor struggles related to dreams of broader social change? As they strove to improve their working conditions and transform their vision into reality, how did they attempt to reconcile the often competing claims of their class, ethnic, and gender identities? Did competing loyalties fragment their movement?

Analysis of these kinds of themes has been limited by the fact that Canadian and American labour historians have frequently neglected key ethnic issues in working-class history, while immigration historians have frequently neglected key class issues in ethnic history.[2] However, a significant historical debate has slowly emerged regarding the relationship between class consciousness and ethnic identity in North America. Many of the participants in this debate have argued that the early twentieth-century working class was intensely fragmented along ethnic lines, thereby precluding the emergence of both a powerful labour movement and a strong radical political movement. Yet some scholars have stressed countervailing historical tendencies which, at times, have brought groups of ethnically diverse workers together in common protest. Rather than conceive of these situations as rare exceptions, some of these commentators have implied that the extent of ethnic fragmentation within the working class as a whole has been seriously overestimated.

Whereas many scholars have contended that intense ethnic identity has generally precluded the emergence of strong class consciousness among early twentieth-century immigrant workers in Canada and the United States, others have emphasized historical situations where key groups of immigrant workers have simultaneously displayed deep class consciousness and a deep commitment to ethnic identity. Important considerations in this whole debate include the character of ethnic prejudices and ethnic loyalties in specific historical circumstances, the extent of social and workplace segregation by ethnic group in particular communities and economic sectors, the tactics used by employers to manipulate ethnic divisions, the ways in which specific union leaders strove to overcome or to accentuate ethnic divisions, and the roles of individual ethnic leaders in either diluting or bolstering working-class consciousness among workers in their immigrant constituencies.[3]

Yet neither the nature of workers' consciousness nor the nature of the labour movement itself can be adequately understood without examining gender identity. Although Canadian and American labour historians have long ignored gender issues, a debate has recently emerged (particularly among feminist scholars) concerning the historical relationship between class consciousness and gender. Much of this debate has focused on explaining why Canadian and American women workers have found it especially difficult to protest their shop-floor exploitation. Disagreements about which factors have been crucial have centred, in part, on the question of whether women workers possessed a significant potential for class consciousness that was frequently thwarted by the sexist attitudes of male unionists. On the whole, these disagreements have taken place in the context of a consensus that women workers have had a notably low rate of unionization, particularly in the early twentieth century. Despite some emphasis on specific situations where women workers were militant, there has been general agreement that the labour movement has been significantly fragmented along gender lines.[4]

Fascination with exceptionally class-conscious women, however, has led to a broad debate about the relationship between socialism and feminism, a debate that has been carried on by contemporary socialists and feminists as well as by certain historians. Commentators have often shared the assumption that because socialists have been attuned to issues of class domination, they would have been sensitive to issues of gender domination as well. These discussants have suggested that the socialists' radical critique of class relations generally leads to a radical critique of gender relations, partly as a result of the socialists' willingness to challenge core social orthodoxies. According to this line of thought, the socialists' emphasis on freedom and equality for working people moves beyond class terms and comes to embrace women's equality as well. Proponents of the natural affinity between socialism and feminism have also often argued that socialists are led to feminism because the very process of women's political mobilization within the socialist movement entails the breaking down of traditional female roles.

By contrast, opponents of this view have argued that socialism's emphasis on the primacy of class struggle undermines the development of feminism – indeed, that the socialist focus on class oppression precludes a genuine analysis of women's oppression *as women*. Proponents of this view have often maintained that socialists have regarded feminism as a threat that divides the working class along gender lines and diverts the energy of sections of the working class towards 'secondary' issues. While these interpretations are the two poles of the debate, certain women's historians have been attempting to carve out some middle ground.[5]

Analyses of the relationship between socialism and feminism could be strengthened by clarifying key terms and concepts (as is also often true of the related analyses of the relationships between feminism and certain other social movements and causes). One might assume that developments that have expanded women's traditional roles are, *ipso facto*, feminist – even when these developments have not actually led to a deliberate commitment to women's equality.[6] A better approach, however, restricts the term 'feminism' to refer to the explicit conviction that women have been (and still are) fundamentally subordinated to men, combined with an explicit commitment to oppose this subordination.

Given this working definition of feminism, one might attempt to rely on terms such as 'incipient feminism,' 'proto-feminism,' 'inchoate feminism,' or 'implicit feminism' to refer to those measures that have enlarged traditional female roles. However, this type of usage implies that 'incipient feminism' quite naturally leads to 'real' feminism; such a progression is, after all, embedded in the very definitions of such terms as 'incipient' and 'proto.' Yet, empirically, one can point to key developments that have enlarged women's sphere, but have not led to feminism. Terms such as 'incipient feminism' could thus be significantly misleading.[7]

Instead, the concept of gender-role elasticity is more promising. Paradoxically, perhaps, the strength of this concept lies in its flexibility. In certain historical situations, female gender roles have stretched beyond traditional confines to enable women to take part in struggles to resolve certain social issues. In such cases, female gender roles have sometimes snapped back into place once the particular contingencies have been dealt with. In other cases, female roles may have stretched so far (or perhaps for so long) that the very conception of what constitutes 'normal' female roles has itself shifted. Indeed, elasticity has its limits: under certain circumstances, female roles may stretch to the point of a far-reaching break with traditional norms. Since the extension of women's roles has led to feminism in certain situations but not in others, historians need to examine the nature of these dynamics more carefully. Careful empirical analyses of issues of gender-role elasticity may help clarify the complex relationship between socialism and feminism and between class and gender more broadly.

On the whole, the class and gender debate and the class and ethnicity debate have taken place in isolation from each another.[8] Yet analyses of the historical relationships among all three – class, ethnicity, and gender – could prove particularly insightful, not only because all three variables are crucial to understanding the Canadian and American working-class experiences but also because there are important parallels between ethnic divisions and gender divisions within the working class.

The history of Toronto's Jewish labour movement provides a critical context for the examination of these issues, particularly because of the highly developed class consciousness, the intense commitment to Jewish identity, and the significant participation of Jewish women in the movement. Concentrated in the needle trades, the Jewish labour movement began slowly in Toronto at the turn of the century and grew significantly during the 1910s as more East European Jewish immigrants streamed into the city. The movement blossomed during the interwar period – the period on which this study concentrates. Jewish workers fought tenaciously against the extremely poor working conditions and low pay that characterized the highly competitive garment industry. For the leaders of the movement and for a significant segment of the rank and file, these shop-floor struggles were closely linked to a broader socialist vision.

In Toronto's needle trades sweatshops, women toiled alongside men, and Jews toiled side by side with non-Jews. By the interwar period, many of the employers themselves were Jews. As this study of the Jewish labour movement demonstrates, the complexity of the interaction between class and ethnicity emerges only through uncovering the original Yiddish sources, for no culture is truly accessible except through its own language. Since women have had to speak through languages shaped by male supremacy, uncovering the impact of gender has been a more difficult task. Although the fragmentary nature of the available evidence has made it difficult to be precise about detailed changes over time, careful sifting of the available materials has led to the emergence of key themes concerning the relationships among class, ethnicity, and gender within the city's Jewish labour movement.

Chapter 1 of this study outlines the background of the Jewish labour movement in Toronto, describing the nature of the immigrant Jewish community, the anti-Semitism Jews faced in this city, the nature of the labour force in the garment industry, the harsh working conditions in this industry, the beginnings of the various needle trades unions, and the highly unstable structure of this sector. Chapter 2 explores the development of Jewish working-class activism within the city's immigrant Jewish community, examining the social, cultural, and political dimensions of the Jewish unions. The chapter stresses the socialist orientation of these unions and analyses the nature of Jewish socialism.

In this context, chapter 3 explores the relations between Jewish workers and Jewish manufacturers in Toronto's needle trades, emphasizing the fierce class conflict between fellow Jews who were relatives, neighbours, and members of the same cultural organizations. This chapter also investigates the use of different kinds of ethnic appeals in the midst of strike situations. Following on this latter theme, chapter 4 examines the divisions between Jewish workers and non-Jewish workers in this industry, focusing on situations where non-Jewish garment workers refused to join Jewish strikers.

Chapters 5 to 7 explore the gender dynamics within the Jewish labour movement. Emphasizing the barriers to women's participation in union and strike activities, chapter 5 centres on the special constraints women workers faced on the shop floor, in their unions, and in their families. Chapter 6 focuses on the dearth of female-oriented organizing strategies and union policies, exploring not only the Jewish unions' general failure to develop special policies to appeal to women workers in particular but also the failure of the Canadian women's movement to provide a feminist counterforce. Chapter 7 examines the activities and consciousness of female union activists through a series of detailed profiles of individual Jewish women who played especially active roles within this movement.

[One of the deepest divisions within the Jewish labour movement centred on a different issue altogether. Within the movement, exponents of the different currents of Jewish socialism engaged in sharp, indeed bitter, political disagreements. These ideological disputes eventually spilled over into the needle trades unions themselves, splitting them into warring Communist and anti-Communist camps. Chapter 8 examines the development of political factionalism in Toronto's needle trades in the 1920s and 1930s, focusing on the Communist party's dual-union phase. This chapter evaluates the impact of these political divisions on the workers' abilities to defend themselves against management aggression on the shop floor.

The study as a whole focuses on the complex interplay of class, ethnicity, and gender, as well as related political ideology, in its analysis of the Jewish labour movement of Toronto. It examines both the sources of strength and the different kinds of divisions within the movement, while situating the analysis within the constraints imposed by the unstable structure of the garment industry and the Depression of the 1930s. In their struggles to envision and create the new Garden of Eden, Jewish activists drew strength from a vibrant Jewish working-class culture that wove together their class and ethnic identities. For the Jewish socialists in particular, their class consciousness and ethnic identity reinforced each other: the intensity of their socialist commitment was based on a two-fold sense of oppression as workers and as Jews. Significantly, the Jewish labour activists' ties to the Jewish manufacturers did not prevent them from protesting their exploitation on the shop floor.]

[The divisions among the workers, however, undermined the Jewish labour movement. Although the Jewish activists were sometimes able to incorporate the non-Jewish garment workers into the Jewish-led unions, the movement was weakened by their inability to incorporate the non-Jews more successfully. Their failure to incorporate many of the non-Jewish needle trades women was pronounced, while their ability to incorporate a significant number of the Jewish women was generally predicated on the Jewish women's implicit acceptance of their own subordination as women.] The employers were able to manipulate not only the deep divisions between Communists and anti-Communists but also these ethnic and gender divisions. Anti-union employers were often further aided by the courts and the police. Although the Jewish labour movement was far richer, broader, and deeper than many sections of the Canadian labour movement in this period, the divisions within the Jewish labour movement, combined with constraints imposed by the harsh economic climate, sharply limited the gains the movement was able to make.

1 A Mound of Ashes in the Golden Land

The Setting

'Like all people who have nothing, I lived on dreams. I burned my way through stone walls till I got to America.

'Nu, I got to America.

'Ten hours I pushed a machine in a shirtwaist factory, when I was yet lucky to get work. And always my head was drying up with saving and pinching and worrying to send home a little from the little I earned.

'Where are my dreams that were so real to me in the old country?'

– Anzia Yezierska, 'The Miracle'[1]

'I wrenched myself away, my dear [mother], from your arms, left the loving nest, to search for good fortune, good fortune in the golden land. And what have I found? Affliction, hardship, misfortune, shame, squalor, loneliness, filthy factories, dismal tenement houses.'

– J. Gordon, 'Fun An Arbayterin's Tog-Bukh'[2]

'Alas! America has turned me into a mound of ashes.'

– Abraham Cahan, *The Rise of David Levinsky*[3]

Like many other Jewish immigrants who flooded into Toronto's needle trades in the early twentieth century, Jim Blugerman had experienced severe hardships before leaving Eastern Europe. Born in the town of Kherson in Ukraine in 1887, Blugerman was the son of a poor, religious shoemaker. While he was still a youth, his family moved to nearby Odessa, where he became a furniture-maker. He was among those who survived the 1905 Odessa pogrom, during which rampaging anti-Semites murdered several hundred Jews, wounded thousands, and reduced many others to beggary by extensively destroying Jewish property. In fact, Blugerman was one of the courageous Jews who, together with some sympathetic Ukrainians, organized a self-defence group that sprang into action at the onset of the pogrom. Several years later, Blugerman joined the stream of Jewish emigrants who were fleeing to North America to escape vicious anti-Semitism and deepening poverty. He himself had an additional reason for leaving: in 1904 he had joined an underground revolutionary group and, like many other Jewish radicals, he decided to emigrate partly to escape Tsarist political repression.

Blugerman did not find 'the promised land' in Toronto. On arrival, he was surprised and saddened to see the impoverishment of the Jewish rag peddlers who trudged along the city streets. To earn his own living, he toiled as a presser's apprentice in Eaton's clothing factory. Before long, he joined both a garment union and a fraternal organization of Jewish socialists. He went on to become an important activist in Toronto's Jewish labour movement.

Blugerman was part of the mass exodus in which approximately one out of every three East European Jews fled their homelands (Tsarist Russia, Poland, Romania, and the Austro-Hungarian empire) in the late nineteenth and early twentieth centuries. Although not all had experienced the violence of pogroms firsthand, most had found their lives severely confined by the many forms of overt anti-Semitism. In the Russian empire in particular, Jewish life was hemmed in by a whole series of discriminatory government decrees, some of the most important of which prohibited Jews from residing in many parts of the empire, from owning land, and from pursuing certain occupations. Harsh restrictions contributed directly to the mass poverty of Jews in Eastern Europe.

These severe problems were compounded by economic and demographic pressures similar to those propelling some of the other Eastern and Southern Europeans to depart for North America in this period. While dramatic population growth produced serious overcrowding in the Jewish quarters of Eastern Europe, many traditional Jewish artisans found their meagre livelihood further undermined by growing competition from

factory-made goods, as capitalism began to develop in their homelands. Many Jews left their *shtetls* (Jewish towns) and either departed directly for the New World or moved to the cities of the Old World. In the latter case, further economic difficulties and anti-Semitic persecution then motivated many urbanized Jews to join the exodus to North America.

Clinging desperately to dreams of attaining freedom and prosperity in the New World, most Jewish emigrants chose to flee to the United States, known to them as *di goldene medine* – the golden land. From 1881 to 1914 almost two million Jews gained entry to America, but the First World War and then increased American immigration restriction in the early 1920s made it harder to get in. Throughout this period, some fled to Canada instead. Between 1891 and 1930 almost two hundred thousand Jews managed to enter this country before Depression conditions prompted Canada as well as other Western states to close the gates firmly, leaving the remaining Jews exposed to Hitler's 'final solution.' During the open-door period, although the United States was usually the Jewish emigrants' first choice, Canada, too, was part of the golden land of opportunity, a land that was richer, freer, and safer than anything they had ever known in Eastern Europe. Yet, for many, the New World was to fall far short of their dreams.[5]

Although there were only 3000 Jews in Toronto in 1901, their numbers grew rapidly during the next several decades. By 1931 over 45,000 Jews lived in this predominantly Anglo-Celtic city. The vast majority of these Jews were either immigrants from Poland and Russia or the Canadian-born children of these immigrants. At this time, Jews constituted almost 7.2 per cent of the city's total population and were Toronto's largest non-British ethnic group.[6] (For further statistical details, see tables 1 and 2 in the appendix.)

Whereas many early twentieth-century Southern and Eastern European immigrants had come to North America intending to stay only long enough to earn enough money to take back home, few East European Jewish immigrants in Toronto (as elsewhere in North America) intended to return to their homelands. The Jews came to put down roots, so there were as many women as there were men within Toronto's Jewish community. The Jewish workers' more permanent orientation to the New World stands in contrast to the temporary orientation of many non-Jewish immigrant workers, who often hesitated to become involved in the labour movement on this side of the ocean because they did not intend to remain here long.[7]

Yet Jewish immigrants' dreams of finding real freedom from anti-

Semitism in the New World were shattered by the reality[Although they faced significantly less discrimination in Toronto than they had experienced in Eastern Europe, the extent of anti-Semitism in 'Toronto the Good' was discouraging.]Joe Salsberg, who came to Canada just before the First World War, provided a number of illustrations of the 'very high degree' of discrimination against Jews in this city. Like many a young Jewish schoolboy, he was assaulted by an anti-Semitic schoolmate. Salsberg used to see anti-Semites openly taunting Orthodox Jewish peddlers in the streets, and he shuddered at signs at public beaches and parks stating 'No Jews or Negroes Allowed.' When he and his wife made repeated attempts to rent a summer place on the Toronto Islands in the 1930s, they were turned down because people there refused to rent to Jews. Ironically, Joe Salsberg was a Toronto alderman at the time, and his ward (which was largely a Jewish constituency) included the Islands.[8]

As Salsberg's testimony indicates, Toronto's Jews faced significant residential, occupational, and social discrimination in this period. They were prevented from renting or buying housing in some parts of the city; indeed, the courts sanctioned restrictive covenants that ensured people would not sell certain pieces of real estate to Jews. At the same time, some factory owners would not employ Jews, department-store managers seldom hired them as salespeople, bank managers were reluctant to have them as clerks, non-Jewish legal and engineering firms would not employ Jewish professionals, hospitals refused to place Jewish medical graduates as interns, and government departments hired very few Jews. Jewish students sometimes encountered discrimination in the public school system and in university programs, and Jews were barred from certain clubs and recreational facilities.[9]

[As in Eastern Europe, Jews in Toronto worried they would become scapegoats for social unrest. In fact, one of the city's major daily newspapers, the *Toronto Evening Telegram,* was particularly prone to blaming Jews. When widespread labour upheaval broke out in Canada in May 1919, for example, the *Telegram* insinuated that the Jews were behind all of Toronto's labour unrest.[10] The *Telegram*'s attacks on Jews were malicious: in 1924, for example, the newspaper declared that 'an influx of Jews puts a worm next the kernel of every fair city where they get a hold.'[11] Later, with the rise of fascism in the 1930s, anti-Semitism in Toronto increased. A new, extremely anti-Semitic newspaper attacked Jews in its pages, and anti-Semites attacked Jews in the streets in a dramatic riot that broke out at the Christie Pits playground. Although the Communist party officially denounced such prejudice, there were even anti-

Semites within Toronto's Communist movement.[12] For Toronto's immigrant Jewish workers, the climate of anti-Semitism in this city, combined with the legacy of harsh discrimination in their homelands, was to shape their interactions with non-Jewish workers on this side of the ocean.

Virtually every page of Toronto's daily Yiddish newspaper reflected Jewish immigrants' concerns about prejudice in Canada and in their places of birth, thereby conveying a strong sense that, despite their divisions, the city's Jews needed to stick together in the face of a common enemy. Of course, immigrant Jews were tied together by more than a sense of common threat. In Eastern Europe, Jews had traditionally lived in tightly knit communities, for the all-encompassing nature of traditional Judaism had bound them together and set them apart from the surrounding culture in a thousand different ways. Although these traditional bonds had then weakened to varying degrees, this legacy remained important. Most of Toronto's Jewish immigrants retained a significant sense of group identity, one that centred strongly on the family, which was seen as crucial to the perpetuation of Jewish heritage.[13]

Jewish identity also centred on the neighbourhood. At first, Toronto's East European Jewish immigrants clustered together in the Ward, a central area bounded by Yonge Street, University Avenue, Queen Street, and College Street. Here they suffered from notoriously poor housing, yet many Anglo-Celtic Torontonians blamed the impoverished 'foreigners' themselves for the Ward's harsh, overcrowded conditions. Somewhat later, Jewish immigrants settled along Spadina Avenue between Queen and College streets, as residential areas of the Ward yielded to more lucrative land use and as more Jews flooded into the city.

The Jewish areas were neighbourhoods in the fullest sense. A relatively high degree of residential concentration meant that Toronto's Jews could speak Yiddish with their neighbours, visit nearby relatives, walk to the synagogues (which was particularly important since the Orthodox were not allowed to ride on the Sabbath), buy kosher food in the neighbourhood, attend the nearby Yiddish theatres, and meet at the local Jewish fraternal associations. Such residential concentration was, of course, partly due to anti-Semitic housing restrictions in certain sections of the city, while economic constraints further limited Jewish options. Yet despite their differences, Jews often clustered together out of choice as well. Living among fellow Jews better enabled them to maintain some of their Old World traditions, as well as providing them with some degree of refuge from local anti-Semitism.[14]

Toronto's immigrant Jewish community contained a rich institutional network, consisting of both religious and secular organizations. Ties between fellow Jews were reinforced through synagogues, philanthropic associations, and mutual benefit societies. One of the most important of these organizations was the *landsmanshaft*, a fraternal association of Jews who had come from the same town or region in Eastern Europe. In the many *landsmanshaftn* in Toronto, fellow immigrants gathered together, seeking familiar company in the strange New World. They would exchange news about their old homes and help each other out. In the *landsmanshaftn*, unemployed members could seek assistance, and a program of sickness and death benefits helped members and their families through hard times.[5]

Unlike many other immigrant communities in Canada, Toronto's Jewish community contained a strong and highly varied component of socialist fraternal and political organizations. The Labour Zionists, for example, believed in the creation of a socialist Jewish state in Palestine. They divided into left and right groups, where each group had its own fraternal association. The Bundists, by contrast, were non-Zionists who believed in a decentralized form of socialism, which they felt would enable Jews to preserve their own culture within multi-ethnic socialist federations. Together with Jewish Trotskyists and Jewish Anarchists, the Bundists belonged to the Arbeiter Ring, a fraternal organization known in English as the Workmen's Circle. An important group of Jewish Communists also emerged and eventually formed their own fraternal organization, known as the Labour League.[6]

As these organizational and political differences suggest, there were serious tensions within the Jewish community. The different types of Jewish socialists disagreed with each other, and the split between the Communists and the other socialists became particularly intense, threatening class solidarity within the Jewish labour movement. Differences between the socialists and the non-socialists and between the secular Jews and the Orthodox Jews also had the potential to produce significant strains.

However, since Toronto did not have a large group of earlier Jewish immigrants from Germany, the Jewish community did not experience the deep divisions that developed in New York City between German Jews and East European Jews. Yet Toronto had become home to a group of middle-class Jews from England who had arrived in Canada in the nineteenth century. By the early years of the twentieth century, the influx of East European Jews had numerically overwhelmed these established English Jews. Tensions that developed between these two groups were partly based on the more assimilated character of the English Jews and were no doubt also related to class differences, particularly since Toronto's East European Jewish community contained a substantial working-class component. Moreover, important class divisions were developing within the East European Jewish group itself, particularly in the needle trades where so many of the immigrant Jewish workers obtained jobs and where a significant number of the East European Jews were eventually becoming small manufacturers.[17]

In Toronto, as in many other North American cities with substantial Jewish populations, Jewish labour was concentrated in the needle trades. Statistics available for 1931 indicate that there were over 5200 Jews in Toronto's clothing industry and that roughly one out of three gainfully employed Toronto Jews worked in this sector, as compared with roughly one out of twenty of all gainfully employed Torontonians.[18] In general, the concentration of Jews in this industry in North America represented one of the highest rates of occupational concentration experienced by any immigrant group.[19] The occupational and residential concentration of Toronto's Jewish workers was to facilitate the growth of the Jewish labour movement in many ways.

Jewish immigrants gravitated towards the clothing industry in the New World partly because many of them had already been doing this kind of work before emigrating. The concentration of Jews in this sector in the Old World was, of course, partly a product of severe anti-Semitic occupational restrictions. This concentration was also related to the religious injunction against wearing clothing that mixed wool and linen, for this meant that religious Jews had to depend on Jewish-made clothing to be sure not to violate sacred law.[20]

In Toronto, Jews continued to concentrate in the needle trades, partly because local anti-Semitism ensured that many other occupations were closed to them. In addition to the experienced tailors who continued this work after emigration, many Jews who needed to find a new trade in the New World entered the clothing industry because it did not take long to learn the less skilled jobs in this sector. New Jewish immigrants who were looking for work were also likely to have relatives or neighbours who worked in the garment shops and would help them find jobs. Toronto's garment shops were often located in the area where many of the city's Jewish immigrants settled, particularly in the Spadina district in the interwar years; this situation reflected the close ties between the Jews and this industry and reinforced these ties, since this proximity helped pull more Jewish workers into the clothing factories.[21]

Jews were drawn into this labour-intensive industry partly because it provided many jobs in this period. In early twentieth-century Toronto, in fact, the clothing industry employed more people than any other.[22] In addition to providing jobs for men, the clothing industry also provided work for women. This was important to impoverished immigrant families, especially since this was a period in which women's job opportunities were extremely limited. Despite legislation designed to curtail child labour, the industry also provided jobs for children, particularly in the first two decades of the twentieth century. Moreover, for Jews with entrepreneurial aspirations, part of the attraction to this expanding industry was the expectation that one could become a clothing contractor or small manufacturer without having to invest much capital. Some Jews became clothing workers in the hope they would be able to accumulate the workplace experience and savings to enable them eventually to open up their own garment shops.[23]

Numerous Jews were attracted to the garment industry because other Jews were already becoming entrenched there. Within certain sections of this industry, many Jews sought to create an ethnic job ghetto that would protect them from the anxieties of living in a non-Jewish and anti-Semitic world. This concentration helped provide a basis for the maintenance of Jewish culture. Religious Jews, for example, sought to work for Orthodox Jewish manufacturers so they would not have to work on Saturday or on other Jewish holy days. In addition, the number of Jews in this sector meant that Yiddish could often be used at work.[24]

Before the influx of East European Jews, the vast majority of Toronto's garment workers were Anglo-Celtic. By 1931, however, Jews constituted roughly 46 per cent of the people employed in this sector in this city, and the proportion of Jews was particularly high among men in this occupational group. More specifically, Jews accounted for 61 per cent of Toronto males in this industry and 30 per cent of females at this time. The non-Jews were still mostly Anglo-Celtic: roughly 43 per cent of the Toronto men and women in this sector in 1931 were of British descent, only 4 per cent were non-Jewish East Europeans (chiefly Poles, Russians, and Ukrainians), and less than 7 per cent were of other ethnic origins (most of whom were probably Italian). Labour activists in the needle trades needed to appeal to these very different groups of workers. (For further statistical details, see table 4 in the appendix.)

As labour organizers were aware, the proportion of Jews varied significantly from section to section of the clothing industry. In Toronto's men's coat and suit branch, which was central to the labour movement in the needle trades, approximately 64 per cent of the 1931 employees were Jews. The Jewish workers also tended to be concentrated in the women's cloak and suit branch and in the fur industry, whereas the custom tailoring branch and the dressmakers' branch remained chiefly Anglo-Celtic.[25]

The vast majority of Toronto's early garment manufacturers, like the city's early garment workers, were Anglo-Celtic, unlike New York, where many of the early garment manufacturers were German Jews. In both cities, however, East European Jews, attracted partly by the low capital requirements, moved rapidly into the manufacturing end of the industry. In Toronto, by the end of the First World War, a significant number of the needle trades employers were East European Jews. Although exact figures are unavailable, it is likely that, by the 1930s, the majority of Toronto's garment shops were owned by Jews.[26]

Many of the city's garment workers were women. In 1911, for example, of the 13,200 people employed in this industry in Toronto, 60 per cent were female.[27] Labour organizers in this sector encountered a situation very different from the many industries where the vast majority of the workers were male. However, labour organizers were also aware that, as with ethnic composition, the proportion of women varied widely between the different branches of the industry. In both the men's coat and suit branch and the women's cloak and suit branch, for example, females probably constituted between one-fourth to one-third of the Toronto workers in the interwar period. In contrast, they made up more than half of the workers in the dressmakers' branch in these years.[28]

The women in the needle trades, as in other sectors of the paid labour force, tended to be younger than their male co-workers. In Toronto's garment industry in 1921 and 1931, for example, more than a third of the women were between the ages of sixteen and twenty-four, while less than a quarter of the men were in this category.[29] Moreover, most of the women garment workers were single. Between 1928 and 1932 (the years for which useful statistics are available), only a quarter of Toronto's needle trades women were married.[30] (Additional statistics are provided in tables 3, 5, and 6 in the appendix.)

The women and men who laboured in Toronto's clothing industry faced notoriously low wages and poor working conditions. The situation at the turn of the century was, in short, appalling. The young William Lyon Mackenzie King, who undertook an investigation of Toronto's needle trades sweatshops in 1897, reported that the pay was so low that 'work from early morn till late at night will scarcely suffice to procure the necessaries of a bare existence.' King focused particularly on the unfortunate plight of those who took in precut pieces of garments to sew together in their own cramped homes. Often whole families did this kind of home work together, and even the young children toiled long hours. He interviewed one man who worked an average of eighteen hours a day. King also visited an old woman who had become crippled from bending over her work and was going blind from the long hours of work in dim lighting. In his 'one brief day' investigating the sweatshops, King was overwhelmed by the many accounts of pitifully low wages and crushingly long hours of labour.[31]

Toilers in the needle trades frequently suffered from unsanitary working conditions as well. In another investigation several years later, King commented extensively on the 'foul and noisome' workplace atmosphere that threatened the garment workers' health. 'A large number of hands were, as a rule, gathered together in small ill-ventilated apartments,' King explained, and these 'hands' suffered from the confinement, particularly 'during cold seasons, when the windows were kept closed and gas irons were used the whole day long.'[32]

Summer was really no better. An organizer for the United Garment Workers uncovered similarly harsh working conditions in Toronto in August 1908: 'For example, in one house in "The Ward" [the organizer] found in one room in the basement, about fifteen feet square, a family of six or seven persons engaged at 11 o'clock at night working on "ready-made" garments, while in the same rooms, used for sleeping, cooking and eating, as well as working, a young girl was lying in bed sick.' The organizer stated that 'there were hundreds of places around Toronto as bad,' and he deplored the fact that 'hundreds of children' were labouring in the city's needle trades. 'Between the hot shop and the filthy conditions I don't see how these people can stand it to sit over the machines nine or ten hours these hot days and live at all,' he exclaimed.[33]

The sufferings of Toronto's garment workers prompted an 'Unemployed Working Girl' to pour out her heart in a letter to the union's newspaper. Explaining that one clothing firm offered an experienced woman worker a mere four dollars per week, this letter-writer exclaimed: 'Imagine, good people, if you can, how a girl is going to find board, room, laundry and clothes out of $4 per week. There are people in this city who give their time and energy rescuing girls from the streets and the vile dens they get lured to. Is it any wonder that girls go wrong? Is it any wonder that there are so many early ill-mated marriages, or cause for surprise that the hospitals and asylums are filled with girls having either half-starved, diseased bodies or nerves shattered and minds wrecked?' She was especially outraged that the manufacturers 'are allowed to rake in a big order with a big profit attached to it, and to rush it through[,] girls must strain every nerve in their bodies and receive in return the munificent sum of $4 per week.'[34]

Because the garment industry was highly seasonal, the workers typically suffered from periodic bouts of unemployment and underemployment that alternated with long hours of hectic work during seasonal peaks. Economic downturns such as the depression of 1913–14 led to further unemployment in this sector. As unionists explained, the long bouts of unemployment (sometimes lasting months) helped clothing employers discipline their workforce, for manufacturers took advantage of the fact that prolonged periods of joblessness could make garment workers 'eager to secure work under almost any conditions.' When accelerated wartime demand for military uniforms pulled the industry out of the 1913–14 slump, for example, workers were compelled 'to put in ninety hours per week [labouring] seven days per week and overtime.' Unionists expressed dismay over the 'miserably low' wages and 'the inhuman conditions under which military clothing [was] being turned out.'[35]

In situations like these, the system of piece work was often used to keep the employees toiling at a frantic pace. Under this system, instead of paying the worker a set fee per hour, the worker was paid according to how many pieces of garment she or he had sewn together that day. To make this system more effective as a speed-up device, piece rates were often reduced when the employers felt that workers were able to earn 'too much' money under the established rates. Factory inspectors as well as unionists stressed that piece work seriously strained workers' nerves.[36]

These considerable problems – speed-ups, low wages, long hours of work during seasonal peaks, unemployment, and unsanitary conditions – continued into the interwar period. Statistical information for 1921, for example, documents the very low wages in Toronto's needle trades. At that time, the city's average adult male garment worker earned approximately $1050 per year, while the average adult female garment worker earned approximately $670 per year. Estimates indicate that, in that year, a family of five needed an annual income of $1655 to rise above the poverty line.[37] Clearly, the family wage – the notion that the male head of the household would earn enough to support the whole family on his own – was a myth in this sector, as in many others.

Although a union organizer had already described the 'rotten' working conditions in Toronto's clothing industry as 'black slavery' in the mid 1920s, the Great Depression made bad conditions far worse.[38] The situation was so bad that a key royal commission reported in 1935 that wages and working conditions in the needle trades 'merit the most emphatic condemnation.'[39]

During the Depression, unemployment and underemployment increased drastically as the sharp decline in the public's purchasing power led to a dramatic decrease in the market demand for new clothing. The industry's peak seasons became shorter and shorter. Sol Abel, a cloakmaker, recalled that in Toronto's cloak trade where there were two seasons a year, a season sometimes shrank to a mere six weeks. Like many others, Abel had to buy many of the necessities on credit when he was out of work. During one slack season he ran up a debt of fifty dollars for milk alone (at a time when milk cost five cents a quart). Although families struggled to economize through such stratagems as basing their diet on potatoes, serious debts accumulated and were not easily paid off once the unemployed garment worker finally managed to obtain some work.[40]

One investigator for the 1935 Royal Commission on Price Spreads focused on the difficulties Toronto's female garment workers experienced in trying to make ends meet: 'We learned of the hardships undergone by a woman factory worker of 19 years' experience ... still in her prime, who has had to begin selling her furniture to cover an unemployment period of three months; or of the girl who has used all her savings during the last three years to supplement low earnings[;] or of the woman whose wages only covered food and shelter, who had to do without firing many a time during the severity of last winter.'[41]

As wage cut followed wage cut, the average pay for a full week's work in Toronto's garment industry fell 30–50 per cent during the first five years of the Depression. The accompanying drastic decrease in the available number of weeks of full-time work per year chipped away further at the garment worker's annual income. Despite provincial legislation that stipulated a specific minimum wage rate for women garment workers, violations of the Minimum Wage Act were widespread in Toronto's garment industry in this period. There is evidence that the Department of Labour itself was deliberately lax in enforcing this legislation.[42]

During the peak seasons, garment workers in the midst of the Depression were forced to toil long hours for their meagre wages. The *Canadian Forum* revealed in 1931, for example, that Toronto dressmakers worked twelve hours or more per day during the height of the season. Ed Hammerstein, a fur worker, remembered when the hours were so long that some of the people would sleep in the plants instead of going home at night. Ida Abel, a Jewish immigrant who worked in the Toronto dress trade in this period, recollected having to work from eight in the morning to midnight for several weeks during the seasonal peak. Her efforts were not rewarded: her employer went bankrupt, so she was never paid for any of this work.[43]

In addition to the long hours, the pace of work was often gruelling. While low piece rates had been used as a method to hurry the workers in the earlier decades, the speed-ups frequently intensified during the Depression. Some employers even prohibited their employees from talking during working hours so they would work faster. As a result of the harsh pace, the strain and fatigue were so great that when an investigator for the Royal Commission on Price Spreads interviewed some of Toronto's women garment workers, 'many of the girls said they were afraid they were going out of their minds.'[44] One woman garment worker, who actually worked in one of the better clothing factories, testified before the commission that the speed-ups were so onerous that 'I would go home nights and I would be so tired I could not eat my supper ... And I would be so tired and stiff going home on the street car, I would just dread getting a seat, because if I sat down, I could not get up again, my knees and my legs would be so stiff.'[45] One of her co-workers had had to be away from work for two months on account of 'nervous exhaustion.'[46] Another co-worker, who had broken down several times and had had to go to the hospital, explained: 'Well you had to work so hard, you were driven so fast ... you were a nervous wreck.'[47]

In addition to nervous breakdowns, other occupational hazards included high blood pressure, anaemia, kidney problems, boils, and skin irritations. There was also a disease known as 'hatters' shakes,' thought to be caused by the mercury used in treating skins that were made into fur hats. (Hence the expression 'mad as a hatter.') Worst of all, there was the dreaded 'tailors' disease' – tuberculosis.[48]

Those who protested against these poor working conditions and low wages risked being seriously victimized by their employers, whereas those who curried favour with their bosses often received small, immediate rewards. In non-union shops using the piece-work system, for example, the employers' favourites might be selected to work on those particular styles of clothing that had the more advantageous piece rates, or they might be given extra jobs to do when work was scarce. Those who sought to ingratiate themselves with their bosses might also be able to get jobs for their unemployed relatives. It was not uncommon for supervisors to require a direct bribe before they would hire anyone.[49]

Throughout the period, union activists risked being fired and blacklisted, except in those rare situations where the union was strong enough to protect them. Joe Salsberg, who got his start in the labour movement as a worker in a Toronto cap factory in the late 1910s, emphasized that in this climate of intimidation early union organizing had to be done in secret. He recalled that one of the activists in his shop was promptly fired when the man's union book fell out of his pocket and the boss found it. Similarly, Sam Kraisman, an activist cloakmaker, recalled the many times he was fired and blacklisted for union activities. Kraisman explained that since the garment industry was concentrated in a small geographical area around Spadina Avenue in the interwar years, the employers could easily spread the word about particular activists.[50]

Although discriminatory hiring and firing could certainly work to the employer's advantage, such intimidation could also backfire, leading instead to worker militancy. In the large 1912 strike in Eaton's garment factory, for example, the strikers' opposition to management was fuelled by the fact that 'any attempt on the part of an employee to so much as dare to protest [had led to] instant dismissal.' 'In short,' stated the strikers' appeal, 'discrimination, intimidation and subjection to the worst prison-like system has been and is the predominant rule of this firm,' a rule they were fighting to change.[51] Similarly, in the large 1931 dressmakers' strike, workers objected to the fact that they had had no protection from being dismissed at any moment 'for any cause or no cause at the whim of their employer.' Indeed, one of the dressmakers' strike demands was the establishment of mechanisms to enable the union to exert considerable control over the hiring and firing process so as to end this kind of discrimination. The striking dressmakers also demanded that the union be allowed to monitor the distribution of work so that favouritism would be eliminated.[52] However, the defeat of both strikes meant these employers could continue to penalize workers whom they disliked.

Employers who fired 'troublemakers' could often replace them with newly arrived immigrants whose newness frequently meant they demanded less from their employers. Even when 'greenhorns' were not readily available, the fact remained that few garment workers possessed job skills that were really scarce; hence those who began to organize unions or who went out on strike were often replaceable. Employers sometimes defeated small strikes by hiring whole new sets of workers. Manufacturers also sometimes undermined strikes at their own shops by contracting out the work. The vulnerability of Toronto's garment workers to employer offensives was heightened by the fact that actual hunger could weaken even the most militant striker's resolve to hold out.

Because many garment workers were scattered in small shops, particularly at the turn of the century, it was difficult for unionists to recruit them and to coordinate their efforts efficiently. Home workers (those who sewed together precut pieces of garments in their own homes) were especially hard to reach, since they worked in isolation. Although this obstacle could be offset somewhat through community ties between workers who were scattered in different workplaces, this was still a drawback that continued into the interwar period. This problem was compounded by the difficulties of organizing workers during the seasonal downturns that characterized this industry.[53]

[Union activists faced further obstacles because the police and the courts often aided anti-union employers, in this sector as in so many others] Some of the leaders of the Toronto branch of the International Ladies' Garment Workers' Union, for example, recalled considerable police brutality during the union's strikes in the early 1930s. Police beat up female strikers as well as male strikers, and the courts were not reluctant to hand out jail sentences for picketing. The threat of deportation added to the intimidation of immigrant workers.[54]

Despite serious barriers, however, activists in Toronto's needle trades struggled to unionize the various branches of the industry. Their initial organizing efforts sometimes resulted in the establishment of small, ephemeral unions that were purely local in character. Eventually, however, the activists' local organizing work linked up with the larger clothing unions that were spreading across the United States and Canada.

The earliest of the important large unions were the Journeymen Tailors' Union of America and the United Garment Workers. In Toronto, these two unions were, in the course of time, dwarfed in importance by the development of the 'Jewish unions' – unions led mainly by Jews and composed largely of Jewish workers while also encompassing a significant number of non-Jewish workers. The Amalgamated Clothing Workers and the International Ladies' Garment Workers' Union were the largest of the four 'Jewish unions'; the other two were the International Fur Workers' Union and the even smaller United Cloth Hat, Cap, and Millinery Workers' International Union. All of these unions were based in the United States, but were known as international unions because they encompassed Canada as well. In the 1930s, however, there were also <u>two purely Cana-</u>

dian clothing unions in Toronto: the Industrial Union of Needle Trades Workers and the National Clothing Workers of Canada. Toronto's garment workers were thus divided among these different unions, some of which competed directly with each other at key points in time. (See table 7 of the appendix for an overview of each of these unions, and tables 8 to 12 for an outline of the key Toronto strikes in this sector.)

Founded in the United States in 1883, the Journeymen Tailors' Union of America (JTUA) managed to establish its first Toronto local in 1891, when a local tailors' union decided to affiliate with it. The JTUA was originally a union for those who worked in the custom-tailoring trade (where clothing was made up according to the specifications of each individual customer) rather than those who worked in the ready-made clothing trade (where clothing was made up in standard sizes). By the turn of the century, however, the highly skilled custom tailors were a besieged group. Their skills were threatened not only by the rapid expansion of the ready-made clothing industry but also by the use of an increased division of labour, which led to significant deskilling in many of the remaining custom-tailoring shops.

This situation eventually led to a radical change in JTUA policy: in 1913 the JTUA declared its new goal of encompassing all garment workers rather than being restricted to the skilled custom tailors. Changing its name to the Tailors' Industrial Union, it called on the other clothing unions to merge with it, but the United Garment Workers refused. A year later, however, the newly formed Amalgamated Clothing Workers hammered out a merger with the Tailors' Industrial Union. Hence, in Toronto, as in many other clothing centres, these two unions began operating as an amalgamated unit.

By mid 1915, however, the custom tailors had changed their minds and pulled out of the merger. Bowing to sharp pressure from the American Federation of Labor, the Journeymen Tailors' Union returned to its original, limited jurisdiction (and its original name). Having turned its back on industrial unionism (the effort to organize all clothing workers regardless of craft distinctions within the industry), the JTUA then dwindled in importance in Toronto, particularly as the demand for custom tailors continued to decline dramatically.[55]

In the late nineteenth century, when the Journeymen Tailors' Union had been unwilling to organize the ready-made section of the clothing industry, a group of American ready-made clothing workers had organized the United Garment Workers (UGW). Founded in 1891, the UGW focused on the men's clothing branch of the ready-made section of the garment industry. The UGW established its first Canadian local in Toronto in 1894, and the union's Toronto branch then developed slowly and unevenly for a time. By 1913, however, the UGW had become fairly strong in this city. An organizing drive in that year led to many successful peaceful settlements and several strike victories. By then, the Toronto branch of the UGW had over twelve hundred members. The establishment of the Amalgamated Clothing Workers in 1914, however, meant that the UGW soon diminished in importance in Toronto.[56]

The Amalgamated Clothing Workers was founded in the United States by a group of secessionists from the UGW who were discontented with the UGW's conservative leadership. The native-born UGW leaders had focused on organizing the overall factories in the small towns of the American Midwest and the American South, principally through convincing the employers to buy the union label. As a consequence, the UGW's leaders tended to neglect organizing work among the many immigrant workers who made men's clothing in the large urban centres of the United States. When these immigrant workers struggled to organize themselves under the banner of the UGW, they frequently felt that the union leadership hindered their efforts. The immigrant activists were hampered, for example, by the fact that the UGW's leaders sometimes even permitted the use of the union label by employers who were not upholding union conditions in their shops. The UGW's leadership had also actively undermined certain strikes that had broken out in the men's clothing factories in several American cities.

As a result, the opposition to the UGW's leadership began to organize itself for a fight for control of the union at the UGW's 1914 convention. In order to control the convention, president Thomas Rickert's group manipulated the regulations so as to reject the credentials of more than one hundred delegates from the opposition. Thus, when the UGW's convention opened in Nashville, Tennessee, in late 1914, most of the opposition's delegates were unseated and barred from participating. In an attempt to prevent the development of sympathy for the ousted delegates (many of whom were Jewish), Rickert's supporters apparently also made anti-Semitic appeals to the native-born delegates from the small American towns. Rickert's ousted opponents, who represented about two-thirds of the UGW's total membership, met together and formally reconstituted themselves under the banner of the Amalgamated Clothing Workers (ACW), a new union for the men's clothing branch of the industry.[57]

The sympathies of Toronto's Jewish garment workers were largely with the insurgents In February 1915, less than two months after the founding convention of the ACW, a group of Jewish clothing workers, led by Jim Blugerman, broke away from the Toronto UGW and established an ACW local. With some help from the Tailors' Industrial Union, these new ACW members struggled to organize more of the city's clothing workers into their new union. The Toronto branch of the ACW then continued to grow even after the Tailors' Industrial Union pulled away from the merger with the ACW. The early growth of the Toronto ACW took place despite the fact that the cutters, the most skilled of the ready-made clothing workers, at first remained attached to the UGW. These cutters, most of whom were Anglo-Celtic, were not attracted to the ACW until 1918.[58]

As the Toronto ACW continued to grow, a key settlement was reached in mid 1919. At that time, a large group of Toronto men's clothing manufacturers organized their own association, the Associated Clothing Manufacturers. This was not a 'union-busting' organization; in fact, four anti-union manufacturers hurriedly left the organization when it became committed to working with the union.[59] The association's first contract with the ACW was ratified by the union at a meeting of several thousand garment workers, setting the pattern for union-management relations in this branch of the Toronto clothing industry for years to come. In addition to establishing mechanisms to determine the wage rates, the 1919 contract established a board of arbitration (headed by an 'impartial chairman') to adjudicate any disputes that might arise between members of the association and members of the union. Arbitration decisions were to be binding on both parties, and the contract stipulated there would be no strikes or lockouts.[60] This commitment to arbitration was an important step in the institutionalization of union-management conflict.

The 1919 contract also established the principle of the preferential union shop. This meant that when employers needed to hire workers, they had to ask the union to supply them with unionized labour. In return, the union agreed it would 'bend its energies to enforce maximum production.' The contract stipulated that 'where the employee acts unfairly with the employer,' he or she would be 'disciplined by the union.'[61]

This pattern-setting agreement brought a little stability to this branch of Toronto's needle trades. Throughout the interwar period there continued to be serious disagreements between the ACW and the Associated Clothing Manufacturers, but the collective bargaining process in this branch of the industry was smoother than in the women's clothing branch (partly because the fewer style fluctuations in men's clothing meant this branch of the needle trades experienced a more stable industrial structure). Conflict developed periodically over the renewal of the ACW agreement, but it usually wound up being renewed with some modifications and covered the majority of the city's men's clothing workers throughout the interwar years. The Toronto ACW engaged in comparatively few major strikes, but tensions were not eliminated and union members experienced numerous dissatisfactions on the shop floor.

Although the union did win some benefits for workers, the ACW was not strong enough to force the employers to make really fundamental concessions in an industry where low wages and harsh working conditions were the norm. This was the case even though the ACW was more firmly established than most of the other garment unions in Toronto. In the middle of the Depression, for example, workers in ACW shops generally experienced better wages and less vulnerability to employer harassment than the non-unionized men's clothing workers, but the workers in ACW shops still faced serious hardships. Even though the ACW was sometimes able to use the collective bargaining process to help the workers, its accomplishments were sharply limited.[62]

The Toronto branch of the International Ladies' Garment Workers' Union (ILGWU) developed much more unevenly than the Amalgamated Clothing Workers. Founded in the United States in 1900, the ILGWU was a union for workers of both sexes who made ready-made women's clothing. The ILGWU attempted to establish a local in Toronto as early as 1903, but it did not last long. Two or three subsequent attempts amounted to little. Part of the ILGWU's difficulty was that, for several years after 1905, it faced competition from the Industrial Workers of the World, a newly formed anarcho-syndicalist union that was also trying to organize Toronto's garment workers. Neither organization was able to make much headway at that time.[63]

In 1909 a group of Jewish members of the Toronto branch of the Socialist party founded an independent union for those who made women's cloaks and suits. Then, when the ILGWU's prestige soared as a result of its success in the huge New York cloakmakers' strike of 1910, many members of the independent Toronto union began to press for affiliation. A deep split developed within the Toronto union over this issue: those close to the Socialist party supported affiliation with the ILGWU, while those close to the Socialist Labour party were opposed. The advocates of affiliation finally won; in early 1911 the independent union officially joined the ILGWU.[64]

For many years the fortunes of Toronto's ILGWU fluctuated widely. The employers in this branch of the needle trades were often particularly intransigent, continuing to challenge the union's existence until well into the 1930s. In response, the union engaged in a whole series of general strikes. (The term 'general strike,' when used to refer to a particular branch of the needle trades, denotes a situation where instead of a strike in one shop, all workers in one branch in a certain geographic area are called out on strike.) Although the union was sometimes able to mobilize considerable support for these general strikes, the gains often melted away soon afterwards. It was not until the second half of the 1930s that the union reached a more stable position.[65]

In the meantime, an altogether different branch of the garment industry was being organized by the International Fur Workers' Union (IFWU). Although efforts to organize the Toronto fur industry predated the founding of the IFWU, these early efforts had not amounted to much. When the IFWU was founded in 1913, a group of Toronto furriers formed themselves into an IFWU affiliate. Despite the Toronto IFWU's initial weakness, the union obtained a key agreement in 1916, covering the vast majority of the city's fur workers. At that time, the fur manufacturers had formed an association and had agreed to union recognition, shorter hours, and a substantial wage increase. Although the fortunes of the Toronto IFWU fluctuated somewhat during the next twenty years, the union managed to retain a fairly firm footing until it was torn apart internally in the late 1930s.[66]

Meanwhile, organizing work had also been going on in another branch of the Toronto garment industry, among the workers who made hats and caps. Founded in 1901, the United Cloth Hat, Cap, and Millinery Workers' International Union began organizing Toronto's capmakers a couple of years later. However, these early attempts floundered. Finally, in 1914, as a result of plans developed by a group of Toronto capmakers who had gathered together on the first night of Passover, the Toronto capmakers' local became more firmly established. Two years later, the union established a local for the city's millinery workers (those who made women's hats). Although the union experienced some ups and downs in the years that followed, the United Cloth Hat, Cap, and Millinery Workers' International Union remained relatively firmly established in both sections of Toronto's small headgear industry.[67]

In addition to these 'international' clothing unions, each of which had its headquarters in the United States, there was, for a time, a purely Canadian clothing union that was Communist led. The Industrial Union of Needle Trades Workers (IUNTW) was established to compete directly with the other garment unions. Founded in 1928, as the Communist party was switching into its dual-union phase, the IUNTW functioned until early 1936, when this phase of party policy was brought to an end. Although the IUNTW was intended as an industrial union to encompass all branches of the needle trades, its Toronto wing was concentrated almost exclusively in the dress trade.[68]

Another Canadian union active in Toronto's needle trades in the 1930s was the National Clothing Workers of Canada (NCWC), an affiliate of the All-Canadian Congress of Labour (ACCL). Founded in 1927, the ACCL was a nationalist labour organization that opposed the role of the 'international' unions in Canada. After an abortive attempt to establish a garment union in Toronto in 1931, the ACCL successfully established the NCWC a few years later. Although the NCWC remained small during the 1930s, it played a significant role in the industry because of its intense competition with several of the other clothing unions. Even though the NCWC was dying out by 1940, the relatively large number of unions in Toronto's garment industry during the first four decades of the twentieth century meant that the city's clothing workers were organizationally fragmented.[69]

In Toronto, Jewish unionists were active not only in the garment industry but also in a number of other occupational sectors. Over the years, organizing efforts were undertaken by Jewish barbers and by kosher bakers, slaughterers, and butchers. There was even some organizing activity among Jews who worked in a large factory where rags were sorted and cleaned. In fact, the large Jewish unions in the needle trades used to help organize the Jewish workers in other occupations. Although the Jewish labour movement included workers from a number of different sectors, the centre of the Jewish labour movement always lay in the needle trades.[70]

Yet the fragmented structure of the garment industry itself placed important constraints on the development of the Jewish labour movement, adding to the difficulties of organizing a labour force that could fragment along the lines of ethnicity, gender, and political ideology. This was a highly unstable industry, partly because of frequent changes in clothing styles and also because of seasonal variations in the demand for clothing. Instability was increased by the fact that the demand for clothing was sensitive to economic cycles, for sales often plummeted during economic downturns. Most importantly, it was a labour-intensive industry. Aspiring entrepreneurs did not require much capital to go into business on a small scale because the machinery necessary for manufacturing clothing was limited to comparatively inexpensive sewing machines. Although certain large firms emerged in this sector in Toronto, small shops continued to proliferate. The result was a high level of competition among firms and great instability.[71]

The use of contractors heightened the competitive nature of this industry. While some clothing manufacturers operated 'inside shops' where garments were completely made up, other entrepreneurs had the fabric cut on their own premises and gave the pieces out to contractors. A man did not require much knowledge of the trade or managerial experience to become a contractor, for the contractors were not involved in buying the material, making the designs, or marketing the finished products. Contractors could go into business even more cheaply than manufacturers. Although the garment unions eventually tried to regulate the practice of contracting work out, their achievements were limited. Toronto's garment industry swarmed with small contractors during much of the period under consideration. Individual contractors would have to agree to make up the garments at extremely low prices to get the business away from their many competitors. The inside shops, competing with the contracting system and with each other as well, were similarly pressured to sell their products at very low prices. Prices were driven down in particular by the purchasing agents of the large retail stores who were in a position to drive harsh bargains in return for large orders.[72]

In addition, some contractors and manufacturers managed to cut their overhead costs by giving out pieces of garments to be made up in the workers' own homes, thereby intensifying competition in the industry. In turn-of-the-century Toronto there was a great deal of home work in the needle trades; even though the garment unions struggled to eliminate this practice, a significant amount of home work remained in this sector in the chaotic 1930s.[73]

The fragmented structure of the industry augmented the difficulties faced by union organizers. Home workers, workers in contractors' shops, and those in inside shops did not necessarily have a strong sense of common interest. Indeed, unionists' efforts to eliminate home work and restrict the use of contractors could pit worker against worker.[74]

The runaway shop also created a serious problem for both the unionists and the Toronto garment employers themselves. If labour costs got too high in Toronto, an employer might try to move his shop to a small Ontario town where cheaper labour was available. Or he might relocate in Montreal, where the garment unions were weaker and the wages lower than in Toronto (a situation Jewish unionists usually attributed to the attitudes of their French-Canadian co-workers). In fact, low-wage competition from Montreal was one of the most serious problems faced by Toronto's garment industry.[75]

The fierce competition in the garment industry had a devastating effect on wages and working conditions. As individual contractors and manufacturers struggled to reduce their costs of production in order to undersell their many rivals, they put a downward pressure on wages, particularly since labour costs constituted a high proportion of the cost of production. The garment industry became notorious for its low wages, long hours, and poor working conditions. Intense competitive pressures also meant that hard-pressed employers were often intransigent in the face of workers' demands. The Toronto garment industry was the scene of many battles as desperate employers faced off against workers who were struggling to make a living.

In these struggles, union activists faced serious constraints. When they pushed particular employers for higher wages and better working conditions, they had to take care not to place their employers at too much of a competitive disadvantage. As Communist activist Joe Salsberg explained, the highly competitive structure of the industry meant that 'the union leadership, no matter how radical it was, had to be realistic' when deciding how far to pressure particular employers for concessions. There was little point in striking for higher wages if the wage demands were such that those shops that acceded to workers' demands would eventually be forced out of business by low-wage competition. In an industry where business mortality rates were extremely high, this was a crucial consideration.[76]

At the same time, the highly competitive nature of the industry provided some impetus for the development of union-management joint action to bring stability to the trade. This motivation was increased by the inadequacies of the sparse government legislation that attempted to limit low-wage competition in this sector in the interwar years.[77] Unionized employers might be interested in working directly with the unions to help protect the 'legitimate businesses' from 'unfair competition.' In an educational manual issued by the ILGWU in 1937, the union's international president, David Dubinsky, addressed this theme:

While in theory the workers and the employers are divided by the class struggle, it is foolish to ignore the fact that at times even sections of the employers favor unionism. [In New York] in 1929, even the employers were interested in strengthening the union because of the keen competition between union shops where standards and conditions were being observed and their non-union competitors and also because of the demoralization that prevailed throughout the industry. These employers, too, realized that the union was in the picture permanently and they therefore favored the extension of unionism to the whole industry.[78]

In Toronto, as in the garment centres of the United States, the ACW and the ILGWU attempted to convince 'legitimate' employers to help them achieve some stabilization by trying to eliminate low-wage competition. Both unions attempted to restrict the use of contractors,[79] but the attitude of Toronto clothing manufacturers towards these efforts was ambivalent. On the one hand, manufacturers as a whole would benefit from a 'healthier' industrial climate if the amount of cut-throat competition in this sector were substantially reduced, and individual garment manufacturers would benefit if unions helped prevent competitors from undercutting them. From this point of view, manufacturers welcomed the unions' attempts to regulate the contracting system. On the other hand, each manufacturer hoped to out-compete the others by keeping his own costs of production low. Individual manufacturers wanted to be unrestricted in their search for contractors who would charge the lowest price, and they disliked the unions' attempts to regulate the contracting system.[80] Unions had to resort to strikes and strike threats, then, in an attempt to force legitimate manufacturers to cooperate over this issue.[81] Union-management cooperation in Toronto was largely a forced cooperation.

Although the unions were able to achieve some gains, real stability was not achieved in this industry. Cut-throat competition continued to exert severe pressure on wages and working conditions in Toronto's needle trades. In some cases, the unions and the employers negotiated temporary truces, but, overall, the war continued.

The activists in the needle trades fought for extremely difficult goals. To reduce the downward pressure on wages and working conditions, they strove to stabilize this highly competitive industry by eliminating 'unfair competition.' They struggled to force employers to grant important concessions to workers who suffered intensely from the long hours, low wages, and poor working conditions for which the industry was infamous. At the same time, realistic unionists had to know when it was unwise to press for further concessions from particular employers because this would be too damaging to the competitive position of these firms.

Jim Blugerman and the other Jewish immigrants who had fled from virulent anti-Semitism and severe economic hardship in Eastern Europe had not found 'the promised land' in Toronto. Far from the fulfilment of their hopes, they found themselves facing the tyranny of the sweatshops. But they were by no means passive victims, for the activists' disappointed dreams fuelled their revolt. Gathering together in the Ward, in the houses and halls of the Spadina district, and in the sweatshops themselves, Jewish workers forged a dynamic labour movement to fight for their interests. Given the composition of the labour force in Toronto's garment industry, their unions needed to embrace non-Jews as well as Jews – in an industry where many of the employers themselves were Jews – and to encompass women as well as men. To be as effective as possible, the Jewish labour movement also needed to bind workers with widely divergent political ideologies together. In their fight for a finer life, Toronto's Jewish labour activists faced many difficulties. This book is the story of their struggles.

2 Pulling in One Direction
The Development of Jewish Working-Class Activism

'If all men pulled in one direction, the world would topple over.'

– Yiddish folk saying[1]

A strong pro-labour current evolved within Toronto's immigrant Jewish community. As the Jewish labour activists struggled to build a militant movement to advance their class interests, their experience of oppression as Jews heightened their political awareness and often sharpened their commitment to activism. For the Jewish socialists in particular, class consciousness and ethnic identity reinforced each other, deepening their commitment to radical social change. Led by the socialists and forged out of a vibrant Jewish working-class culture, the Jewish labour movement was a dramatic departure from the more conservative unionism that characterized many sections of the Canadian labour movement in this period.

The activism of Toronto's immigrant Jewish community was reflected not only in shop-floor struggles but also in strikes by Jewish schoolchildren and consumer boycotts by Jewish housewives. Around 1914, for example, in the context of deep concern within the Jewish community about the activities of aggressive Christian missionaries, Jewish children from several Toronto schools went out on strike to protest having to sing Christmas carols in class. The children triumphantly returned to school when the board of education reluctantly agreed they need not sing the carols.[2] In 1918 another strike of Jewish schoolchildren broke out in a classroom where the teacher, a non-Jew, refused to hang up the Jewish flag along with other national flags that decorated the room. While the flag incident triggered the strike, the Jewish students felt this teacher had acted unfairly towards them on other occasions as well. According to the city's Yiddish newspaper, the children won their battle.[3]

[In both cases, the schoolchildren's strikes had centred on ethnic rather than class issues, but the line between the two areas was not always sharply drawn. Children who learned to adopt an activist orientation in one area could carry these lessons into the other area] In fact, Joe Salsberg, the religious twelve-year-old who led the protest against singing carols, went on to become a key labour leader. Moreover, many of the striking schoolchildren had probably already heard about strike tactics from parents or neighbours involved in shop-floor battles.

Toronto's Jewish children may well have learned some of their activism from their mothers as well as their fathers, for Jewish women, in their role as housewives, participated in a whole series of consumer boycotts during the first four decades of the twentieth century. The women launched these boycotts to combat sharp increases in the prices of particular kosher food products, and these protests often gathered wide support within the immigrant Jewish community] This class activism focused on 'the point of consumption' rather than the 'point of production,' for the activists saw this tactic as an important way of standing up for the interests of working people. The boycotts were a focal point for female militancy, and often the women's efforts succeeded.[4]

[The kosher-meat boycott of 1924, for example, indicates the seriousness with which Jewish housewives mobilized the community to protest against a price increase.] The decision to launch this boycott was made at a meeting of women from a wide range of Jewish organizations, including representatives from the women's auxiliaries of various benevolent societies as well as women from the socialist groups. Consumer activists set up picket lines in front of the butcher shops, began negotiations with the butchers, and sought to mobilize additional support through the Jewish unions. They even discussed forming a cooperative butcher shop to supply meat at reasonable prices. Some of the women were beaten up while picketing, but the boycott succeeded and, within two weeks, the butchers reluctantly agreed to lower their prices.[5]

Another kosher-meat boycott, this time in 1933, stands out as a dramatic example of Jewish housewives' militancy. When the price of kosher meat increased sharply in this year, seven hundred indignant Jewish women gathered at a mass meeting and decided to organize a boycott. They made plans to picket the butcher shops and chose a committee of fifty women to direct the protest. As the boycott progressed, the leaders issued leaflets each day and held frequent mass meetings to discuss strategy. Approximately two thousand Jewish women joined the boycott, and hundreds of women picketed the butcher shops, sometimes as early as five or six in the morning, holding their ground when the butchers tried to drive them away. Scuffles broke out between the picketers and the customers as well, particularly when zealous picketers snatched packages of meat out of the customers' hands and threw the meat in the mud. The protest was so effective that, within a week, the butchers decided to reduce the price of meat substantially.

Bessie Kramer, one of the boycott leaders who was struck in the face by an angry butcher, stressed that this boycott was a women's action. Although there were male supporters, all of the leaders and picketers were women. Sadie Hoffman, another boycott leader, explained it was a women's action because, 'meat that you have to cook, it's a woman's item.' She felt the women 'showed by action' they were capable of such militancy.[6]

In fact, the Jewish women of Toronto had been showing their capabilities by action for quite a while, for they had been involved in a whole range of successful boycotts over the years. Housewives have frequently been viewed as a conservative group, one that is difficult to mobilize for political action. Indeed, historians have commonly assumed that immigrant women in particular have been passive. Thus the militancy of these boycott activists is all the more significant, testifying to the important activist element of Jewish working-class culture. The housewives' attempts to fight for working people at the point of consumption, as well as the schoolchildren's strikes, indicate a context of broad activism within Toronto's immigrant Jewish community, a context that would have been missed by the traditional labour historian's narrow focus on the point of production.

The activist tenor of the city's East European Jewish community, indeed the vibrancy of Jewish working-class culture, was also reflected in Toronto's main Yiddish newspaper, the *Yiddisher Zhurnal*, which was established in the early 1910s. On the one hand, the editors of this paper, the only daily Yiddish newspaper in the city, saw the *Zhurnal*'s mission as representing the interests of the Jewish community as a whole. In fact, they often saw themselves as mediating between the conflicting interests within the community in order to promote the good of the entire community in a nonpartisan fashion. On the other hand, this newspaper was actually pro-labour. This pro-labour orientation constituted a reversal of the usual brokerage politics, so common in other newspapers in Canada in this period, where labour's interests were portrayed as sectional while business interests were equated with the national interest.

The *Zhurnal*'s approach sometimes required peculiar juggling acts, as is apparent, for example, in an editorial that appeared during the 1919 general strike in the city's cloak trade. In this editorial, the writers indicated they had tried to bring both the Jewish workers and the Jewish manufacturers in the cloak industry together to work out a settlement. The editorial insisted that the *Yiddisher Zhurnal* was an independent and impartial newspaper which took an impartial stand regarding the cloak-makers' strike. The editorial continued, however, by stating: 'if we are partial, it is only in one sense – to help the oppressed to receive justice and, in general, to raise the standard for a better, nicer, and more comfortable life.'

Notwithstanding the newspaper's own convoluted claims to impartiality, the paper's coverage of the various garment strikes was clearly pro-labour. Abraham Rhinewine, the main editor of the paper for years, was a socialist and a Jewish nationalist who supported the city's Jewish labour movement, and the *Zhurnal*'s editorials commonly presented the strikers' demands as fair and equitable. The paper usually presented its strike reports from the union's point of view and, in the middle of strikes, habitually refrained from including any information that might have harmed the strikers' cause. The pro-labour orientation of the newspaper was also apparent in the Yiddish poems it printed, poems that stressed the sufferings of the workers, praised stalwart strikers, and promoted visions of a future society where real freedom and justice would prevail.

In addition to prominent strike reports and workers' poetry, the *Yiddisher Zhurnal* usually carried a special weekly section on the labour movement. This section not only supported trade unionism, it was also often socialist in tone. An article that appeared during the 1935 cloakmakers' general strike, for example, agreed that the strike was justified because the workers needed higher wages, but added: 'It would seem that workers already have had enough experience to know that the struggle, to tear several more cents per garment out of the wolfish teeth of the employers, helps them very little, because as fast as they get the raise, the capitalist wheel turns, and the [cost of the] necessities of life increases again, and [the workers] must immediately fight again for higher wages, because [their earnings] are not enough to live on.' The writer concluded that 'with economic struggle alone, one cannot fundamentally improve the position of the worker. The worker[s] must realize that they must also fight politically in order to be able to establish another order, in which the products of human hands should be divided among the producers according to their needs.'[9]

By the interwar period, the pro-labour current within Toronto's immigrant Jewish community was so deep that a Jew who was a strike-breaker may well have found himself spurned by neighbours and friends. Sol Abel, an activist cloakmaker in the city's ILGWU in the 1930s, declared: 'There [were] very few Jewish people that would go strike-breaking, very few. And if there was the odd one, the community ... rejected him. You see, he couldn't keep his head up high.'[10] Joe Salsberg agreed: 'The general atmosphere was such that ... a "scab" was almost to be outlawed.'[11]

Yet not all immigrant Jewish workers were part of this Jewish working-class culture. Some, of course, harboured entrepreneurial ambitions. Some did not share the activists' commitment to the labour movement for a variety of other reasons. Although it is important not to exaggerate the extent of class culture within the immigrant Jewish community, liberal Jewish historians have minimized its importance for far too long. A strong Jewish working-class culture developed in Toronto, as in New York and in certain other key North American cities. Even though this culture did not encompass all Jewish workers, it encompassed many. The depth and vibrancy of this culture are crucial to understanding not only the development of the Jewish labour movement but also the nature of the immigrant Jewish experience more broadly.

The vigorous pro-labour current within Toronto's immigrant Jewish community did not mean, of course, that the unionization of the Toronto needle trades was easy or problem free. In a period where employers and the state actively discriminated against unionists, where the threat of actual hunger was ever present, where legislation did not exist to force employers to abide by contracts they themselves had signed with the union, Jewish workers (like other Canadian workers in this period) were not always able to stick to their unions. Then, too, the fact that they often worked for Jewish bosses complicated the question of class allegiance, as will be explored in the next chapter. In view of the many cross-pressures and deterrents, the extent of Jewish working-class activism in Toronto was remarkable, particularly in the 1920s and 1930s.

Even the _landsmanshaftn_ could be used as vehicles for reinforcing class culture by censuring Jewish strike-breakers and building strike support, for many of Toronto's Jewish workers were grouped together in these mutual benefit societies for co-religionists who had come from the same parts of Eastern Europe. Ed Hammerstein, a local activist from the fur workers' union, stressed that these organizations were pro-labour and explained that, in the midst of strikes, labour activists within the *lands-manshaftn* would mount pressure to expel any strike-breakers from these organizations. Many of the *landsmanshaftn* actively supported the Jewish unions by making donations during strikes and by setting up welfare measures to aid impoverished strikers.[13]

The Jewish unions themselves were based on an outlook that was far more than the 'trade unionism pure and simple' of Samuel Gompers (president of the American Federation of Labor for many years) and his many followers. The Jewish labour movement emphasized building a 'union with a soul' in each branch of the needle trades, a union that would speak to the needs of the workers on more than a simple economic level. For example, a leader who had been active in the Toronto fur workers' union for years explained: 'The Furriers' Union is far more than an association for economic purposes. It is a workers' organization that possesses a soul and a mission. Many of its leaders and members came to the movement in the pursuit of an ideal: to eliminate the sweat-shop and to have a new way of life, one with dignity and pride.'[14]

By the interwar period the Jewish unions served as vital social and cultural centres, providing an important form of community for many of these recent immigrants. Since so many of the Jewish workers lived in the garment district, it was easy for Jewish men to drop by the union halls to socialize with their fellow workers. This kind of informal socializing increased after the Labour Lyceum was built on Spadina Avenue in the mid 1920s to house the Jewish unions. The lyceum operated explicitly 'as a Union Institution to serve the Union Workers for their social and cultural requirements ... as a place where the laborer can meet his fellow men.' In an era in which television was non-existent and radios and movies were hard to afford, in a time when recent immigrants were living in crowded, poorly heated flats, the Labour Lyceum was an attractive place for men to visit with their friends. Moreover, the seasonal nature of the garment industry meant that the men had a lot of time to sit and socialize and plan strategies during seasonal downturns. Jewish men would drop by the lyceum to chat, discuss politics and policies, sip coffee, or perhaps play dominoes.[15]

While the Jewish unions drew strength from being built around the Jewish neighbourhoods in the Spadina district, not everyone participated in this informal social network. The non-Jewish garment workers seldom participated, partly because they tended not to live in the garment district and partly because the Canadian-born workers, unlike the recent immigrants, already had their own established social networks. Nor did Jewish women tend to drop by the union halls to socialize. They were included in the more formal social and cultural events, such as the lectures and concerts that took place in the auditorium of the Labour Lyceum.[16]

Although the unions' lack of sufficient strength meant there were limits to what they could do in the cultural field, Toronto's Jewish unions sponsored a variety of educational and recreational activities in the interwar years. As a Toronto ILGWU official explained, these programs were mainly designed 'to enable [the members] to better understand the problems that confront the working class in their struggle for a better social order.'[17] In 1924, for example, the ILGWU's speakers' series included a lecture on Lenin by John MacDonald (national secretary of the Communist Party of Canada) and a lecture on the English Labour government by James Simpson (an activist in the local Independent Labour party). The courses launched by the various Jewish unions in this period were often taught by instructors from the University of Toronto and held at union headquarters. Over the years, course topics included English-language instruction, public speaking, 'Group Singing Instruction for Men and Women in Labour Songs and Modern Compositions,' trade union history, and the 'History of Economic Development of Society Beginning with Primitive Society to the present Capitalist System.'[18]

These course topics reflected the fact that the Jewish unions were more than collective bargaining agencies. As a local leader of the International Fur Workers' Union explained in 1937: 'We do not only limit our work to securing better conditions for our membership, but we also aim to educate them both culturally and politically.'[19] In addition to serious political education, the unions eventually organized athletic clubs, particularly baseball teams.[20] These educational and recreational activities, as well as the informal socializing at the union halls, helped build worker solidarity. All these activities reflected the broader nature of the city's Jewish labour movement.

The Jewish 'unions with a soul' were socialist in orientation. The constitutions of unions like the Amalgamated Clothing Workers and the United Cloth Hat, Cap, and Millinery Workers' International Union contained ringing proclamations against the capitalist system. This was not just empty rhetoric, for the socialist nature of these constitutional proclamations was reflected in the Toronto locals of the Jewish unions. Leaders of the Toronto capmakers' local in 1918, for example, stressed the union's efforts not only to improve working conditions but also to take 'a very active part in all important socialist campaigns.' Many Jewish labour activists viewed strikes as more than just a way to get a few cents more per hour; they saw strikes in the needle trades as an intrinsic part of the class struggle that would one day bring about a socialist society.[1]

Unlike the leaders of many other Canadian unions, the leaders of Toronto's Jewish unions were committed socialists. The men who founded the Toronto Cloakmakers' Union in 1909, for example, were Jewish immigrants who had been radicalized in Tsarist Russia, particularly in connection with the revolution of 1905. Within the Jewish labour movement, the leadership's commitment to socialism was true not only during the early period but during the interwar years as well. These leaders were drawn mainly from the Bund, the Labour Zionist movement, and the Communist party. Socialists constituted a substantial portion of the rank and file of the Jewish unions as well.[2]

In contrast to this situation, activist Jewish workers in trades that were not predominantly Jewish sometimes complained about the more conservative unionism in their industries. In 1932, for example, Toronto's Jewish barbers criticized the union to which they belonged:

It is true that the [barbers'] union does nothing. Because one must not forget that the Barbers' International [Union] is a 'pure and simple union' and follows in the path of the A. F. of L. This fact alone is enough to make one understand that [the barbers' union] is against strikes, against each revolutionary action which it is sometimes necessary to adopt. [This union] is content that it provides for the members when they are sick and for their families after death. And, really, when you speak with an English worker, he is quite content with his union. Of course, this cannot satisfy us [the Jewish barbers] whose attention to unionism is altogether different.[23]

Jewish barbers had been organized in a sublocal of the Toronto section of the Barbers' International Union and had been putting forth 'demands which the Christian barbers saw as Utopian.'[24]

While the 'pure and simple unionism' of certain non-Jewish unions alienated key Jewish activists in those sectors, the socialist character of the Jewish unions did not generally alienate the Orthodox Jewish garment workers from the Jewish labour movement. Although Orthodox Jews disapproved of the atheism of Jewish socialists, there was not a sharp division between the two groups within the Jewish unions when it came to shop-floor issues. This is illustrated, for example, in the experience of Leah Stern, an Orthodox garment worker. Stern, in fact, was so Orthodox that when she once fell and broke her knee on the Sabbath, she refused a ride to the hospital, limped home, and did not phone a doctor until after sundown. (Religious Jews are not permitted to ride in a car or use the telephone on the Sabbath. Stern wound up having to have a knee operation.) The depth of her religious convictions meant that it was crucial that her employer permit her to avoid working on the Sabbath. Faced with an uncooperative boss, Stern turned to her union organizer to help her with this fight. This organizer was a Communist Jew who did not personally believe in religious observance of the Sabbath, but he nevertheless supported Stern. She won her fight and praised this man as a good union leader. 'He was a lefty,' she added, 'but that didn't bother me because he fought for my rights.'[25]

Orthodox convictions could thus lead to pro-union convictions. In fact, the Orthodox garment worker's struggle for a day of rest on the Jewish Sabbath should perhaps be seen as part of organized labour's long-standing tradition of pushing for the shorter work week. Moreover, Orthodox and socialist Jewish workers drew together around other shop-floor demands as well. Although the socialists were the more active unionists, the two groups of Jewish workers often walked off the job together when a strike was called. As Leah Stern explained, religious Jewish workers generally appreciated that socialist union leaders 'fought for the rights of the working person.' Although there may have been some minor friction between the Orthodox and the socialists with respect to the Jewish unions, the Jewish labour movement was not significantly fragmented along these lines.[26]

The pro-labour current within Toronto's immigrant Jewish community stemmed partly from the fact that a significant number of East European Jewish immigrants had already learned about trade unionism before emigration, in contrast to many of the other immigrant groups from Southern and Eastern Europe. Whereas many of these other North American immigrants had come from agricultural backgrounds in the Old World, Jewish immigrants tended to come from more urbanized and industrialized settings. Very few Jews had been farmers because they had been forbidden to own land in Tsarist Russia, and they had also been forced to live within a particular section of the empire, known as the Pale of Settlement. In the cities of the Pale, some Jews acquired trade union experience, which then facilitated the building of the Jewish labour movement on this side of the ocean.[27]

In both the Old World and the New, Jews often experienced class and ethnic oppression as closely intertwined. Impoverished Jews traced their economic hardships not only to their class position but also to anti-Semitism, which blocked them from access to better occupations. Even though anti-Semitic restrictions were, of course, more severe in Eastern Europe, anti-Semitism in Toronto meant not only that real upward mobility was difficult for Jews in this period but also that it was difficult for Jewish workers to enter even the better-paying blue-collar jobs. Although some of Toronto's first-generation Jewish immigrants did achieve upward mobility (largely by scraping together enough money to open a small retail store or a small garment factory), many Jewish workers continued to feel blocked both by anti-Semitism and by their class position. This experience of sharp, dual constraints led a significant number of Jewish workers to seek collective remedies through the Jewish labour movement.

Many Jewish labour activists viewed anti-Semitism and class oppression as closely intertwined in another way as well, declaring that Canadian capitalists deliberately stirred up racial antagonism to discredit class-conscious Jewish workers and to undermine the development of class consciousness among non-Jewish workers. This emphasis emerged, for example, in the context of the *Toronto Telegram*'s efforts to blame Jewish 'agitators' for the attempted general strike in Toronto in May 1919. At that time, an editorial in the *Yiddisher Zhurnal* explained: 'They, the most relentless enemies of labour, know that the demands for a shorter work week and collective bargaining are popular demands ... and they search therefore to fight against the just demands with incitement, with searching to bring in race-hatred, and so to draw away attention from the real strike issues.'[28] Although some Jewish workers may have concluded they should avoid labour activism so as to avoid providing an 'excuse' for anti-Semitism, others drew the opposite conclusion, taking active roles in the Jewish labour movement in order to fight back. The analysis of anti-Semitism as endemic to the capitalist system led some Jews to embrace socialism.

The depth of Jewish socialist commitment stemmed, in fact, from the double dimension of Jewish radicalism, for Jewish socialists were often radicalized both as workers and as Jews in response to their dual oppression. Many of the socialists within Toronto's immigrant community 'had already experienced the school of the labour movement in the old home' and had joined underground revolutionary societies before coming to the New World. Their passionate commitment to socialism was fuelled by their direct experience of the virulent anti-Semitism which erupted periodically in violent pogroms and which was systematically enforced through discriminatory legislation in Tsarist Russia. Their radical commitment was heightened by their direct awareness of the dire poverty experienced by Jews in the Pale.[29]

For example, Ed Tannenbaum, a long-time activist in one of Toronto's garment unions, was originally radicalized during his youth in Poland. Tannenbaum was brought into the underground movement at the age of eleven or twelve when he was asked to bring some of his classmates to a meeting of the Left Labour Zionists in his home town. He joined this movement, both as a response to Polish anti-Semitism and to the sheer drudgery and hardship of his life as a garment worker. Responding deeply to the egalitarian promise of socialism, he joined this particular wing of the Jewish left because he felt, at the time, that the only satisfactory solution to anti-Semitism was the construction of a socialist Jewish state in Palestine.

Tannenbaum emphasized the arduous working conditions in the needle trades in his town in Poland, where the Jewish clothing workers toiled from 5 AM until midnight during the busy seasons, longing for fresh air and sunshine. 'Personally, I said to myself when I came home [from work at night]: "if I have to continue living like this, and if I have no other way, I wouldn't like to live at all."' He became active in the struggle to establish a union in his town, and his pro-socialist inclinations were strengthened by the fact that the Jewish socialists were the driving force in the fight to establish the union.[30]

Sol Abel, another activist in Toronto's Jewish labour movement, similarly helped organize tailors while still in Poland and came to Canada as an experienced radical trade unionist. As a youngster in Poland, Abel joined the Bund in rebellion against the difficult lives Jews were forced to lead there. He declared that Polish anti-Semitism was the main reason why he became a Bundist. For him, socialism held out the promise of a new society in which everyone – including Jews – would be equal.[31]

Unlike Tannenbaum and Abel, Bessie Kramer did not become a committed socialist until after emigration. Nonetheless, Kramer stressed similar issues, and her deeply rooted socialist convictions guided her activism in Toronto's Jewish labour movement. She explained that she joined the Young Communist League in Canada largely because she felt that Communism would solve the related problems of anti-Semitism and harsh taxation that Jews continued to experience under the Polish régime. She stressed that she had been radicalized as a Jew: 'I joined [the Communist movement] for [the] reason that [at] that time, we thought that the best solution for the Jew is in the Soviet Union. That was right after the revolution. And I joined for that reason, that I wanted my *people* should be equal with every other people. And that was the slogan of the Communist Party, that in the Soviet Union, all the citizens are the same.'[32]

Joe Salsberg, one of the key leaders of Toronto's Jewish left, gave similar reasons for eventually joining the Communist party. He came to Canada at the age of ten or eleven and joined the youth section of Toronto's Left Labour Zionist movement several years later. In the mid 1920s he left the Labour Zionists and became a Communist. This was partly because he felt that even if the British could be persuaded to allow more Jews into Palestine, other measures were needed to solve the problems faced by those Jews who would remain in Eastern Europe. At that time, Salsberg became convinced that the Soviet Union embodied the solution: 'The early few years of the Soviet power created what later on appeared to have been illusions, but which at the time were very real and very attractive and very promising, as far as Jews and other minorities in the old Tsarist Russia were concerned. What happened? The new government of Lenin ... declared anti-Semitism as a criminal offence, punishable in the severest way that a state power has at its command.' Salsberg was impressed that 'for the first time in the history of Jewish life in Eastern Europe, all educational institutions were opened up for Jews to attend.' He believed that secular Jewish culture was blossoming in the Soviet Union – with the encouragement of the Soviet state. Thus Salsberg asserted that he, along with many others, joined the Communist movement 'both as very conscious Jews and also as very conscious socialists.'[33]

Concern for the fate of Jews remaining in Eastern Europe was closely linked to concern about the hardships of immigrant Jewish life in the New World. Jewish radicalism was reinforced by intense dissatisfaction with the harsh working conditions and low pay that so many Jewish workers encountered in Toronto, particularly in the notorious clothing industry where many of them were concentrated. Although the Canadian state was a decided improvement over Tsarist absolutism and although immigrant Jews were freed from the violence of pogroms, the New World fell far short of the immigrants' dreams, for labour activists still faced significant state repression here and immigrant Jews still faced significant prejudice. The sense of thwarted expectations about life in the New World strengthened the socialist convictions of a significant number of Jews.[34]

Some of these concerns are apparent in the experience of Jacob Black, who came to Canada at the age of thirteen. In explaining his own radicalization, Black stressed both the harsh economic conditions in Toronto and the anti-Semitism in Russia:

I was born in Russia, and I saw the pogroms in Russia in 1917–1918 and so on. So I was naturally affected by that. And when I came here and had to go to work in a [garment] factory when I was seventeen years old and being exploited – my first wage was five dollars a week – I realized that I had to do something about it, and I joined the union immediately, in 1926. That's how I became radicalized. And it wasn't too hard for me to combine [fighting for] my Jewish rights as well as my rights as a worker. And that's why I found my place in the Left Poale Zion [the Left Labour Zionist movement]. It gave me a home for both my strong beliefs.[35]

Ed Hammerstein, too, stressed the radicalizing impact of sweatshop conditions in Toronto and, focusing on the 1930s, also explained that 'the world situation radicalized people.' 'Don't forget,' he declared, 'Hitler came to power, [and] there was the Spanish Civil War.'[36]

For the immigrant generation, radicalism was sometimes reinforced by the dramatic transitions many experienced in their work lives. In Eastern Europe, the Jewish workers had generally toiled in small artisanal work-shops; thus immigration often meant an abrupt transition to the harsh discipline of the factory. This was a radicalizing experience for some, particularly since significant deskilling could heighten the abruptness of this transition. Although some of the Toronto garment shops did not depart dramatically from the labour process of the Old Country, many Jewish immigrants encountered a highly subdivided labour process in Toronto's needle trades, especially in the larger men's clothing firms. Here, the worker who used to make a whole garment was often reduced to sewing one particular seam on garment after garment, without variation.

Ed Tannenbaum, for example, described how the Jewish tailors in his home town in Poland in the 1920s toiled in small workshops where there would be only one or two sewing machines. In this setting, the typical machine operator usually did all the stitching on each garment by himself. This contrasted sharply with the sectionalized system of production Tannenbaum encountered when he emigrated: in the larger men's clothing shops in Toronto in the late 1920s, at least twenty or thirty people worked on different sections of the same coat. Tannenbaum was confined to stitching one small part of each coat. Labour historians have noted the radicalizing effect of rapid deskilling among groups such as the shoe-makers, but a similar point needs to be made about these garment workers as well.[37]

The Jewish workers' experience of the traditional artisanal labour process had other important implications. A vision of a socialist society, where capitalist employers would not be needed, probably made particular sense to workers who knew how to make up complete garments by themselves. For them, the process of production was not mystified, as it often was for workers who toiled in the large automobile assembly plants, for example. In the garment industry, where workers could become bosses after scraping together some money and gaining experience on the shop floor, workers generally understood the role of the employer clearly. This understanding made it easier to envision a socialist transformation.

Socialism also had a special appeal for Jewish needle trades workers in particular, because of the limited gains that the garment unions could make. The highly competitive structure of this labour-intensive industry set strict limits on what could be gained through collective bargaining; after all, pushing for decent wages ran the risk of driving one's employer out of business. Hence radical workers became even more convinced that the whole economic system needed to be changed.[38]

In addition to sharp changes in their work lives, Jewish socialists often experienced sharp changes in the religious sphere, for the development of radical convictions represented a break with key tenets of traditional Judaism. The Jewish socialists were commonly atheists, and some of them defiantly spurned the Jewish religion. Ed Tannenbaum was one such worker. As a youth in Poland, he openly rebelled against his religion, engaging in defiant acts he now thinks were tactically unwise. On Yom Kippur, the holiest fast day of the year, he and his friends would walk bare-headed along the streets, eating and smoking. On Passover, they would sing revolutionary songs and eat bread (which is forbidden) 'as a rebellion against the old way of life.' Ironically, Tannenbaum's mother had wanted him to become a rabbi, but he studied Marx instead.

At the same time, there were important continuities between traditional Judaism and the socialists' beliefs. Tannenbaum's discussion of the Bible reveals this link. 'Moses was a fighter for freedom,' he explained, 'but we peel out what we consider to be historical facts and throw away the legends.' 'So we do also, say, with Isaiah ... We embraced his teaching [on social problems], not his religion ... He warned the kings of his day, for suppressing the people, that they'll never get into heaven because of what they are doing. He wanted a better deal for the people. We want a better deal for the people; we are against the kings. Then he spoke against the wars, against the war-makers, whether they were Yiddish or not Yiddish, and he preached a community of the whole human race, of brotherhood of all nations.' 'We are for the same aims' as Isaiah, Tannenbaum concluded, 'now and forever, regardless of his religiousness.' Instead of promoting these aims 'in the name of God,' he explained, the Jewish socialists promoted them 'in the name of humanity.' Thus despite his opposition to religion, the values to which Tannenbaum dedicated his life were the values of Moses and Isaiah – minus the emphasis on God.[39]

For Joe Salsberg, socialist conviction sprang from especially deep religious roots. He came from an Orthodox home, like many other Jewish socialists, and was pious in his younger years. He explained: 'The earliest motivation in my young life then [regarding] social problems and social evils really came from my Jewish studies ... I did study the Bible – it wasn't a matter of reading, it was studying – and, above everything, the prophets ... I've concluded that Amos and Isaiah had more influence on me than socialist thinkers. [In my younger days,] Marx was nothing; it was an abstract name.' As a youngster in the Labour Zionist movement, Salsberg felt this movement stood for the idea that 'the Palestine that we want will be based on socialist prophetic thinking ... a Jewish socialist commonwealth.' In those days, he tried to justify his socialist ideas in discussions with his father and his father's Orthodox friends. 'In addition to the general socialist conception which I had begun to imbibe,' Salsberg explained, 'I also justified [my ideas] with the preachings of Amos and chapters of Isaiah which condemned the rich.'[40]

Numerous quotations can be drawn from the books of Amos and Isaiah to support Salsberg's assertions. These two prophets continually emphasized the need to 'seek justice' and to 'relieve the oppressed.'[41] They repeatedly stressed that the Lord was angry with those who 'oppress the poor' and 'crush the needy.'[42] They praised those who 'despiseth the gain of oppressions' and preached that the people must 'undo the bands of the yoke ... to let the oppressed go free.' The Lord, they explained, required that 'ye break every yoke.'[43]

Salsberg remained impressed by the prophets' 'dedication to social ideals,' and, looking back over his life, he stated: 'Sometimes I think that, after all I did, I am basically, all my life, an advocate and an activist in the realm of realizing Amos ... Call it democratic socialism now ... My writing and my activity are all reflections ... of a basic desire to change the world so that people stop exploiting people. And that brings [us] back to Amos, the starting point, without the religious dogma.'[44]

Moe Levin, a member of Toronto's Left Labour Zionist movement, made similar connections. Asked how the Orthodox Jews felt about unions, Levin replied: 'Well, my [Orthodox] father was for unions because he was a working man. Although he was a Jewish scholar, but he was working. He believed in the prophets, way back ... I would say he had socialistic ideas – not from Marx here, [but rather] way back, from the prophets ... He believed in social justice, and so did I. And that's the secret of it.'[45]

In addition to the prophets, other aspects of traditional Jewish belief were appropriated by some of the Jewish socialists to legitimate their radical convictions. The coming of the Messiah was transformed, for some, into a socialist vision. The socialist world, which they envisioned, was seen as a new Garden of Eden. They also drew parallels between Moses liberating the Jewish slaves from the tyranny of Pharaoh and the attempt to liberate the workers from their slavery in the sweatshops. Jim Blugerman, an important Toronto unionist who eventually became a Communist, recalled that his religious parents were sympathetic when he joined an underground revolutionary student group in Russia in 1904. His mother believed that, after all, Moses himself had been a socialist.[46] There was, in fact, a fundamental clash between traditional Jewish values and the mores of industrial capitalism. Religious ideals of social justice and community responsibility conflicted with the profoundly materialistic and individualistic nature of Canadian society. Although some Jews embraced the competitive materialism of the New World, the disjunction between the two sets of values helps explain why many immigrant Jewish workers became ardent unionists, seeking justice (and a sense of community) through the labour movement. This disjunction was also potentially radicalizing. Given the shortcomings of industrial capitalist mores as measured by traditional Jewish ideals, some concluded that the whole socio-economic system needed to be radically changed.

Salsberg's commitment to 'Amos socialism' represents a Jewish development that was roughly analogous to the radical wing of the Christian Social Gospel movement in the early twentieth century. There are further parallels, as well, between the religious roots of Jewish socialism, as analysed here, and the ways in which 'radical criticism and labor discontent [were] sanctioned by an appeal to Christian tradition' on the part of certain late nineteenth-century American workers, as analysed by historian Herbert Gutman.[47] Yet the double dimension of Jewish radicalization distinguished the Jewish socialists' commitment to radical social change.

Moreover, the development of working-class Jewish socialism was also a product of the unique role played by Jewish intellectuals. Unlike the common attachment of intellectuals to the dominant class, many Jewish intellectuals had become socialists in Eastern Europe partly in response to the anti-Semitism which sharply limited their own opportunities.

Although there were deep divisions between the Jewish socialist intellectuals and the Jewish masses in the Old World in the earlier period (particularly in the decade preceding the pogrom wave of 1881–2), close ties had developed between the two groups by the early twentieth century, both in Eastern Europe and in North America.

The immigrant socialist intellectuals gravitated to New York City in particular, where many initially worked in the needle trades sweatshops to earn a living. They articulated class grievances and an alternative socialist vision for their fellow workers, and helped give the Jewish labour movement a radical cast. In New York City they played leading roles in establishing not only the Jewish unions but also the Yiddish socialist press and the Jewish socialist political and fraternal organizations. Toronto had some of its own socialist intellectuals, and the close links between the Toronto and New York Jewish communities meant that the New York intellectuals strongly influenced the Canadian Jewish labour movement as well. More broadly, the ability of the socialist intellectuals to exert such influence over their fellow Jews stemmed, in part, from the decreased authority of the rabbis under the impact of rapid social change in Eastern Europe and especially in North America.[48]

The socialist currents within the immigrant Jewish community, in Toronto as elsewhere in North America, were also reinforced by certain aspects of secular East European Jewish culture, particularly Yiddish literature. For example, Molly Fineberg, an activist in Toronto's Jewish labour movement, explained that her own radicalization was partly due to the fact that 'the subjects, the stories that are written in the Yiddish books are so socialistically inclined. They write about the poverty; they write about the difference between poor people and wealthy people. And it's very democratic ... Peretz [one of the greatest Yiddish authors] was already a rebel.' Fineberg's own family 'lived very poorly' in Toronto, so Peretz's stories resonated with her own experience. Joe Salsberg, too, stressed that I.L. Peretz's writing strongly condemned the exploitation of working people and inspired many readers.[49]

Scores of examples could be cited from Yiddish literature to illustrate the anger at oppression and the call to rebellion. In New York City at the turn of the century, there was even a school of 'sweatshop poets,' including such well-known Yiddish socialist writers as Morris Rosenfeld, Morris Winchevsky, and David Edelstadt. Their verses were often set to music and sung by Jewish workers in Eastern Europe, the United States, and Canada. Edelstadt's '*Vacht Oyf*' ('Awake'), for example, was widely sung:

How long, oh, how long will you
slaves yet remain
And bear the shameful chain?
How long will you glorious wealth create
For him, who robs you of your bread?

How long will you stand with your
backs bended low
Humbled, homeless, and wan?
It dawns! Awake and open your eyes!
And feel your iron might![50]

Toronto's Jews had their own Yiddish sweatshop poets, the most famous of whom was probably S. Nepom. Nepom's poem, 'In the Shop,' conveyed the disparity between the rich and the poor, and called on the poor to rebel:

Needles flashing, dancing and excited,
Machines rushing noisily, which eat up
 the days.
The shop smells sweaty, like a jail.
And a hundred hands, tired out, hot –
They create good fortune, they create joy,
For those who have round bellies,
For those who whiten their polished hands ...

The shop is full with unrest, with rushing,
Machines sing songs of the sweatshop and of
 hardship –
And over all the heads and shoulders
The sun of freedom sang, so red.
Needles flashing, dancing and excited,
Fifty tailors in the shop, by the machines.
'Straighten out your backs!' someone sang,
'Unite together!' – dawn is about to
 break through.[51]

Another of Nepom's poems, 'A New Mankind,' envisioned the coming of the new order where 'The slaves who yesterday were severely oppressed/ Today have heroically reached their good fortune.'[52]

[In the struggle for the 'new mankind,' a network of socialist Jewish fraternal organizations in Toronto reinforced Yiddish socialist culture and actively supported the Jewish unions. Not only did most of the Jewish labour leaders belong to these organizations but a significant number of the rank-and-file Jewish garment workers also belonged. In the early years, most of the different types of Jewish socialists joined the Arbeiter Ring (Workmen's Circle). The first Toronto branch of this organization had been established in 1908, largely with the help of Jewish members of the Socialist Party of Canada. In the period from the mid 1920s to the early 1930s, however, a number of factions split off from the Arbeiter Ring to form their own fraternal organizations. Those who were oriented towards the Communist party in particular left to found the Labour League. The left Labour Zionists and the right Labour Zionists each developed their own fraternal organizations as well. Although serious divisions emerged between certain Jewish socialist groups, these fraternal organizations enriched Jewish working-class culture in many ways.[53]

The Arbeiter Ring organized a whole range of cultural activities, setting up reading clubs for adults to learn more about socialism, for example, and bringing prominent Yiddish speakers from New York to Toronto to give talks. The organization also had a summer camp where workers could socialize with each other while vacationing with their families. The depth of the Arbeiter Ring's commitment to the future of the Jewish socialist movement is apparent particularly in the network of Yiddish schools that it established. These schools, known as the Peretz Shuls, taught the children about secular East European Jewish culture and about socialism and the labour movement. There was even a special children's version of 'The Internationale' for these young pupils to sing in Yiddish. 'We are children, all equal,' they sang. 'We are all one for the other; there are no poor ones, no rich ones,' they proclaimed. Through songs like these, as well as through more formal classroom education, the Arbeiter Ring strengthened the ranks of the Jewish socialist movement.[54]

As a Toronto activist explained in 1922, the Arbeiter Ring was founded 'to introduce proletarian self-help' in order 'to free ourselves from bourgeois philanthropy' and 'to create a labour family where all the members should live peacefully, despite the variety of ideas [among them], inculcating a spirit of brotherhood and friendship.'[55] Within the organization, the different types of Jewish socialists would all be tied together, according to the Arbeiter Ring's declaration of principles, by the belief that the existing system was unjust and by the obligation to fight for the establishment of a socialist system.[56]

As the 'Red Cross of Labour,' the Arbeiter Ring provided various support services for the workers, ranging from social fellowship and members' sick benefits to active strike support. In fact, Toronto's Arbeiter Ring supported Jewish strikers vigorously, providing financial aid and help on the picket lines as well as moral support. In addition to fundraising and picketing, female members of the Arbeiter Ring, like Molly Fineberg, would try to obtain donations of meat and bread for the strikers. Even the Peretz Shul children sometimes helped out by singing workers' songs and folk songs at a special concert for the strikers. In addition, since some of the Arbeiter Ring's branches were organized around specific trades (such as the capmakers' branch), the Arbeiter Ring's structure helped provide a basis for union activities in these particular trades.[57]

Like the Arbeiter Ring, the Communist-oriented Labour League was a social and cultural organization that also served as a mutual aid society and a support network for the Jewish labour movement. The Labour League had its own cultural activities, including a Yiddish choir that performed songs about socialism and the labour movement. There was also a network of schools where the children were taught left-wing politics and working-class history as well as Jewish history and the Yiddish language. The Labour League had special branches organized for members of particular trades, and it played an active role in strike-support work. Organizations like the Arbeiter Ring and the Labour League helped reinforce the needle trades unions by threatening to expel any members who served as strike-breakers. In addition, the fraternal organizations of the right and left Labour Zionists similarly helped support the Jewish labour movement, providing funds for strike relief and joining in picketing and mass demonstrations. Although there were serious divisions among the Jewish socialists, these socialist Jewish fraternal organizations formed an important part of the Jewish labour movement, supporting various union activities and reinforcing values that encouraged union militancy.[58]

Toronto's Jewish labour movement was based on an activist, Jewish, working-class culture. A deep pro-labour current flowed through the immigrant Jewish community and led to much more than 'trade unionism pure and simple.' The Jewish unions served as social and cultural centres and were explicitly socialist in orientation. Whether motivated by the teachings of the prophets, by the children singing 'The Internationale' in Yiddish, by the poetry of Morris Rosenfeld, or by the hardships of life in the sweatshops, many Jewish workers responded to their plight with activism.

3 Uncle Moses and the Slaves
Relations between Jewish Manufacturers and Jewish Workers

'[Uncle Moses, owner of the garment shop, said:] "At my place, men don't work on the Sabbath or on the holidays ... At my place, the people are *landslayt* [from Uncle Moses' home town], family ...

'"I don't need this," [he said,] pointing to his shop. "I spend money on it. I support this only because of you, that my *landslayt* should be able to make a living. What would you do without me? Who brought you to America? To whom did you come for a ship ticket, for money, when you needed to bring your families here? To whom do you come when you have trouble? When one of you becomes, God forbid, sick?" Uncle Moses shouted so loudly that the *landslayt* trembled. [He continued:] "To whom do you come? Everyone comes to Uncle Moses, heh? Is it so? And this one wants to establish a union at my place. Not at my place, brother!"'

– Sholem Ash, *Onkel Moses*

'And Charlie [the union organizer at Uncle Moses' shop] again became the "Moses" who is going to free the Jews from "Pharaoh, King of Egypt," and from under his heavy yoke. Charlie again became the redeemer, the liberator of the *Kuzminer landslayt* [the Jews who had come from Uncle Moses' town of Kuzmin].'

– Sholem Ash, *Onkel Moses*'

'What's the matter with the Jew?' asked union activist Ike Gilberg in 1913. Writing in the newspaper of the Journeymen Tailors' Union of America,

Gilberg argued that North America's Jewish workers needed to realize the complete irrelevance of the ethnic bond between themselves and the Jewish manufacturers in the clothing industry. 'The mind of the Jewish working people has been for generations subverted and confused by religious and racial superstitions and persecutions, perhaps more so than the minds of any other race,' he maintained. As a result, Jews belonging to 'the master class' were able to 'appeal to the Jewish working people from their racial pride and religious superstitution [sic]' in such a way as to dampen workers' militancy in the clothing industry. 'What my people need,' concluded Gilberg, 'is to be educated to their class interests ... My object in life for the past 26 years has been to teach my people who make their living by the sweat of their brow, that they do not belong to the Jewish race, but that they belong to that great International Family, the Working class.'[2]

Gilberg's promotion of a single-minded class allegiance is simplistic. In Toronto, class-conscious Jewish workers – people such as Bessie Kramer, Ed Tannenbaum, and Jacob Black – emphasized their Jewish identity as well as their working-class identity. Their Jewishness was crucial to them. Indeed, many of these Jewish socialists had become radicalized not only as workers but also as Jews, particularly in response to anti-Semitism. Although there were probably a few Jewish workers in Toronto who would have agreed with Gilberg, most of them would have been appalled by his call for the complete renunciation of their ethnic heritage. Moreover, 'that great International Family, the Working class' did not welcome Jewish workers with open arms.

Although many of the Jewish clothing workers were employed by non-Jews in early twentieth-century Toronto, the proportion of Jewish clothing workers who worked for fellow Jews had increased significantly by the interwar years. By the 1930s in particular, Jews probably owned the majority of the city's garment shops. This development altered the dynamics of labour-management relations in Toronto's needle trades.

Although the limitations of fragmentary evidence make it difficult to be precise about detailed changes over time in the nature of the relationships between Jewish workers and Jewish manufacturers, key themes emerge. Overall, class relations within Toronto's Jewish community were shaped by ethnicity in ways far more complex than Gilberg suggests. The significant ties between Jewish workers and Jewish manufacturers were shaped, for example, by the fact that the Jewish garment unions did certain kinds of work to promote the interests of Jews as a whole.

Although it is true, as Gilberg indicates, that Jewish workers' militancy was sometimes dampened by the common ties with Jewish employers, it is also true that these ties sometimes rendered Jewish employers less intransigent. In situations of conflict, appeals to ethnic interests were not simply designed to force concessions from Jewish workers, for different representatives of the Jewish community appealed to Jewish ethnic interests in different ways in the midst of strikes. On the whole, although the common bonds sometimes dampened class conflict, fierce conflict often erupted between Jewish workers and Jewish manufacturers in the city's needle trades.

In contrast to Gilberg's union (the Journeymen Tailors' Union of America), the Jewish needle trades unions were explicitly concerned with Jewish issues as well as with working-class issues. In 1925, for example, one of Toronto's ACW leaders emphasized this aspect of the union's activities. Reviewing the work of the city's ACW locals over the course of the preceding ten years, he stressed that 'the Amalgamated [Clothing Workers], whose Jewish membership is from sixty to seventy per cent, must also, from time to time, attend to special Jewish problems and needs.' He explained that the Toronto ACW, which eventually became an affiliate of the Canadian Jewish Congress, had done relief work for unfortunate Jews in Eastern Europe and had pushed for equal rights for Jews in 'the oppressed lands.'[3] Surely the Jewish manufacturers approved of this kind of union activity.

In the interwar years, Toronto's Jewish unions helped mount several large demonstrations against anti-Semitism. In 1919, for example, they joined a number of the city's Jewish organizations in planning a day of mourning and protest against the intense wave of pogroms in Ukraine and called upon all their members to join the protest demonstration. Similarly, Toronto's Jewish unionists helped organize against Naziism and Fascism in the 1930s. They were active, for example, in carrying out a large Toronto demonstration in 1933 against the persecution of Jews in Germany. Jewish garment manufacturers willingly cooperated with the unionists by closing their shops for half a day to allow everyone to go to this demonstration.[4] Here was a cause that united Jews of different classes.

The ties between the city's Jewish employers and Jewish employees in the garment industry were also shaped by the fact that the economic gap between these two groups was not usually very large. Although the gap increased in cases where Jewish manufacturing firms prospered, a significant number of Jewish employers were only somewhat better off than their workers. Aspiring entrepreneurs needed only limited capital to become a clothing manufacturer, and cut-throat competition in the industry often squeezed their profits severely, so Jewish manufacturers often ran small shops that did not do very well, particularly in the depressed 1930s. Commonly, the Jewish clothing employer had recently been a worker himself, and, given the high rate of business mortality in the industry, he might soon become a worker again. Then, too, the unemployed garment worker, despairing of ever finding someone to hire him, might try to scrape together enough money to start up his own little business. Thus, although there were some substantial Jewish garment firms in Toronto, the distinction between the two classes was sometimes fairly fluid, especially because of the unstable structure of this industry. Jewish workers and Jewish manufacturers were often tied together as neighbours, relatives, *landslayt* (Jews from the same region of Eastern Europe), members of the same synagogues, or members of other Jewish community organizations. Although Jewish residential patterns were beginning to develop some differentiation based on class, 'the actual extent of class-based spatial segregation' among Toronto's East European Jews was still 'decidedly weak in 1931,' as geographer Daniel Hiebert has demonstrated. Although some Jewish manufacturers prospered, moved to better areas, and joined the more prestigious synagogues and community organizations in these years, many Jewish manufacturers remained more closely linked to working-class Jews in the interwar period. Often, when Jewish immigrants first came to Toronto, they depended directly on relatives or *landslayt* for employment. Many interviewees recalled working for a relative in the needle trades when they first arrived. 'And generally in the plants, it wasn't absentee employers,' Ed Hammerstein recalled. 'The employer would be standing side by side with you, working at the bench or doing whatever is necessary.' Focusing on the small garment shops, Hammerstein stressed the close nature of the relationships between the Jewish manufacturers and their Jewish workers.[6]

The ties between relatives and between *landslayt* were particularly important in immigrant Jewish culture. Jewish tradition was (and still is) highly family oriented. Indeed, in the context of the stresses of mass immigration, extended family ties could be crucial in helping a person to emigrate and to adapt to life in the New World. Similarly, the *landsmanshaftn* played key roles in helping Jews adapt to this country. As Joe Salsberg pointed out, the *landsmanshaft* 'was important to [Toronto's Jewish immigrants], first because it was a warm corner where they met people they knew, [people] they grew up with. Second, they received moral and social assistance and support from their groups. And in many instances they even established a little synagogue of their own.'[7] The material assistance one could receive from the *landsmanshaft* was particularly important in a period where there were no programs such as unemployment insurance or government health plans.[8]

As the Yiddish novelist Sholem Ash portrayed in the character of Uncle Moses, some Jewish employers made a particular point of hiring relatives and *landslayt*, and, in some cases, the manufacturers had even helped these workers to emmigrate. Sometimes these manufacturers employed such people as part of a deliberate strategy to try to ensure a docile workforce, but some manufacturers were motivated by a sincere desire to help people to whom they were closely tied. As Salsberg explained, 'it was old loyalties, old relationships, family ties, and so on' that made employers feel like helping people from their old homes come to Canada. 'Undoubtedly,' Salsberg declared, 'there were [those] such as Levinsky,' a well-known fictional character who employed his *landslayt* as a conscious strategy to keep the union out. 'But there were also others who would help a *landsman* come [because] maybe they went to school together, they were on the same social level at home. And he helped get him a job.'[9] Indeed, these two types of motivation were not necessarily mutually exclusive. Some Jewish manufacturers may have sincerely desired to help old friends by providing passage money and jobs while, at the same time, hoping to profit personally from having a workforce closely tied to them.

The religious bond was also important, particularly between Orthodox workers and employers. Religious Jews, who wished to observe the traditional Sabbath, often sought to work for Jewish bosses who would close their shops on Saturday. Traditional Judaism also stressed the importance of praying three times a day in a group that included at least ten males, so, in some shops, work would temporarily halt at sunset, while the Orthodox – both employers and employees – prayed together.

Ironically, Toronto's Jewish bosses and Jewish workers were further tied together by the fact that a significant number of the bosses had recently been active unionists themselves. Jewish unionists became manufacturers for a number of reasons, including cases where blacklisted activists opened their own little shops because no one would hire them. Moreover, some of the Jewish manufacturers had been ardent socialists in their earlier years, and some of them asserted that they remained committed socialists even after making the transition from worker to boss. In fact, some of these socialist employers remained members of radical organizations such as the Arbeiter Ring and the Labour League.[11]

These close ties dampened class conflict somewhat. Indeed, Toronto's Jewish manufacturers were called upon to help fund the new building for the Jewish unions. In 1924 the city's Jewish unions were raising money to build their own Labour Lyceum, a 'Jewish workers' home' where all these unions would have their headquarters. In the *Yiddisher Zhurnal*, the unions' fund-raising committee appealed to Jewish businessmen to provide financial help, arguing, from the point of view of the businessmen, that 'the Jewish businessmen of today are the workers of yesterday. Most of us have not broken off our relations with the mass of workers; if we are not tied to them through business, we are belonging with them in various societies and organizations. In each family, there are male and female workers.' The appeal also indicated that Jewish workers and Jewish businessmen were further tied together by the fact that 'we are [all] enslaved by big capital.'[12]

This appeal emphasized that the Labour Lyceum would serve as a focal point for Jewish cultural life. Maintaining that Jewish businessmen were, of course, interested in the institutional life of the Jewish community, the text of the appeal explained that 'the workers are building now an institute which will be a source of pride for all Jews; they're building not only a home for workers, but also a comfortable place where many Jewish societies and organizations will be able to have their meetings and undertakings on a big scale.'[13] Subsequent newspaper reports on the progress of the fund-raising drive indicated that the Jewish president of Tip Top Tailoring, the largest firm in the men's clothing industry, had contributed a substantial amount of money.[14]

The many ties between Jewish workers and Jewish manufacturers meant that they sometimes found it disturbing to take a hard stand against each other. The Jewish manufacturer, who would meet his workers at the synagogue, at the *landsmanshaft*, or even at the Arbeiter Ring, must have felt uncomfortable about being intransigent on shop-floor issues. In some cases, this meant that the manufacturer was more inclined to reach an accommodation with the union. For example, one of the Toronto leaders of the furriers' union, a man who was a member of the Left Labour Zionist group, was able to get some good contracts, without resorting to strikes, because he was friendly with certain employers through the Zionist movement.[15]

The ties between Jewish workers and Jewish manufacturers sometimes also meant certain manufacturers did not resort to recruiting strikebreakers in the midst of strikes. For example, Jacob Black, who stressed the sharp class conflict between fellow Jews in this industry, indicated that some of the Jewish manufacturers, especially those who had recently been workers themselves and who belonged to progressive organizations, 'were easier to get along with.' Black recalled the general strikes in the various branches of the needle trades that hit both the more sympathetic and less sympathetic employers. 'Now maybe [the more sympathetic employers] didn't operate a factory with scabs, like some of the others tried to do,' he explained, but there was still serious conflict between these employers and their workers. In such cases, common ties dampened class conflict to the extent that strike-breakers were not recruited (which was, after all, a significant concession), but not to the extent that a strike was avoided.[16]

Joe Salsberg illustrated just this type of occurrence in a lengthy recollection about two Jewish brothers in Toronto, the older of whom had been a union activist and had then opened up his own millinery factory where he employed his younger brother and sister. The older brother belonged to the employers' association, and when the association refused to renew the collective agreement on the basis of the union's demands, 'a strike/lockout situation' resulted throughout the millinery trade. The two brothers slept in the same room, and, when the dispute broke out, the older brother woke up the younger brother early in the morning to remind him not to be late for picket duty. The younger brother, who was the union's shop chairperson at the older brother's shop, went out to picket this shop with the sister. 'It's hard to believe,' exclaimed Salsberg in retrospect, 'but that's what happened! And there were similar cases.'

Salsberg stressed that the older brother 'didn't attempt to employ non-union labour during the strike. But the picket line had to be there, according to union rules. And [he] knew [this] because he had been a founder of the union ... and had no intention of actively participating in an anti-union act [sic].' Although other manufacturers recruited strike-breakers, the older brother kept his shop closed. Here again, class conflict was significantly dampened – but was by no means eliminated.[17]

Jewish workers, too, must have found it uncomfortable to be aggressive on the shop floor, in view of their ties to the Jewish manufacturers. In some cases, workers were reluctant to push for higher wages because they were relatives of the owners. This was the case, for example, in a particular Toronto cloak shop where ILGWU officials had trouble persuading the workers to bargain with the employer for better wages. The key worker in this shop was the employer's brother-in-law, who felt that he could not argue with his boss for higher wages.[18] Similarly, when ILGWU officials reported problems in a particular Toronto dress shop, they explained that 'this shop is too much of a family affair, and consequently the prices and conditions are very bad there.'[19]

To a certain extent, such ties must have facilitated the development of arbitration machinery in certain branches of the clothing industry. The establishment of arbitration boards depended partly on the ability of unionists and manufacturers to agree on a person who could act as 'impartial chairman.' One such person was Sam Kronick, a manufacturer who sympathized with the unions. Joe Salsberg recalled Kronick's helpfulness in the early 1920s, in a period when Salsberg was the organizer for the millinery workers and before Kronick became impartial chairman of one of the arbitration boards in the clothing industry. Recollecting how Kronick helped the union organize other shops, Salsberg stated: 'In Toronto, we had the odd experience of the largest millinery shop was the American Hat, and the owner [Sam Kronick] was ... a very liberal person (with a small "l"), a very nice man. His shop was unionized because he couldn't bring himself to resist. [He was a] Jewish man. He was not considered an opponent. In fact, we worked with him, hand in hand, both in our efforts to organize Montreal, which he was very anxious to see come about, and in Toronto.'[20] Salsberg also described how, during negotiations between the union and the millinery manufacturers' association, Kronick would help convince the other unionized employers to give in to certain of the union's demands. Kronick's sympathy for the union was perhaps partly due to a belief that the manufacturers should work with the union to help stabilize the industry by reducing low-wage competition, but Salsberg felt that Kronick was favourably disposed towards the union particularly because he sympathized with his workers.[21]

The development of formal arbitration machinery in certain sections of the clothing industry received part of its impetus from the tradition of using the rabbi as arbitrator in the *shtetl* (Jewish town in Eastern Europe). Rather than use the Gentile courts to voice complaints against their co-religionists, Jews in Eastern Europe frequently depended on their own religious leaders to adjudicate disputes. The rabbi was called upon to pronounce judgments not only in religious matters (as narrowly defined) but also in cases of monetary disputes. The rabbi's judgments were made on the basis of the laws set forth in the Jewish sacred writings, laws that covered a wide range of issues, including an edict that a man must be paid enough to live on. In the *shtetl*, the people sometimes also called upon other community leaders to arbitrate disputes.[22]

Toronto's immigrant Jews remained concerned that public quarrels between fellow Jews would damage their image in the eyes of non-Jews, thereby fuelling anti-Semitism. This concern surfaced frequently during industrial disputes between Jewish workers and Jewish manufacturers.[23]

Thus, to a certain extent, the eventual development of arbitration machinery in certain branches of the garment industry reflected the traditional reliance of East European Jews on the arbitration of disputes within their own community.

In the midst of strikes, various Jewish community leaders appealed to the community's ethnic interests in very different ways. One approach was typified by the early actions of Rabbi Jacobs ('of the assimilationist synagogue') who, according to a local ILGWU leader, played an 'ugly role' in a 1910 cloak strike 'with his sermons that Jews must not rebel and that this is a disgrace in the eyes of the Gentiles.'[24] Solomon Jacobs was the rabbi of Holy Blossom Synagogue, which represented mostly the old community of middle-class, English Jews (very few of whom were involved in the needle trades). Although there was tension between the English Jews and the more recent East European Jewish immigrants, some of the more prosperous East European Jewish manufacturers had been joining the prestigious Holy Blossom.[25]

A few years after Rabbi Jacobs had been so outspokenly anti-union, he tried to play a more conciliatory role that harked back to the traditional role of the rabbi as mediator in Eastern Europe. During the large Eaton strike of 1912, the rabbi, together with magistrate Jacob Cohen and Mayor George Geary, tried to arrange a conference with representatives of the strikers and Eaton officials. In this case, the many striking garment workers were Jewish while the owners of the firm were not. Management adamantly refused to negotiate. When the rabbi's attempts to mediate the dispute failed, he and magistrate Cohen tried to persuade the strikers to repudiate certain negative statements about the company nonetheless, and the two of them issued a statement in which they 'assured [the strikers] that they could rely on the generosity and consideration of the firm and that they could expect nothing but fair and just treatment.' The strikers had a different opinion of management's commitment to justice. Moreover, one of the key managers of Eaton's garment factory, Sigmund Lubelsky, was a member of Holy Blossom and a chief opponent of the strikers. Thus East European Jewish workers increasingly felt that Holy Blossom represented interests opposed to them.[26]

Despite the workers' distrust of Rabbi Jacobs, he continued to play a high-profile role in needle trades disputes, in contrast to most of the other Toronto rabbis who seldom took public positions in industrial disputes in the clothing industry. During the ILGWU's general strike in 1919, for example, he was involved in an arbitration committee that worked out a settlement for the city's dressmakers. In this case, Rabbi

Jacobs, together with Edmund Scheuer, represented the manufacturers during the arbitration. Scheuer, a relatively wealthy Reform Jew from Alsace, had been one of the leaders of Holy Blossom for years. Although both Jacobs and Scheuer had represented the manufacturers in this case, Jacobs assumed a different role when it came to working out a settlement for the striking cloakmakers a few days later. At that time, he acted as mediator and chairperson in a conference between both sides.[27]

As for Cohen, another community leader from Holy Blossom, his initial interest in helping mediate needle trades disputes soon gave way to a harsh attitude towards striking Jewish workers. A prominent East European Jewish immigrant, Cohen had been a peddler in his early days in Toronto, and his upward mobility was largely due to Tory patronage. As justice of the peace, Cohen used his official position to harass Jewish strikers. During the ILGWU's general strike in Toronto in 1919, he meted out stiff fines to Jewish picketers and even threatened them with deportation. He declared that he was deliberately imposing large fines in order to stop the trouble that strikes caused.[28]

By 1919, however, the *Yiddisher Zhurnal* was providing strong community leadership that countered the influence of men like Jacobs, Scheuer, and Cohen. In response to Cohen's actions during the ILGWU's general strike, the *Zhurnal* published a sarcastic editorial, mocking Cohen as a pretentious 'peacemaker' who was attempting 'to rid the world of the strike plague' by using the 'solution' of more and bigger fines. Not surprisingly, the editorial concluded that Cohen's strategy would not work and that, if he really wanted to help his friends, the cloak manufacturers, he would have to come up with something better. The editors also berated Cohen for attempting to intimidate strikers by threatening they would be thrown out of the country if they did not behave.[29] Deportation was an extremely serious threat, particularly in the context of the new wave of pogroms that was sweeping across large parts of Eastern Europe in the aftermath of the First World War. Yet here was the spectacle of one Jew threatening fellow Jews with deportation. The ties between Jews could become very strained indeed, especially as class differentiation increased within the city's Jewish community.

As Jewish manufacturers squared off against Jewish workers, the *Zhurnal*'s editors appealed to the community's ethnic interests in ways that were diametrically opposed to Jacobs's 1910 anti-strike sermons. The newspaper's editorials frequently called upon Jewish employers to make concessions to their Jewish employees to contribute to the welfare of the Jewish community as a whole, stressing that Jews needed to stick together in a hostile world. During the 1919 general strike in the city's cloak trade, in particular, the paper's editors tried to appeal to Jewish employers to break with the intransigence of Christian manufacturers and settle with their own workers. Jewish manufacturers were asked how they could, in all good conscience, conspire with the Gentiles against fellow Jews: 'You don't want to admit it ... but even from your silence one finds out that you, Jewish cloak manufacturers, lick no honey in your [Toronto Cloak Manufacturers'] Association where Mr Merrick and several large Christian manufacturers are the main policy-makers. You are quiet about this, but indirectly you complain, you know, about the anti-Semitism which predominates in the Association where they so hate you[,] exactly as they hate the Jewish tailors.' 'How many times has it unwillingly slipped out,' the newspaper's editors asked, 'that you don't go to the meetings of the Association because you can no longer endure the insults?' 'How many times,' they continued, 'have you yourselves admitted that it is not right for you to have anything to do with men who believe all Jews are Bolsheviks and who, at their meetings, make the worst accusations against Jews?'[30]

The editors tried to strengthen their appeal by arguing that, in this case, the economic interests of the Jewish cloak manufacturers – as well as their ethnic interests – dictated that they should give in to the demands of the workers. Trying to drive a wedge between the Jewish manufacturers and the Christian manufacturers, the editorial claimed that the two groups were in a different position economically. 'We write these words because we want to warn you about the catastrophe which awaits you,' declared the editors to the Jewish employers:

You don't want to see that the big Christian [cloak] manufacturers try, with the Association, to shoot two hares at once [kill two birds with one stone]. They want to fight the union *and also to destroy the small Jewish manufacturers*. Therefore, they are for lengthening the strike, to draw it out longer, in order to accomplish both things, to become free from both the union and from you, their competitors.

In your anger at the workers, incited by the Merricks and their like, you don't want to see it, and you let them lead you – *to your own grave*.[31]

The moral, of course, was that Jews should ally with their own kind and beware of trusting Christians. Editorials in the *Yiddisher Zhurnal* also tried to appeal directly to Jewish manufacturers on the basis of the common fear that public fighting between Jews would arouse anti-Semitism. During the 1935 general strike in Toronto's cloak trade, for example, the editors called on the manufacturers to give in to the demands of the workers, declaring: 'We are concerned about the current strike in the cloak industry [in particular] because they, the factory-owners and also the workers are Jews, and it seems, to this non-Jewish city, that only Jews make scandals, that only Jews fight each other, and only Jews shed blood ... Besides the fact that both sides suffer directly from the strike, the whole Jewish community also suffers [from it].'[32] Although it was an exaggeration to state that Gentiles felt that 'only Jews make scandals,' the fact that there had been some serious fighting on the picket lines undoubtedly gave Jews more of a negative image. While the editorial pressured the manufacturers, it did not call on Jewish workers to make concessions to bring an end to the fighting. Yet Jewish manufacturers and Jewish workers may both have felt more compelled to reach an accommodation with each other, in view of this fear of inadvertently contributing to the increase of anti-Semitism. However, the *Zhurnal*'s detailed coverage of these strikes testifies dramatically to the intense class conflict that broke out between fellow Jews in this sector.

Thus, although the common ethnic tie sometimes dampened class conflict in Toronto's needle trades in the interwar period, sharp conflict did erupt frequently between Jewish workers and Jewish manufacturers. In attempting to explain these bitter conflicts, one Jewish garment worker proclaimed: 'Why should I feel better if I am exploited by a Jew?' For her, this was a rhetorical question. Having been oriented towards the Communist party for years, this woman defined herself as a secular, left-wing Jew. Despite the fact that being Jewish was an important part of her identity, she felt it was essential to fight against all forms of economic exploitation, whether or not the exploiter was Jewish. Many Jewish socialists would have agreed.[33]

Yet the issue was not so simple. Some Jewish workers may actually have felt 'better' about being exploited by Jewish employers. A worker might have felt that if some boss was to make a profit from her or his labour in any case, it would be better if the boss were at least a Jew – who might donate some of his money to the *landsmanshaft*, the synagogue, or Mount Sinai Hospital, thereby reducing the level of exploitation in terms of the 'social wage.' Although 'proletarian self-help' was an important goal for many Jewish workers, it might still have been significant that the Jewish manufacturer might plough some of his profits back into local Jewish community institutions (including the Labour Lyceum) or into financial aid for Jews desperately trapped in Europe.

Designing and cutting room, Eaton's garment factory, c.1910. The electric cutting machine shown here could cut 250 layers of light cloth at a time.

Needle trades sweatshop, c.1890s

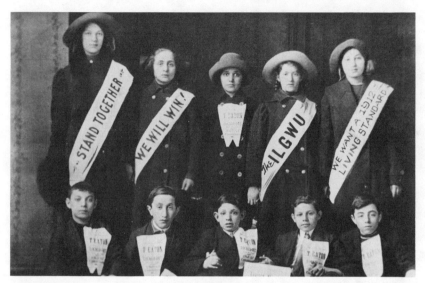

Supporting the strike by the International Ladies' Garment Workers'
Union against the T. Eaton Company, 1912

Cellar dwelling on Teraulay Street in 'the Ward,' 1913. Living conditions in this basement were so poor that the Department of Health
had closed down the premises once, but other tenants had
subsequently moved in.

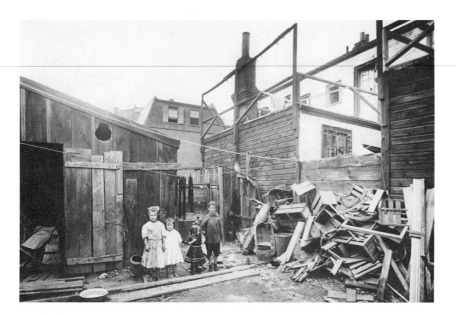

Price's Lane in 'the Ward,' 1914

Members of the Arbeiter Ring, a key socialist Jewish fraternal organization, c.1915

Presser, 1916

Factory buildings of the T. Eaton Company, c.1919

Employees' tribute to Sir John C. Eaton, 1919. Thousands of Eaton employees in Toronto express thanks to the president of the company for granting them Saturdays off in July and August and a half-day holiday on all other Saturdays.

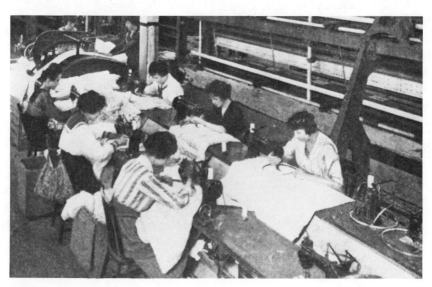

Embroidery workers, c.1910s

Spadina Avenue at Queen Street, looking north, c.1926

Joshua Gershman,
prominent Jewish
Communist and
activist in the
needle trades, 1923

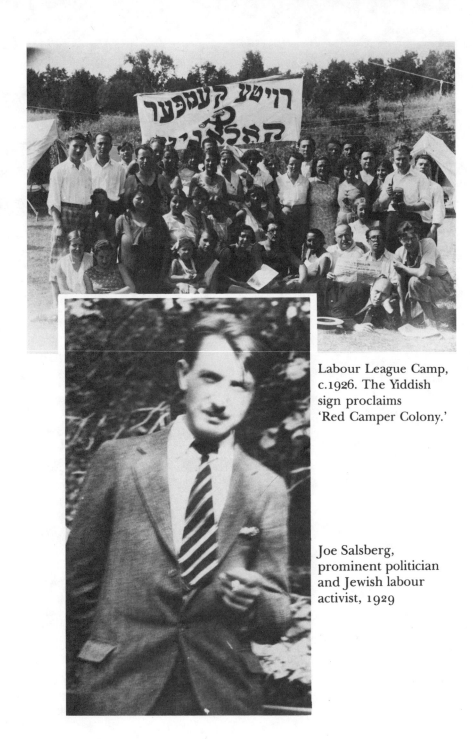

Labour League Camp,
c.1926. The Yiddish
sign proclaims
'Red Camper Colony.'

Joe Salsberg,
prominent politician
and Jewish labour
activist, 1929

Although it would be simplistic to discount the ties between Jewish workers and Jewish manufacturers entirely, it is important to emphasize that these ties did not prevent the emergence of serious class conflict in this period. The manufacturer, who had brought over his *landslayt* and given them jobs in his shop, often tried to appeal to them, in times of strike, on the basis of all the help he had already given them. As Salsberg explained: 'There would be the cry, "Look, I brought you to [the New World] and look what you're doing to me!"' Although such a plea sometimes worked with some of the workers, the effectiveness of this appeal often decreased sharply because the workers desperately needed higher wages. As Salsberg explained, when they found that they could not make a living and that the boss, their *landsman*, would not increase their pay, their gratitude towards him often shrank dramatically. Tenacious strikes resulted.[34]

In fact, when Jewish workers and Jewish manufacturers belonged to the same *landsmanshaft*, 'the [class-based] animosities were carried over there,' explained Salsberg.[35] During strikes, for example, if the intransigent employer was a leader within the *landsmanshaft*, the workers would often try to overthrow his position of leadership within the organization.[36] Ed Hammerstein, too, recalled the tensions within Toronto's *landsmanshaftn* during strikes: 'There would be some heated arguments and heated exchanges. [The Jewish bosses and the Jewish workers] still would stay in the same organization. Perhaps during the period of the strike, the employer would absent himself from attending meetings and so on, because he certainly wouldn't be very welcome. And pressures would be put on him by the organization, by leading members of the organization, to try to settle.'[37] Salsberg even recalled a case where a Jewish manufacturer 'was expelled from a fraternal organization, that he [had] belonged to as long as he was in the country, because he allowed a strike in his plant.' Although this employer was 'terribly hurt' by his expulsion, his fraternal ties with the Jewish workers had not prevented the strike.[38]

As Salsberg emphasized, it was by no means rare for Jewish workers to be organizing against – and even striking against – manufacturers who were close relatives of theirs. Indeed, the fact that the young David Dubinsky (who later became president of the ILGWU) had joined a strike against his own father's bakery 'was held up as a model of labour consciousness [and] dedication.'[39]

Moe Levin, for example, recalled trying to unionize his own uncle's shop. When Levin first came to Canada he got a job in his uncle's Toronto shirt factory. At that time, the Amalgamated Clothing Workers had begun to mount an intensive drive among the city's shirtmakers, and Levin became active in the organizing drive. Levin told his uncle that 'business is business and family is family' and that the two things were quite separate. (What Levin did not say was that his uncle might have made a similar speech and fired him.) The uncle was highly annoyed that Levin was trying to organize his shop, and Levin himself indicated that he felt 'very uncomfortable' about being in this position vis-à-vis his uncle. But Levin was strongly pro-labour and, despite his discomfort, had no doubt where he stood. He told his uncle: 'If working people have a right to be organized and have a right for a union, then I'm with them. I'm a worker.'[40]

Similarly, Alex Levinsky recalled organizing against his uncle. After coming to Canada at the age of fifteen, Levinsky learned the capmaking trade as an employee of his uncle's. Shortly thereafter, there was a strike at the shop, which Levinsky joined. He became an active striker, walking the picket line for months, until the workers finally had to give up. Afterwards, family ties reasserted themselves and Levinsky's uncle eventually hired him back.[41]

Other workers were not as fortunate as Levinsky; when a strike generated animosity within a family, the animosity could be long-lasting. Salsberg recalled a revealing incident where a young man was brought over by an aunt whose husband and sons owned a large Toronto factory where the young man was given a job. 'After a couple of months of the young immigrant's experience as an industrial worker in Toronto, a strike broke out in that plant. He had already imbibed somewhat of working-class consciousness in Poland before he came. And he knew that a strike is a strike is a strike. And the duty of every working man is to [walk] out. And he joined the picket line.' Although 'the aunt tried to defend him that he's a foolish boy,' her sons were not prepared to make allowances for him. They declared: '"He'll never enter this plant [again]. We brought him here. We paid his passage. We took him into our home and to the factory. And there he goes and joins on the picket line!"' Family ties were sacrificed to class interests, and the young man never did get his job back.[42]

The sharpness of class conflict within Toronto's Jewish community was highlighted in a revealing incident that took place during the 1919 general cloak strike. The union's strike leader, Samson Koldofsky, described this incident to a reporter from the *Yiddisher Zhurnal.* Pointing to 'an emaciated, pale-faced Jewish youth,' Koldofsky explained that the young man had just been fined forty dollars (or sixty days in jail) by magistrate

Cohen for allegedly battering 'two big strong non-Jewish Poles' who were acting as strike-breakers for a Jewish manufacturer. Koldofsky puzzled over this incident:

'How can one explain such a phenomenon[?] The proprietor who made the complaint against this Jewish youth is a member of the Labour Zionist Party. [He is] a Jew who complains about the terrible position of Jews in Poland and who seeks to protect Jews from the wild barbarism of non-Jewish Poles.

Here, in free Canada, [he] hires big healthy Polish scabs to rob the Jewish workers of their little piece of bread.

And at the word of such scabs, a Jewish judge punishes such a hunched-over Jewish youth for beating up such big non-Jewish Poles.[43]

The importance of immediate economic interests is apparent in a dramatic incident, recalled by Joe Salsberg, that took place during a Toronto capmakers' strike. The workers were striking against a large firm headed by a man who had once helped found the socialist-oriented Arbeiter Ring. The head of the firm drove his 'big open car to pick up a key strike-breaker who lived in the Jewish area' and found that 'the workers were picketing the house of this man, hoping to prevent him from going to work.' Then, 'the strikers surrounded the car and made menacing threats, of course. [So the head of the firm] stood up on the seat, and in his hand, he held the old [engine] crank ... which was a heavy piece of iron ... Here is this man, [who,] twenty-five years before, was the founder [of the Arbeiter Ring]; now he stands symbolically, with a chunk of iron in his hand, threatening the people that he was going to clobber them if they come close to his car.'[44] For Salsberg this graphic image symbolized the intensity of class conflict and the compelling nature of class interests within the Jewish community.

The man with the chunk of iron was not unique, for many of the 'socialist Jewish employers' actually engaged in bitter conflict with their workers. Socialists who became employers often argued that they were still committed to the ideal of socialism but that, in the meantime, they had to make a living in this world, under the present capitalist system. Salsberg recalled they would say: 'Well, listen, I've got to defend my place, but it has got nothing to do with my beliefs.' Salsberg even remembered a Jewish socialist employer who developed a more convoluted rationalization for anti-labour behaviour. This employer, who was 'a very devout believer in democratic socialist ideas' and 'agitated socialism to all who would listen to him, on Spadina,' had a bitter strike in his plant:

And he was approached during the strike. They'd say: 'What are you doing? You're a manager; you're a socialist!' He says: 'Of course, I'm a socialist. And I will be a socialist as long as I live. But ...' And he gave a cynical answer. The answer was: 'How many of those workers that you pulled out are socialists?' And he said: 'These backward characters will only be taught to turn to socialism if they suffer a little more than they do.' That was another rationale. 'Let them get out on the picket line; then maybe they'll begin to use their heads!'[45]

Class conflict within Toronto's Jewish community was so intense that a significant number of Jewish garment manufacturers adopted especially harsh measures against the Jewish garment workers. The *Yiddisher Zhurnal* angrily reported cases of Jewish manufacturers refusing to hire Jewish workers, contributing directly to anti-Semitic stereotypes by smearing all Jewish workers as dangerous Bolsheviks, and fomenting anti-Semitism specifically among the non-Jewish clothing workers to try to keep them away from the Jewish unions.

In early 1919, for example, a group of unemployed Jewish workers complained in a letter to the *Zhurnal* that Jewish manufacturers were discriminating against their fellow Jews. The letter explained that when members of this group went to some of the Jewish employers who needed new workers, 'to our astonishment, we were told that they are looking for other workers, not Jewish workers. When we explained to them that we are content to work like the others, for the same prices, they scoffed at us and left us.' These unemployed Jewish workers stressed that their families were going hungry and appealed to the Jewish manufacturers: 'We want to ask, through your newspaper, those Jewish employers who employ no Jews: if you, Jewish employers, refuse to employ Jewish workers, what should the non-Jewish employers do? The non-Jewish drive us [away]. We have, perhaps, no claims on them, but you, who are yet the leaders of community institutions, do you think that this is right? To let Jews go hungry when you have work to give.'[46] Although this refusal to hire Jews might have occurred partly because the Jewish manufacturers may have felt worse about trying to take advantage of their co-religionists on the shop floor, the main reason for this discriminatory policy was that Jewish workers had a reputation for being more militant than non-Jewish garment workers.[47]

Half a year later, the *Zhurnal* reported that some Jewish manufacturers were attempting to discredit the Jewish unions by publicly branding Jewish workers as traitorous Bolsheviks. Although it is true that there were many Jewish radicals (including Bolsheviks), public denunciations of Jews as Bolsheviks contributed directly to a prevalent anti-Semitic stereotype. When some Jews themselves engaged in such denunciations, much of the Jewish community perceived this as a betrayal. During the 1919 general cloak strike in Toronto, for example, Jewish manufacturers raised the cry of Bolshevism and refused to negotiate with the union. As described by an ILGWU official:

[Union] President Schlesinger visited Toronto this week and tried to confer with the manufacturers but met with failure. The only reply of the manufacturers was that the 'Jews are Bolsheviki and undesirable citizens, and that they are only fit to do tailoring but not to be conferred with.' The striking thing about this situation is that of the thirty odd manufacturers who are affected by this strike, only five are Gentiles, the rest are all Jews, and these are the ones who make the statements that the Jews are undesirable citizens![48]

The *Yiddisher Zhurnal* was scathing in its denunciation of this kind of conduct by Jewish manufacturers. An editorial in this newspaper exposed the vilifying of Jewish workers that took place at a meeting of the cloak manufacturers just before the 1919 general strike began. According to the editorial, a particular Jewish manufacturer ('whose whole Jewishness consisted in this that he sometimes takes in his brother on a Friday evening to eat a piece of *gefilte fish*') stated: 'You know, the Jewish workers are guilty in all our troubles. At the time when Canadians shed their blood on the fields of slaughter, [the Jewish workers] were slackers, and, as mice, they resisted going to serve [in the war]. Furthermore, they didn't want to give even one cent for a patriotic goal ... Now, they are in the front ranks of the Bolsheviks. It is the Jewish workers who are guilty in all this unrest.' According to this account, 'when this hero, whose own children call their father "sheeny," finished his sermon, a second Jewish manufacturer got up, a Jew who said more with his hands than with his broken English, and he continued the first one's sermon.' A Christian manufacturer then joined in the denunciation of the Jewish workers, explaining that he had previously refrained from speaking about this issue because he was afraid of offending the Jewish employers, but that he now felt free to agree with what the two Jewish manufacturers had stated.[49]

Although several of the other Jewish employers were offended and eventually walked out of the meeting, the *Zhurnal* focused on the two outspoken Jewish manufacturers, branding them as 'contemptible creatures' who were smearing the reputation of all Jews with lies in order to show off in front of the Christians. 'All of Jewry stands in a volcanic fire now,' the editorial declared, 'and here come ignoramuses, who have had the fortune to be "allrightniks," and pour oil on the fire, in order to find favour in the eyes of [the Christian manufacturers].' 'Know, however, you denouncers, that the whole Toronto Jewish community despises you and sends you its curse,' the editors proclaimed.[50] In a follow-up editorial, the *Zhurnal* maintained that the cloakmakers' strike was a purely economic conflict and that the issues of Bolshevism and patriotism had nothing to do with it. They warned the manufacturers to stop dragging in irrelevant issues so as to soil the reputation of Jews.[51]

A few days later, another *Zhurnal* article took up the same theme. 'In their fight against the strikers, some bosses from the cloak shops are losing even the least responsibility which elementary justice requires,' the article stated, for 'the workers are being besmirched in a criminal way.' The article portrayed 'conniving' bosses who had themselves entered Canada illegally a few years earlier, after the American government had refused them admittance on the grounds of dishonesty. According to this account, these 'connivers' 'scream that the loyal and quiet older [Jewish workers] are Bolsheviks and that they should be driven out of Canada.'[52] Strong class interests thus shaped the harsh behaviour of these Jewish manufacturers.

These incidents were not unique. Several years later, Jewish shirt manufacturers in Toronto strove 'to undermine the [ACW's] organization of the shirtmakers ... by voicing plans to weed out all the Jewish workers in their shops,'[53] while Jewish cloak manufacturers sought to 'bring in racial hatred in their shops and use anti-Semitic methods in their fight against the union.' The *Zhurnal* reported that some of these cloak manufacturers 'incite the female Christian workers against the Jewish workers. They tell the girls fabricated stories [claiming] that the union, which consists of "foreigners," does not want to have [Christian girls] as members.'[54]

A public controversy over similar issues erupted during the 1925 general cloak strike as well. J.M. Leiderman, a Jewish employer who was acting as spokesperson for a group of local cloak manufacturers, was extensively quoted in Toronto's English-language press on the subject of the group's preference for non-Jewish workers. According to the *Globe*, Leiderman 'threw some light upon conditions in the large factories. He claimed that experiences of employers in recent years with members of the radical Jewish unions, whose members, he said, were endeavoring to get control of the industry through shop committees, had been such as to force employers to turn to Gentile labour. This had resulted in a more stable condition in the industry.'[55] According to the *Star*, Leiderman stated: 'We are willing to employ Jewish operatives at any time, but we will not employ them while they are controlled by radical leaders. For five years we had all Jewish help in the factory without ever securing a feeling of security or of reasonable give and take to meet conditions as they arise in the industry.'[56]

Leiderman maintained 'that the attitude now being assumed by a number of Jewish garment manufacturers toward Jewish [workers] in the business is not based upon anything but objection to control of the union workers by a radical element.' He further proclaimed: 'I have publicly stated ... that in religion and social life I am a Jew, but that when it comes to business I am a Canadian, and being such I have no fear in giving true statements regarding our industry. I am naturally averse to making any statement that might be misinterpreted as derogatory of my own race. This is not a social or religious matter, but a purely economic one.'[57] While an ILGWU leader responded to Leiderman's remarks by maintaining 'that the reason the Gentile workers are so beloved is that they can be hired [for significantly lower wages],'[58] Leiderman publicly levied a more serious charge against the union: 'To give you some idea of the tactics of some of the union officials, I can give you my experience with an international organizer ... This man came to Toronto and visited me, offering to give me Jewish labour from the union if I would discharge Gentile labour. My employees had given me satisfaction. I frankly told him I would not force them into the street. The man was simply endeavoring to take advantage of racial prejudices.'[59]

Leiderman's remarks created a storm within the Jewish community. He was accused of lying, and his actions were interpreted as an attempt to incite racial hatred among the non-Jewish workers. The reaction against Leiderman within the Jewish community was so intense that even the president of the Toronto Cloak Manufacturers' Association, Bernard Sutin, publicly declared that Leiderman's charge was false. According to the *Globe*, Sutin 'regretted the injection of racial disputes in the strike, and said he had known no instance in recent years of a Gentile being refused work and preference given to a Jew, although the needle industry was largely in Jewish [employers'] hands.'[60] For their part, cloak union officials hotly denied that Toronto's ILGWU sought to push Christian workers out of the trade and pointed to the multicultural membership of the ILGWU in the United States. In particular, Mary McNab, who had been hired by the union to help organize Toronto's non-Jewish cloakmakers, 'objected strongly to [Leiderman's] statement that the union had asked him to discharge his Gentile workers and take on Jews. This, she said, was false, that it was an endeavor to introduce the racial question into the strike.'[61]

Despite this condemnation of Leiderman, some of Toronto's Jewish manufacturers continued to act harshly towards Jewish workers. In 1927, for example, the ILGWU's newspaper reported that Jewish cloak bosses in Toronto were again attempting to stir up anti-Semitic prejudice among the non-Jewish workers. These Jewish employers tried to discourage the non-Jews from joining the ILGWU, partly by telling them that this was a purely Jewish union where Gentiles did not belong.[62]

In 1932 Toronto's Yiddish newspaper reported that 'every day, people come to the office of the *Zhurnal* with complaints and report horrible facts of discrimination against Jewish workers and [by] none other than Jewish bosses.' The newspaper's editorial condemned the local Jewish manufacturers who refused to hire Jews and proclaimed that while 'we raise big protests ... when it is a question of boycotts and discrimination against us in Poland, Rumania, Germany and other countries where we suffer on all sides merely because we are Jews, [we must also] give a look at how we conduct ourselves [towards each other].' The editors pointed out that there were, of course, anti-Semitic Gentiles who refused to employ Jews unless they were absolutely forced to do so. As for the Jewish employers, some of them refused to hire fellow Jews because they 'believe the cynical and banal expression [that] "one should live among Jews, but one should do business with Gentiles."'[63]

The editorial focused primarily, however, on Jewish manufacturers who 'do not want to hire any Jewish workers because Jews are too progressive, too developed, have larger demands and are "too clever."' According to this argument, such manufacturers preferred to 'employ backward, unorganized workers and enslave them.' The editors protested: 'When a Jewish worker asks for a job from a Jewish manufacturer who needs workers, and the latter gives [jobs to] Slavic workers, Poles, Russians, Ukrainians and others of this type, merely because they are less developed than the Jewish worker and [because they] work for less, then this is dangerous discrimination.' Moreover, 'we know of cases where Jewish workers have asked Jewish bosses for work, asking to work at the same price as the Polish or Ukrainian worker, and [the Jewish workers] were given no work because the Jewish manufacturers wouldn't believe the Jewish workers, having in mind that a Jewish worker cannot be enslaved for long.' The editors explained: 'We do not say that a Jewish manufacturer must only employ Jewish workers and no others. We are not so narrow-minded and also not so narrow-hearted. But discriminate?' The editorial forcefully called on the Jewish community to pressure these manufacturers to end this discrimination:

The only cure for this plague is clearness, daylight, the uncovering of this and the putting forth of this in its full ugliness for all of public opinion. If we are power-less against widespread anti-Semitism, public opinion can, however, react to such discrimination ...

We add that under the current capitalist system, the dollar plays the [largest] role, and gold is faith and God. But when a Jewish worker is prepared to work for the same price as the non-Jewish, then [how can one] discriminate? Such a one [a person who discriminates] is not worthy of the name human.

'Jewish public opinion,' the editorial concluded, 'should accurately evaluate such creatures and show them their places.'[64] Although the *Zhurnal* thus tried to mobilize the Jewish community against such behav-iour, the very existence of this behaviour testifies to the intensity of class conflict within the community.

In general, despite Gilberg's bold proclamation that Jewish workers belonged not to 'the Jewish race' but solely to the 'great International Family' of the working class, there clearly were significant ties between Toronto's Jewish workers and Jewish manufacturers. These bonds did sometimes dampen class conflict in the needle trades. At times, Jewish garment workers became less militant because of reluctance to adopt a hard stand against employers who were relatives, neighbours, or *landslayt*. But the impact of these ties was more complex, for Jewish manufacturers themselves sometimes became more conciliatory for similar reasons. Moreover, in situations of potential or actual conflict, Jewish manufac-turers often tried to use their ties to their Jewish workers to pressure the workers to be more tractable, and Jewish workers sometimes tried to use a similar approach to pressure the manufacturers to make concessions. In the midst of strikes, other representatives of Toronto's Jewish commu-nity, particularly Rabbi Jacobs and the *Zhurnal* editors, differed distinctly from each other in the nature of their appeals to the alleged interests of the community as a whole.

Clearly, then, in spite of the significant ties between Jewish workers and Jewish manufacturers, bitter class conflict often erupted between them in Toronto's needle trades, testifying to the militancy of Jewish working-class culture. Immediate economic interests often determined the Jewish manufacturers' course of action. Indeed, at times, some of these employers took strong actions against Jewish workers, as when they refused to hire Jews or when they tried to use anti-Semitism to turn non-Jewish workers away from the unions. Jewish workers, too, were strongly motivated by their own economic interests, and a significant number of them were also compelled by their conception of working-class solidarity and by their socialist visions. In fact, some Jews were probably led to emphasize the need for socialism all the more because of the discomfort they experienced in fighting against class opponents who were their fellow Jews. These socialists sought to abolish capitalism partly because they felt it pitted people against one another and made true 'brotherhood' impossible.

- conflict causes btw Jewish manufacturers and Jewish workers

4 'Mixing with People on Spadina'
The Tense Relations between Non-Jewish Workers and Jewish Workers

'God Protect Us from Gentile Hands and Jewish Wits.'

– Yiddish folk saying[1]

Armed with knuckledusters, two unemployed Toronto ILGWU members assaulted two of the union's leaders in October 1936, beating them badly. The victims were both Jews, the assailants were not. 'The attackers, in a statement to the police, which the press featured, attempted to create anti-semitic feeling, by the contention that they were being discriminated against, because of being Gentiles,' reported another local Jewish union leader. 'This is without foundation, of course,' the official declared, explaining that 'we countered with a statement in the press by the Gentile Local repudiating this, stating that discrimination does not exist in our Union.' He was so concerned about the incident that he immediately called the union members together in a mass meeting and also made a point of visiting each shop 'to pull out as much poison as possible.' Although he believed 'the base instincts of some elements among the membership have been put to flight,' he felt that 'generally speaking the incident was rather injurious [to the union].'[2] When David Dubinsky, president of the ILGWU, learned 'the startling news,' he, too, stressed that this was an explosive issue, adding: 'This, in my judgment, is the effect of the propaganda being disseminated by Father Coughlin and other groups, who are interested in stirring up racial prejudice.'[3]

This assault was only one of the more dramatic manifestations of the serious divisions between Jewish workers and non-Jewish workers in

Toronto's needle trades. Although, initially, the vast majority of the city's garment workers were Anglo-Celtic, the proportion of Jews in this sector had increased to slightly less than half by 1931. Among the male garment workers in particular, the proportion of Jews had risen to a little under two-thirds by that year.[4]

The language barrier was only one of the many ways in which Jewish workers stood apart from their non-Jewish counterparts, but the language problem itself was no minor matter. Yiddish-speaking immigrants had seldom learned any English before emigrating, and, once here, they found that learning English involved mastering a whole new alphabet as well as the different syntax and vocabulary. Beyond the language issue, the separateness of Jewish workers reflected, in part, the legacy of relative isolation Jews had experienced for centuries in Eastern Europe in the context of vicious anti-Semitism. Even though prejudice against Jews was less severe in Toronto, the city's immigrant Jews still experienced significant discrimination. Contrary to a common present-day misconception, anti-Semitism in Toronto (as well as in Canada as a whole) constituted a serious problem not only during the rise of Fascism in the 1930s but during the preceding three decades as well. Jewish experiences of persecution in Eastern Europe, combined with the very real presence of anti-Semitism in Canada, made Jewish workers wary of their non-Jewish co-workers.[5]

Traditional East European Jewish culture had, of course, set Jews apart from Christians in absolutely fundamental ways. Although this culture was in the process of being transformed, most Jewish immigrants continued to have a strong sense of being different from non-Jews. To a large extent, this was the case even for those secular Jews who were socialists, for they often sought to combine a commitment to proletarian internationalism with a commitment to preserving Jewish identity. As indicated in chapter 2, Jewish working-class culture in Toronto was consciously and deliberately Jewish. In this context, Toronto's Jewish garment workers did not commonly differentiate between the different types of non-Jews in this sector, often lumping together the Anglo-Celtic workers (who constituted the majority of the city's non-Jewish garment workers) and the Italians, Poles, Ukrainians, and others (who, together, constituted a mere one-fifth of the non-Jews in this industry in 1931).

By the interwar years in particular, Jewish workers tended to live in Jewish neighbourhoods in the garment district, socializing at the union halls, in the Jewish socialist fraternal organizations, and in the *landsmanshaftn*. Since non-Jewish garment workers usually lived in other parts *as separateness*

of the city and seldom dropped by the union halls for informal socializing, their social lives tended to be separate from their Jewish co-workers.]

The structure of the garment unions often reflected the distinctness of the two groups. Within most of Toronto's needle trades unions, Jewish workers and non-Jewish workers were organized in separate union locals. Although this was expedient because of the many Jews who were not comfortable using English, many workers preferred this arrangement because of deeper discomforts as well. Moreover, within a given union, the local leadership often used separate organizers for the Jews and the non-Jews. Here, again, this system was partly due to the language problem, but, as well, union activists often shared a strong sense that Jewish workers would respond better to one of their own kind, while other workers would respond better to a non-Jewish organizer.[8]

[The leaders of the needle trades unions did, however, try to overcome the relative separateness of the two groups of workers by appealing to the ideal of working-class solidarity. The need for class solidarity was, of course, very real, particularly since Jews and non-Jews often toiled beside each other on the shop floor in this sector. Within a particular union, separate locals may have eliminated some problems, but representatives from each local had to work together on their union's joint board. More broadly, of course, union members needed to function smoothly together at many levels.]

In some cases, there were leftist political links between some of the Jews and some of the non-Jews, who might have been connected through the CCF, the Communist party, the Socialist party, the Social Democratic party, the Trotskyist movement, or the Anarchist movement. Partly because there were relatively few non-Jewish garment workers involved in these political groups, however, ethnic divisions among the city's needle trades workers were difficult to bridge.[9]

Indeed, the many appeals to the need for working-class solidarity testify to the depth of the ethnic divisions. For example, a 1937 ILGWU organizing manual, written by the International's Educational Department, wrestled with 'what can be done by the union to resolve these nationalistic biases.' The Educational Department recommended that all ethnic groups be carefully included in organizing campaigns and strikes and that 'a balance [be] maintained among them so far as committees, etc., are concerned, so that one particular group does not dominate.' As well, 'if the workers, or large numbers of them still "think" in their own language even though they have a certain grasp of English, it is a good thing to have speakers or interpreters who can talk to them in their own tongue' not only to facilitate understanding but also because 'they feel more confidence in a union that has the backing of their own people, and their sense of nationalistic pride is pleased.' This manual particularly advised unionists: 'Most important of all is to drive home the point that the workers' chief quarrel is not with one another over differences arising from the accident of birth in this country or that, but with those who stand between them and the higher wages and better conditions that they all want. They should be warned that the bosses may try to play off one nationality against another to the ultimate harm of both, and that anyone who, in the crisis of a strike, stirs up racial or national enmity is consciously or unconsciously helping the boss to break the strike.'[10] Similar editorials in the various garment unions' newspapers indicate that ethnic tensions generally created problems in the clothing centres of North America.[11] Toronto was no exception.

The friction between Jewish workers and non-Jewish workers was, in part, related to issues arising out of the differences in the skills involved in their work. In Toronto, such issues became particularly important for male workers in the men's clothing industry in the 1910s. In this particular period, the conflict between Jews and non-Jews was also heightened by interunion rivalry in this section of the industry. A detailed examination of the development of the Amalgamated Clothing Workers highlights not only the conflicts of the 1910s but demonstrates also the problems of ethnic conflict that continued into the 1920s and 1930s, resulting in further interunion rivalry in the midst of the Great Depression.

In the 1910s the three rival unions were the Journeymen Tailors' Union of America (JTUA), the United Garment Workers (UGW), and the Amalgamated Clothing Workers (ACW). The JTUA had been established for those involved in custom tailoring (a process whereby clothing was made up according to the specifications of the individual customer). The other two unions competed sharply in the ready-made branch of the men's clothing industry, for the ACW had been formed by a group of secessionists from the UGW in 1914. In Toronto, as in many of the other clothing centres in Canada and the United States, the ACW was composed mostly of Jews from the beginning of its formation. In contrast, the members of the JTUA tended to be non-immigrants, as did the members of the UGW.[12] (Table 7 of the appendix summarizes the important characteristics of each of these unions, including the relations among them.)

Shortly after the formation of the ACW, the JTUA worked out an agreement with it, merging the two organizations into one industrial union (see chapter 1). This merger led, in fact, to a lot of friction between the two groups, both in Toronto and elsewhere. As a result, the merger was liquidated not long after it had been established. During the period of the merger, the Toronto members of the JTUA had been involved in attempts to organize the ready-made men's clothing workers, together with the ACW.

Much of the friction between the two groups stemmed from the ways in which employers used the Jewish immigrants as part of the deskilling process in this period. The traditional custom tailor was highly skilled and made the whole garment either by himself or with the help of an apprentice. This craft was being seriously undermined, however, by the increasing popularity of ready-made clothing as well as by the dramatic increases in the division of labour in the remaining custom tailoring establishments. Many of the skilled custom tailors resented those workers who made clothing according to these newer – and cheaper – systems of production. The custom tailors looked down on those whom they viewed as far less skilled than themselves, and they saw these newcomers as a threat to their own positions. In Toronto, as elsewhere, many of the workers who did these less skilled jobs were Jewish immigrants. Ironically, a considerable number of these Jews were themselves victims of deskilling, for they had done skilled tailoring before emigration and then found themselves relegated to less skilled roles in the newer production processes on this side of the ocean.[13]

An American report in the UGW's newspaper in 1907, for example, emphasized the connection between deskilling and the use of immigrant labour, maintaining that 'the effect of the use of machinery and of the minute subdivision of labor in the clothing industry ... has been the employment of unskilled immigrants as operatives in place of the oldtime skilled journeymen tailors.' 'The Jewish immigrants,' the report asserted, 'displaced the native and the Irish garment workers.' In general, many JTUA and UGW members resented the immigrants as encroaching on their trade.[14]

In Toronto, James Watt, a key JTUA official, experienced serious difficulties during the brief JTUA–ACW merger, when he tried to help his organization unionize the less skilled men's clothing workers. 'The section worker [the person who puts together only one section of the garment] finds it as difficult to understand the journeyman tailor as it is for the journeyman tailor to understand the section worker,' declared the frustrated Watt in 1915.[15] The difficulties were compounded by the fact that Toronto's journeymen tailors were usually Anglo-Celtic, while many of the section workers were Jewish.[16] Ethnic tensions were directly related to the specific role many Jewish workers played in the labour process.

In the context of these tensions, Watt requested the JTUA's head office to send a Jewish organizer, Max Sillinsky, to Toronto because 'it will certainly take a Jew to get the best results out of the Jewish wage earners in this or any other city.'[17] The head office's reply indicates ambivalence about this approach: 'No doubt a Jewish Organizer is necessary, but this should not deter you from doing whatever you can. Eventually we must develop men who can undertake the work among all Nationalities. As long as we cater to national or racial feeling we will find it difficult to harmonize the different elements into an Organization. The workers should not be appealed to from a national or racial standpoint but from an industrial standpoint.'[18] However, Watt found that, by himself, he was able to make little headway among the Jewish workers. He explained to headquarters: 'The question of a Jewish Organizer seems to be uppermost in the minds of the Jew Workers, but they always want something. Have been doing the best I can amongst them, but it is slow work. Have often thought that the more we cater to the Nationalism of these people on a language basis, the more we may [have to continue doing so]. And the same applies to Italians and others.'[19]

Sillinsky eventually did come to Toronto and was soon able to report that his arrival had 'brought life into the Jewish tailors.'[20] A little while later, Watt reported that, before Sillinsky could return to the head office, 'it is necessary that [Sillinsky] should establish the machinery that will provide for further organizing and a proper understanding by all parties Jew and Gentile.'[21] Given that there were misunderstandings between these two groups of workers, it is no wonder that the Jewish workers had been insisting on a Jewish organizer.

In fact, there was considerable strain between the JTUA's skilled non-Jewish workers and the ACW's less skilled Jewish workers in Toronto during the JTUA–ACW merger. Watt reported to the JTUA's head office that the non-Jewish tailors were grumbling about having to spend money to help organize the Jewish workers. He indicated that, if the non-Jews were not reimbursed quickly: '[They] will simply holler[:] "Same old game always begging or borrowing. Never have anything to pay half expense for committee rooms or anything else as long as they can get *white* men to pay for it." The result will be that we will not be able to get the members to take joint action under any circumstances[.]'[22] Watt's report highlights the perception that Jews were not really 'white,' and Watt was quite right that the non-Jewish tailors might reject joint action, particularly since their anti-Semitism was apparently heightened by their concern that

Jewish immigrants were becoming an integral part of the deskilling process. When the Journeymen Tailors' Union held a referendum across North America, Toronto's original JTUA members, along with many of their counterparts in other locales, voted to end the merger with the ACW.[23]

In the meantime, both during and after the short-lived merger with the JTUA, Toronto's Amalgamated Clothing Workers concentrated on recruiting all the ready-made clothing workers in the city's men's clothing industry. This involved trying to persuade workers they were better off in the ACW than in the United Garment Workers. At the international level, the founders of the ACW had seceded from the UGW largely because of the anti-immigrant attitudes of the UGW's head office.[24] Indeed, Jewish readers of the UGW's newspaper might well have been offended by the occasional anti-Semitic jokes it contained.[25]

In Toronto, as well, there is evidence of the UGW's insensitivity to the Jewish garment workers. Sam Landers, the union's organizer for Toronto and its most important Canadian organizer in this period, was hardly in a position to inspire confidence in Jewish workers. Originally a Jew, Landers had joined the Salvation Army, and he publicly referred to Jews as 'Kikes' in the pages of the UGW's newspaper. Other indications of the UGW's insensitivity include the fact that, in 1915, the Toronto branch of the UGW held an important organizing meeting at the same time that the city's Jews had scheduled a mass meeting to organize relief for their persecuted co-religionists in Poland.[26]

In the contest between the ACW and the UGW in Toronto, ethnic differences were sometimes reinforced by skill differences. In 1917, at a time when the city's ACW had seven hundred dues-paying members, not even one cutter had joined this union. The ACW's organizer reported that the cutters had their own UGW local and that it would be a 'mighty hard job' to organize the members of this highly skilled occupation into the ACW. In this branch of the city's needle trades, almost all of the cutters were non-Jews. Thus the ACW organizer suggested that the union renew its efforts to organize them by hiring a local non-Jew, someone who would be 'well known amongst the Gentile element in Toronto' and well known among the cutters in particular.[27]

Although some of the cutters had joined the ACW by the following year, there was friction between them and the other ACW members. More broadly, it was still difficult for the ACW to 'make any progress at all among the English speaking element.' The union strove to remedy the situation by setting up a separate office for the non-Jews.[28]

[In addition to the cutters, other non-Jews eventually began to join Toronto's ACW, partly to work in the shops where the employers had signed contracts with this union. This ethnic mix led to further tensions within the union itself. In 1920, for example, certain English-speaking union members reportedly had a constant 'feeling of irritation' that they did not yet have their own separate local.] These anglophones had temporarily been placed in a sublocal of the Jewish coatmakers' local, and their Jewish co-workers did not object to their request for their own local. When the manager of Toronto's ACW wrote to the union's head office to emphasize the need for a separate local, he explained that the new local's 'designation cannot be properly placed for any particular branch of the industry, and the only distinction seemingly can be made that they cannot under any circumstances meet with the Jewish Speaking element; to them it's a matter of a moral prestige.'[29]

Several years later, after the new English-speaking local had been established, the anglophone members of Toronto's ACW continued to press for more separation from the Jewish ACW members. The executive board of this English-speaking local, together with the executive board of the English-speaking cutters' local, protested to the ACW's Toronto Joint Board 'against the disorderly conduct of some members at the mass meeting in the Standard Theatre. [They] recommend[ed] that in the future separate meetings shall be arranged for the Jewish and English speaking members.'[30] Although the union's records do not indicate the nature of this 'disorderly conduct,' the non-Jews' call for separate meetings highlights the serious ethnic tensions within the union.

Relations between these two groups of ACW workers remained strained. In the context of a 1927 joint board decision to ensure that all union members were up to date with their dues payments, for example, the ACW's English-speaking local pointedly asked the board 'why the English membership is being checked up more on the dues than the others.' Although the board replied there was no evidence of discrimination, the anglophones clearly felt they were being discriminated against.[31] Another incident in the same year illustrates that Jews, too, were concerned they were being discriminated against within the union. In this case, 'Brother Beckerman,' an executive member of local 233, expressly asked the joint board to clarify whether this particular local was 'a Gentile Local or an English-speaking Local.' Beckerman decided to push for this clarification after attending one of the local's executive meetings where 'an English-speaking woman who was Jewish by nationality applied for membership [in local 233] and some of the members of [the local's] Executive tried to refer her to the Jewish Locals.' When he objected to her treatment, 'stating that every English-speaking person has a right to belong to the Local,' 'he was denounced, even by Brother Tovey,' the union's anglophone business agent. 'By what right did Brother Tovey tell him that he would expel him from the Organization?' Beckerman indignantly inquired.[32]

Further problems developed. Several years later, for example, an ACW official reported that, in Toronto, 'an attempt has been made to disrupt loyalty [to the union] by bringing in the element of antisemitism.' 'That is being checked, however,' he optimistically declared.[33]

While Toronto's ILGWU experienced its own difficulties with 'the Jew Gentile problem,'[34] tensions between Jews and non-Jews in the men's clothing industry continued to plague the ACW, leading directly to the establishment of the rival National Clothing Workers of Canada (NCWC). The NCWC was the product of the All-Canadian Congress of Labour (ACCL), a central labour body founded in 1927 in explicit opposition to the international unions that were based in the United States and included Canadian locals. While advocates of the ACCL maintained they were fighting to free the Canadian labour movement from American domination, much of the motivation for the formation of the NCWC was far less noble.[35] (Characteristics of the ACW and the NCWC are outlined in table 7 of the appendix.)

Although the ACCL had made some efforts to organize Toronto garment workers in 1931, it did not gain a significant foothold in this sector until the NCWC was launched in early 1934, arising out of a struggle with the ACW at Ontario Boys' Wear. This struggle began in late 1933 when more than one hundred workers struck this Toronto shop for recognition of the Amalgamated Clothing Workers and for a substantial wage increase. After the strike had dragged on for several months, the employer turned around and signed a closed-shop agreement with the ACCL's newly formed National Clothing Workers of Canada. The NCWC supplied the firm with workers, while the ACW continued to picket for a time.[36]

The owner of Ontario Boys' Wear himself had been a key initiator of the formation of the NCWC at this shop. In the midst of the strike, Mezza Finch (soon to become president of the NCWC) contacted the ACCL's head office to explore the possibility of forming an ACCL affiliate at this firm. She explained that 'the firm [is] determined against the amalgamated [the ACW] and ap[p]ealed to me as a worker against them.'[37] Since Finch was already associated with the ACCL at this time, the employer was apparently turning to her in the hopes that an ACCL local could be formed in his shop to enable him to avoid having to settle with the ACW.

The collusion between management and the pro-ACCL workers at this shop was based on ethnic prejudice. The ACCL's newspaper pointedly asserted that Ontario Boys' Wear was 'almost the only non-Hebrew shop in Toronto.'[38] In the letter to the ACCL's head office in which Finch first explored the possibility of forming an ACCL affiliate at this firm, Finch explained that 'the employees [of Ontario Boys' Wear] are all gentiles and they are a gentile firm.' 'The firm,' she continued, 'does not wish to employ any but gentiles.'[39] Neither Finch nor her correspondent, the secretary-treasurer of the ACCL, objected to management's plans for continued discrimination. This employer apparently preferred the ACCL over the ACW partly because the ACCL was liable to go along with his discrimination against Jewish workers.[40] The ACCL's NCWC was formed out of this collusion.

This incident raises crucial questions about the nature of the Canadian nationalism of the ACCL. Finch, who became a member of the national executive board of the ACCL, saw herself as British and appears to have been highly ethnocentric. Her brand of Canadian nationalism was not a multicultural brand, and her belief in Canadian unionism seems to have been rooted in a more xenophobic form of nationalism. Finch's opposition to what she saw as the foreign domination of Canadian labour implied not only opposition to American control but also opposition to control by immigrants inside Canada – and Jews were considered to be foreigners by definition.[41] Moreover, Finch was not the only such nationalist labour leader opposed to Jews. Ernest Smith was another nationalist who played a leading role in the ACCL's work in the Toronto needle trades. In an attempt to discredit the ACW, Smith wrote to Ontario's attorney-general, describing the ACW as 'an American union controlled by Russian Jews.'[42]

The NCWC's ethnically based collusion with the boss at Ontario Boys' Wear led to significant collusion around low wages as well, for the NCWC attempted to block government officials from investigating low pay at the firm. In the late 1930s these government officials were attempting to ascertain whether this shop was violating the legal minimum wage rates, but the NCWC, which still had a closed-shop agreement with Ontario Boys' Wear, refused to allow the officials to question union members. Finch, leader of the NCWC, believed that the ACW was determined to put both Ontario Boys' Wear and the NCWC itself out of business. She apparently feared this could be done by forcing the firm to increase wages to meet the minimum wage rates stipulated in the Industrial Standards Act. Thus she wound up fighting the act as well as the ACW.[43] Meanwhile, it was the boss himself who had profited from exploiting the divisions between Jewish and non-Jewish workers in Toronto's needle trades.

Tensions between these two groups of Toronto garment workers were pronounced not only among the men's clothing workers but also among the furriers. A detailed examination of the development of the city's International Fur Workers' Union (IFWU) further illuminates the nature and sources of these interethnic tensions from the 1910s through the 1930s. In the early years the IFWU was weak, consisting of only a handful of non-Jewish cutters in local 35 and a handful of Jewish operators in local 40. As a result, Toronto's IFWU leader suggested to the head office in 1915 that they dissolve local 40 'until times improve' and that the Jews from that local join local 35.[44] He soon realized, however, that the non-Jews found this unacceptable. He wrote to the head office: 'I am given to understand that local #35 does not want Jews as members, and that bringing them in would most likely cause a decrease in the already small membership of local 35. Local 35 committees have [repeatedly] declined to invite Jews [in] local #40 to partake in the social gatherings of local 35. Hence I don't believe local 35 will accept them. Further local #40 prefers its own Charter [and] Union.'[45]

By the late 1920s there were three IFWU locals, all of which were in the fur-coat branch of the industry. Local 40 was a Yiddish-speaking local for all the Jewish workers, regardless of skill and gender. Local 35 was for the non-Jewish cutters mainly, although it also included some non-Jewish men who were blockers and operators. There was also local 65, which was mainly for non-Jewish women. Ed Hammerstein, an IFWU activist, recalled there was a great deal of tension between the non-Jewish locals and the Jewish local: 'The Joint Board consisted of the three locals, and, as you can well see, that [the Jewish] local 40 was a ... minority group. And there were some very heated arguments and battles that took place at [the Joint Board] meetings, so much so that the Labour Council of Toronto had to appoint a person to act as chairman, to sort of mediate between these groups. Otherwise, they would've never been able to come to any [agreement].' Hammerstein explained: 'The decision there arrived at was that, in order to bring some equality and balance, [they should] organize the [fur] collar and cuff workers. So, aside from it being an organizing drive to help workers who were terribly exploited, it also served sort of a political purpose insofar as the union was concerned in order to equalize the strength of the two [groups].' The union succeeded in organizing the collar and cuff trade and set up local 100 for these workers, who were mostly Jewish men. However, according to Hammerstein, 'the problem wasn't resolved when local 100 was formed because then you had a balance. And because you had that balance, they could very seldom come to terms on issues.' As a result, the IFWU again turned to the Toronto Labour Council, which assigned a person to chair the IFWU joint board meetings 'so this sort of broke the constant tie votes that took place.'[46]

By 1931 'the difficulties and misunderstandings' between the Jews and non-Jews had assumed such a 'serious character' that the local IFWU leaders were appealing to the union's president to come to Toronto to help them straighten out the situation. As the IFWU minutes reveal, the local officials warned the union's head office that the two non-Jewish locals were 'threatening to engage their own business agent and also to hire an office for themselves.'[47]

The tensions between the Jewish and non-Jewish members of Toronto's IFWU exploded a year later during a general strike in the city's fur industry. As the union prepared for the strike, some of the bosses succeeded in influencing around two dozen members of the non-Jewish local 35, the cutters' local, to break away from the IFWU and form their own union. A key Jewish IFWU leader denounced this breakaway union as a tool of the manufacturers and declared it was being used against the other workers.[48]

The *Yiddisher Zhurnal* was nonetheless optimistic about developments in the IFWU. A week before the strike began, the newspaper reported that the union's head office had succeeded in uniting the four Toronto IFWU locals under one joint board that would take over negotiations with the manufacturers. Locals 35 and 65 had apparently agreed to give up their own office and work closely with the two Jewish locals, but it soon became clear that the non-Jews were not honouring this agreement. At that point, the leaders of the two Jewish locals announced that if the manufacturers signed a contract with locals 35 and 65, the Jewish locals would not honour it. The Jewish unionists felt that a strike was becoming necessary not only to win better wages but also to force the manufacturers to recognize the joint board of locals 40 and 100.[49]

When the 1932 general strike began in Toronto's fur industry, hundreds of Jews walked off the job while most of the non-Jewish workers refused to join the strike. The local Jewish IFWU leaders enlisted the support of the union's head office to try to solve the problem of 'the two locals which didn't join the strike and [which], with their deeds, hindered the organization of the fur workers.'[50] The local IFWU strike leaders had even tried, to no apparent avail, to appeal to the Trades and Labour Council of Toronto to pressure the strike-breakers into cooperating.

Although the Jewish workers eventually won the month-long strike anyway, this general strike provides one of the most graphic examples of the conflict between Jewish workers and non-Jewish workers in Toronto's garment industry.[1]

Recalling the clashes between these two groups in Toronto's IFWU, Ed Hammerstein indicated that the hostility stemmed from the fact that 'the Jews who were coming into the industry were, in the eyes of the Gentiles, threatening their position.' He felt that much of the friction arose because the non-Jewish fur workers were less militant than the Jews:

Well, basically the Jewish worker[s], who had come over here with a tradition of fighting for issues and demands ... were occupying lesser positions in the industry. They were newcomers in the industry; they were working for lower wages than the others who had been here a long time, the cutters and the people in locals 35 and 65. And the position of the Jewish worker[s] was that they should be entitled to some of the same type of wages that the others are getting. And the only way to achieve that would be by strike action. And the others were quite happy with their lot, and they could get increases in wages as a result of their experience and expertise. And this created the conflict.

Employed in the better section of the industry and 'secure in their jobs,' the non-Jews 'didn't cotton to this militancy that was developing' among the Jews.

When Hammerstein was asked if he had experienced anti-Semitism within the union, his reply emphasized the way in which ethnic differences were reinforced by skill differences (at least as far as the male workers were concerned): 'You'd find there might be some latent, incipient type of anti-Semitism on the part of individual fellow workers, particularly, as I said, people who were in local 35, your cutters, who would sort of look down upon you not only as a result of a racial approach but also denigrate your type of work and everything else. So you found that. But it wasn't *overt*; it may have been *latent* and covert. But certainly you didn't feel it in the sense that you'd have to take up arms and fight them.'

As Hammerstein explained, the Jewish workers and the non-Jewish workers had two very different conceptions of trade unionism. The Jewish IFWU leaders, who were themselves divided into rival Communist and CCF camps in the 1930s, felt that unions should be seriously involved in progressive political action. In contrast, the non-Jewish members, who, in any case, often voted Liberal or Conservative, did not think the union should be involved in any political activity. The fact that the non-Jewish IFWU leaders were generally opposed to socialism added to the friction between them and their Jewish counterparts.[52]

Jacob Black, another Jewish activist in the furriers' union, similarly emphasized that the non-Jewish IFWU leaders were less militant than the Jewish leaders. As an illustration, he described an incident that took place when the joint board was discussing calling a particular strike. During this discussion, an Anglo-Saxon woman expressed concern that it would not be 'nice' to call a strike at a time when the employers had to make their samples. Moreover, Black, who was himself a supporter of the CCF, also stressed that the non-Jewish IFWU leaders were politically conservative. Very few of them would have supported the CCF. According to Black, these non-Jewish leaders were 'the old-timers ... mainly the Anglo-Saxon types,' who were 'old Orange people.'[53]

Differences between Jewish furriers and non-Jewish furriers were also heightened by the fact that Jacob Black, along with many of the other Jewish IFWU leaders, worked to involve the union in political actions that had special significance for Jews. The non-Jews, for example, tended to be relatively indifferent to the fight against world Fascism, whereas the Jews were highly concerned about this issue. Some of the Jewish IFWU leaders were also involved in support work for the Jewish labour movement in Palestine, which did not generally interest non-Jewish workers.[54]

In the context of ethnic tensions within the various needle trades unions, many of Toronto's garment manufacturers employed a 'divide and conquer' strategy, attempting to pit non-Jewish workers and Jewish workers against each other, particularly during strikes. In so doing, these garment manufacturers were acting like many other employers in Canadian industry who strove to manipulate ethnic divisions within the workforce to their own advantage. Indeed, early twentieth-century Canadian immigration policy had been strongly shaped by key Canadian entrepreneurs whose insistence on the open-door policy stemmed partly from their plans to benefit from an ethnically diverse labour force. Within Toronto's garment industry, even some of the Jewish manufacturers tried to capitalize on ethnic divisions on the shop floor (see chapter 3). Many of the non-Jewish employers, in particular, did not hesitate to try to discredit the Jewish unions through appeals to anti-Semitism.[55]

These issues surfaced, for example, during two key Toronto strikes in 1912. In the midst of the JTUA's lengthy general strike in that year, the union's newspaper emphasized – and denounced – the bosses' 'shallow schemes' to create 'dissension in our ranks by appeals to race prejudice.'[56] Appeals to prejudice were even more pronounced during the large Eaton strike of the same year. As the ILGWU's newspaper reported: 'Those affected [by the dispute at Eaton's] are almost entirely Jewish: and the chief slogan by which it was hoped to cut off public sympathy was the report ... that this is "only a strike of Jews." The appeal to race and creed prejudice has succeeded, too, in so far as it has prevented the Gentile Cloak Makers from joining in the sympathetic strike.'[57] In fact, the non-Jewish cloakmakers' failure to join the strike, together with the firm's recruitment of additional non-Jewish strike-breakers, were key factors contributing to the union's defeat.[58]

Toronto's garment manufacturers used various tactics to inflame ethnic divisions in the workforce. During a shop strike in 1920, for example, one of the bosses apparently reported to the police and the magistrate that the strike was caused by the strikers' refusal to work with Christian workers. The unionists denied this was the case, and the *Zhurnal* interpreted this charge as yet another slur against Jewish workers. 'Racial denunciations have already been dragged in,' explained the *Zhurnal*, because 'the bosses realized that they cannot fight the workers with the usual [economic] methods.'[59]

'The bosses have plainly become anti-Semites,' reported a Toronto ILGWU official a few years later. 'They incite the English workers against the Jewish workers, using such expressions as "we want to get rid of the damned Jews."'[60] As the employers continued to stir up racial hatred among the garment workers, Toronto's ILGWU prepared for a cloak-makers' general strike, appealing in the *Zhurnal* to the Jewish cloak-makers to support the union. This appeal explained: 'At each strike ... such ugly deeds of the bosses are noted, when they try, through racial hatred between Jews and non-Jews, to incite one against the other. On you, union members, lies the obligation to enlighten the non-Jewish workers that a fight for the union means only an economic, not a racial fight ... Explain to [the non-Jewish workers] also the significance of strike-breakers [and the importance of unity].'[61] Toronto's garment manufacturers also sometimes threatened Jewish union members that if any of them protested too much, they would replace them with non-Jewish women.[62]

The manufacturers' attempts to exploit ethnic divisions were particularly apparent during the 1934 strike in a dress department of Eaton's garment factory. The employees of this department were non-Jews, and several of the women strikers testified that when they became interested in the ILGWU, '[management] would try to bring in [the] racial question, about the Jewish people, telling us we should not belong to the union at all that was controlled by Jews.'[63] The women were allegedly 'out of [their] class' because, in seeking the help of ILGWU officials, 'they were mixing with people on Spadina.'[64]

The manufacturers' interest in trying to keep the non-Jewish workers from 'mixing with people on Spadina' stemmed partly from the fact that, by the interwar period, Toronto's Jewish garment workers were generally more militant than the others. In the earlier years, however, the pattern of militancy was more complex. In the early to mid 1910s, in particular, the JTUA found it difficult to organize Jews, while Jewish unions such as the ILGWU found it difficult to organize the non-Jews in Toronto's needle trades. More specifically, although there was not a simple pattern of non-Jewish strikers pitted against Jewish strike-breakers during the JTUA's large, lengthy strike in 1912, some of the strike-breakers were drawn from 'the scab Jewish element.'[65]

Jewish garment workers tended to be less militant in the early part of the twentieth century than they were to become in the interwar years. Indeed, this increase in Jewish militancy took place despite the fact that the proportion of clothing manufacturers who were Jews was significantly higher in the interwar period. In the earlier period, when the percentage of Jews in Toronto was much smaller, Jewish working-class culture was just beginning to put down roots in this city. By the 1920s, as organizations such as the Arbeiter Ring became more firmly established, Jewish militancy was strengthened by a more solid cultural base. As Jewish workers increased in numbers and became organized in unions that were predominantly Jewish, their union activities tended to increase.

Yet even in the early 1910s there were situations where Jewish workers – mobilized by the Jewish unions – were significantly more militant than their non-Jewish counterparts. Not only the Eaton strike of 1912 but also the Puritan strike of 1911 presented a pronounced pattern of Jewish strikers and non-Jewish strike-breakers. The strike of cloakmakers and skirtmakers at the Puritan factory began when forty-five males and females walked out in protest against wage cuts and the employer's discrimination against ILGWU members. 'Who takes the place of the workers in this factory?' asked *Cotton's Weekly*, the newspaper of the Social Democratic Party of Canada. Dramatically, the newspaper exclaimed:

In British Columbia, when miners rise up in rebellion against the shameful conditions, Chinese are brought into the mines. In this and other Western provinces, Japs, Hindoos, and Indians fill the places of the white toilers because they live on cheaper food and under such intolerable conditions no white people can stand it. Half-castes, ignorant, poverty-stricken and oppressed, slave in Southern mill-yards, plantation fields and swamps.

No nation is supposed to be so advanced as the British nation, no race so progressive as the white. BUT HERE IN TORONTO NO CHINESE, NO HINDOOS, NO JAPS, NO INDIANS, NO BLACKS, NO FOREIGNERS NEED BE IMPORTED. WHITE GIRLS AND MEN OF BRITISH BIRTH BREAK THE STRIKES. Capitalists need not take the trouble to send to other lands for scabs. WE HAVE THEM ALWAYS READY IN TORONTO. LOYAL, PATRIOTIC CANADIANS, ANXIOUS TO KEEP THEIR JOBS, REFUSE TO GO OUT with strikers who are brave enough to struggle for human treatment. CANADIAN GIRLS ARE HANDED WORK THAT JEWISH GIRLS REFUSE TO DO.[66]

Puritan's non-Jewish cutters apparently refused to join this strike, and *Cotton's Weekly* concluded that 'Craft Unionism was shown up as selfish and incompetent, for men of other unions refused to even attempt persuading the English speaking cutters to go out, when asked to do so by the Jewish, who cannot speak English very well.'[67]

This newspaper's account of the strike focused particularly on the non-Jewish women who were doing work that formerly had been done by the Jewish strikers. According to this account, 'this union realizes that as they are Jewish, racial and religious prejudices are animating the girls to take their places and to decline to go out on strike with Jews.'[68] The newspaper declared:

We are disgusted to find that our Canadian girls are not unwilling to slave 'faithfully' and 'diligently' at the very work our Jewish comrades who are in the overwhelming majority in this Union would scorn to touch ...

But this is no unusual feature in our strikes. The girls and women who have been taught to sing 'Britons never never shall be slaves,' put to shame the worst of lackeys in their endeavor to 'keep in with the boss' and 'have nothing to do with Unions or strikes.'

'In every strike it is the same,' declared *Cotton's Weekly*. 'Gentile girls break them. English speaking workers are unwilling to struggle for better conditions, shorter hours or higher pay for fear of losing "my job."'[69]

Here, ethnic and gender concerns intertwined significantly: the newspaper's indignation against the female strike-breakers was heightened by 'the injustice of [the girls'] act in taking the places of these family men who cannot live on ten dollars per week, a wage that is considered exceptionally good by a single girl.' 'OH TORONTO WORKING WOMEN, WHY BE SO

BLIND, SO SELFISH SO HEARTLESS? SHAME ON THE VAUNTED WARMTH OF WOMANLY HEARTS IF JEWISH WORKINGMEN CAN BE REPLACED BY CHEAP FEMALE LABOR!' exclaimed *Cotton's Weekly.*[70]

ILGWU activists continued to find that Toronto's non-Jewish garment workers tended to respond less favourably to their appeals than did the Jews. In 1916, for example, the *Industrial Banner,* an Ontario labour newspaper, reported that this union had experienced difficulties in trying to capture the interests of the non-Jewish workers. Although the newspaper optimistically declared that the ILGWU's new Gentile organizer was stimulating the non-Jews to become enthusiastic about the union,[71] the problem was by no means solved. In 1917 Toronto's ILGWU was carrying out an ambitious organizing campaign, when some of the employers, including Eaton's, responded by making concessions to try to keep the workers away from the union. Eaton's reduced the work week, increased wages, and instructed its supervisors to be more polite. According to the ILGWU's newspaper, 'these concessions, instead of keeping the Jewish workers away from joining the union, enthused them all the more, but [the concessions] influenced a certain number of the gentile women workers in the trade, mainly in the T. Eaton shops.' In response, the ILGWU's leaders were relying on the aid of two new non-Jewish organizers, one female and one male, to try to recruit more of Toronto's non-Jewish garment workers.[72] However, these workers remained a problem for the ILGWU.[73]

Toronto's Amalgamated Clothing Workers experienced similar difficulties. In 1918, for example, the *Yiddisher Zhurnal* reported that the city's ACW was hiring non-Jewish organizers 'for the non-Jewish [workers] in the trade, whom no one had ever been able to organize.'[74] A while later, the ACW and the manufacturers' association signed a new contract that stipulated non-union workers in the association's shops had to join the union. The signing of this agreement 'brought into the ranks of the Amalgamated about 1000 members English speaking, the majority of whom had never previously belonged to a trade union.' The ACW was faced with the need for a massive internal educational campaign. Although the ACW's anglophone business agent felt that the union was succeeding in instilling 'the principles for which we are organised into [the] hearts and minds' of these non-Jewish workers,[75] the non-Jews continued to lag behind.

In 1925, for example, when Toronto's ACW was in the midst of an organizing campaign, the non-Jewish locals were apparently less involved in the campaign and had to be specially urged to participate.[76] Similarly, a year later, when the ACW was involved in two important shop strikes, a union official reporting on strike-support work declared: 'What is really wanted now is a little more co-operation from the English speaking members and a special committee will have to be organized for that purpose.'[77]

The Jewish needle trades unions continued to experience these kinds of difficulties in the 1930s as well. During the ILGWU's 1931 general strike in Toronto's dress trade, for example, the *Canadian Forum* reported that 'the shops employing mostly gentile help' did not join the strike.[78] Non-Jewish workers apparently also posed a problem for the Communist union that was organizing Toronto's dressmakers. In 1935, for example, at a time when the Industrial Union of Needle Trades Workers had contracts with most of the city's dress shops, 'nearly everyone of the workers employed in [the] open shops are Anglo-Saxon.'[79]

The Jewish unions' difficulties with the non-Jewish garment workers thus took a number of different forms. In some cases, particularly in the early period when these unions were weaker, many of the non-Jews stayed away from the Jewish unions altogether. In other cases, these workers were members of the unions but were significantly less active than their Jewish counterparts. At certain times, such as during the Eaton strike of 1912 and the ILGWU's dress strike of 1931, non-Jewish workers even served as strike-breakers while Jews went out on strike. The deep divisions between the two groups emerged particularly sharply during the large 1932 fur strike, when non-Jews acted as strike-breakers against their Jewish fellow unionists.

Although Jews still constituted less than half of Toronto's garment workers in 1931, they clearly predominated in the labour movement in the city's needle trades in the interwar years. The non-Jewish garment unions, particularly the JTUA and the UGW, were dwarfed by the Jewish unions in this period. Jewish workers tended to be more militant than non-Jews, partly because the activism of the Jewish workers was deeply rooted in a vibrant Jewish working-class culture. The Jewish workers' loyalty to their unions was further reinforced by the ways in which the Jewish unions served a number of special functions for them, over and above the function of collective bargaining. These unions addressed specifically Jewish concerns, such as relief work for Jewish refugees in Eastern Europe and protests against the rise of world Fascism. The unions also served as social and cultural centres for the Jewish immigrants in the strange New World.

While these factors bound the Jewish workers more closely to their unions, however, they probably alienated the non-Jewish workers to a certain extent, thereby deepening the rift between the two groups. The more the unions addressed specifically Jewish concerns, the more the non-Jewish union members may have felt themselves to be outsiders. As a consequence, the non-Jews tended to be less active in the Jewish unions.

The lower level of militancy of the non-Jewish garment workers was also partly a product of language problems. In the 1920s and 1930s, many of the Jewish workers could speak Yiddish in the shop and at the meetings of their locals. In contrast, most of the various non-Jewish, non-English-speaking workers were lumped together in a local that conducted its business in English. Since their command of English was often not good, members of these different ethnic groups had trouble understanding what was going on at union meetings. It is not surprising that this kind of a miscellaneous local, within both the ACW and the ILGWU, had a reputation for being weak.[80] Although most of the non-Jewish garment workers were Anglo-Celtic, this particular aspect of the language problem was significant.

The leaders of Toronto's Jewish unions made some efforts to eliminate the friction between the Jewish and non-Jewish garment workers. These efforts included carefully recruiting non-Jewish organizers and business agents, appealing to union members for understanding, and sometimes even entreating officers of the Toronto Trades and Labour Council to help mediate. However, the Toronto leaders of these garment unions did not make the kinds of major efforts that historian Steven Fraser claims to have found in his study of Jewish-Italian relations in the ACW's major centres. Fraser argues that the ACW leaders worked hard to reconcile Jews and Italians in the men's clothing centres of North America, contending that these efforts were critical because of the predominance of these two ethnic groups in this branch of the needle trades. Even if he were right about the extent – and success – of the ACW's efforts to unite these particular ethnic groups in New York City (and he would need more evidence to prove his case), clearly these extensive efforts were not being made in Toronto.

This was perhaps partly due to limited local resources and perhaps also to the different ethnic composition of the workforce in Toronto's men's clothing industry, where Italians were a small minority. It may have been an easier task to bring Jewish and Italian immigrants together in early twentieth-century polyglot New York than to unite Jewish and Anglo-Celtic workers in the predominantly Anglo-Celtic city of Toronto. Particularly important is the absence of strong, class-conscious anglophone leadership within the Toronto branches of the 'Jewish unions.' Although there was an assortment of Anglo-Celtic organizers, business agents, and members of the various unions' joint boards, the Toronto branches of these unions lacked strong, dynamic non-Jewish leaders who might have made major efforts to bring the non-Jews and the Jews closer together.[81]

Throughout the period under consideration, Jewish workers and non-Jewish workers in Toronto's needle trades continued to constitute two fairly separate groups, customarily speaking different languages and organized in separate union locals. Despite the ideal of – and the real need for – working-class solidarity, serious ethnic tensions persisted within the garment unions and often emerged as key factors in the rivalries between particular unions in this sector. In some cases, these tensions were reinforced by the different roles the two groups played in the labour process. The manufacturers often attempted to heighten these tensions, particularly by using anti-Semitic appeals to try to keep the non-Jews from uniting with more militant Jewish workers in the interwar years. Although the anti-Semitism of non-Jewish garment workers did not usually lead to assaults with knuckledusters, this prejudice was an important factor not only during the 1930s but during the earlier part of the twentieth century as well. The ethnocentrism of both the Jewish and the non-Jewish workers also constituted an important factor. Consequently, it was extremely difficult to overcome the deep ethnic divisions within the workforce.

5 'Better Material to Exploit'
The Barriers to Women's Participation in the Labour Movement

'The factory is scarcely a proper setting for romance. It is one of the battle-fields in our struggle for existence, where we treat woman as an inferior being, whereas in civilized love-making we prefer to keep up the chivalrous fiction that she is our superior.'

– Abraham Cahan, *The Rise of David Levinsky*

When the strike-breaker set out to cross the picket line, Bessie Kramer sprang into action. Kramer, an ILGWU activist, tried at first to convert her opponent, explaining that the strike at this Toronto cloak shop was a fight for better working conditions. The indignant strike-breaker, a woman in her forties, demanded to know what right Kramer had to tell her what to do. Kramer, a younger cloakmaker, replied that her own working conditions would be affected by the outcome of this strike, but the other woman was not impressed. Tempers flared. Suddenly, Kramer felt that her adversary was about to hit her, so Kramer struck first. 'Sometimes, you know, when I'm alone in the house and I start looking back,' Kramer recently mused, 'I just wonder: how did I, or somebody else, do things like this?' For her the issue was age, not femininity: 'I was brought up to respect an older person, and here I picked my hands up and [hit her]!' Why? 'Because I knew that if I wouldn't protect my job and somebody else is going to take it away, I wouldn't be able to make a living.'[1]

This dramatic incident raises key questions about women's roles in the labour movement in the needle trades. Did women often act as strike-breakers? Or did they commonly take an active part in the unions? What

barriers did women face on the shop floor and within the labour movement itself? Did male union leaders vigorously encourage women's activism? And did the women develop feminist perspectives of their own
experience?

Although there are, as yet, few detailed historical studies of women's
militancy in other sectors of the Canadian economy, women garment
workers were apparently more militant than their counterparts in most
– perhaps all – other sectors. Indeed, Linda Kealey's analysis of women's
strike patterns in early twentieth-century Canada concludes that 'the
clothing industry was arguably the most important sector of women's
strike activity.'[2] A 1925 government report drew corresponding conclu-
sions: the women in the clothing industry were union members in larger
proportion than were women in any other industry in Canada.[3] This was
due mainly to the fact that the activist Jewish women in the needle trades
were rooted in a militant Jewish working-class culture. Even so, however,
women workers in this sector, as in other sectors, faced special barriers
that made their participation in the labour movement especially difficult.

'Women, as is well-known, [are] always more difficult to organize,'
declared an article in Toronto's Yiddish newspaper in the context of a
campaign to organize the millinery workers in 1924.[4] This comment
echoed similar remarks in the Yiddish Communist press. More pointedly,
an English-language labour newspaper, stressing the problems of organizing Toronto's garment workers, attributed these difficulties to the many
females in this sector, since 'it is very hard to keep them in line.'[5]

The Jewish union activists commonly considered the non-Jewish women
to be especially difficult. The *Yiddisher Zhurnal*'s report on a particular
strike in a large men's clothing firm in 1919, for example, indicated that
this strike was considered unique because the non-Jewish women workers
had actually joined the strike. During the general strike in the city's cloak
and dress trades later that year, the *Zhurnal* reported that 'in the shops
where males were in the majority, everyone came out on strike. But there
were certain dress shops which employed only women, mostly Gentile
girls and women. In those shops, some remained at work.'[6]

Although such difficulties existed, women garment workers did become
militant on occasion, and some, like Bessie Kramer herself, were committed militants who were deeply dedicated to the labour movement. Joe
Salsberg, for example, recalled a mixture of reactions when his union
undertook the initial efforts to organize the women in Toronto's millinery trade. Although some of the women did not want to join the union,
most of the women workers were, in fact, pro-union. Salsberg explained

that the non-joiners would say: '"I'm not here for my whole life; I'm here until I get married." Or "I'm here until my husband gets a job." But the vast majority wanted to be part of the union.' In speaking about Toronto's women needle trades workers more generally, Salsberg exclaimed that some women were 'fighting cats' on the picket lines. Many of the other male union leaders would have agreed.[7]

Bessie Kramer herself stressed that there were female activists in her union but that 'some of [the female union members] took a little the back seat.' Kramer recalled that a significant number of women joined the picket lines during the cloakmakers' strikes but 'the fact is that we had a big local and there was only a handful of women that were active in the local ... Some of them, they came to a meeting, paid their dues, and that's all. And they waited [for you to] fight for them, to get an increase in wages or so.' Although 'there were [also] some men that weren't active,' on 'the whole, there [were] more women that took that attitude: "I come to the meeting, I pay my dues, and that's all."'[8]

Because women faced serious barriers, the sections of the Toronto needle trades that were the most unionized tended to be those in which the proportion of male workers was relatively high. Thus the garment unions in the interwar years tended to be concentrated in the cloak, fur, headgear, and men's fine-clothing branches of the industry. In general, although women constituted the majority of the city's garment workers during most of the period under consideration, they seem to have been a minority of the unionists in this sector. This pattern was related to ethnicity as well, for the proportion of Jews was significantly higher among the men than among the women. Moreover, although the available evidence is fragmentary, there were at least a few cases where women were clearly underrepresented in general strikes in Toronto's clothing industry.[9] Yet the pattern was not simple, for women struck roughly in proportion to their numbers during the general cloak strike of 1933 in particular.[10] Women may have had difficulties mobilizing for labour struggles, but their mobilization was not impossible.[11]

The vast majority of the strikes in Toronto's needle trades included many women strikers as well as men. Although it is not often possible to ascertain whether women played key roles on occasions where they struck with men, the Lowndes strike of 1905 provides an interesting example of women's militancy. When the management of the Lowndes Company tried to introduce a new system of speed-ups, the workers who attended a special shop meeting voted overwhelmingly to strike. The next morning, three women picketers were on the scene and persuaded at least forty more people to join the walk-out. Altogether, the strikers, most of whom were Russian Jews, totalled about 125 women and 75 men. In the early stages of the strike, the cutters and pressers (the men who were the most skilled workers) had continued to work, although they were reportedly just about to join the strike when it was announced that the company had capitulated.[12] The key role of the three women picketers in this strike suggests that in situations where women and men struck together, the women workers were not necessarily just following along after male militants.

The fact that Toronto's women garment workers were not simply trailing along on the coat-tails of male militancy can be seen in cases where women struck alone. These cases tended to take place in the earlier part of the twentieth century because greater union involvement during the interwar years generally meant that workers' militancy was more coordinated, so women and men struck together more often. In 1903 seventy-two women walked off the job at the Wyld-Darling Company protesting the price they were being charged for thread used in factory production. No union – and no male workers – supported these women strikers. A committee of the women managed to work out a quick settlement through a series of meetings with the heads of the firm.[13]

There were other early examples of women striking alone in Toronto's clothing industry. These incidents included the strike of fifty women against new regulations at the Crown Tailoring Company in 1905 and the strike of twenty-five women for higher wages at Andrew Darling & Company in 1907. In 1910 sixty women at T.E. Braime & Company initiated a strike on their own and then received help from the United Garment Workers after the strike had begun. Four years later, one hundred unionized women workers testified to the potential for women's militancy when they struck the Dominion Cloak Company under the banner of the International Ladies' Garment Workers' Union.[14] Despite the serious barriers women garment workers faced, they played militant roles in workplace struggles on a significant number of occasions.

To the extent that women were considered 'an element which it is very difficult to organize,' what was needed was an informed analysis of the barriers women workers faced. Such an analysis could have formed the basis for developing special policies to recruit women in particular. In fact, however, male union leaders seem to have had little insight as to why it was difficult for women to participate fully in union and strike activities.[15] Yet women workers' difficulties stemmed not only from their vulnerable position on the shop floor but also from the ways in which household obligations restricted their ability to participate fully in the labour movement. Moreover, within the needle trades unions themselves, women faced the sexist attitudes of male unionists. Significant factors included the male culture of union halls, some ambivalence towards women's presence in the paid labour force, certain union policies that privileged men, and the male monopoly of leadership positions.

Women's vulnerability on the shop floor was partly a product of the fact that female needle trades workers seldom possessed scarce skills. In the men's fine-clothing branch of the industry and in the women's cloak and suit branch, for example, women were generally confined to jobs as finishers, liners, sergers, and basting pullers. All of these positions could be relatively easily replaced in strike situations because there was usually an oversupply of workers with the necessary skills to do these jobs.

The basting puller, who took out temporary stitching, required little training, as did the serger, who sewed the edges of seams to avoid fraying. Finishers did the hand-sewing, such as basting (temporary stitching) and putting in hooks, buttons, and belts and sometimes linings as well. Young women who had learned how to use a needle at home could easily become finishers. As for the liners, the women who specialized in lining the garments were regarded as less skilled than the finishers. Because so many women had learned to do sewing at home before entering the paid labour force, the skills necessary to do these jobs were common. Even women who performed more complex jobs as sewing-machine operators in the dress trade lacked the clout that the possession of rare skills might have provided. Thus, although an employer would value a woman worker who was particularly fast and efficient at her job, most female garment workers were fairly replaceable from the employer's point of view. This perspective was related to the low valuation of women's household skills carried over into their jobs in the garment industry.

In contrast, the pressers and cutters constituted a male job preserve, and their skills were highly valued because of their scarcity and because these workers played crucial roles in the production process. A good cutter could save his employer money on cloth by laying out the patterns economically and cutting the cloth accurately. Since the quality of the cutting was also crucial in determining the fit and final appearance of the garment, this was considered the most skilled job in the clothing industry. The presser's job, too, was central to the quality of the end product, for he had to be able to handle a heavy iron to smooth, shape, and mould each garment. As a result, the pressers and the cutters, men who were the 'aristocrats' of the trade, had much more clout in attempting to enforce their own demands on the shop floor.[16]

The vulnerability of relatively unskilled women workers was something they shared with those men in the trade who also held relatively unskilled jobs. Unlike the men, however, women were generally restricted to these types of jobs. Women workers also tended to be more vulnerable because they were often less experienced in the world of paid labour than their male counterparts. This was partly because, on the whole, the women were younger than the men. Many were single women who left the paid labour force when they married. Furthermore, older, married women sometimes moved in and out of the paid labour force in a pattern of their own. A married woman might leave paid employment just before her child was born and re-enter it several years later, once the child was in school. Even then, she might have to leave her paying job each summer to stay with the child when school was not in session. Compared with the men, even married women workers were less likely to build up continuous workplace experience. The fact that the women tended to have less experience on the shop floor no doubt made it harder for them to engage in collective protests.[17]

In addition, women workers often faced special intransigence from their employers. Manufacturers tended to be particularly stubborn towards their female employees because often the reason they had hired women in the first place was because they could pay them lower wages. Given the highly competitive structure of the garment industry, these employers counted on low-wage female labour, and they were especially opposed to women's organizing activities. At the same time, the manufacturers were sometimes able to pursue a 'divide and conquer' strategy by setting female and male workers against each other and by buying off male workers at the expense of the women. While women clearly faced special constraints, these developments roughly paralleled the employers' attempts to use different ethnic groups, and especially 'greenhorns,' to cheapen wages, facilitate deskilling, and divide the workforce.

The newspaper of the United Cloth Hat, Cap, and Millinery Workers' International Union, for example, called attention to this 'divide and conquer' strategy in the late 1910s by pointing out that 'as in other trades the bosses try to instigate the workers of one nationality against those of another, so here [in the New York headgear trade] they created a hatred between the opposite sexes.'[18] As this newspaper emphasized in a subsequent article about several other American cities, gender and ethnic divisions often intertwined: 'As soon as our organization campaign developed, the employers started a vicious campaign to keep the women from the organization, both by coaxing and threatening and by sowing religious, racial, and sexual hatred. [The employers and their agents tried to convince the girls that the movement to increase wages and shorten hours is a man's movement or a Jewish movement, and that it does not behoove American girls to organize along with men for the defense of their rights or Gentiles to organize with Jews, etc.]¹⁹

[Focusing on Toronto, William Lyon Mackenzie King's 1897 newspaper report on the 'sweating system' recorded a dramatic example of buying off male workers at women's expense. When King asked a manufacturer of ready-made clothing what he paid his help, this Toronto manufacturer replied: '*I don't treat the men bad, but I even up by taking advantage of the women.* I have a girl who can do as much work, and as good work as a man; she gets $5 a week. The man who is standing next to her gets $11. The girls, however, average $3.50 a week, and some are as low as two dollars.'²⁰

Joe Salsberg's recollection of events in the Toronto millinery trade in the early 1920s provides a vivid example of employers' attempts to utilize a 'divide and conquer' strategy. Salsberg, who was an organizer for the United Cloth Hat, Cap, and Millinery Workers' International Union at the time, discussed the early efforts to organize the finishers. When Salsberg decided to establish a local for these unorganized women, he found that he had to work 'to overcome a silent resistance from the men' in the union. When asked if the men really did not want to have the finishers organized, he replied: 'Well, there was nobody that would voice opposition openly because that would be reactionary. But they *knew* that it is perhaps easier for *them* to get concessions than it will be if they become part of the union ... with the girls, with the women.' Salsberg explained that the employers tried to drive a wedge between the male and female workers: 'The bosses, some of them, warned the men: "Look, [if] you're gonna get these girls in [the union], it'll be [at] your expense, because there's only so much we can pay for the production of a hat or we can't sell [the hats]."' The manufacturers' threat – that if they were forced to grant higher wages to the newly organized women, they would compensate by keeping the men's wages down – was credible, particularly in view of the intense competition from unorganized Montreal firms.

Although Salsberg himself gave special consideration to the women because he felt they were underpaid, the other male unionists were much more ambivalent. 'It took me a little while, a year or so, to finally get the [union] leadership to agree' that the women should be organized, Salsberg explained. When the finishers did join the union, the demand for increases in their wages led to a number of shop strikes. In the negotiations that preceded these strikes, the employers were willing to grant wage increases for the males only. The male unionists 'weren't very happy' about striking for higher wages for the finishers, declared Salsberg, 'but they struck.' In this case, the union seems to have been able to overcome the employers' divisive tactics, for the unionists finally succeeded in winning agreements that included wage increases and union recognition for the women as well as the men.[21]

In addition to employers' machinations, women workers faced other obstacles in their efforts to organize, obstacles that often centred on the nature of home life. Women's household responsibilities, in particular, frequently limited the time and energy available for union activities. Unmarried women wage-earners were significantly burdened in cases where they had to keep house for male relatives who did not have wives, and single women who had immigrated without their mothers usually had to look after their own household needs even if they were not looking after male relatives as well. Of course, the married women in the paid labour force faced particularly heavy household responsibilities. Bessie Kramer, for example, emphasized how hard it was to do all the housework, look after her child, work full-time in the cloak shop, and still do a great deal of work for the union and for the Communist-oriented Labour League. For many Jewish women, the extra effort involved in keeping kosher made housekeeping an even more time-consuming task.

Leah Stern, another mother who worked in the needle trades, emphasized how difficult it was to ensure that her child got proper care. Although she arranged for a woman to look after the boy for part of the day, she herself still had difficulty combining her work in the shop with her maternal responsibilities. As an illustration, Stern explained how tiring it was to have to rush home every day to feed her young son lunch. She would rush by street car from the shop to his school, walk home with him, feed him lunch, take him back to school, and then hurry back to her work in the shop.[22]

Molly Fineberg, too, found it difficult to juggle the competing demands on her time, even though she had some help from her mother who lived nearby. Fineberg's activities in the Arbeiter Ring were demanding. She recalled that when she rushed home after doing work for this organization, the neighbours warned her that her son was not being properly looked after. Fineberg worked for a time in the retail end of the dress trade, and she stressed how difficult it was to work long hours in the store on top of all her other commitments. Much of her housework had to be done on her 'day off.' She explained: 'On Sunday, I was lying on the floor, washing the floor, and [I] went down to the basement and did the wash. Instead of going out to eat, [I would make all the meals]. So who could afford to go out to a restaurant to eat? So I was busy. *Sunday was the most difficult day.* I had to clean up the house, and then I had to cook and bake and wash and what-not. It was a very, very hard life.'[23]

In some cases, women were further burdened by the disapproval of male relatives. Sadie Hoffman, an activist in the Labour League, recalled: 'With my first husband, I couldn't be as active [politically] as I would have liked to be, because he didn't let me.' Since she was a dedicated socialist who displayed remarkable courage in her political activities, the fact that she felt restricted by her husband is all the more significant. Other male relatives could also be a problem. Hoffman, for example, recalled that her father did not ensure that she would learn to read and write Yiddish. This was not because her father promoted assimilation. When she was young, he was reluctant to spend money on a basic education for her not only because of tight financial circumstances but also because he did not feel her education was important. He displayed a typical Old World attitude: 'So my father said, "[Sadie] will get married anyway." He didn't worry about me getting married. And that was all that counted; that was all that mattered.' Then, when Hoffman began to teach herself to read the Yiddish newspaper, her brother teased her about her efforts. Hoffman stuck to her goal nonetheless.[24]

Although Yiddish literacy skills were not a prerequisite for an active role in the Jewish labour movement and the Jewish left, a woman who could not read Yiddish would, of course, have been at a considerable disadvantage as an activist. The brother who ridiculed a sister's attempts to teach herself to read may well have also ridiculed her attempts to become informed about union matters. He may have turned into the sort of husband who would try to restrict his wife's political activities. Although some women did not run into these problems with their male relatives, a significant number of women faced the risk of active discouragement.

Partly because of women's subordination in the home, the labour movement in the needle trades was male-centred. Union officials and labour reporters, almost all of whom were men, hardly ever mentioned the women garment workers. The frequent invisibility of women in the historical record has, by now, become something of a commonplace among certain historians, but the recurrent invisibility of women in this case is particularly remarkable, precisely because there were so many female clothing workers. The available documents seldom mentioned these women, either in the Yiddish or the English sources.

When male union officials did mention the women, it was often the women workers' physical appearance that seemed most noteworthy to the men. Descriptions of the ILGWU's general strike in Toronto in 1919 provide an illustration. During this strike one writer, aided by the union, wrote a series of personalized accounts of the strike in the *Yiddisher Zhurnal*. His account of what the strike meant to the women workers explained that, on an ordinary working day, the women were in such a hurry to get to the shop punctually that they did not have enough time to fix themselves up really nicely. But all this had changed because of the strike: 'Now, blessed be God, there is enough time to stand by the mirror and perform one's toilet. Yesterday, Khayke, the finisher, really was prettier than usual, simply shining like the bright sun in summer.' The article went on to describe Khayke's attractive manners and then discussed how the strike had changed dating habits. When the striking 'girls' dated male strikers, they could no longer expect the men to pay for both of them. As a result, each paid his or her own way. However, 'it is, you know, not nice that a lady with a gentleman should pay, so she [slips] him the money for her share. And he treats with it, and she gives him a good time.'[25]

This was all that this writer had to say about what the strike meant for the women workers. Yet women as well as men were being arrested on the picket lines in the midst of this dispute.[26] Furthermore, interviews with female activists reveal that a significant number of women garment workers were, in fact, dedicated unionists. Women's dedication was being maligned by a fixation on face powder and dates.

The orientation of the above account was mirrored in a Yiddish poem, 'My First of May,' which appeared in the *Zhurnal* during the same year:

I march in the streets
On the first of May,
My soul flutters
Like a bird, free.
I see: girls, girls,
Girls – row after row:
Daughters of labour –
Proudly they march ...

The girls ask me
About Capital –
I answer them: 'Engels,

Karl Marx, Lassalle –
All of these didn't
In all of their years
Possess a penny,
They only served amour' ...

Their eyes glow,
Become blazing, large;
I choose for myself the prettiest
Of the girls.
Both of us go
Deep among the trees
And from class-struggle
I give her an idea[.]
'Leave those behind?'
She asks quietly and gently;
I reply: 'Yes, we must
Be the avantguard ...
And in my eyes
My child, tall and free[,]
Read the proclamation
Of the first of May.'

We kiss
Each other communistically;
'Don't be economical!' –
I ask of her.
'Over-production may
Be valid in love;
See, my heart flutters
Like a red flag!'
My lips ring out
The Marseilles
On her white neck. –
She calls me Juares ...
Without a revolution
We feel free;
And we are fortunate
On the first of May.[27]

Such stereotyping of women may well have bothered the female Jewish activists of this period. One wonders how the women felt, for example, when they read a supposedly humorous account in the millinery union's newspaper about how the male union leaders in Montreal were having trouble hiring a female organizer because their aesthetic standards were too high.[28]

In many ways, union culture in the needle trades was male culture. Although women attended some of the movement's more formal social and cultural affairs, such as the concerts and lectures held in the Labour Lyceum's auditorium, women did not generally take part in the informal socializing at union halls. If women were to feel welcome in the Lyceum, even such a small matter as cleaning the women's washroom should have been regularly attended to. In fact, some of the women workers had to complain that the washroom was not being well cleaned.[29]

Jewish men went to union halls to chat with their friends, sip coffee, and play dominoes, but Jewish women did not take part in such informal socializing partly because of their domestic responsibilities. Indeed, when Bessie Kramer was asked why women did not join this social network, she felt the explanation was obvious: '[The Jewish men] used to come and have a chat and play cards ... No, women didn't do this. It stands to reason. The women, they were always busy. If they didn't have work in the union, they used to go home and do the work. And the man would sit [in the union hall]. He knows his wife is going to prepare his dinner. He can sit and play cards and have a chat with the other men.'[30] As Ida Abel pointed out, even the unmarried woman worker would often have to rush home to cook dinner for herself or do her own laundry.[31]

Yet the women's lack of participation in this particular social network was a product of more than just household responsibilities. Another reason for women's being left out is suggested by Sol Abel's reply when asked if Jewish women were part of this network: 'No, there [were] no women [who] came in there to play dominoes. There, no women came in to socialize. They ... What could they do there? There was nothing to do. Well, there was nothing to do but sit and play dominoes. What kind of a social life is that?'[32] Thus, while Jewish men seemed to find the social life at the union halls satisfying, men like Sol Abel considered it an unsatisfactory social life for women. This kind of informal socializing represented a male domain that served important functions, providing the male workers with more opportunity to get to know one another and discuss union issues. Such companionship reinforced a male-centred solidarity.

– women have more responsibilities

Whereas female workers hurried home to attend to domestic chores, male workers hurried to the union halls partly because 'it was a way of getting away from home,' as Joe Salsberg revealed.[33] Salsberg explained that Jewish men would especially gravitate towards the union halls during the slack seasons, gathering together to chat, read, and play cards because the laid-off men had nothing much to do at home. They viewed the home as a woman's domain, and the men apparently felt they needed a social network separate from their homes. Yet since these male workers had considerable free time during the slack seasons, they could have remained home for more of the time to help do the housework and look after the children. Sharing these household responsibilities was clearly not on the men's agenda.

One way of involving women more in the Jewish labour movement would have been through the establishment of women's auxiliaries for the wives of the male unionists. A woman who had worked in the needle trades before marrying a male garment worker would have been better able to retain her connection with the union had there been an active women's auxiliary for her to join after leaving the shop floor. Although being part of an auxiliary might have involved a second-class status, these organizations could have played an important role in bringing working-class women together. United in women's auxiliaries, these women might have been able to help make the unions more responsive to the needs of the female workers. In fact, however, Toronto's needle trades unions seldom had women's auxiliaries. The ILGWU's cloak makers, for example, never established a women's auxiliary during the period under consideration.[34]

The city's International Fur Workers' Union did not establish a women's auxiliary until the late 1930s. When this auxiliary was finally set up, it was led by Pearl Wedro, a long-time fur worker who was an outstanding activist in her union and in the Labour League. According to Ed Hammerstein, this organization, established 'to involve the women in the life of the union,' was primarily for the wives of male workers.[35] The women who worked in the fur shops themselves were also free to join the auxiliary. In addition to setting up meetings where speakers would provide members with information about the labour movement, this auxiliary also did important strike-support work. Indeed, a Toronto IFWU official reported in 1938 that he was well pleased with the activism of the auxiliary: 'We have organized a Ladies' Auxiliary which has a membership of over a hundred. This organization was one of the most helpful in our struggle, not only in picketing but they even assisted us in the strike.

They had an affair for the benefit of those who served jail sentences. This was a great success.'[36] Yet despite the fact that women's auxiliaries could serve important functions, the city's needle trades unions generally failed to establish such organizations.

[The male-centred nature of the needle trades unions was closely related to the fact that during the first four decades of the twentieth century, many people in Canada felt that the workplace should be a male domain. Woman's 'proper place,' they argued, was the home. This attitude was particularly strong at the beginning of the century.] Although single women's participation in the paid labour force became fairly acceptable by the 1920s, there continued to be strong opposition to married women's paid employment. Moreover, as historian Veronica Strong-Boag has emphasized in her study of Canadian working women in the 1920s, 'in the final analysis acceptance of any kind [even for single women in the paid labour force] was in large measure predicated on the continuation of women's inferiority in the labour force.' While this point remains relevant to the subsequent decade as well, the Great Depression dramatically heightened the over-all antipathy to women's paid labour.[37]

In 1910 Sam Landers, key organizer for the United Garment Workers in Toronto, publicly proclaimed that no one denied the 'truism' that women belonged in the home. Speaking to a female audience, Landers announced: 'There would be no need of the advocacy of equal rights or suffrage for women were they permitted to remain in their *natural* sphere, the home, but the present competitive system, the greed for wealth by corporate and other employing interests had driven the women and the girls out into the commercial and industrial field to such an extent that there were as many or even a greater percentage of females earning a living at trades and callings than there were men; and if so, why should they not have some say in the legislation that shaped their destiny?' Landers continued: 'If some of our "women's rights" opponents, who use the now stereotyped phrase, "Women should remain in the homes," were to get down to business and grapple with some of the political and economic problems that drive women out of the homes, they would be doing a practical service instead of theorizing without relief.' Landers then added that he deplored the fact that women were entering new areas of work that had traditionally been reserved for men. He found it offensive for women to work not only at core-making in iron moulding shops but also at typesetting and at ticket-taking in railway stations.[38]

Landers's support for women's rights was decisively limited. Although he did not comment on the gender division of labour in the needle trades shops, the logic of his opposition to women ticket-takers would have extended to opposing women's entry into traditionally male jobs in the garment industry. As well, his sharp exaggeration of the extent of women's participation in the paid labour force suggests a deep unease. He seems to have wanted women to return to their allegedly natural sphere, although he realized that much would have to change before this goal could be realized. It may well have been difficult for the women in his union to deal with a leader who held such convoluted views. More broadly, the women garment workers must have found it hard to participate fully in shop-floor struggles when the very legitimacy of their presence in the workplace was so much in dispute.

As for Toronto's working-class Jewish community and the Jewish unions in the interwar years, although men's attitudes towards women's paid labour were generally not extreme, there were some challenges to the participation of women – particularly married women – in the paid labour force. A 1922 article in the *Yiddisher Zhurnal,* for example, argued against married women going out to work. Written by a man, this article charged that married women workers were seriously endangering the family by leaving their children during the day. The article focused on married women who could allegedly have been supported by their husbands. The writer argued that when these women went out to work, they worked for 'pin money,' taking desperately needed jobs from men and from unmarried women. The writer went on to explain that the employers profited by hiring these married women because they did not have to pay them much. As a result, according to this argument, the employers were keen to hire these women and were making up pseudo-philosophical justifications for these hiring practices.[39]

The views expressed in this *Zhurnal* article, however, were not necessarily typical within the Jewish community. While some people shared this writer's concern that married women's paid employment would weaken the family, others had a more matter-of-fact attitude towards married women's work. The views of Jacob Black and Moe Levin, for example, provide an interesting contrast. Black felt that the question of married women's work outside the home involved the issue of the centrality of family life rather than being simply a matter of economic calculations. When he was asked if Jewish women continued to work in the needle trades after getting married, he replied: 'Some of them continued to work after they married, and others started having children and stayed home because there was more attachment to the family in those days than today.' Black himself viewed single women's paid labour differently from married women's paid labour. He presented the issue of paid labour for single women as a straightforward economic matter: 'Many Jewish women, young girls, had to go to work because they had no other way of supporting themselves. They came from poor families, and they had to go to work.'[40]

Unlike Black, Levin viewed both married women's and single women's paid labour pragmatically in economic terms. When he was asked if the Jewish community felt that married women should not work outside the home, he replied that the answer was self-evident: 'If [married women] had to work, they had to work.' He suggested that, in the face of economic necessity, there was no question of moralizing about woman's proper place; he did not suggest that married women's paid labour was a sign of weak attachment to the family. He also pointed out that during the Depression of the 1930s, families often could not survive on the husband's wage alone.[41]

Yet the low wages of female needle trades workers frequently reinforced the domestic ideology. As Sol Abel pointed out, it often did not pay for married women to work in the needle trades instead of staying at home. His wife, Ida Abel, a finisher in the dress trade in the late 1920s and early 1930s, did try working in the shop for a few months when her child was still young. She found that after paying the babysitter and her carfare to and from the shop, there was little left of her wages. As a result, she left paid employment.[42] In cases like this, although becoming a full-time housewife freed women from the double burden of wage-earning and household labour, it made them more dependent on their husbands. Since women's low wages acted as a disincentive for mothers to 'work,' they also helped reduce the threat that women would stream into the paid labour force in severe competition with men.

However, some men still felt threatened. Within the Canadian labour movement as a whole, sharp opposition to women's paid labour became a fairly common theme as the Depression of the 1930s deepened. Joe Salsberg recalled that, at that time, many male unionists unashamedly advocated returning women to the home: 'At the [Toronto] Trades and Labour Council, I heard those idiots get up, you know, [and say:] "We gotta send *all* the women back to the kitchen!" ... *You heard it in every union!* It was an open cry: "Send them back to the kitchen!" ... If [the man's] out of work and a woman is working, so he's going to solve it like the primitive man with the club ... We don't use clubs now. But we got a union; we can tell the women to go back.' Salsberg declared that these men were 'primitives in economics' who 'didn't understand the cause of the crisis.'[43] Salsberg's own position suggests that a left analysis of the causes of the Great Depression could foster shifting the resentment and blame from the women workers to the capitalist system.

In discussing this 'primitive' defensiveness, Salsberg drew an interesting parallel between attitudes towards women workers and attitudes towards young male workers. In the millinery trade, the sewing-machine operators were originally all men, but women were gradually beginning to obtain jobs as operators by the early 1920s, when Salsberg was an organizer in this branch of the needle trades. When he was asked whether the men resented this competition from the women, he replied that the male unionists were generally not resentful, but 'you might have found an odd screwball who said: "we don't want women in here."' In this context, Salsberg explained there were 'also males that I knew in the men's union who objected to apprentices, *male* apprentices,' because they 'didn't want competition!' Salsberg went on to describe how male unionists in this particular union sought to reduce job competition by attempting to curtail the number of male apprentices allowed in union shops. As a young man, Salsberg himself had had to learn to be a cutter in a non-union shop because no places were available for him in a unionized factory. After learning this job, he then applied to join the union. However, the union would not take him in at first, because certain unionists felt there was no need for new cutters in the union.[44]

Salsberg stressed this parallel between opposition to women workers and opposition to young male workers because he felt that present-day feminists tend to be 'too simplistic' in evaluating the attitudes of male unionists. 'It's so easy to fall into the trap of [attributing everything to] either male indifference or male domination,' he argued.[45] It is true that male unionists were often on the defensive, desperately trying to improve their wages and job conditions in a difficult situation. It needs to be emphasized, however, that restricting women's access to paid employment was part and parcel of women's subordination in the home. After all, Salsberg himself indicated that in his union, 'certainly there was fear that the women are going to become masters over men. You know, you had backward people. It still persists in Jewish homes and in other homes.'[46]

Although some men, like Joe Salsberg and Ed Tannenbaum, argued against the view that women workers should be sent 'back to the kitchen,' this view persisted among certain members of Toronto's ACW as well. Tannenbaum recalled that during the Depression, men did not openly advocate this view at meetings of his ACW local because they were aware they would be accused of being reactionaries. The implication was that class solidarity should extend to female workers. [In the shop, however, Tannenbaum would hear men saying that the women should be removed from the workplace in order to provide jobs for men.] He himself considered such opinions reactionary. He would argue with the exponents of these views, explaining that there were women working in the shops who did not have any husbands to support them and that there were also women workers whose husbands were unemployed. When faced with one particular male worker who argued that women should be sent home, Tannenbaum replied that this attitude was 'poison' because 'each person has a right to a job, the same right as you have. Since when have you decided that you are the person to have a job, the right to work, and the other person, [who] is in a dress, has no [such right]?'[47]

The minutes of the joint board of Toronto's ACW reveal concern that, in the decade of the Depression, women were 'unfairly' occupying jobs. In 1931, for example, the Jewish coatmakers' local 'decided that married women who are working in the trade who have husbands who are employed, also men who are working in the trade who have [other] business where they can make a living through their business, should be removed from the shop.'[48] Although the local recommended that the joint board endorse and implement this policy, there is no record of the board's decision at that time. Another ACW local, the Jewish vestmakers' local, expressed similar concerns about married women two years later, but this time there was no corresponding concern about male workers who had other sources of income. The Joint Board adopted the vestmakers' recommendation 'that girls who are getting married and wishing to continue working should appear before the executive and the executive [should] determine whether their husbands can provide for them.'[49]

Some union members, however, felt that this provision was inadequate. Hence the members of this ACW local took up the issue once again in the spring of 1939, stating that 'the joint board should deal on [sic] the question of married women working in our shops whose husbands are also working and making a good living.' In response, the joint board 'decided to leave this question in abeyance for the time being,' but the board added that 'the Secretary is instructed when sending girls to work to use his better judgment by giving preference to single girls.'[50] Since the unionized employers did their hiring through the union, the union secretary's 'better judgment' would have had considerable weight in placing – or not placing – women in jobs. The secretary's instructions thus suggest discrimination against married women, whether or not their husbands were employed.

The fact that these ACW resolutions were all directed against married women suggests that, officially at least, men in this union saw single women as having a right to their jobs. However, the family wage, earned by the male breadwinner, was expected to take care of most married women. Because of this assumption, women were not being treated equally; it was considered legitimate to deny jobs to people who wore dresses.

The lack of more substantial opposition to female needle trades workers in general is, of course, also significant. In part, the absence of greater opposition reflects the legacy of the *shtetl* (Jewish town in Eastern Europe), where many Jewish women used to work to earn money for their families. The lack of more substantial opposition to women's work in the clothing factories also reflects the fact that women had been entrenched in this particular sector of the Canadian economy for a relatively long time. Moreover, female garment workers usually perform-ed jobs in female job ghettoes. Women were often considered to have a legitimate right to certain jobs within the clothing sector; indeed, these were thought of as 'women's jobs.' This was apparently the case, for example, with regard to operators' jobs in the dress trade. Hence when Moe Levin, one of the relatively few male dress operators, was asked if men in his trade felt women were taking jobs that should have gone to men, he replied: 'No, men felt that this is a woman's trade.'[51]

In the fur industry, as Ed Hammerstein stressed, the division between women's jobs and men's jobs was pronounced, 'so there never was that problem of [men's] fear of women taking their jobs.' Hammerstein explained that, in the fur shops, there were no women blockers and no women cutters. He added that there were just a few women operators, so few that the men did not really fear an influx of women in this job category. When asked about the other branches of the needle trades in the 1930s, Hammerstein replied that he did not sense much fear that women were taking men's jobs. In this period, he explained, women did not invade the male job preserves of the pressers and cutters.[52]

Although, in general, the written record tends to confirm Hammerstein's point that male needle trades workers were not afraid of being replaced by female labour, Hammerstein's generalization is too sweeping. There were, after all, some expressions of this kind of resentment. In 1932, for example, on the brink of a key strike in the fur industry, a male Jewish union leader announced in the *Yiddisher Zhurnal*: 'Jewish fur employers are discriminating openly against Jewish workers, merely because they [the Jewish workers] are good union men. [The Jewish manufacturers] will sooner hire an English girl than a Jewish family man, simply because the girl is better material to exploit.'[53] Here, ethnic and gender divisions again reinforced each other. Opposition to the hiring of women in this case was based not only on ethnic loyalties but also on the contention that women were being used to undercut union activism. The opposition to hiring women was heightened by the assumption that the jobs should go to the men because the men had families to support. Yet the fact that the legitimacy of women's place in the paid labour force was not solidly established must have made it difficult for women to become active unionists.

Although most male garment workers in the interwar period did not vigorously oppose women's employment in this sector, it is significant that there was still some opposition and considerable ambivalence. As indicated by activists like Jacob Black, Joe Salsberg, and Ed Tannenbaum, there was some concern that married women's paid employment would weaken the family and that women were taking jobs that should have gone to men. Particularly during the Great Depression, some men in the Jewish unions clearly wished to send women back to the kitchen full time. Although most of the men were not so extreme, the fact that some men had these attitudes must have made it hard for female workers to participate fully in shop-floor struggles. Women workers must have found it difficult to stand up against their bosses for their rights on the shop floor when these struggles necessitated trying to unite with those male fellow workers who were opposed to – or even just ambivalent about – women's right to be on the shop floor at all.

Women workers thus faced important constraints that served to hinder their participation in the Jewish labour movement. As workers who were relatively unskilled, women were particularly vulnerable on the shop floor. Compared with the men, the women workers were relatively inexperienced in the world of paid labour. Yet the women faced special employer intransigence and were particularly vulnerable to 'divide-and-conquer' strategies. At the same time, female workers had less time and energy to devote to union activism because they were often burdened by heavy household responsibilities. In addition, some of the women faced active discouragement from male relatives, and, within the unions themselves, they sometimes faced sexist male attitudes. The male culture of the union halls, for example, meshed with the occasional stereotyping of women and with some men's ambivalence towards women's participation in the paid labour force. Although some women (especially some of the Jewish women) were 'fighting cats' on the picket lines, other women found these barriers insurmountable. Toronto's Jewish labour movement was thus significantly fragmented not only along lines of ethnicity but also along lines of gender. The movement was particularly weakened in situations where ethnic and gender divisions reinforced each other.

6 'Just as a Worker'
The Dearth of Female-Oriented Strategies

'Another thing I learned during the years I was organizing was that to get women into the trade union movement required a technique that was different from organizing men. From the very beginning, I myself worked with men very successfully both in the factory and in the trade union movement, but I appreciated the difficulties that women met with, and I knew that in general they should have different treatment than men.'

– *Woman at Work: The Autobiography of Mary Anderson*[1]

'The regular machinery of our organization was not sufficient to arouse the interest of the women in the work of our organization and attract them to join it,' announced the ACW's general executive board to the union's Canadian and American locals in 1916. To attract the women workers, 'some sort of special machinery, which would apply not to all workers in the industry, but to the women particularly and exclusively, must be created,' the board concluded. Hence the head office advised the locals to organize 'women's clubs and other auxiliary organizations in order to promote the organization of women in the industry and educate those already organized.' Although the board specifically asked the union locals to take 'immediate action' and to submit frequent progress reports on this matter, there is no evidence that Toronto's ACW paid any attention to this unusual appeal.[2]

Throughout the period under consideration, Toronto's Jewish unions generally failed to develop special policies to appeal to female workers in particular, and the Canadian women's movement did not provide a feminist counterforce. The union leaders' failure to develop 'some sort of special machinery' stemmed not only from conventional attitudes towards the gender division of labour in the home and on the shop floor but also from the nature of their class analysis. Fashioned by a male-dominated leadership, the policies of the Jewish unions were commonly male oriented. At the same time, the Canadian women's movement rarely allied with Toronto's female garment workers. Initial efforts to found a cross-class women's alliance on behalf of women workers quickly failed here, leaving the city's female garment workers without the support some of their counterparts received from the National Women's Trade Union League in the United States. Thus, with few exceptions, Toronto's women garment workers continued to encounter only 'the regular machinery' of the Jewish unions.

The significance of the traditional division of labour in the home emerges, for example, in Ed Hammerstein's discussion of the position of women in his union. Hammerstein indicated that although women took their turns on the picket lines, 'there weren't too many women [who] were active in the [furriers'] union in the sense of getting up at union meetings and speaking up, being on strike committees, or things of that nature.' He then explained that there was 'not too great an effort' to involve the women more 'because there was an acceptance of the fact that women had to go home and do whatever has to be done, you know, look after homes and things like that.'

Although male unionists were aware that women's household roles restricted female activism, they did not question women's traditional responsibility for housework and child care.[4] Even the men who supported radical social change in other areas did not consider sharing household labour or trying to make communal arrangements that might have been able to cut down on the individual woman's housework. Issues such as having the union provide child care during union meetings, to encourage women workers to attend, were simply not on the unions' agendas.

The nature of the Jewish activists' class consciousness meant that they generally focused on what they saw as the common oppression of all workers, ignoring the fact that women workers faced special constraints. When union activists were asked if the unions had special policies to appeal to women workers, the question surprised them, for the notion of the particular interests of women workers was foreign to their class analysis. Typically, the unions appealed to each person 'just as a worker!' as Moe Levin proudly exclaimed.[5]

Yet this was not really a gender-neutral construct, for the prototype of *the* worker was the male worker. Although men usually constituted less than half of Toronto's garment workers, the 'masculine conception of class' (which scholars such as Joan Scott have recently emphasized in other historical contexts) operated even in the labour movement in this sector. Men were able to shape the conception of the 'typical' garment worker in their own image, partly because the female workers were seen as temporary and hence less 'central' to both the industry and the unions. The male union leaders appeared to speak for and represent working-class interests as a whole, but the definition of class was gender biased. This bias was not questioned.[6]

In their efforts to win wage increases for Toronto's garment workers, male union leaders did little to try to reduce substantial pay differentials that were based on gender. Indeed, the unions' wage policies often served to increase these gender-based differentials. Regardless of the fact that male unionists generally did not see women workers as having special problems on the shop floor, women workers were commonly confined to jobs that paid substantially less than jobs performed by men. In Toronto's needle trades, on the whole, the average female worker's wage usually fell between one-half to two-thirds of the average male worker's wage. In 1921, for example, the city's average adult female garment worker earned only 58 per cent of what her male counterpart earned.[7] Fifteen years later, the average woman in Toronto's needle trades earned a scant 52–53 per cent of what the average man earned.[8] Women's average earnings sometimes even dipped below the halfway mark, as in Toronto's cloak trade in 1933, when the average woman made only 44 per cent of what the average man made.[9]

Women garment workers often did not earn enough money to enable them to be self-sufficient.[10] The inability to earn a 'living wage' – which, of course, reinforced the institution of marriage – is evident in the experience of Ida Abel. Abel worked as a finisher from the mid 1920s until she got married in the mid 1930s. Because her parents had not emigrated to Canada, Abel shared her lodgings with another young woman in order to economize in those years. Although Abel's way of life was humble, her two brothers had to supplement her earnings to help cover her living expenses.[11] Moreover, during the Depression in particular, many female garment workers were not even earning the legal minimum wage, an amount that had been established by the Ontario Minimum Wage Board as the sum of money judged necessary for a self-supporting single woman.[12]

Yet the wage policies of Toronto's needle trades unions often widened the gap between women's earnings and men's earnings, thereby reinforcing women's subordination. These unions often fought for pay raises that were formulated in terms of an across-the-board percentage increase for all workers. Such an increase meant that the dollar difference between the average woman's wage and the average man's wage would actually become larger. In 1920, for example, when the average wage in the city's ACW shops was $21 per week for women and $34 per week for men, the union simply demanded an across-the-board increase of 33 per cent.[13] Although the average woman's wage would have remained at 62 per cent of the average man's wage, the gap between her wage and his wage would have increased from $13 to $17. Because women generally could not enter the better-paid jobs, the very structure of these wage demands disadvantaged women further.

The garment unions' tendency to formulate wage demands in terms of such across-the-board percentage increases was widespread.[14] This practice cropped up often during the course of union-management negotiations, and union demands for across-the-board percentage increases featured in individual shop strikes as well as in general strikes.[15] Moreover, there were also cases where the unions, in demanding flat wage increases of so many dollars, actually demanded a significantly lower increase for female workers than for male workers. In the 1933 general cloak strike, for example, at a time when pre-strike wages were listed as $16 per week for men and $7 per week for women, the ILGWU demanded a $1 per week increase for men and only a 50 cent per week increase for women.[16] Such a strategy again served to increase the actual dollar difference between the average male wage and the average female wage. Thus, although there were exceptions, the unions' wage policies generally privileged men further by widening the pay gap.

While Toronto's women garment workers were generally confined to the less-skilled and low-paid jobs, there were some cases where women and men did the same kind of work. In some of these cases, the workers were on piece work, and the same piece rates applied to females and males who performed the same jobs. In formal terms, this meant equal pay for equal work, although, in practice, some of these women workers sometimes earned less money per week than their male counterparts. This disparity occurred at times because the men had usually been at the job for a longer period of time and, consequently, some of them were faster at the work. In addition, some of the men tended to be faster because they had had more training in the tailoring trade before emigrat-

ing from Eastern Europe. Perhaps some of the women were slower because they were tired out from heavy household responsibilities as well.
In Toronto's dress trade in the 1920s and 1930s, for example, female and
male operators did the same kind of work and received the same rate for
each piece they completed. Thus the actual weekly earnings of each
person depended on how speedily the particular individual could work.[17]

In the needle trades as a whole, however, there were revealing situations where unequal pay for the same work prevailed. In an 1897 investigation of government clothing contracts, for example, Mackenzie King
reported: 'The time has not yet arrived, at least in the clothing trade,
when a like service commands a like remuneration irrespective of the sex
of the person who performs it. The reward for female labour is still
greatly at a discount as compared with that of the opposite sex.' King
pointed out that since there were many women clothing workers available
at low wages, this meant that few men were hired for these jobs.[18]

Two decades later, female labour was still 'greatly at a discount.' In the
unionized shops in Toronto's men's fine-clothing industry in 1920, for
example, there were cases where women and men performed the exact
same jobs and were on time work rather than piece work. In these cases,
the women's wages were invariably considerably lower than the wages of
their male counterparts. In some of these cases, the women did have less
experience than the men who did the same work. Male buttonhole-
makers, for example, had an average of nineteen years of experience and
received an average wage of $36 per week, while female buttonhole-
makers had an average of seven years of experience and received an
average wage of $22 per week. Other women who found themselves in
similar situations were those who did various kinds of basting jobs and
those who made collars and lapels.[19]

Although the women's fewer years of experience provided some sort
of rationale for their lower pay, the soundness of this line of reasoning
is questionable. It is doubtful that these women were so much less skilled
than their male counterparts as to merit such wide pay differentials. After
all, one could learn to be a fairly fast and efficient buttonhole-maker in
less than seven years. Indeed, a 1920 Ontario government publication on
vocational opportunities in the needle trades declared, in another context, that 'the maximum speed on a single [sewing-machine] operation
will generally be attained in one or two years.'[20]

Moreover, in these unionized men's fine-clothing shops in 1920, there
were actually a few cases where women and men performed the same jobs
and where the women had experience equal to or greater than the men

in those jobs. In such cases, the women were still paid considerably less than the men. Consider the case of the pants operators. The men in this job averaged seven years of experience and made an average of $39 per week, while the women averaged fourteen years of experience and made an average of $22 per week. Similarly, male pocket operators averaged eight years of experience and made an average wage of $40 per week, while female pocket operators averaged ten years of experience and made an average of $26 per week.[21] In these particular cases, the Amalgamated Clothing Workers, the union involved in these shops, appears to have made no attempt to rectify these instances of grossly unequal pay for equal work.[22]

Such cases indicate that women's lower wages cannot be seen simply as a product of a lower level of skill on the part of women who did not generally stay in the trade as long as men. Indeed, these particular cases suggest that there were other powerful forces acting to dampen women's wages. In a society where women were being systematically devalued, it is not surprising that these women workers were not being paid what they were worth. Sadie Reisch, a rare female leader at the ILGWU's head office, maintained that 'the [pay] rate is customarily less for women than for men even on the same job' because of 'a hangover of the old idea of masculine superiority.'[23]

Part of the rationale for women's low wages was the expectation that male breadwinners were obliged to support families, while female workers were not expected to do so. Stripped to its core, this meant that women were expected to be dependent on men. And these expectations were married to necessity. In Toronto's needle trades, as in many other sectors in this period, low wages for women workers often meant that a woman could not even fully support herself, let alone support children or aging parents. By making economic independence impossible for most women, women's low wages served to reinforce – even as they reflected – the systematic subordination of women.

Feminist scholars have commonly considered equal pay for equal work to be a progressive measure, for it challenges the devaluation of women and sexist assumptions about the primacy of the male breadwinner.[24] However, policies of equal pay for equal work have sometimes been a Trojan Horse, a poisoned gift. Historically, union enforcement of equal-pay provisions has sometimes directly resulted in the displacement of women workers. As explained by Sam Landers, leader of the United Garment Workers in early twentieth-century Toronto, 'equal pay for equal work has a tendency to lessen the employment of women at least in the

organized trades, as employers when they must pay the same wage, prefer
men.'[25] Although it is extremely difficult to document deliberate inten-
tions, some male union leaders who promoted equal pay may have been
motivated by this tendency. In general, women workers could be hurt
both in situations where they received significantly lower pay than men
performing similar work and in situations where unions' insistence on
equal pay, without programs like affirmative action, served to drive wom-
en out of certain jobs.

Toronto's needle trades unions seldom actively promoted equal pay for
equal work. Indeed, unequal pay was sometimes incorporated in union
contracts, as, for example, in the 1934 IFWU contract that provided for
lower minimum wages for female workers than for male workers in the
same job categories.[26] The Amalgamated Clothing Workers in particular
had apparently remained silent with regard to the equal-pay issue in 1920,
despite the glaring inequities that existed. Nine years later, when leaders
of the Toronto ACW and the manufacturers' association were negotiating
a new agreement, 'the conference [between the union and the associa-
tion] also dealt with the request of the Union to strike out from the wage
scale the difference between the male workers and female workers.'[27]
However, this was not one of the union's more central and well-public-
ized demands. When no agreement was reached on the issue at this
conference, the ACW appears to have dropped the demand.[28]

For most of Toronto's women garment workers, equal pay for equal
work was not a central issue because they were largely confined to
low-paying 'women's jobs' within the industry. Recognizing the system for
what it really was, Ed Tannenbaum recently labelled it 'discrimination
against women.' He recalled that in his union there was never any talk
about trying to expand women's job opportunities on the shop floor. The
other Jewish unions were the same. 'Women knew their place,' exclaimed
Ed Hammerstein, 'insofar as the hierarchy of employment [was con-
cerned].'[29]

The unions' failure to challenge the gender division of labour in the
needle trades was, of course, partly due to the fact that the male unionists
themselves profited directly from the restriction of jobs available to wom-
en. Moreover, if the unions had championed women's rights, they would
have met with significant opposition from the garment manufacturers
themselves. The employers in this highly competitive industry depended
particularly on low-wage female labour; thus their determination to 'even
up by taking advantage of the women' would have been hard to fight.
The unions were in a highly precarious position in this period, having to

struggle hard for gains that often proved to be meagre. For all these reasons, the unions were not in a strong position from which to do battle with employers for women's rights.]

Union records, however, do not give the impression that male union leaders were seriously attempting to support women's rights but were finding their hands tied by the employers. Instead, the available evidence suggests that male union activists were not particularly concerned with women's rights. Despite a few minor exceptions, the garment unions basically did not try to alter gender-based pay differentials or indeed alter the gender division of labour itself. This standpoint must be seen not only as a product of the very real constraints that the garment unions faced in this period but also as a product of male unionists' attitudes towards women. These attitudes were conditioned, in part, by the fact that male workers' immediate interests often ran directly counter to the interests of women workers. Since the men led these unions and usually outnumbered the women within the rank and file as well, males were in a strong position to fashion union policies in their own interests.

The nature of male unionists' attitudes towards women can be explored more fully by examining the garment unions' internal monetary policies with regard to special assessments and benefits. Here, after all, was an area of union policy where the unions were able to operate relatively free from constraints imposed by the employers. Although the available evidence is fragmentary, it is clear that these monetary policies were far from consistently fair to women workers. What was at stake here was not just a matter of principle, for more equitable policies might have significantly strengthened women's allegiance to the unions.

If union activists had felt it was unfair for women to earn so much less than men, they could have structured strike benefits so that female strikers received the same as male strikers. This seldom happened.[30] The rationale for lower strike pay for women was that women earned less than men on the shop floor. However, this same rationale should have meant that women's union fees were lower than men's fees. Yet, in many cases, the women had to pay the same fees as the men.[31] Notwithstanding minor variations between the unions and within particular unions over time, the overall pattern is that the Jewish unions did not make a point of advancing progressive policies in these areas. The inequitable treatment of women was not imposed by the manufacturers alone; it was imposed as well by the unions.

In addition to the unions' failures to frame their monetary policies more to the benefit of women, there were other ways in which the needle trades unions failed to help women workers. The women, for example, were vulnerable to sexual harassment from male supervisors. Since there was little public discussion of this issue in this period, it is difficult to document the extent to which women needle trades workers faced this problem. It is clear, however, that this was a real problem for them.

During the 1912 Toronto Eaton strike, for example, the *Western Clarion* reported that 'young girls on starvation wages have been subjected to gross insults and temptations from [the] foreman and examiners.'[32] Alice Chown, a local women's rights activist, similarly depicted the plight of the women in the Eaton garment factory at that time. According to Chown, the women strikers explained that female workers who went out with the foreman would get the best jobs while those who would not comply with the foreman's wishes would be penalized.[33] Presumably, it was this kind of sexual harassment that Mackenzie King had been referring to when his report on Toronto's needle trades sweatshops alluded to 'instances ... where foremen and contractors had taken a more terrible advantage of those anxious to secure enough work for a livelihood.' These instances, exclaimed King, were 'too hideous to admit of publication.'[34]

Indeed, sexual harassment was (and still is) often seen as an issue 'too hideous to admit' at all, and this attitude has made it difficult to deal with. As far as the records indicate, none of Toronto's garment unions made any attempts to protect women workers from this kind of harassment. Yet union leaders could have promoted union involvement in the hiring process as a way of minimizing employers' opportunities to extort sexual favours in return for a job. Although the unions did promote union regulation of employers' hiring and firing practices, no such appeal to women's specific interests was made. The unions' failures to help combat sexual harassment meant that the burden of the problem – and often the blame itself – continued to rest with individual women.

Although Toronto's needle trades unions did not generally address issues of special relevance to women workers, there was one dramatic strike where the union's demands were formulated particularly in terms of women's interests. In this case, the union's unusual demands stemmed from a special set of circumstances rather than from a major shift in female-male relations. It was the large 1912 strike in Eaton's clothing factory that was so exceptional in this respect. At the time of the strike, Eaton's employed the majority of Toronto's cloakmakers, and most of these garment workers were Jewish. Although Eaton's was not a union shop, a significant number of the firm's garment workers were members of the International Ladies' Garment Workers' Union. Owing to low

128 Sweatshop Strife

wages, long hours, blatantly unfair supervisors, and the firm's exploitation of child labour, dissatisfaction had been mounting in this factory for several years before the outbreak of the strike.[35]

The strike began in one department of the firm's clothing factory when sixty-five male sewing-machine operators refused to follow new orders to sew in the linings of women's coats on their machines. These men, all of whom were ILGWU members, had been making 65 cents per garment without sewing in the linings, and management was now insisting they do the extra work without any increase in pay. Previously, the linings had been sewn in by hand by female workers who were known as finishers. The new order from management amounted to more than a pay cut for the men – it meant women were going to lose their jobs. Male self-interest and female self-interest now coincided, and the activists presented the strike in terms of male solidarity with women workers.[36]

This solidarity was emphasized by the Toronto District Labour Council when it passed a resolution objecting to Eaton's locking out workers for refusing 'in the interests of their sister workers, to do work which did not belong to them.'[37] Indeed, this solidarity between women and men became one of the main themes of the strike. 'Remember,' stated Joe Salsberg, 'the Jewish tailors in Toronto went on their first big strike in defense of *undzere shvester* – our sisters.' Salsberg explained: 'The reasoning of the men who worked at Eaton's was a simple one: that these [women workers] will lose their jobs, and ... maybe they felt that they didn't want to do these jobs that the women are now doing, maybe their wages will come down [if the men were to sew in the linings by machine] because the rates fixed for those operations were always traditionally lower because women did [those operations]. I never rule out the element of selfishness and self-interest – which is also human.' Salsberg stressed that one of the strike slogans 'became the folksy expression of simple, honest working men ... in Yiddish particularly: *Mir vellen nisht aroycenemen dem bissle fun broyt fun di mayler fun undzere shvester* [We will not take the morsel of bread from the mouths of our sisters].'[38]

The ILGWU's newspaper, too, stressed the men's solidarity with the women, portraying the men's action as more than a simple matter of self-interest. According to the newspaper, union officials believed in the early stages of the strike that 'management would have increased the price of operating [on] the garment, but the operators, with admirable solidarity, insist that the finishers shall not be deprived of their share of the work.'[39] Since Eaton's never made a clear offer of extra pay to the men for doing the extra work, this was never put to the test. Indeed, given the company's obstinate refusal to negotiate as the strike dragged through the first two months, such an offer was highly unlikely.

[Moreover, while the men's refusal to do 'women's work' supported their female co-workers, male reluctance may have stemmed partly from a sense that this work was beneath them.] The men probably viewed the extra work not only as unremunerative but also as less skilled. The male strikers were, in effect, taking a stand to maintain the gender division of labour on the shop floor. This system of labour-market segmentation privileged the men themselves.

In the meantime, the strike had built up considerable momentum. When the sixty-five male operators protested against sewing in the linings by launching their own sit-down strike, management fired them and physically threw them out onto the street. Almost immediately, more than one thousand of their fellow workers from Eaton's factory went on strike to support them. About one-fourth to one-third of these strikers were women, and the ILGWU's head office sent two women organizers to Toronto to help lead the female strikers. The sympathy strike spread beyond the ILGWU to include members of the United Garment Workers who worked in the men's clothing departments of the Eaton's factory. And it spread beyond Toronto: some workers at Eaton's clothing factory in Montreal also struck in sympathy with the Toronto workers, and Hamilton's garment workers threatened to join the strike if any of Hamilton's clothing firms attempted to do work for the T. Eaton Company.[40]

The Eaton strikers received wide support within Toronto's immigrant Jewish community in particular. The Associated Hebrew Charities provided food for the strikers, the Jewish mutual benefit societies donated funds, as did the Arbeiter Ring, and the local Jewish women's organizations took up street collections for the strikers until city officials stopped them.[41] When the assault on Fort Eaton was reinforced by the call for a nation-wide boycott of the company's goods, many 'Jewish patrons of Eaton's ... transferred their custom to the Robert Simpson Co.'[42] The force of the boycott within Toronto's immigrant Jewish community depended on the support of women in particular, for they were the ones who were primarily responsible for family shopping. Here, women's role as consumer was used strategically to support the struggles of producers of both sexes. The boycott also received some support from other groups; indeed, the *Industrial Banner* reported that Eaton's mail-order business suffered as customers across the country mailed back their Eaton's catalogues in protest.[43]

However, the strike was significantly weakened by the fact that Eaton's non-Jewish cloakmakers continued to work while the Jews struck. The company also managed to obtain strike-breakers directly from England. Thus, after the strike had dragged on for sixteen weeks, the unionists were forced to admit defeat. The effect on Jewish workers was devastating. The ILGWU was seriously weakened, and, as one union official recalled, 'for a very long time [after this strike], the T. Eaton Company would not hire any Jews.'[44]

Despite the loss, the 1912 Eaton strike was an outstanding example of male solidarity with female workers in a situation where the self-interest of the male workers meshed well with the interests of the women. In this case, the solidarity between Jewish men and Jewish women, however, was not matched by solidarity between Jews and non-Jews. Although the ILGWU's demands had been formulated specifically in terms of the concerns of women workers in this particular case, this development was the product of a unique set of circumstances. Such emphasis on women workers' special concerns was rare within the Jewish labour movement.

Although the Communist Party of Canada (CPC) occasionally highlighted the need to organize female workers during the party's dual-union phase, the nature of this emphasis requires careful analysis. As the CPC moved to establish its own 'revolutionary unions' under the umbrella of the Workers' Unity League, the *Worker* proclaimed that 'only the Communist Party and the left wing has the virility and the desire to organize the mass of exploited unorganized workers, whether they be men, women or the youth.' A 1931 CPC plenum resolution echoed the theme, while, at the same time, also criticizing the party itself for not having done enough to organize women.[45]

Within the garment industry in particular, the Communists formed the Industrial Union of Needle Trades Workers (IUNTW), and the IUNTW leadership similarly reiterated the need to organize the unorganized, including women, youth, and French Canadians.[46] Yet this was not a strong emphasis on women, for the coverage of the IUNTW in the Communist press only occasionally contained one-line statements on the importance of organizing the female garment workers. In 1931, for example, Myer Klig, one of the IUNTW's leaders, raised this issue briefly in the party's Yiddish newspaper. Writing about the union's second convention, Klig declared that in addition to more work among the youth in the garment industry, 'special attention must be paid to work among women.' 'Until now, nothing has been done in this area,' he added.[47] Such statements were usually only short remarks within articles that did not otherwise focus on women workers. Significantly, articles such as Klig's did not go on to explain what steps the union could take to appeal specifically to women. Nor did they explain why the IUNTW had not yet done anything in this area.

This scarcity of references to women was in spite of the fact that the IUNTW in Toronto came to focus on organizing the dressmakers, the majority of whom were female.[48] A 1930 plea to dressmakers to join the IUNTW, for example, contained no special appeal to female dressmakers and, in fact, made no mention of women at all.[49] More broadly, the Worker's and Der Kamf's coverage of the IUNTW's general dress strikes seldom even mentioned women.[50]

In this context, Annie Buller's retrospective account of the 1931 IUNTW strike is instructive. In a 1951 article in National Affairs, Buller, a former IUNTW organizer, described the union's activities during this attempted general strike in the Toronto dress trade. She charged that the International Ladies' Garment Workers' Union had refused to organize the dressmakers in 1931 because these 'reformist leaders' felt it was not possible to organize women workers. Yet, apart from this charge, her article made no further mention of women. Given this specific accusation against the ILGWU, Buller's failure to examine whether the IUNTW took special steps to organize the women in particular calls into question the actual nature of the party's commitment to this task.[51]

Although the CPC was progressive in that it did sometimes call attention to the need to organize women workers in this period, the party's appeal to female workers seems to have been no different from its appeal to male workers. The Communists did not view female workers as having significant separate interests from male workers, since women were not seen as having special interests outside their class interests. The party's goal was to mobilize women as part of the class struggle.

The Communist party was clear and insistent on this point, proclaiming in the Worker in 1931: '[Working-class women] can be drawn into the entire struggle of the Canadian workers for relief from their present misery. The women workers have no interests apart from those of the working class generally. There is no room for "feminism" in our movement. There is only place for unity and solidarity on the basis of the joint struggle against capitalism.'[52] 'Exactly right!' exclaimed Joshua Gershman when asked to comment recently on this quotation. Gershman, one of the main IUNTW leaders, stressed that this excerpt from the Worker accurately expressed how he, together with the other Communist-oriented IUNTW members, felt about women's issues in this period.[53]

Asked whether the IUNTW had special policies to bring female workers into the union, Gershman replied that the union did not really have a particular program to attract women, although he added that the IUNTW did fight for equal pay for equal work. He indicated that the leaders of the Communist union movement in this period did not think in terms of having a special plank for women workers. Nor did Gershman make the argument that women could only be liberated after capitalism was abolished. Instead, his replies indicated that there was not much concern with women's issues and women's rights.[54] For the Communist movement in this period, the focus was clearly on class struggle. Although the CPC press carried a few articles that asserted that women were truly free in the Soviet Union,[55] this apparent concern with women's equality was not reflected in the thought of IUNTW leaders.

In discussing women and unions, however, Gershman added that during the party's dual-union phase, the Communists did argue that there were not enough women in union leadership positions. In this context, Gershman pointed out that the Workers' Unity League, the central labour body of the Communist-led 'revolutionary unions,' had female organizers.[56] With regard to the IUNTW (an affiliate of the Workers' Unity League), the most prominent woman leader was Annie Buller. During her brief connection with the IUNTW, Buller played an important role in the needle trades.

Buller was a working-class woman who courageously devoted her life to the Communist Party of Canada, serving as a member of the party's national executive for years. Before becoming an IUNTW organizer in 1929, she had already done various other kinds of arduous organizing work for the party, and she later became involved in heroic efforts to recruit support for such causes as the Estevan miners' strike and the On-to-Ottawa Trek. Buller was a member of the IUNTW's general executive board for a time, and she helped lead the IUNTW's general strike in the Toronto dress trade in 1931. She was centrally involved in IUNTW affairs for two or three years, but later shifted her focus to other party activities.[57]

Buller's leadership role clearly did not provide the IUNTW with a focus on women's issues. Deeply committed to the class struggle, Buller apparently was not concerned with women's issues in this period. This can be seen, for example, in her answer to a 1928 request for a speaker on women's rights. 'Wouldn't a real topic be better than the woman question – say the war danger, modern imperialism, China, or a colonial question?' she replied.[58]

Apart from Buller, women were not well represented in the IUNTW leadership despite Gershman's concern that it was important to have female leaders. In 1931 the top three officers of the IUNTW were men, although women were better represented at the next leadership level. Of the thirteen IUNTW general executive board members representing Toronto, four were women, one of whom was Annie Buller.[59] By 1935, however, there were hardly any women on the union's general executive board, and the board's two top officers were men. By this time, Annie Buller had left the IUNTW, and, of the eleven IUNTW board members representing Ontario, only one was a woman.[60] Buller's departure from the IUNTW thus meant that women became less well represented at leadership levels, despite the fact that Toronto's IUNTW had come to focus particularly on the dress trade, a branch of the needle trades in which over half of the workers were women.

Although the party deserves credit for organizing female and male dressmakers, the Communist needle trades union was little different from the other garment unions with respect to women. The Jewish Communists' focus on class struggle, a focus by no means foreign to other branches of the Jewish left, precluded the mobilization of women workers around separate women's issues. From their class perspective, it would have been too divisive to mobilize for women's special interests within the labour movement and on the shop floor. According to this view, such an emphasis on special women's issues was likely to have weakened the working class significantly, by dividing male workers and female workers. There was also 'no room for "feminism" in [the Communist] movement' because any vision of the common oppression of women, which transcended class, threatened to dilute the class struggle. From this Communist perspective, such an emphasis on women's oppression was tantamount to advocating an interclass alliance of women, which could only have obscured the interests of the working class. Thus, given the party's emphasis on the working class as the central revolutionary agent, Communists in the Jewish labour movement would have viewed the mobilization of women workers around separate women's issues as 'counter-revolutionary.'

The non-Communist needle trades activists, like the Communists, did not seek to mobilize female workers around women's issues. They did not place a priority on recruiting women into union leadership positions and the key positions in Toronto's needle trades unions were generally monopolized by men, as was the case in many other Canadian organizations in this period. During the ILGWU's 1919 general strike in the city's cloak and dress trades, for example, there were no prominent female union officials. Samson Koldofsky was the main leader of the strike, and Tom Black, a non-Jew, served as the organizer for the ILGWU's English-speaking workers. In addition, males served as heads of all the committees that were organized to help with the various aspects of the strike. Although the piano player was female, even the head of the entertainment committee was male.[61]

The leading male unionists, however, sometimes realized that a woman union leader might be better able to appeal to women workers, so they did occasionally use women organizers. From time to time they placed a woman organizer on the local staff of one of the garment unions or relied on their unions' head offices to parachute a woman organizer into the city during a particular crisis. In the context of so many more male organizers, this occasional use of women organizers amounted to little more than tokenism. While there was a vague sense that a woman organizer might occasionally be useful to impart a 'woman's touch,' this did not act as a catalyst to develop special policies to appeal to the female workers. The infrequent use of women organizers did not provide a focal point for the articulation and promotion of women's interests as workers who faced special forms of oppression by virtue of their gender.

The intermittent awareness of the need for a woman organizer can be seen, for example, in a report of a 1913 meeting of the Toronto joint board of the ILGWU. The report declared: 'The question of a lady organizer came up and the statement was made that the Board could not proceed with their organizing work, unless the girls in the skirt trade be first organized, because they are in the majority, and the moment that the male members make an attempt to organize they are fired. The Locals are absolutely helpless and can do nothing for their members in the skirt trade unless they have a lady organizer to assist them. [It was], therefore, recommend[ed] that a lady organizer be sent to Toronto.'[62] Instead of stressing the need to help female workers because the women were exploited, this account emphasized organizing the women workers in order to reduce the vulnerability of the unionized male workers. Although the union did advertise in Cotton's Weekly for a female organizer,[63] it seems that a woman was not actually hired at that time. It appears that the union's commitment to hiring a woman was relatively weak.

There were only a few cases where one of the unions' head offices actually sent a woman organizer to Toronto to help out on a short-term, emergency basis. In 1931, for example, the head office of the International Ladies' Garment Workers' Union sent Sadie Reisch to Toronto during the union's general strike in the dress trade. Reisch, a dressmaker who had become an organizer for the National Women's Trade Union League and had been 'loaned' by the league to the ILGWU, helped organize Toronto's women dressmakers while the strike was in progress. In the aftermath of the strike, Toronto union officials requested their head office to send a 'girl organizer' to do further work among the city's dressmakers, but there is no evidence that the head office complied with this request.[64]

Although there were occasionally women organizers on the local staff of Toronto's Jewish unions, they were but a small minority within a predominantly male officialdom. Toronto's Amalgamated Clothing Workers briefly had a woman organizer on staff in 1923, for example. Sarah Gold, the daughter of a poor immigrant Jewish family in Toronto, was hired as the ACW's organizer for the city's shirtmakers, who were mostly women, and she was also expected to 'do other work amongst the women in the clothing industry.' Although Gold was reported to have been making 'considerable headway' within a month or two of having been appointed organizer, there was already talk of dispensing with her services. In fact, Gold was dismissed from her position after only six or seven months because the head office felt a new male organizer would be able to take over her work in addition to his other responsibilities. At the time of her dismissal, no mention was made of the earlier consideration that a woman organizer would be particularly appropriate for dealing with the many shirtmakers who were women.[65]

Mary McNab was another of the rare female organizers in this period. McNab, who was later to work for the ILGWU in Toronto, began her connection with the needle trades unions when she served as organizer for a Hamilton ACW local for about a year in 1917. While in this position, she played a central role in a dramatic strike of women garment workers in the nearby town of Dundas. 'When I think of the splendid spirit of these girls,' wrote McNab in connection with this strike, 'I am proud I am a woman.'[66] Yet, as a woman, she earned approximately half of what the union's male organizers were earning at this time. Before long, McNab felt forced to resign her position because, according to her own account, she was undermined by an important male ACW organizer who told the membership that she 'did nothing but take money out of the Local for nothing.' Although the reason for this man's antipathy to her remains unknown, her value as an organizer was supported to by the fact that the union's head office asked her to reconsider her resignation. She felt she had to resign nonetheless.[67]

As the Toronto cloakmakers were embarking on a new organizing campaign in the summer of 1924, the ILGWU hired Mary McNab as organizer for the English-speaking workers. During the course of this campaign, McNab played a central role in mobilizing the non-Jewish women in particular. When the cloakmakers undertook a general strike in February 1925, McNab was actively involved. As part of her strike-support work, she represented the ILGWU at a meeting of the Toronto Trades and Labour Council, where, according to the Toronto *Star*, she 'caused quite a bit of excitement in asking for the support of the council [for the] strike.'[68] She also served as one of the ILGWU's delegates to the Trades and Labour Congress. Although little is known of the difficulties McNab may have faced in such a male environment, one male unionist recalled that when shorter skirts came into fashion, the male delegates to the Toronto Trades and Labour Council used to stare at her during council meetings, trying to look up her legs.[69]

Women were also significantly outnumbered by men in various other kinds of official union leadership positions. For example, although there were many women in Ed Hammerstein's IFWU local, Hammerstein, who held various leadership positions within this union in the 1930s, recalled that there were hardly any women on the local's executive board. Similarly, Sol Abel, a cloakmaker who was a member of the ILGWU's joint board in the 1930s, remembered that, as a rule, there would be only about two women on a board that was composed of approximately thirty people. This was at a time when women made up one-quarter of the city's cloakmakers.[70] This pattern was repeated in the Jewish unions' other locals and joint boards. For example, the ACW's Toronto joint board, which was composed of approximately twenty representatives from the various locals, usually included only one woman in the interwar years – despite the fact that women constituted about a third of the ACW's membership. In fact, at a number of points during the interwar period, there were no women at all on the ACW's joint board for months on end.[71]

In contrast to the lack of measures to ensure that women would be systematically included in the leadership of the Jewish unions, the unions had specific measures to make sure that certain other constituencies, particularly non-Jews, would be represented. In Toronto's ACW, for example, it was common practice to have one Jewish business agent and one non-Jewish business agent. Both of these positions were almost always filled by males. Since the two business agents played a central role in the union, this careful ethnic balance was highly significant. Sometimes the Jewish unions even had special provisions to balance the leadership between the Communist and anti-Communist factions, as, for example, in the dressmakers' branch of the ILGWU in the late 1930s. At that time, there was a deliberate policy that one of the dressmakers' two business agents would be a member of the Communist faction while the other agent would be drawn from the anti-Communists. These two positions were always filled by men even though the majority of the dressmakers were female. These provisions contrast dramatically with the lack of systematic provisions to ensure that women would have ongoing representation within the leadership of these unions.[72]

In contrast to the situation in the Jewish unions, one woman played a central role in the National Clothing Workers of Canada, a small All-Canadian Congress of Labour (ACCL) affiliate that competed directly with the other needle trades unions. As explained in chapter 4, this union was first established in 1934 in Toronto, when Mezza Finch, a female serger, led a deputation of clothing workers to call on the ACCL to help them organize a union for a particular group of the city's garment workers. When an ACCL charter was issued for these non-Jewish workers, Finch was elected president of the new union, a post she held for six years. During part of this time, she was also a member of both the executive committee of Toronto's ACCL council and the national executive board of the ACCL, where she was apparently the only woman. Finch thought of herself as unique as a woman union activist. In writing to the ACCL's secretary-treasurer about whether she would be able to attend the upcoming ACCL convention, she stated: 'It lends Prestige to the delegation to have a woman representative as there are so many industries who employ female help and [there] are hundreds of women in the field but women do not take the interest in Labour which they Should.'[73]

The scarcity of female union leaders requires a more complex explanation than simply blaming women for not taking enough interest in the labour movement. Since Toronto's women garment workers, like most other women workers, faced significant barriers to their participation in the unions, special measures were necessary to recruit and promote women. The male-centred needle trades unions, however, failed to develop policies to appeal to women.

For the anti-Communist as well as the Communist leaders of the Jewish labour movement, the lack of special policies was partly due to the concern that measures of this kind would weaken the movement by dividing the working class along gender lines. Yet, in the absence of specific policies to attract women to the unions, the labour movement in this sector was significantly fragmented along gender lines anyway. Clearly, the proportion of female garment workers who were unionized was dispro-portionately low. Part of the explanation lies in the male-oriented nature of the Jewish unions.

In this respect, the Jewish unions were hardly unique. Such male-centredness was common in many other sections of the Canadian labour movement, as well as in many other types of Canadian organizations in these years. Within the Canadian labour movement, the Jewish unions were not the most extreme. Craft unionists at the turn of the twentieth century frequently sought to exclude women from the traditionally male crafts and, in situations where women did engage in such work, the leaders of the craft unions often opposed the organization of women in a variety of ways. As Ruth Milkman has emphasized in the American context, 'efforts to exclude women were most vigorous in trades they were just beginning to enter and in which men had predominated for some time. In industries where it was clear that women were a permanent part of the labour force ... excluding them was a hopeless endeavor,' whereas organizing them might help avert a general lowering of wages.[74]

Hence, unlike the classic craft unions, the early twentieth-century clothing and textile unions included skilled and unskilled, male and female workers, on both sides of the border. The rise of the CIO in the late 1930s, a development the garment unions promoted, led to the increased unionization of women workers, but discrimination against women persisted within the labour movement. Although the scarcity of in-depth studies of gender dynamics in other unions makes detailed comparisons difficult, a general pattern emerges: despite the fact that the position of women within the Jewish unions was an improvement over the situation in the craft unions, the male-centredness of the Jewish unions seems to have paralleled developments in the other unions that included a significant number of female workers in these years.[75]

While the male union activists were problematic allies for Toronto's women garment workers, the local women's movement seldom allied with these working-class women at all. When the female workers strove to overcome the many barriers and to struggle against their exploitation on the shop floor, they simply could not count on much support from the feminist movement, as the unfolding of the Eaton strike of 1912 demon-strates. In the midst of this strike, the labour movement appealed to various women's groups for support. The Toronto District Labour Coun-cil, in particular, asked 'Women's Clubs [and] Suffrage Associations ... to defend the rights of the [Eaton] workers.' Although the ILGWU's newspaper optimistically reported that 'associations of leisure class women' promised to support the strike, this optimism was premature.[76]

With few exceptions, meaningful solidarity between women appears to have stopped at the class border, as the strikers continued to struggle against the Eaton Company. Alice Chown, a local women's rights activist, stressed the difficulties she encountered when she tried to persuade middle-class women's groups to support the Eaton strikers: 'I tried to interest the various women's clubs, but I was amazed because they had no sympathy with the strikers, unless I had some tale of hardship to tell. The common, everyday longings for better conditions, for a life that would provide more than food, clothes and shelter, were not recognized as justifying a strike. I had to tell over and over the old, old story of the bosses who favored the girls whom they could take out evenings, girls who had to sell themselves as well as their labor to get sufficient work to earn a living.'[77]

Chown highlighted the unwillingness of female suffragists to support female strikers, stressing the suffragists' fear that strike-support work would tarnish the appeal of their main cause. In a thinly disguised account of a special meeting of the Equal Franchise League, she depicted the audience's lack of sympathy for the strikers: 'During the [Eaton] strike I had to preside at a meeting of the Woman's Political League. I asked [the woman], who had been sent from New York to conduct the strike, to speak to our association. She made a very wise and illuminating speech. I did not expect an audience who had never considered that justice to working people was a higher virtue than charity, to respond any more cordially than it did.' At this meeting, Chown 'asked all who were willing to try to awaken interest in the strike to remain ... But [she] aroused a great deal of hard feeling amongst the zealous suffragists, who were afraid that their pet cause would be hurt through being linked with an unpopular one.'[78]

Although Chown managed to gather together several women to try to raise money for the 'displaced working girls,' this fund-raising appeal was not notably successful.[79] The unpopularity of the strikers' cause in Chown's circles no doubt stemmed, in part, from the fact that the vast majority of the Eaton strikers were Jews. In these years, the Canadian women's movement, like many other facets of Canadian society, was steeped in nativism. Organizations such as the main women's suffrage societies, the Woman's Christian Temperance Union, and the Young Women's Christian Association sought to uphold values that were, as many of their names suggest, explicitly Christian. In this context, first-wave feminists sometimes viewed Jews as a threat. The newspaper of the Woman's Christian Temperance Union, for example, even went so far as to reprint anti-Jewish material from Henry Ford's viciously anti-Semitic *Dearborn Independent.* More common was the standard suffrage argument that it was unfair for the 'ignorant' male 'foreigner' to have the vote when 'decent' Anglo-Celtic women did not. As Mariana Valverde has demonstrated in her recent work on English-Canadian moral reformers in the late nineteenth and early twentieth centuries, 'feminism, Christian chauvinism, and ethnocentrism were for [Nellie] McClung and her fellow feminists a unified whole.' Hence, the members of the main women's organizations were not predisposed to make common cause with Jewish strikers.[80]

Chown's difficulties in recruiting support for the strikers were also related to the fact that, in Canada, there was no group similar to the National Women's Trade Union League (NWTUL) in the United States. Consisting of a cross-class alliance of women, the NWTUL sought to improve the conditions of American women workers by working with the established labour movement and by pushing for protective labour legislation. In cities such as New York and Chicago, the NWTUL succeeded for a time in mobilizing significant middle-class, female support for the union activities of early twentieth-century women garment workers.[81] The absence of a similar organization in Toronto was symptomatic of the fact that few early twentieth-century Canadian women reformers were sympathetic to the problems of working-class women.[82]

Although there had been some interest in forming a Women's Trade Union League in Canada, efforts along these lines failed to develop very far. In 1917, as the ILGWU's special organizing campaign in Toronto encountered particular difficulty recruiting non-Jewish women workers, the union's newspaper optimistically reported that 'with the aid of Miss Hugh[e]s we have lately started organizing a Trade Union League of the progressive and influential women in [Toronto], with good results. We hope that this will help us much in organizing the gentile women workers in our trade.'[83] Laura Hughes, a middle-class suffragist, had become sympathetic to labour, partly as a result of having taken a factory job in a knitting mill in 1915 in order to examine working conditions in connection with the war effort. An activist in the Independent Labour party of Ontario, Hughes had participated in a variety of union drives and was also helping to organize 'the girl workers' for the United Cloth Hat, Cap, and Millinery Workers' International Union in Toronto. Although she did help the garment unions recruit new members, she apparently could not find enough 'influential women' who would support a Women's Trade Union League.[84]

Yet some interest in creating an alliance remained. In a 1918 article in the official journal of the National Council of Women of Canada, Saul

Elstein, an important figure in Toronto's Jewish labour movement, called for the creation of a Canadian National Women's Trade Union League. Arguing that 'women in industry as well as in commerce have come there to stay,' Elstein stressed that women workers, like all workers, needed unions to improve their working conditions. He declared that male unionists had such 'a hard and uphill struggle' to win gains for themselves that they did not have enough time and energy left to help the female workers.[85]

To whom, then, could the women workers turn for help? According to Elstein: '*To organize women for direct and for effective action, and to get for them the necessary legislative protection, it is necessary that the work should be undertaken by a body especially formed for that purpose,* and composed mostly of women workers and their sympathizers. We should have in every large industrial centre and in the country as a whole, an organization with the same objects, and working on similar plans as are the objects and plans of the "Women's trade union league" in England and in the United States.' Asserting that the English and American leagues were 'open for membership to men and women of whatever class,' Elstein approvingly explained that the non-working-class members of these groups believed that 'such help [for women workers] is necessary as a measure of justice on the part of the consumers and of those who are "better off" towards the man and especially the women and children who toil to earn a living.' League members, according to Elstein, believed this kind of help was crucial 'to sustain our individual and social wellbeing.' He ended his article by calling for the establishment of a similar organization in Canada, proclaiming: 'Surely we have in this country a sufficient number of men and especially women of all classes whose sympathy are with the workers and who are willing to help the wage working women and children to obtain better conditions of labour.'[86] He was overly optimistic.

In fact, Toronto's women garment workers received support from middle-class women's groups on rare occasions only. During the 1910 strike at the T.E. Braime clothing factory, for example, the limited encouragement the female strikers received was itself unusual. While these sixty women workers were out on strike in protest over having to pay for the thread they used in factory production, they were invited to visit the headquarters of the Suffrage Club. Although many of the strikers accepted the hospitality of the club for an evening, the available records suggest that, apart from Flora MacDonald Denison's efforts, the suffragists' hospitality did not develop into more active support for the strike. However,

Denison herself, an important figure in the women's suffrage movement, worked with the strikers to help publicize their cause. The daughter of a lower middle-class family, Denison was more sympathetic to the labour movement than were many of her contemporaries in the various suffrage organizations.[87]

The role of women's groups during the ILGWU's attempted general strike in Toronto's dress trade in 1931 was more ambiguous than Denison's earlier efforts. Although women's groups seldom became involved in industrial disputes in Toronto's needle trades even during the Great Depression, the *Canadian Forum* reported that 'a group of women's organizations in the city became interested in [this particular 1931] strike, as a matter which particularly concerned women.' Representatives of the Young Women's Christian Association, the Local Council of Women, the University Women's Club, the Women's International League for Peace and Freedom, and the Big Sister Association decided to investigate conditions in the dress shops and obtained the cooperation of both the union and the manufacturers' association. The *Forum*'s article was apparently based on the results of this investigation.[88]

This article stressed the hardships caused by low wages but did so in the context of concern about the employers' problems in this highly competitive sector, arguing that 'to a great extent, [the manufacturers] as well as employees, are victims of causes over which they have no control.'[89] Indeed, the article asserted that the dispute between the union and the manufacturers' association 'was characterized by the most complete misunderstanding between the employers and the strikers; a profound ignorance, real or assumed, of the case on the other side; and an all too apparent distrust and hostility.'[90] Although the article did concede that the manufacturers should make some changes, such as trying to reduce the irregularity of working hours and standardizing the pay rates, this was far from a solid endorsement of the strikers' demands. Furthermore, apart from undertaking this investigation of the strike, there is no evidence that these women's groups did any real strike-support work.[91]

During a strike in one department of Eaton's clothing factory in 1934, however, women's groups were unusually supportive. This exceptional support stemmed partly from the fact that, at this time, the Royal Commission on Price Spreads was focusing public opinion on the negative impact of department-store policies in the midst of the 'Dirty Thirties.' Indeed, the commission's highly publicized hearings singled out the T. Eaton Company in particular for harsh condemnation. More broadly, the intense sufferings of female garment workers in the depths of the Depression heightened public sympathy for them. The unusual support for the striking Eaton workers no doubt also stemmed from the fact that, this time, unlike in 1912, the female strikers were all non-Jews.[92]

This particular industrial dispute began when thirty-eight female dressmakers, members of the ILGWU, stopped work because Eaton's management refused to grant an increase in the very low piece rates for a particular set of dresses. These women left the factory to consult with union officials, but when they attempted to return to work the next day, management locked them out. They replied by declaring themselves on strike against the company.[93]

While the CCF's provincial executive tried to help the women strikers, the role of key CCF women was particularly important in mobilizing strike support. Jean Laing, the CCFer who was hired as an ILGWU organizer, was probably the main link between these two female groups. Party activist Dr Rose Henderson also helped lead the strike-support campaign. According to the CCF newspaper, a committee of women worked to drum up active strike support by organizing mass meetings to publicize the injustices perpetrated by the Eaton Company. At a rally at Queen's Park, for example, both Henderson and Laing played prominent roles. The CCF paper proudly reported that the committee of women 'who stood by the strikers ... organized both park and street meetings, as well as three very successful dances in the Labor Temple to raise money to augment the strike pay.'[94]

Beyond this, the strikers received rare support from the Local Council of Women (the Toronto branch of the National Council of Women). This development was partly due to Laing's and Henderson's efforts to persuade council members to take up the strikers' cause. The Young Women's Christian Association (YWCA), one of the local council's important affiliates, also helped bring this strike to the council's attention. The YWCA's Winifred Hutchison was in an especially good position to know about labour relations in the needle trades, for she became an investigator for the royal commission and eventually was to testify before the commission concerning the appalling wages and working conditions of Toronto's female clothing workers. Hutchison urged the president of the local council to use the council's resources to support the striking Eaton women. Another link between the local council and the women strikers may have been forged by Margaret Gould, a council member who, previously known as Sarah Gold, had served as an ACW organizer in 1923, before anglicizing her name and moving into other circles.[95]

As a result of a special local council meeting that three of the women strikers attended, the council decided to endorse the strikers' demands prominently. The organization also offered to arbitrate the dispute and attempted to influence government officials. In a letter to the Ontario minister of labour, the president of the council stressed that the women workers in this Eaton's department had been forced to accept a relentless series of wage cuts and speed-ups. She indicated that council members had investigated the situation, listening to both sides of the dispute, and were concerned that the constant speed-ups had led to nervous break-downs. 'At the end of the day's work,' this letter declared, 'the girls were unfitted for any personal life, for recreation, or home duties, lacking even the energy to eat their meal.' 'A good many of the women are married,' she continued, 'with children and homes to care for when they returned from work. For these life was a constant torture.' The letter ended with a strong statement of the council's position: 'We feel that if the working conditions which the management wishes to impose are permitted, that these will lead to physical and nervous breakdowns, and to greater social cost later. We feel that to impose such harsh conditions particularly on women, who are child-bearers, or potential child-bearers, is most deplor-able.'[96] The council's concern thus focused particularly on the threat to the women's maternal capabilities and duties.

The strike built up considerable momentum, and a special appeal was made to female shoppers. Union leaflets, which were issued to publicize the dispute, called on all women to support the female strikers and declared that before any woman buys a new dress, she should make sure it was made under fair working conditions. The leaflets indicated that in addition to support from the Trades and Labour Council and a number of trade union auxiliaries, the women workers were being supported by the Local Council of Women, the Women's International League for Peace and Freedom, and another women's organization.[97]

But the company would not budge. Thus, despite the unusual support the strikers received, they were eventually forced to give up. This was partly because so many of the women workers in the same Eaton's depart-ment had failed to join the strike in the first place. In addition, since this department did not have a lot of orders to fill and since work could easily be contracted out, management was not forced to settle with the union. In the aftermath of the defeat, there was considerable tension between union officials and the committee of women that had been supporting the strikers.[98] Since women's groups seldom offered support to female strikers in this sector, the leaders of the garment unions were not used to cooperating with such female support networks.

The absence of a women's trade union league in Canada did not merely mean that Toronto's women needle trades workers lacked an important source of support for their struggles for better working conditions; it also meant that an important avenue for raising feminist consciousness was closed to women workers. In the United States, the NWTUL was an explicitly feminist organization that came to emphasize feminist concerns about the ways in which female workers were in a different position from male workers. In this context, League women sought to make the American women's movement more responsive to the needs of women workers.[99]

As a cross-class alliance of women, the league sought to encompass working-class women and their middle-class 'allies,' and helped to develop American women workers' consciousness of feminist issues. As a feminist organization that was specifically concerned with the plight of women workers, the league also helped to make the American women's movement more attractive to working-class women. Although the league's influence was limited and although class and ethnic tensions emerged within the organization itself, the league influenced several exceptional female needle trades activists in particular, namely Pauline Newman, Fannia Cohn, and Rose Pesotta, all of whom were Jewish immigrants living in the United States. While these three women union leaders generally felt that class struggle took precedence over women's issues, there was a significant feminist component to their consciousness. Historian Alice Kessler-Harris's account of their lives suggests that their awareness of feminist issues was heightened by their contacts with the league.[100]

As Colette Hyman has demonstrated in her recent work on the Chicago branch of the NWTUL in the period from 1904 to 1924, the league focused on the particular needs of women workers, pioneering the development of special methods for organizing women. As Hyman explains: 'In contrast to the established unions, the [Chicago] WTUL took into account the whole of women's lives, not just their lives as wage-workers. The strategies that the league developed encompassed women's domestic responsibilities as well as cultural standards that severely limited women's participation in activities outside the home.' For a time, the Chicago WTUL, which was very involved with women garment workers, emphasized such women-centred organizing strategies as home visits to educate women workers about the labour movement, special social gatherings to help solidify networks of women, personal testimonies of women labour activists, and special training for women unionists. The league's publications sought to inform women workers about suffrage campaigns as well as to provide practical instruction about how to conduct union business. Although the league subsequently shifted away from these organizing strategies and focused on agitating for protective labour legislation instead, the initial development of specific female-oriented organizing techniques was important.[101]

In contrast, there was hardly any emphasis on the special needs of women workers in Toronto's Jewish labour movement. Whereas male Jewish intellectuals helped shape the Jewish labour movement along socialist lines in both Canada and the United States, female intellectuals (who were rare in any case) did not generally ally with Toronto's female garment workers and did not motivate the women workers to shape the Jewish unions along feminist lines. Without a women's trade union league, there was less opportunity for the female workers to develop a sympathetic awareness of feminist issues. Without such a cross-class organizational alliance, the Canadian women's movement seems to have been more narrowly focused on middle-class concerns.[102] Thus, in Canada, the women's movement appears to have been less attractive to women workers than in the United States.

With regard to Jewish women workers in particular, the Canadian women's movement was perhaps even less attractive because of its emphasis on maternal feminism. Although both the Canadian and American women's movements contained equal-rights feminists and maternal feminists, and although the lines between these two feminist strands could become blurred in practice, the American women's movement seems to have had a deeper equal-rights tradition than its Canadian counterpart, partly because of the early ties between the abolitionist movement and the early women's rights advocates in the United States. Many Canadian feminists tended to argue that women should be given more of a say in public affairs because society badly needed the special virtues mothers 'naturally' possessed. In contrast to American feminists, Canadian feminists seem to have been less likely to argue that women should be entitled to participate in the public sphere because all human beings should, *a priori*, have equal rights.[103] Maternal feminism, with its emphasis on the moral superiority of females, was foreign to traditional East European Jewish culture, with its emphasis on the moral superiority of males. The fact that Toronto's Jewish women workers seldom saw themselves as feminists was partly due to the way the Canadian feminist movement was strongly, though not exclusively, shaped by middle-class, Anglo-Celtic, maternal feminists.

Perhaps because Toronto's Jewish women felt more beleaguered *as Jews* than did their counterparts in New York City, Toronto's female Jews may have been less inclined to develop gender-based alliances with Anglo-Celtic middle-class feminists or even with non-Jewish women workers. Jewish women's close identification with Jewish men may have been heightened in Toronto not only because Toronto's Jewish population was so much smaller than New York's but also because, in contrast to the high proportion of non-British immigrants in the major American cities where Jews congregated, Toronto's population was so overwhelmingly Anglo-Celtic. Moreover, Jews had significant political power in New York City, unlike the situation in Toronto in this period. These demographic and political differences probably increased Jewish feelings of vulnerabili-ty in Toronto and reduced Jewish women's openness to alliances with female non-Jews.[104] Yet the significant difference between the two situations should not be exaggerated. American historians who have written about female Jewish garment workers – without seriously examining Yiddish sources – may well have underestimated the importance of Jewish identity and the impact of anti-Semitism in their analyses of these American Jewish women.[105]

The relative weakness of the Canadian women's movement in the 1920s and 1930s was also significant, for this was the central period in the development of Toronto's Jewish labour movement. Not long after women's suffrage was granted federally at the end of the First World War, the Canadian women's movement grew weaker, remaining comparatively weak throughout the interwar period. Whereas the women's movement had tended to unite around the push for the vote in the earlier stage, the interwar years witnessed a more fragmented feminist movement.

The impact of these changes was paradoxical. On the one hand, the very weakness of the movement during the 1920s and 1930s probably lessened the likelihood that the movement could or would help develop female garment workers' consciousness of women's issues or aid these needle trades women in their struggles against their employers. On the other hand, the movement's shift away from the earlier intense focus on suffrage diminished the concern, which was so evident during the 1912 Eaton strike, that the appeal of the movement's main cause would be tarnished if feminists aided striking female workers. This shift helped provide some leeway for certain women's groups to aid the non-Jewish Eaton strikers in 1934. The activism of the CCF women, in particular, made an impact on this distinctive strike and emphasizes, as well, the increased diversity of the interwar women's movement. Nevertheless, despite important differences between the pre- and post-suffrage women's movement, the main point remains: women's groups hardly ever aided striking female garment workers in Toronto in the first four decades of the twentieth century, nor did they make significant efforts to bring these female workers into the women's movement itself.

This study calls into question the readiness of many women's historians to emphasize the notion of a distinct cross-class, cross-ethnic women's culture. As American historian Nancy A. Hewitt has demonstrated, 'the notion of a single women's community rooted in common oppression' has 'become increasingly paradigmatic ... in American women's history' even as it 'has become increasingly problematic.'[106] Toronto's female Jewish garment workers clearly do not fit into this paradigm of universal sisterhood. In the field of Canadian women's history, assumptions of sisterhood and strong commonalities need to be tempered by a greater willingness to examine the conflicting interests and contrasting cultures of different groups of women.[107]

Of course, while Toronto's female garment workers were not simply women, they were not simply workers either. Yet, by the Second World War, Toronto's Jewish unions still had not developed 'some sort of special machinery' to mobilize the women garment workers in particular. The fact that the unions appealed to female workers 'just as a worker' meant that the special barriers women faced were not being taken into consideration. The unions were basically male-centred, as was apparent not only in the male monopoly of leadership positions but also in the many cases where union wage policies privileged the men by widening the pay gap between females and males on the shop floor. On the basis of a male-oriented class analysis, Jewish union leaders sought to bring women into the class struggle while ignoring the fact that women encountered special forms of oppression specifically as women.

In the meantime, the Canadian women's movement seldom reached out to Toronto's female garment workers. Whereas the Women's Trade Union League had developed female-oriented unionization strategies in early twentieth-century New York and Chicago, there was no comparable Canadian women's organization to help develop similar strategies in Toronto. The gap between the Canadian women's movement and the women garment workers was wide, especially where ethnic differences reinforced class differences. Toronto's female garment workers were left in a particularly difficult position.

7 Doing Things That Men Do
Women Activists in the Needle Trades

'She was busy with the strike all day, and far into the night ... One
night she came home with a bandage around her head. Two
Italian gangsters and an Irish policeman hired by the Jewish
bosses had attacked her.

'"But how we scratched their faces," she chuckled grimly. "They
will remember us girls."'

– Michael Gold, *Jews without Money*[1]

Despite all these difficulties, there were a significant number of women
whose militancy helped make the growth of Toronto's needle trades
unions possible. Together with the male unionists, they joined strikes and
took their turns on the picket lines. In addition, some Jewish women were
especially dedicated to the Jewish labour movement, playing more active
roles within the movement despite the self-sacrifices involved. The activism of these Jewish women drew on the legacy of East European Jewish
culture, which did not define women as passive, fragile, house-bound
beings. Detailed profiles of several female Jewish activists reveal not only
their pride in their own assertiveness but also their deep commitment to
the struggles against class oppression and anti-Semitism. As these profiles
disclose, the Jewish women activists did not develop significant feminist
perspectives of their own experiences on the shop floor or within the
Jewish labour movement itself. The fact they did not do so was partly a
product of the deeply patriarchal nature of traditional East European
Jewish life. Although the socialist Jewish women challenged other aspects

of traditional Jewish culture, they did not fundamentally challenge its patriarchal character.

In traditional East European Jewish culture, women were distinctly subordinated within the religious sphere but played assertive roles in the marketplace. Although the increasing urbanization of Jews in Eastern Europe meant that many of Toronto's Jewish immigrants did not come to the New World straight from the *shtetl*, the traditions of the *shtetl* shaped the attitudes of the immigrant Jewish community in significant ways. In the traditional *shtetl*, the religious sphere was defined as the most important. Although women were responsible for certain religious rituals in the home, the synagogue – the centre of religious study and prayer – was clearly and simply a male domain. Women did not gather there to study with the men, and when women did attend religious services, they were segregated behind a special partition. The more important aspects of worship took place in the men's section, and prayers were said in Hebrew, a language females were taught to recite for religious purposes but were not taught to comprehend.[2] Indeed, a woman who became too involved in religious study was ridiculed and considered to be unnatural, as was reflected in the harsh *shtetl* proverb: 'When the hen begins to crow like a rooster, it's time to take it to the *shoychet* [the ritual slaughterer].'[3] The 'World to Come,' a kind of Jewish version of Heaven, was pictured as a glorious house of study where the men would sit together, rapturously pouring over the holy texts, while their dutiful wives would sit silently at their feet. The ideal Jew was a religious scholar, a role from which women were deliberately excluded.[4]

Jewish women, unlike Jewish men, were responsible for looking after the home, but the women were not limited to that sphere. In traditional East European Jewish culture, Jewish women had a legitimate role to play in the marketplace. As one detailed historical study of *shtetl* life has emphasized, 'the economic area [was] more nearly an extension of the woman's domain [the household] than of the man's [the domain of Jewish study and prayer].'[5]

If a woman's husband was a talented scholar, it was incumbent upon her to earn the family's income while the husband devoted his time to study and prayer. Men who were less talented scholars, or who could not afford to be full-time scholars, might spend some time working to contribute to the family's income while still spending part of the time in the house of study. In such cases, wives would still have to do their share to earn a livelihood for the family. The wife who earned money so that her husband could study was considered to be performing a *mitsva* (a good deed).[6] Although the ideal of the husband as full-time scholar was remote from the realities of the lives of many Jewish families, the fact that East European Jewish culture stressed this kind of ideal legitimated women's role as direct contributors to the family income.

Dire poverty also legitimated a bread-winning role for women. In the context of widespread poverty within the Jewish communities of Eastern Europe, both wives and husbands often needed to do work that contributed directly to the family income. In the *shtetl,* the large majority of women were engaged in some kind of gainful employment, as were the large majority of men. No dishonour was attached to this kind of work for women. Children were also frequently called upon at an early age to help contribute to the family economy. The earnings of each family member belonged to the family as a whole, rather than to the particular individual who had earned that money.[7]

Yet the fact that women were not restricted to the domestic sphere did not mean they were able to occupy important political positions within the community. In the *shtetl,* the community leaders were male. In large part, this was due to the way in which religion, an area in which women were distinctly subordinated, permeated every aspect of life. In traditional East European Jewish communities, the synagogue served as the centre of self-government, for, as a group of Jewish scholars has pointed out, 'no clear-cut distinction [was] made between religious and secular functions, since for the *shtetl* Judaism [was] not a religion but a way of life.' The rabbi served as the most important legal authority within the community, basing his judgments on traditional Hebrew laws that had been set down in the sacred writings. Of course, no woman could ever be a rabbi.[8]

Although Jewish women were clearly subordinated to Jewish men, gender roles in traditional East European Jewish culture were fundamentally different from those embodied in the Victorian 'cult of true womanhood.'[9] In view of this contrast, some feminist scholars need to rethink their assumption that this Victorian ideal applied to all kinds of women. The fact that Jewish women were not confined – either in terms of the ideal or the realities of their lives – to the private sphere of domesticity contrasts sharply with the Victorian emphasis on the domestic ideology. Although Jewish women were considered intellectually weak, East European Jewish culture did not view women as too fragile for venturing outside the safety of the home. (Nor did the home provide much safety in a region where pogroms could quickly erupt.) Indeed, in a culture where religious scholarship, not physical strength, was valued in men, Jewish women were not seen as particularly fragile.[10] Thus, given the extent to which the domestic ideology was foreign to traditional East European Jewish culture, it is no wonder that the women interviewed for this book failed to exhibit a sense that women did not belong in the paid labour force.

Lack of confinement to the domestic sphere did not, of course, amount to liberation. The Jewish woman who contributed directly to the family's earnings was burdened, as a matter of course, by a second job at home, looking after the children and the housework. Like her Victorian counterpart, the Jewish woman was defined primarily in terms of her family duties, as a wife and mother. The difference was that the Jewish woman's family duties often included working to contribute directly to the family's income, whereas the Victorian woman was told that her duties to her husband and children meant she should not engage in paid labour.

The sharp contrast between the two traditions is further highlighted by the fact that the Jewish women who were interviewed were able to dismiss the notion of having been restricted by the need to be ladylike. Although Jewish women were supposed to be subordinated to their husbands,[11] they differed from the Victorian lady in that they were not socialized to be docile and passive.[12] In fact, Jewish women needed to be outspoken and assertive in the marketplace, as they worked to contribute to the family income within the harsh context of the *shtetl* economy.[13]

In addition, the Jewish woman was not seen as more pure, noble, and pious than the man. On the contrary, East European Jewish culture viewed the man as the one who was closer to God. In Jewish tradition, it was the woman, not the man, who was associated with the material as distinct from the spiritual world. Thus the notion of women being too pure for this world was entirely foreign to East European Jewish tradition. In fact, the Jewish woman was often seen as the one who had more practical sense than the man, for the ideal Jewish man was expected to have an other-worldly quality. Lacking the Victorian notion of the superior purity and piety of women, East European Jewish culture also lacked the highly idealized Victorian conception of the home as a 'haven in a heartless world.'[14]

The particular brand of feminism that relied on the notion of woman's moral superiority was basically a Christian development. This kind of feminism, usually called social or maternal feminism, was based on the argument that women should be entitled to participate in the public sphere because society badly needed woman's moral influence. According to this argument, women were to become engaged in social housekeeping, using their special virtues to help clean up society.[15] Since the conception of women's moral superiority was lacking in Jewish tradition, it is not surprising that this kind of argument was not being made within Toronto's immigrant Jewish community. And, since the Canadian women's movement was often led by middle-class, Anglo-Celtic maternal feminists, it is no wonder that most Jewish women workers did not see themselves as feminists in this period.

In order to understand more about the consciousness of women needle trades workers, more research is needed regarding the extent to which the Victorian cult of true womanhood, which arose as a middle-class ideal, may have permeated the anglophone working class in Canada. To the extent that working-class anglophone women may have subscribed to the notion that woman's 'proper place' is in the home, this would have served to undercut the possibilities of women's activism within the labour movement. Belief in the domestic ideology, even if modified by the acceptance of an interval of paid labour between school and marriage, would have meant that anglophone women workers would have placed less emphasis on their roles as workers and would therefore have been less interested in labour activism.

Studies are needed to explore the extent to which working-class anglophone women may have been restricted by confining notions of being ladylike. One Jewish woman, a labour activist in Toronto's millinery trade, recalled that the many non-Jewish women millinery workers 'thought that the union was beneath them.'[16] These women may have felt this way not only because union membership meant associating more closely with Jewish immigrants but also because, as evidence recently unearthed by American feminist scholars suggests, there may have been a sense that unions were not respectable places for proper young ladies.[17] Indeed, a 1937 educational manual, published by the ILGWU's head office, explained that, in organizing women workers, it was necessary to combat 'the idea that "it isn't nice" to even belong to a union, let alone go on the picket line.'[18] Anglophone working-class women cannot have been altogether free of middle-class anglophone notions of feminine docility and fragility, notions that would have clashed with the qualities necessary for taking a stand against male employers.[19]

Given the nature of women's roles in traditional East European Jewish culture, Jewish women workers were probably less constrained by these kinds of ideological barriers to women's labour activism. Although the increased division between the home and the 'workplace' in the more industrialized New World meant there was a developing tendency for married Jewish women to refrain from 'working,'[20] the fact that East

European Jewish culture had traditionally legitimated women's gainful employment remained significant. The traditional assertiveness of Jewish women in the marketplace probably helped prepare Jewish women garment workers for a militant role in the labour movement. The traditional subordination of women within the family and within the most important aspects of traditional Jewish culture, however, did not predispose these women to challenge the male leadership of the Jewish labour movement.

The following profiles of several female Jewish activists provide an opportunity to explore in detail the activities and consciousness of women who were especially dedicated to Toronto's Jewish labour movement. The bold, assertive women who appear in these pages were remarkable activists, at the cost of considerable personal sacrifice. Their deep class consciousness and ethnic identity contrast with the lack of developed feminist perspectives.[21]

Pearl Wedro was a spirited union activist. A Jewish immigrant who had become interested in socialism in Poland, Wedro remained intensely active in the Jewish labour movement for most of her life. While working in a fur shop in Winnipeg during the 1920s, she had helped to organize the city's first local of the International Fur Workers' Union and had served as an officer of that local for a time. In 1931, unable to get a job as a result of being blacklisted for union activities, Wedro moved to Toronto where she lived for years. In Toronto she continued to earn a living as a fur worker, and, having joined the Communist party, was active in the Industrial Union of Needle Trades Workers as well as the IFWU. She also participated in other Communist party work, helping to organize the unemployed and doing a lot of work to help party candidates in their campaigns for government office.

Active in the Workers' Unity League, Wedro was one of the Toronto members of the IUNTW's general executive board. She participated in IUNTW organizing campaigns and was particularly active in the WUL's drive to organize the fur dressers and dyers at the Hallman and Sable Company in 1933. Divided into a number of different ethnic groups, the two hundred workers in this shop had been suffering from poor sanitary conditions and low pay. Wedro recalled that the members of each particular ethnic group would not trust members of other ethnic groups, so she and her friends had to try to organize each group separately. Wedro herself was working full time in another fur shop and used to visit the homes of the Hallman and Sable workers in her spare time to talk to them about the union. In a number of homes, she was asked to leave because, as she explained, the people 'were so poor they were afraid to take a chance [on the union].' Finally, however, the diligent efforts of Wedro and her allies succeeded. The WUL called these workers out on strike and won higher wages and better working conditions.[22]

In the meantime, Wedro had remained remarkably active in the International Fur Workers' Union. Her IFWU activism increased after the Communist faction won control over Toronto's IFWU in 1937. She served on the union's political action committee and also served as secretary of the IFWU's joint board for a time, remaining active in the union through the 1940s and 1950s as well. Over the years, she won election to the Toronto joint board a number of times – often as the only woman on the board. She also served on the union's negotiating team and recalled how the union's male negotiators frequently put aside the demand for equal pay for equal work for women and men. She specifically remembered a Toronto fur strike in the 1940s where the union's male negotiators wanted to agree to a settlement that did not include equal-pay provisions, but she insisted they hold out for equal pay. In this case, she felt vindicated because the manufacturers conceded equal pay after the strike had continued for two further days.

Deeply dedicated, Wedro also continued to do unpaid organizing work for the union while continuing to earn her own living by holding on to her full-time job in a fur shop. In the Second World War period, she helped tannery workers in Kitchener organize into the leather workers' division of the IFWU. According to her account, the IFWU's official organizers were not themselves interested in taking on the task of organizing these tannery workers, for they felt this was a lost cause. Without any monetary support from the union, Wedro used her personal savings to finance her organizing efforts in Kitchener. As an unofficial organizer, she also faced the difficulty of having to make special arrangements to take time off from the shop where she was employed. Her efforts paid off, however, for the tannery workers eventually won union recognition and better conditions.

In 1949 Wedro finally obtained a job as a paid IFWU organizer in Winnipeg, and, a year later, she was transferred to Vancouver, where she served as a paid organizer for a short period before becoming temporarily physically incapacitated. She felt that the organizing work had proceeded well in both cities at that time. She then returned to Toronto, where she resumed her activities as an unpaid union activist.

Wedro recognized that, as a woman who was so active in the labour movement, she was unusual. She pointed out that, throughout this period: 'Usually in unions, women took a backward seat. And they weren't elected, and they were kind of looked [on] as people who paid their dues, they come and go ... It was out of the ordinary that a woman should develop and do this type of thing.' In addition to being often the only woman on the IFWU's Toronto joint board, she was one of the very few women at conventions of the Canadian Congress of Labour. She took pride in all these achievements.

Yet Wedro also felt that within her own union she had been discriminated against as a woman. She resented the fact that she was not made a paid organizer until 1949, for, until then, she had found it difficult to juggle her organizing activities with the hours at her job on the shop floor. Looking back over the period during which she had done so much successful organizing work in her spare time, she felt that the union leaders had often hired less qualified men as full-time organizers while she herself had been passed over because of their reluctance to hire a woman. She felt that some of the male union officials resented her organizing activities and seemed to see her as a threat to their offices. Thus she stated: 'I always felt, it's left with me now, that even [in] progressive-led unions, a woman's chances are less than a man's. There's always somehow resentment to let to the very top a woman. And although our International was led by progressives and our own union ... but I don't think, due to my ability and contribution, that I got a proper deal. If I was a man, I think I would have been placed with the highest responsibility and having a chance not to sit in the shop but really make the *full* contribution. But that was not the case.'

Despite these frustrations, Wedro devoted her life to the labour movement. She never married. She explained that her aunt, who was her closest female relative, used to tell her that by remaining unmarried she was destroying her own life. Her aunt could not understand why a woman would make what seemed to her to be such a big sacrifice. Wedro herself simply stated that she never married because she had not fallen in love and because her involvement in the labour movement had not left much time for developing her personal life.

Ironically, Wedro's unmarried status was turned against her and used to disparage her within the very movement she supported so resolutely. At one particular Communist party meeting, a man involved in a political disagreement with Wedro sought to humiliate her by calling her, in Yiddish, an 'old maid.'[23] Within immigrant Jewish culture, this was considered a particularly sharp insult. On another occasion, a man who was a prominent anti-Communist leader of the fur workers called Wedro a

'Stalinist fish wife.'[24] Yet although some men stooped to such sexist insults, other male comrades were deeply impressed both by Wedro's self-sacrificing devotion to the cause and by the effectiveness of her political work.[25]

[Wedro's dedication to the Jewish labour movement was basically a product of her deep concerns about class and ethnicity. Like many other Jewish radicals, she defiantly embraced Communism because she felt it would end the exploitation of the working class. As well, she apparently believed that, by establishing a society based on real justice and equality, Communism would also put an end to anti-Semitism.]

Although Wedro mentioned her support for equal pay, she did not generally portray herself as a champion of women's rights. She personally felt that the male leaders of her union had discriminated against her as a woman, but she did not articulate a broad conviction that female workers were in a different position from male workers. When she discussed union organizing, for example, she made no distinction between the approaches used to organize women and the approaches used to organize men. When she discussed her own strengths as an organizer, she indicated that she was as capable as the male organizers; she never argued that she had a special contribution to make as a woman organizer. Further, although she mentioned her aunt's judgment that it was a tragedy to remain unmarried, Wedro discussed this issue in terms of the particular circumstances of her own life, rather than grappling with the issue of gender roles more broadly.

Thus, on the whole, although her personal experience made her aware of certain instances of discrimination against women, this awareness was not articulated at a more general ideological level. These specific experiences did not lead her to a developed commitment to feminism.

Nonetheless, her own sense of womanhood was not constrained by notions of docility and fragility. Her union activism reflected a strong sense of self-competence and effectiveness, as well as a willingness to take difficult and important risks. She strove for, and sometimes achieved, leadership positions that were seldom attained by women within Canada's labour movement. Moreover, she bravely took up Communist party work at a time when party members were often the targets of harsh repression. For Pearl Wedro, a woman's 'proper place' – if she were working class and Jewish – was in the fighting ranks of the Jewish labour movement.

Sadie Hoffman, another activist in the Jewish labour movement, was an ardent socialist. When one interviewer began by asking her a series of background questions about her childhood, Hoffman interjected: 'I'm anxious to start telling you about how I became a socialist because that's my life.' In 1905 Hoffman had immigrated to Canada with her family as a young child. Her early political development had been heavily influenced by her older sister, who was swept up in the 1904–5 wave of radicalism in Russia at the age of fifteen. In Toronto the older sister used to take Hoffman along to Socialist party meetings and labour events. Hoffman even remembered that as a child she marched along with her sister in a labour parade during the Eaton strike of 1912, wearing signs proclaiming: 'We don't patronize the T. Eaton Company.' When the Russian Revolution took place, Hoffman was deeply impressed by it. By 1923 she had become a Communist.

In the meantime, Hoffman had started working in a box factory at the age of thirteen, and then, during the First World War, she had obtained a job in a large firm that made army uniforms. At the uniform company, she was a bookkeeper and also sometimes cut basting threads. When the Amalgamated Clothing Workers began to organize the factory workers at this firm, she helped with the unionization campaign even though, as an office worker, she was not part of the bargaining unit. Her dedication to the union was reflected in the fact that she eventually resigned over union issues.

Hoffman left the paid labour force when she married, and did not return to paid work until her son was six years old. At that time, she got a job as a sewing-machine operator in a sportswear shop, where she remained until just before the birth of her second child six years later. She helped unionize this sportswear shop for the United Garment Workers. Even after she left the paid labour force a second time, she used to help her second husband in the organizing work he was doing for one of the needle trades unions.

Sadie Hoffman was especially active in the Jewish Communist movement, and she stressed the many sacrifices she and her friends made for the movement over the years. She recalled how they gave their last few pennies to *Der Kamf* (the Communists' Yiddish newspaper) even though they were all so poor. In addition to doing extensive fund-raising work for the party, she did a lot of work recruiting votes for the Communist candidates in their campaigns for government office. She and her female friends also sometimes helped out resolutely on the picket line, as, for example, during an IUNTW dress strike when she was arrested for picketing. During certain protest demonstrations, Hoffman displayed extraordinary physical courage in trying to stop the police from beating male comrades. She would rush in front of a man who was being beaten and try to shield him with her body, hoping that the police officers would not hit a woman.

Hoffman also worked to mobilize women around consumer issues. She played a leading role in the kosher meat boycott of 1933, and she later worked with both Jewish and non-Jewish women in protesting the high prices of key household items. She became an executive member of a housewives' organization that was established at the end of the 1930s with branches in every ward of the city. In this organization, she worked together with non-Communist women to protest against the high cost of such items as milk and household gas.

Hoffman recalled how she and her women friends in the movement sometimes used to take their young children with them while doing political work. As one of the women canvassed house-to-house for party candidates in local elections, for example, she would be pushing a child in a baby carriage. The attempt to combine child-rearing with intense political activity must have been frustrating for these women, however, for Hoffman sadly indicated that some of the children of activist mothers felt neglected because of their mothers' time-consuming devotion to political work.

When one interviewer asked Hoffman about the extent to which the radicalism of the Jewish Communist movement encompassed a commitment to women's liberation, her answers revealed that a developed commitment was lacking. This can be seen, for example, in the uncertainty of her reply to the specific question whether Communist men had had a more progressive attitude towards women in this period: 'I don't know. They should have [because] they wanted everybody to be freer. They should have. Whether they did ...' She continued: 'Mind you, [it was] not like [things] are now. I know that if a couple works, the husband tries to help [with household responsibilities] now, because he feels [he should help] because she works. But in those days, it wasn't that way. Those women worked in the shop, and they worked [at home].' In the 1920s and 1930s, there was no discussion of men sharing household responsibilities. Hoffman herself felt fortunate because her second husband simply liked to 'help' her, especially with child care, but she pointed out that this made him 'an exception to the rule.'

In her discussion of her intense commitment to socialism, Hoffman never indicated that she had been drawn to this movement because either she or the movement itself stood for women's rights. Yet when the author recently asked Hoffman what she thought of the present-day feminist movement, she replied: 'I think if I were younger, I would probably be involved [in it].'

Distinguishing between the two time periods, Hoffman asserted that the Jewish labour movement focused specifically on working-class economic struggles – not women's rights struggles – because everyone was so desperately poor in that period. Overwhelming poverty, she declared, meant that activists in the movement necessarily concentrated on fighting for direct economic gains such as higher wages and unemployment insurance. She particularly stressed the crucial need to build up the unions, pointing out how weak the unions were at that time.

Hoffman was proud of the role women played in these demanding struggles and spoke about the important accomplishments of the Yiddisher Arbeiter Froyen Fareyn (known in English as the Jewish Women's Labour League). Oriented towards the Communist party, the Fareyn was an organization of working-class Jewish women, most of whom were housewives who were not engaged in paid labour. This organization had been founded in 1923, with Hoffman as one of the original members. Hoffman explained that the Fareyn women helped found a Jewish workers' children's camp where, in addition to recreational activities, the children received instruction about socialism. The Fareyn women especially did a lot of electoral work, canvassing for Communist candidates such as Joe Salsberg. In addition, they raised money for the party's Yiddish press and for the Jewish colonization efforts in Birobidzhan (a remote region of the Soviet Union). The Fareyn women thus made important contributions to the political work of the Jewish Communist movement.[26]

When one interviewer asked Hoffman if the Fareyn was at all feminist, she replied: 'There wasn't too much talk about that in those years. There really wasn't. There wasn't too much talk like there is today.' Although this women's organization was clearly not a feminist organization, the Fareyn women appear to have had some sense of not wanting their organization to be merely a women's auxiliary. The Fareyn had been formed as a separate women's organization at a time when the husbands of these women were still in the Arbeiter Ring (AR), fighting within the AR to orient that organization towards a more pro-Soviet line. By 1926 these men had broken away from the AR completely and formed the Labour League. Once the Labour League was established, however, the Fareyn did not immediately become an affiliate.

Speaking of the Fareyn women at that time, Hoffman explained that 'we were afraid that if we joined the Labour League, they'll make an auxiliary out of us [and] we didn't want to be an auxiliary.' In part, their reluctance to join the Labour League may have reflected a general tendency of organizational groups to try to retain a considerable amount of autonomy. In this particular case, however, there also seems to have been some concern that they would be subordinated as women, for Hoffman explained that the Fareyn women watched as other women joined the Labour League, and were reassured when they found that the women within the league were being well treated. After that, the Fareyn became a branch of the league. Thus, although the Fareyn had not been focused on feminist activities at all, the women in this organization were not altogether lacking in concern about the ways in which women were subordinated to men.

Like Wedro, Hoffman did not become a committed feminist. Yet both of them shared a sense of strong womanhood that enabled them to take part in the arduous task of building the Communist wing of the Jewish labour movement. Although Hoffman struggled to combine her political activism with her family responsibilities, she, too, fought boldly and courageously for the cause she so deeply believed in.

Like Hoffman, Bessie Kramer was a devoted member of the Jewish Communist movement for years. Having emigrated from Poland in the mid 1920s, when she was seventeen years old, Kramer became acquainted with the Canadian Communist movement through an older sister who had joined the movement before Kramer had arrived in this country. Deeply troubled by the anti-Semitism she had experienced in Poland, Kramer joined the Young Communist League soon after arriving in Canada, primarily because she felt that the Communist movement promised real equality for the Jewish people. She remained a party member for over thirty years, until the Stalin revelations of the mid 1950s.

Together with other women in the Labour League, Kramer did extensive fund-raising work to help finance the party's Yiddish and English press and the league's Yiddish school. Like Hoffman, she was also involved in diligent door-to-door canvassing to recruit support for party candidates for government office. In addition, she and her friends did vital strike-support work, both within the Jewish community and beyond it. If one of the local unions was on strike, they would help with the picketing. During the 1926 British general strike, they raised money to buy food for the strikers' children, and they collected canned goods for the strikers at Oshawa's General Motors plant in 1937. Kramer was also one of the leaders of the 1933 kosher meat boycott.

In the meantime, Kramer had been working as a cloak finisher. Having arrived in Canada without a trade, she had soon found a job as a finisher in a large shop owned by her uncle's relatives. She worked in this trade until she married several years later. In the early 1930s, when her child was two years old, she resumed work as a finisher because the family was having a hard time living on her husband's income. She remained in this trade until shortly after the Second World War.

During her seventeen years of working in the garment industry, Kramer was highly active in the cloakmakers' section of the ILGWU. She served as the finishers' representative on the union committee that went from shop to shop settling prices, and, during the 1930s, served as secretary of her local for five years. She was a member of the joint board for five years as well. In addition, she was particularly active on picket committees during the various cloak strikes.

She proudly recalled the hard work and dedication required during these frequent strikes: 'There was never a stop [to the work]. Once you were on a committee for the picket line and you know that you are responsible, you didn't care how cold it was, how late it was, or how early it was. This was a job you had to do [well]. And [especially] being a member of the Communist Party, you had to show your loyalty to the working class because the policy of the Communist Party put the working class first.' As she described picketing in the bitter cold at six o'clock in the morning, she also stressed the camaraderie on the line: 'When we used to have the strikes, we also used to have a lot of fun ... When you went out on the picket line, you went out with pride. You are going on the picket line because you wanted a better life for you and a better life for your fellow workers.'

Kramer's recollections add to the evidence that many women in the Jewish labour movement were not seriously constrained by notions of feminine passivity. When the author asked whether anyone felt it was unladylike for a woman to participate in union activities, Kramer replied by focusing first on her own sense of pride for standing up for her rights on the shop floor. She was proud that she fought for herself instead of meekly depending on others to fight for her. It had never occurred to her to feel ashamed of her assertiveness. Kramer then declared that the idea that a woman should not seem too aggressive was 'old-fashioned.' She added: 'You know, some people, maybe years ago they would have that approach: "Oh, a woman is not supposed to go on the picket line or do this and that" ... But [the women] knew that if they want to eat, they have to work for it!'

Group of activist Jewish fur workers, 1920s. The man standing on the left is Max Federman. The man kneeling on the right is holding a copy of *Der Kamf*.

Making men's clothing at Tip Top, 1931

Toronto joint board, Amalgamated Clothing Workers, 1930s

Hat, cap, and millinery workers marching in May Day demonstration, early 1930s

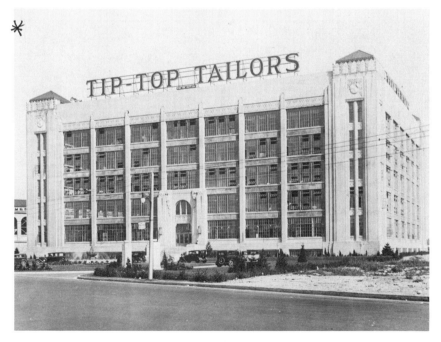

Tip Top Tailors' factory building on Lakeshore Blvd West, 1930s

Second convention of the IUNTW, 1931. Seated in the first row (from left to right) are (6) Annie Buller, (10) Myer Klig, (11) Pearl Wedro, (12) Joshua Gershman, and (13) Jim Blugerman.

Group of workers leaving the headquarters of the Industrial Union of Needle Trades Workers to head for the picket line, 1932

Members of the Industrial Union of Needle Trades Workers marching in the May Day parade on College Street, 1935

Picket line during the dressmakers' general strike, led by the Industrial Union of Needle Trades Workers, 1933

Picnic of members of the cloakmakers' branch of the International Ladies' Garment Workers' Union, 1938

Toronto joint board, International Ladies' Garment Workers' Union, 1936. Seated in the first row (from left to right) are (1) Abe Kirzner, (2) H.D. Langer, (4) Sam Kraisman, and (5) Abe Megerman.

Joe Salsberg (on right) relaxing at the Toronto Islands, late 1930s. Anti-Semitism prevented him from renting a summer home there.

Socialist Day at the Arbeiter Ring's Camp Yungvelt, 1936. Seated in the second row (from left to right) are (2) David Lewis, (3) Sophie Lewis, (4) Lucy Woodsworth, (5) J.S. Woodsworth (leader of the CCF), (6) Norah Coldwell, and (7) M.J. Coldwell (prominent CCFer).

Pearl Wedro, Jewish
Communist activist, 1944

Toronto union organizer Sam Lapedes at Treblinka, 1962. Nazis
murdered approximately 850,000 Jews, 2000 Gypsies, and 3000 other
victims at this notorious death camp. Lapedes stands at the left of the
monument to the victims from the Polish town where he was born.
Within the space of fifteen days in 1942, the 40,000 Jews of this town
were deported to Treblinka's gas chambers.

In this context, Kramer brought up the kosher meat boycott of 1933, stressing that Jewish women received credit for fighting back against the high price of meat. With regard to the beginning of the meat boycott, however, she indicated: 'In those days, the people [didn't] realize that women could do a thing like this – to go on a picket line, have a fight with the butcher, and go to court ... A lot of people didn't think [that women could engage in such militant action]. "What do you mean you're going out on a strike? You're going to fight with the butchers, with the men?" I [said]: "Why not? Why couldn't women do things that men do?"'[27] Many women apparently agreed with Kramer's assessment of women's capabilities, for they joined the boycott. As the women picketers stood up to the male butchers (and the few male customers), the majority of the East European Jewish community approved of their actions. Moreover, the Jewish women of Toronto had actually been doing 'things that men do' for quite a while, since, over the years, they had participated in a whole series of militant and successful boycotts.

Overall, Kramer felt that the need to fight for a better deal took precedence over any 'old-fashioned' restrictive notions of femininity. Although Kramer indicated that some women believed that militant behaviour was not entirely appropriate for a woman, she minimized the importance of this attitude. Clearly, she herself did not feel personally constrained by ladylike docility. Indeed, she expressed satisfaction that, in the Jewish Communist movement, she had learned to fight assertively for what she believed: 'I learned one thing [especially]: if I get slapped on one side of my cheek, I wouldn't put my other [cheek] up, but I'll give two [slaps] back. This goes for everything, wherever I'm active. If [there's] something I don't like or I see something is wrong, I wouldn't talk behind anybody's back. I'll come out and I'll say to them right in the front, "this is not to be done, and this wasn't right" ... And that's what we learned in the left-wing movement.' Kramer was certainly a bold and dedicated activist.

At the same time, Kramer's discussion of her union and party activities revealed that neither she herself nor her associates in the Jewish labour movement viewed gender issues as important in this period. When, for example, the author asked her why union records and labour newspapers seldom mentioned the female workers in this trade, Kramer replied that the explanation was straightforward: women were not specifically mentioned because members of the Jewish labour movement (including Kramer herself) felt they were all workers together and, therefore, felt no need to differentiate between female workers and male workers. According to this argument, what really mattered was that they were all working

[handwritten annotation: no differentiation btwn females & workers]

class. A similar sense of the relative unimportance of gender issues also emerged when the author asked if there was ever any discussion about having a female business agent to better organize the women workers. 'No,' she replied, 'it wasn't the policy of the union that we have to put women in to do this and this work. We [all] worked together.'

Within this general context, however, there was some sense of needing women on the picket line during strikes. Some activists felt that women had a 'different approach' when it was a question of talking to strike-breakers, particularly female strike-breakers. According to Kramer, the concern to have women on the picket line meant it was a good idea to have some women on the picket committee. However, this awareness of the need for women on this specific committee did not mean it was important to make sure that women were represented in other union posts. Indeed, as the discussion of the business agent indicates, there was little sense of a broader need for female union leaders.

Apparently, there was little awareness that women workers might have had special concerns of their own. When the author asked Kramer whether union activists discussed specific issues to help bring women into the union, she replied they did not: 'We were interested to get the members into the union. We didn't care [whether] they are women or men.' When the author asked specifically if there were any particular issues that women would have been interested in, she answered: 'No, we were interested that nobody should take our work away and that we should get paid what we deserved.'

Even though the women garment workers earned especially low wages, Kramer revealed that neither she nor other activists felt that women's work was being unfairly undervalued in a systematic way. To a certain extent, the issue was obscured by the prevalence of piece work. Rather than focus on a comparison between the average woman's pay and the average man's pay, Kramer pointed out that if a cloak finisher was particularly adept and speedy, she might be able to make more money than some of the operators, the overwhelming majority of whom were men. Apparently, no one at that time was articulating a critique of the fact that, in the cloak trade, women were being confined to jobs that were generally low-paying.

Even so, Kramer's emphasis on the highly proficient finisher also suggests that women, too, could develop a sense of pride in good 'workmanship.' Kramer herself took pride in her sewing abilities and in her crucial financial contributions to her family's well-being. The importance of her job to her was part of the motivation for her commitment to the union.

In discussing her own activism, Kramer brought up the fact that she had had a hard time juggling political work with her household responsibilities and her full-time job in the shop. As she discussed this issue, she exclaimed: 'And I did [all of] it! I don't know *how* I did it, but I did it ... Sure it was hard ... [But] when you're devoted to something, [when] you believe in something, nothing comes hard. I believed in my cause [at] that time. All right, I was [eventually] disappointed [about] what happened to the Jews in the Soviet Union. But when I was in the left-wing movement and I worked for the left-wing movement, that was my belief. Nothing was too hard for me.' Kramer had brought up the difficulties of juggling all these demands in order to demonstrate how dedicated she was to the cause. She did not suggest it was unfair that women were burdened by all these household responsibilities. In fact, here again, what emerges is a sense of strong womanhood.

When the author asked Kramer if anybody was talking about men sharing household responsibilities back then, she replied: 'In the 30s and the 20s, we didn't talk about it. I'll tell you why. *Because it was [a] very tough time to make a living.* We were interested in how to make a better living ... But you would never think: "If I'm working and he's working, why can't we both help each other [with the housework and the child care]?" I never even thought of it.' Instead, she simply assumed that, in addition to bringing in part of the family income, she was responsible for running the household. Yet she remarked approvingly that 'the women now have a different outlook [on] life [from what] we had ... Now, I think it's a very good thing,' she declared, that some of today's husbands share domestic responsibilities with their wives.

Kramer's discussion of these issues harkened back to women's roles before immigration. In explaining what life used to be like for Jewish women in Eastern Europe, she focused on her mother's household labour: 'We were six children in our home. And my mother, her job was to look after the children, to do the cooking [and the cleaning] ... There was no dishwasher; there was no ... washing machine. You had to do everything by hand. A woman in the Old Country, a Jewish woman, worked very hard ... The mother had the most work.' Kramer also described how she and her sisters began to help with her mother's housework when they were ten or eleven. Her mother had made a point of emphasizing how important it was for girls to learn how to look after a home because they would have to care for homes of their own one day.

When the author asked Kramer whether she recalled Jewish women contributing directly to the family income in Eastern Europe, she answered: 'Oh, yes. My mother helped my father. We used to buy wheat ...

and sell it ... The farmers used to come in from out of town ... and they would bring their wheat and corn and everything to sell. My mother would go out and buy it, just like my father would do. And [later], when my father passed away, I used to help my mother. I was a young girl [at that time] ... But,' she continued, 'if a woman has six children, or five children, or four children, believe me, she's got enough responsibilities without even thinking of helping [the man make a living].' Although Kramer emphasized that it would have been easier for women to focus on their domestic work full time, her testimony indicates that, in Eastern Europe, women like her mother also worked to earn money for the family as a matter of course. Kramer's own role in the New World was, in many ways, a continuation of her mother's role in the Old World.

In order to investigate continuities and changes in 'appropriate' gender roles, the author also asked Kramer about attitudes towards married women working in Toronto's needle trades in the 1930s. In response to the specific question whether there was any grumbling that married women were taking jobs away from men in the middle of a depression, she replied that she did not run into this kind of attitude, partly because finishing was considered to be a woman's job anyway. In general, she seemed to feel that people understood that married women had to work if the family really needed the money. She herself did not feel that her neighbours disapproved of her for leaving her young child with a baby-sitter while she worked in the cloak shop, for the neighbours were well aware of her family's financial need.

Like many immigrant Jewish women, Kramer emphasized the centrality of the family as a whole. This focus applied to both daughters' and wives' paid work. When the author asked Kramer whether, years ago, a single Jewish woman who lived with her parents would feel significantly more independent when she obtained a paying job, the notion of independence in this context seemed foreign to her. Emphasizing the family, not the individual, Kramer indicated that such a women would feel she was rightfully contributing to the family income. Kramer confirmed that it was the general practice for unmarried children to hand their entire pay envelopes over to their parents, and she felt this was as it should be. Her thinking, in fact, closely reflected traditional Jewish values, which prescribed that any money earned by a particular family member belonged to the family as a whole rather than to that particular individual.[28] Moreover, since very few young Jewish women would have earned enough to live on their own, the emphasis on the family group was reinforced by straitened economic circumstances.

Similarly, married women's jobs in the needle trades were seen in terms of the economic needs of their families. During the entire discussion of married women's jobs, Kramer never suggested that these women might have had their own private reasons for wanting paying jobs. Although it is true that the available jobs were often not attractive, the main point is that such a suggestion would have been alien to Kramer's emphasis on the family as a whole. Even though Kramer herself derived some pride from her job in the needle trades, this was not why she went out to work. Kramer's way of conceptualizing the family meant that the needs of Jewish working-class women were generally collapsed into the needs of their families. Thus Kramer never expressed an interest in power dynamics within the family. Moreover, the importance of the family group must have been reinforced by the importance of Jewish identity for Kramer, for the family was seen as central to the perpetuation of Jewish culture.

The collectivities of class, ethnic group, and family were central to Kramer. Her strong emphasis on assertiveness, on the importance of fighting back, was focused on her deep commitment to oppose the oppression of workers and Jews. In contrast, she never spoke of the need for Jewish women to assert their own interests as women, either within their own families or within the Jewish labour movement more broadly. Focused on these other collectivities, she did not really see women as having important special interests of their own.

The nature of Kramer's class analysis is important in explaining why she did not see women as having special interests of their own. As indicated previously, Kramer felt that female workers and male workers were basically the same because they were all members of the working class. Yet Kramer's own experience as a woman contradicted this notion of sameness, particularly since she spent years in a typically female job that was considered unskilled. Even while asserting that the workers were all the same, she was mentioning that she had difficulty juggling her household responsibilities with her other activities. She raised the issue of household responsibilities to discuss how dedicated she was to the cause, not to point out that women were in a different position from men. In other words, her own experience as a female worker was significantly different from that of male workers, but this difference was being denied at the ideological level. Kramer's testimony suggests that even for female members of the Jewish labour movement, the tendency to view the dynamics of their situation in terms of a class analysis helped create – as it also reflected – a blindness to gender dynamics.

A highly active member of Toronto's Arbeiter Ring for years, Molly Fineberg had come to Canada from Poland in the mid 1920s at the age

of twenty. In Poland her family had been relatively comfortable economically. She had received a high school education at the local Polish gymna-
sium, even though her parents had objected to the fact that the school
had held mandatory classes on the Jewish Sabbath. Soon after she arrived
in Toronto she was drawn into a Left Labour Zionist youth organization,
where she began to learn about the Jewish labour movement. Before
long, she married a Toronto fur worker who was devoted to Left Labour
Zionism.

Although she did not fundamentally disagree with the Left Labour
Zionist movement and although her husband remained active, Fineberg
soon joined the Arbeiter Ring. She stressed that both groups were part
of the Jewish socialist movement and that they did certain kinds of cultural work together. In fact, they became allies in the fight against the
Communists. She explained that the main difference between the Left
Labour Zionist organization and the Arbeiter Ring, which was led mainly
by Bundists, was that most Arbeiter Ring members disapproved of the
idea of a Jewish state in Palestine. Although she herself strongly believed
in the establishment of such a state, she was drawn to the Arbeiter Ring
largely because she was impressed by its Yiddish school and Yiddish camp.

Like many Jewish women of that period, Fineberg looked after the
household tasks while her husband toiled in the needle trades
sweatshops. When his income was inadequate to meet all of the family's
needs, she obtained a job as a salesperson in a dress shop, where she
worked long hours for low pay.

Although Fineberg never worked in a garment factory, her vital strike-
support work and her notable activities within the Arbeiter Ring meant
that she was certainly a part of the Jewish labour movement. Along with
other women from her organization, she used to help out during various
strikes, including a number of strikes in the dress and cloak trades.
Sometimes they helped by getting donations of food for local Jewish
strikers; sometimes they joined the picket lines, as, for example, when
they supported striking Jewish bakers by picketing the bake shops in an
attempt to stop customers from buying bread. In addition, Fineberg
diligently raised funds for the Arbeiter Ring's Yiddish school. She also
helped with other Arbeiter Ring projects such as sending money to
pogrom victims in Poland.

Fineberg thrived on the sharp political differences within the Arbeiter
Ring, an organization composed of Social Territorialists,[29] Anarchists, and
Trotskyists, as well as Bundists. When the author asked if all these differ-

ent groups got along well inside the one organization, she replied: 'No, they didn't. That's why it was so interesting – because I listened to all the discussions ... They weren't personal insults, but they were political discussions, and they were very interesting ... I was curious to learn and to find out about everything.' She did not merely listen to the political debates; she participated boldly in them, especially in trying to convince reluctant Arbeiter Ring members to support certain Zionist efforts.

Within the Arbeiter Ring, Fineberg held a number of important leadership positions over the thirty years during which she belonged to this organization. She served as president of her women's branch and as the branch's financial secretary and recording secretary at other times. She was the secretary of the Arbeiter Ring's city committee, a kind of joint board that linked the various Toronto branches together. She also served as secretary of a special school committee and acted as secretary at some of the Arbeiter Ring's regional meetings. In short, Fineberg was a remarkable activist.

Fineberg believed in socialism. She became a socialist, she explained, primarily as a response to the poverty she had seen among working-class families in both Poland and Canada. She did not feel it was fair for working-class people to have to struggle so hard to make a meagre living. In discussing why she became a socialist, Fineberg did not bring up the issue of women's rights. When the author specifically asked if her becoming a socialist had anything to do with women's issues, however, she replied that she had been attracted to the socialist movement because she felt socialists believed in equal rights for women. Similarly, when Fineberg spoke about the ideology and the activities of the Arbeiter Ring, she did not bring up the subject of women's rights on her own. Yet when specifically asked whether Arbeiter Ring members used to talk about equal rights for women, she replied they did. She recalled hearing Emma Goldman lecture on this topic. Despite expressing a general belief in women's rights, Fineberg did not go on to portray this issue as a dynamic aspect of the movement to which she was so committed. Instead, she returned to the more familiar subject of socialism and stressed the socialist slant of Yiddish literature, with its emphasis on the injustices faced by the impoverished. When the author asked if she remembered any Yiddish stories that talked about women's equality, she did not.

Fineberg said it was not common for women to hold executive positions on the Arbeiter Ring's important committees. She felt that as a woman who had served as secretary of the city committee, she herself was fairly exceptional. She attributed her position to the fact that others thought she was very capable, and she took pride in her achievements. When the author asked if she had ever felt that women should have been better represented on the executive, she seemed to find the question surprising. Presumably she felt that candidates for the executive were to be evaluated on the basis of their experience and their political commitments and that gender was not the issue.

Speaking of her own leadership positions in the Arbeiter Ring, Fineberg declared: 'And everybody said [to me], "Where do you get the time? Who looks after your son?" ... I managed ... [It was] hard, but I was quite active. I was quite active and willing and interested in so many things. The labour movement was very, very interesting to me.' Although her mother helped her look after her son, Fineberg was concerned that her own intensive political activism meant that the child was not getting as much supervision as he needed. She also recalled how difficult it was to do so much of the housework on Sunday when she went out to work during the week. Yet she proudly stated: 'Even when I went [out] to work, I didn't open up a can. We ate a good meal.' Like Bessie Kramer, Fineberg was deeply satisfied that she had been dedicated, capable, and strong enough to do it all.

Fineberg's sense of strong womanhood was also apparent in her response to questions about views of femininity in the Jewish community in the 1930s. When the author asked if people felt that it was not ladylike for a woman to be on a picket line or to speak up at political meetings, she replied: 'No ... This is *farshimilt* [old-fashioned]. This is a very old idea. It's not ladylike? I never heard of that!' She dismissed the idea that Jewish women were being held back by notions of feminine docility.

In general, Fineberg's testimony suggests that a belief in women's rights was, at most, a subtheme within the sections of the Jewish socialist movement encompassed by the Arbeiter Ring. The fact that she was never the one to bring up the topic of women's rights during the course of the interview indicates this was not a major area of focus. For Fineberg, as for so many other courageous activists within the Jewish labour movement, the main themes were class and ethnicity. Fineberg's description of her intense political activities did not include active involvement in women's rights struggles. However, in responding to direct questions about women's rights, Fineberg did indicate that a belief in women's equality was a part of her socialism. In part, she was picking up on the author's own interests. Thus, although she was surprised to be asked about the extent to which women were represented in leadership positions within her organization, she remarked later that the governor general was a woman, 'so we [women] are going somewhere.'[30]

Although class-conscious activism required special sacrifices for women, a significant number of Jewish women were prepared to make these sacrifices. Socialist women like Pearl Wedro, Bessie Kramer, Sadie Hoffman, and Molly Fineberg actively participated in Toronto's Jewish labour movement even though, for some, it meant a lessening of marriage prospects in a period where 'old maids' were disparaged. They continued their activism even though, for others, it meant uneasiness about whether their children were being neglected. It also often meant that these women were hard pressed to perform a triple day of labour – juggling a full-time job in the paid labour force, full responsibility for household tasks, and the time-consuming demands of political activism. The remarkable dedication of these women testifies to the depth of their class consciousness. Yet, given the nature of these sacrifices, it is not surprising that some women workers were too busy with a double day of labour to participate more actively in the Jewish labour movement.

A significant number of female Jewish workers were highly conscious of themselves as members of a working class in opposition to the bosses. For example, Leah Stern, an Orthodox Jew, stressed the need to 'fight for the rights of the working people,' and faithfully joined the picket line whenever a strike was called.[31] Moreover, for women like Wedro, Kramer, Hoffman, and Fineberg, this consciousness was augmented by the vision of an alternative socialist society, a new Garden of Eden.[32] The socialist women were deeply committed to fighting to help bring about the new society, and, as part of this battle, they actively participated in the struggles of the Jewish unions. Even when they were housewives who were not engaged in paid labour, they did important strike-support work.

Their roles in the family, in the paid labour force, and in the Jewish labour movement reflected the ways in which the process of immigration had led to a combination of changes and continuities in female gender roles. Whereas married Jewish women had typically combined domestic responsibilities with income-generating activities in the Old World, this was gradually becoming less common in the New World. Many immigrant Jewish wives earned money by taking in boarders or laundry, helping with a small family business, or doing homework in the needle trades (if such work was available), but there was a growing tendency for married Jewish women not to work outside the home.

In the less industrialized setting of the Old World, it had been easier for Jewish women to combine childrearing and income-generating activities because there was less of a division between the home and the 'workplace.' In the *shtetl*, workshops and stores were often located inside the homes or nearby. It was also more difficult for Jewish mothers to go out to work in the New World because female relatives were not always available to help out. Child care arrangements, in particular, were made more difficult by the fact that members of the extended family, who would have been relied on to help watch the children in Eastern Europe, might not have made the journey to North America.

In addition, the domestic ideology was to become more compelling for Jewish immigrants as the pressures of assimilation undermined certain aspects of Jewish religious tradition. In particular, reverence for the traditional male scholar was declining in the New World. As assimilation proceeded, albeit unevenly, and male status in the New World derived less from religious learning and more from financial achievement, the 'non-working' wife was becoming an important status symbol. Although many immigrant Jewish families could not yet afford such 'status,' this factor was to become increasingly important in the period after the Second World War when the Jewish community was to experience much more upward mobility.[33]

Meanwhile, in the interwar years, to the extent that Jewish wives were becoming less likely to combine paid work with domestic responsibilities in the New World, this dimension of female gender roles was in the process of contracting, for better or worse. However, married women workers such as Leah Stern, Bessie Kramer, and Molly Fineberg were, in effect, resisting this contraction and preserving more continuity between Jewish women's roles in the Old World and the New. Moreover, the activist women were not simply continuing traditional Old World patterns in the new settings: they were expanding women's roles beyond the legacy of the *shtetl*. Whereas the *shtetl*'s community officials had been men, both the married and the unmarried women who played active roles in Toronto's Jewish labour movement were expanding women's sphere by carving out the legitimacy of female participation in the civic life of the community in the New World. Although this process had begun in the Old World as new currents such as Bundism were bringing in changes, the activities of female militants in Toronto's Jewish labour movement nonetheless signified an important expansion of Jewish women's roles. By taking on militant political roles in the public sphere, the female Jewish activists were displaying a notion of womanhood that stood apart from the conventional notions of their new country as well.[34]

This expansion of Jewish women's roles took place because of the activist women's dedication to the struggles to end the exploitation of the working class and the oppression of Jews. In this case, gender-role elasticity did not lead to a developed commitment to feminism. Despite the very real differences between the position of working-class women and the position of working-class men, and despite the significant shifts taking place in Jewish women's roles, the female activists tended not to be particularly self-conscious or reflective about gender roles in these years. Theirs was a much more practical approach, pitching into the fray to advance the Jewish labour movement.

Many Communist women, like Bessie Kramer, felt that the important point was that female and male workers were all members of the working class and that, in this context, issues of gender were irrelevant. Some, like Sadie Hoffman, had a limited awareness, at times, that women were treated as second-class beings, an awareness that was generally submerged in their emphasis on class oppression. Others, such as Molly Fineberg, had more of a belief in women's rights, but this was not a concern they emphasized or fought for. Class considerations were seen as far more important.[35]

The available written records substantiate much of what these female interviewees have recalled concerning perceptions of the position of women within the Jewish labour movement. The dearth of references to women workers in the written record suggests that many shared Bessie Kramer's sense that gender issues were relatively unimportant in the context of an emphasis on class analysis. Had female workers been conscious of themselves as having separate interests from male workers, some of this would presumably have been reflected in the union records, even though union records were usually written by men.

Had women members of the ACW, for example, been sending delegations to the joint board meetings to put forth special women's demands within the union, the ACW minutes would probably have noted these developments – even if male union leaders never took any real action on such demands. Instead, the available ACW joint board minutes, which cover seventeen years of the period under consideration, record only two minor cases where women workers specifically expressed their concerns as a distinct group. In March 1924 a representative of a meeting of woman workers recommended that 'no more apprentices should be permitted in the trade, especially in the finishing line as the trade is overcrowded.'[36] Several months later the women members of one of the ACW locals asked the board what was being done about members who had worked on Good Friday.[37] Indeed, this concern about the Christian holiday suggests tensions between Jews and non-Jews rather than being specifically a gender issue.

Moreover, in the local Yiddish press, there was no sustained discussion about the position of women in society. In 1923, however, an exceptional letter to the editor appeared in the *Yiddisher Zhurnal*. In this letter, a woman writer raised a number of interesting points about women's roles:

I want to say here a few words about the relation and opinion of men with regard to women. I believe that men have an incorrect opinion of women.

In truth, women are the most important element in the human family. In real life, a woman has, however, little significance.

The new times have brought forth a woman problem. And one should relate to this problem with more seriousness and not babble so, for no good reason, about women.

It is a pleasant phenomenon that women are organizing themselves everywhere. By us in Toronto, a dozen women's organizations have been established in the last several months. The Chenstechover Society has founded a women's auxiliary. The Rumanian women have done the same. The Zion Benevolent [Society] has followed the same example.

This shows that there is a necessity to form women's organizations and to express the special needs of the woman, as a person and as an active person in the community.[38]

Although this woman ended her letter by asking for other suggestions and calling upon the readers to think seriously about these matters, subsequent issues of the *Zhurnal* contained no further consideration of the 'woman problem.' Within the city's immigrant Jewish community, there was apparently not much concern regarding the position of women.

Moreover, although the writer of the 1923 letter was optimistic about the formation of women's organizations, there were no special organizations specifically for Jewish women workers. This, in itself, says something about the lack of interest in women's issues among these women. Indeed, the writer of the 1923 letter focused only on women's auxiliaries of mutual benefit societies.[39] The Yiddisher Arbeiter Froyen Fareyn, despite its name (which translates literally as the Jewish Women Workers' Association), was composed mostly of housewives who were not engaged in paid labour. An organization of Jewish women who were oriented towards the Communist party,[40] the Fareyn did important left-wing political work, as Sadie Hoffman has explained, but it was not concerned with issues of women's rights.

The Declaration of Principles of the Fareyn makes it clear that this organization sought to bring women into the class struggle and was not concerned with women's oppression as women. The declaration began: 'Recognizing that the development of capitalism has pulled the woman into all branches of industry and placed her *in the same position* as the male workers, and also recognizing that the imminent liberation of the working class as a whole is also tied to the liberation of the woman worker, we are therefore interested in organizing the Jewish women workers and preparing them for the joint struggle of the whole working class for its imminent liberation.' Defining the organization's work in the economic field, the declaration stressed 'prevail[ing] upon the women workers to join the unions in their trade and having joined, to fight for the minimum wage'; it also emphasized that 'the women themselves should prevail upon their men to belong to their unions.' The declaration also described the Fareyn's responsibility 'to take part in all campaigns which are directed by the revolutionary part of the working class, namely to help elect labour representatives.'[41]

As Bessie Kramer indicated, the Fareyn was not really involved in work within the needle trades unions. Kramer, whose sister was a member of this organization, explained that there were some Fareyn women who worked in the needle trades and who would have been involved, as individuals, in union work in their own shops, but these women were not using the Fareyn to help develop strategies for their work within their own particular unions.[42] After all, the majority of the Fareyn women were housewives who did not work in the garment shops.[43] The Fareyn was clearly not an organization devoted to furthering the particular interests of women workers within the Jewish unions.

The Fareyn did, however, do valuable support work during strikes of the Industrial Union of Needle Trades Workers. The party press credited the Fareyn women with helping to build the IUNTW, especially through joining the picket lines and raising money for strike relief.[44] Moreover, on the occasion of the Fareyn's eighth anniversary in 1931, *Der Kamf* called on the Fareyn to help fight for unemployment insurance, for old-age pensions, for lower rents, and against the eviction of tenants. The writer of this article also stated that the Fareyn should help organize women workers into the Workers' Unity League. The writer explained: 'This does not mean a lessening of its old work (camp, children's school), but this means that the camp and school and general cultural work must *be co-ordinated and used for the central task:* to draw the working women into the economic fight for the improvement of their situation, to draw them into the general revolutionary fight.'[45] The Fareyn did play an important role in mobilizing women for working-class political action. In its strike-support work, in its work for the children's camp and school, and in its attempts to draw women into 'the general revolutionary fight,' however, the Fareyn did not focus on issues of women's oppression as women.[46]

The fact that there were no special organizations specifically for Jewish women workers was perhaps partly a reflection of the difficulties women faced in taking on additional organizational work. However, it also suggests that Jewish women workers did not see themselves as having special interests distinct from the interests of their male counterparts. Although the women were, with few exceptions, systematically confined to the less-skilled and lower-paying jobs in the needle trades, these women did not develop a critique of their own position on the shop floor.

The explanation for this attitude is twofold. Women workers such as Bessie Kramer interpreted their own experience through the framework of a class analysis that emphasized the common oppression of all workers, regardless of gender. This obscured the fact that women workers faced special constraints. At the same time, the implicit assumption was that it was fitting for male workers to have the better jobs because men were the primary breadwinners in their families. Married women workers, regardless of their differing political and religious views, explained their paid labour in terms of going out to work because their husbands were not able to make enough money to support the family. The assumption that the men were rightfully the primary breadwinners presumably provided a powerful rationale for men's exclusive rights to the better jobs within the clothing industry. Although this was not something that was frequently articulated, it was an implicit – and significant – assumption. Indeed, to the extent that it was an assumption that was widely shared, it did not need to be explicitly articulated.

Certainly there was a contradiction here. On the one hand, there was the ideological emphasis on the common oppression of all workers, regardless of gender. This preoccupation tended to obscure any differences between female and male workers. On the other hand, there was the assumption that female workers were different from male workers because male workers were the primary breadwinners for their families and therefore deserved the better jobs. However, in a period when gender issues were seldom examined or questioned, it is not surprising that there should have been contradictions in people's thoughts.

The lack of emphasis on women's emancipation was not the product of a deliberate tactical choice. It was not as if many of these women actually possessed a developed feminist consciousness and had made a strategic decision to focus their energies elsewhere. During the interviews, these women were not saying that they were oppressed as women but that they could not focus on women's rights because they were so closely linked together with male workers in the fight against the bosses. Nor were they saying that women's issues had to be consciously downplayed because the women themselves were closely linked to Jewish men in an anti-Semitic world. Instead, there was little awareness of feminist issues in the first place.

Neither did these women say that women's emancipation could only be achieved in a socialist society and, therefore, the class struggle had to come first. Yet Becky Buhay, a prominent Communist party official, did make this kind of argument. In a 1930 article in the *Worker*, for example, Buhay proclaimed: 'ONLY THE COMPLETE SMASH-UP OF CAPITALISM and the victory of the workers can bring about economic, political, and social equality between the sexes.'[47] Calling upon women to fight together with men against the capitalist system, Buhay contrasted the 'tremendous achievements of the women of the Soviet Union' with the 'growing rottenness of the condition and status of the working woman in Canada today.' In this 1930 article, Buhay even stated: 'To enable the working woman to take active part in all channels of activity, industrial, political and cultural[,] the workers['] state has done its utmost to free woman from the drudgery of the kitchen by instituting communal restaurants, laundries, creches and kindergartens, nurseries and summer homes, etc.'[48] Yet, as historian Joan Sangster has recently pointed out, most Russian communal kitchens had been closed by the mid 1920s, and, by the end of the decade, the debate on women's issues had been silenced within the Soviet Union.[49]

Unlike Buhay, none of the Communist women interviewees stressed the idea that women were achieving equality in the Soviet Union in the interwar period.[50] Pearl Wedro, for example, did not even mention the idea that the Soviet Union was said to have been promoting women's equality. Regardless of her attendance at a women's conference in the Soviet Union at the beginning of the Depression, Wedro did not discuss the Communist movement in feminist terms.[51] More significantly, none of the women who were interviewed made the argument that women's equality could only be achieved after the fight for a socialist society had succeeded. Instead, they were not especially interested in issues of women's rights.

While historian Joan Sangster has convincingly demonstrated that certain individuals within the Canadian Communist party expressed support for women's rights within the context of their overall emphasis on the class struggle, her work situates these sentiments within the broader framework of party policy. Sangster emphasizes these expressions of support for gender equality but also discusses 'the peripheral status of the woman question within the Party.'[52] The kinds of feminist sentiments she highlights were not reflected within the Communist wing of Toronto's Jewish labour movement. In fact, key Jewish Communist leaders such as Joshua Gershman expressed antipathy to feminism (see chapter 6).[53] These findings suggest that Sangster may have underestimated the extent to which the party as a whole obstructed the development of feminist tendencies.

Partly because of the impact of pressing economic hardships, the Canadian women's movement has tended to be middle class. Although working-class, left-wing, Finnish women seem to have developed feminist views in early twentieth-century Canada, they appear to constitute an exception to the broader pattern.[54] For women like Sadie Hoffman and Bessie Kramer, their families' serious economic difficulties led them to emphasize working-class economic struggles to the exclusion of women's rights struggles. Even for non-politicized working-class families, working-class economic issues loomed large in the context of poverty and harsh working conditions. Although the economic security of middle-class women has been tenuous to the extent that it has usually depended on their husbands, these women have been relatively free from the same kinds of pressing necessities. Thus they have more readily been able to turn their attentions to issues that were defined in feminist terms. In addition, middle-class women have usually been in a better position to devote their energies to women's political causes because, unlike working-class women, they could afford maids, 'cleaning ladies,' or new labour-saving household appliances.

Yet working-class women themselves faced special, gender-conditioned, economic hardships, particularly due to the discriminatory gender division of labour in the workforce. Even the full-time housewife was not necessarily immune to discriminatory labour practices. In addition to having usually engaged in paid labour before marriage, the full-time housewife could be propelled back into the paid labour force by the unemployment, illness, death, or desertion of her husband. Even her husband's particularly low earnings could drive her out to work. Nonetheless, working-class women like Hoffman and Kramer focused on the welfare of the family as a whole and looked to class gains to improve their families' lot, both in the short and the long term. For them, economic issues were not defined in terms of gender.

 Moreover, working-class Jewish women were less apt to develop a feminist critique of their position within the immigrant Jewish community, because they shared a common sense of oppression with many of the men in this community, not only as fellow workers but also as fellow Jews. Because of the threat of anti-Semitism, there was often an emphasis on the interest of the Jewish community as a whole. This context made it less likely that Jewish women would develop a sense of their own oppression as women within this beleaguered community. Indeed, the contrast with the working-class immigrant Finnish women highlights the impact of Jewish identity all the more.

The radicalism of the Jewish socialists did not extend to a critique of women's responsibility for household labour. Dishwashing and child care were hardly ever seen as political issues in those days; after all, the feminist insistence that 'the personal is political' is largely a contemporary development. Both women and men generally felt that political issues were restricted to matters of the public sphere. As Jewish women's roles expanded to include political activity in the public realm, their men's roles did not expand to include sharing household responsibilities. With respect to the participants in the Jewish labour movement, female gender-role elasticity was not matched by male gender-role elasticity.

In general, then, some Jewish women overcame significant obstacles and played especially active roles in Toronto's Jewish labour movement. They were highly class-conscious and dedicated themselves to building the movement, despite the personal hardships this entailed. Their assertiveness stemmed, in part, from the strong economic roles women were accustomed to in traditional East European Jewish culture, for, unlike Victorian culture, Jewish tradition did not define women as passive, delicate, and exclusively domestic. These militant women were also expanding female gender roles beyond the legacy of the *shtetl* by carving out a place for themselves in the civic life of the community. The women activists often stressed not only their commitment to the class struggle but also their commitment to fighting against anti-Semitism. They were not active in women's rights struggles and seldom developed feminist perspectives of their own experiences. Although they challenged other aspects of traditional East European Jewish culture, they did not fundamentally question its patriarchal nature. The activist women made crucial contributions to the Jewish labour movement, without substantially challenging the movement's male-centred character.

8 Pulling Apart
Divisions over Political Ideology

'Wherever there were two Ukrainians there would be a
mandolin orchestra, two Finns guaranteed a steam bath and a
co-operative, and two Jews meant three political parties.'

– Peter Hunter, *Which Side Are You On, Boys: Canadian Life
on the Left*[1]

'Let us once and for all liberate ourselves from the parasites [in the
clothing factories],' proclaimed a fiery letter to the editor of one of the
Yiddish newspapers in 1931.[2] Other articles in this paper echoed this
theme, calling on Toronto's Jewish garment workers to free themselves
'from the paws of ... the principleless creatures who suck the blood from
the workers daily.'[3] Denunciations were heaped upon the enemy who
used 'terror' and 'the whip of discrimination' to 'suppress any discontent
and any protest from the workers.'[4] But who exactly was the enemy?
Although the Communists certainly saw capitalists as their class opponents
and although other articles in this newspaper graphically denounced the
clothing manufacturers, these particular phrases were not being used to
describe the bosses in the garment shops. Instead the Communist press
was describing the leadership of the 'right-wing' needle trades unions.

Toronto's Jewish labour movement was fragmented not only along the
lines of ethnicity and gender but also along the lines of competing political ideologies. The especially deep ideological division within the movement was not between the socialists and the non-socialists. Instead, the
most pronounced ideological division was between those Jews who were

Communist party adherents and those who were socialists and opposed the Communist party in particular. In the needle trades, as in other sectors, Communist party supporters appropriated the term 'left wing' for themselves and labelled their opponents the 'right wing,' but the terminology is misleading since the 'right-wing' needle trades activists were socialists, not conservatives.[5]

Moreover, the 'right wing' itself was not ideologically uniform, for the anti-Communist activists represented a variety of different types of Jewish socialists, particularly Bundists,[6] Left Labour Zionists, Right Labour Zionists,[7] Trotskyists,[8] and Anarchists.[9] There were substantial differences between all these different sections of the Jewish left, leading to an ongoing debate within the left concerning the best strategies for the class struggle and the struggle to end the oppression of Jews, and also concerning the precise relationship between these two struggles. In contrast to the complexity and intensity of this debate, there was no comparable debate about strategies to promote women's rights or about the relationship between women's rights and these other struggles, for gender was simply not considered an important issue.

Within the Jewish left, important aspects of the debate focused on the question of Zionism as well as competing opinions on the lot of the Jews in the USSR. The Labour Zionists' antipathy to the Communists, for example, was heightened by the Soviet Union's opposition to the establishment of a Jewish homeland in Palestine. For their part, the Jewish Communists condemned the Labour Zionists as 'bourgeois nationalists' and maintained that 'the Jewish question' was being solved with the building of the Communist state in the Soviet Union. The anti-Communist Jewish socialists, however, were increasingly opposed to the Communists because of concern that there was significant anti-Semitism in Stalin's Russia, an allegation the Jewish Communists vehemently denied in this period. Thus the intense divisions between the Communists and the anti-Communists in the needle trades were deepened by the sharp disagreements between these two groups as to whether the Soviet Union really represented *the* solution to the plight of the Jews.

Yet while conflicting opinions on the solution to 'the Jewish question' intensified the split between the 'left-wing' Communist Jews and the 'right-wing' anti-Communist Jews, the sectarianism of the Communist party itself played a central role in heightening the conflict. After all, the Bundists and the Trotskyists, for example, were distinctly opposed to Zionism but were able to unite with the Labour Zionists in the anti-Communist camp nonetheless. Although there were serious ideological divi-

-conflict

sions between the different types of non-Communist Jewish socialists, they were all able to work together within the Jewish unions. In contrast, the ideological differences between the Communists, on the one hand, and the non-Communist socialists, on the other hand, led to fierce conflict within the needle trades unions, largely because of the Communist party's sectarian policies.

CCP's
.policy

During most of the 1920s, the Communist Party of Canada (CPC) generally pursued a policy of 'boring from within' the established unions, in the garment industry as in most other industrial sectors. Within the ILGWU, the ACW, the IFWU, and the United Cloth Hat, Cap, and Millinery Workers' International Union, Communists vied for leadership with anti-Communist activists. During this period, Canadian Communist groups within the established unions were linked together in the Trade Union Educational League (TUEL).[10] Communist sectarianism intensified dramatically, however, when the policy of the Communist Party of Canada underwent a significant change in response to the Sixth World Congress of the Communist International, held in mid 1928. On the basis of an analysis that humanity was entering a new revolutionary phase, the Sixth World Congress announced an emphasis on organizing new radical unions.[11] At about this time, the Industrial Union of Needle Trades Workers of Canada (IUNTW) was formed under Communist leadership.[12] By the end of 1929, the Communist Party of Canada had inaugurated the Workers' Unity League (WUL), which, superseding the TUEL, was intended to be the country's 'revolutionary trade union centre.'[13] In the words of the WUL's Draft Constitution, the Workers' Unity League was 'pledged to a program and policy of revolutionary struggle for the complete overthrow of capitalism and its institutions.'[14] The IUNTW soon affirmed its adherence to the WUL and then became an official affiliate in 1931.[15]

The IUNTW was intended as an industrial union that would encompass all branches of the needle trades, competing directly with the 'right-wing' garment unions. At its first convention, in mid 1929, the Communists optimistically reported that the IUNTW had already established Canadian locals of cloakmakers, capmakers, furriers, men's clothing workers, dressmakers, and raincoat-makers. It soon became clear, however, that, despite the Communists' ambitions, the IUNTW had become concentrated almost exclusively in the dress trade, both in Toronto and Montreal.[16] Because the Communists were not as strong in the other branches of the needle trades, the party's dual-union policy had to be modified considerably. This meant that although the broad outlines of the Communists' dual-union policy had been drawn in Moscow, the actual implementation of the policy varied between the different branches of the local clothing industry. Hence each union will be considered separately in the sections that follow. (Background information on each union is available in table 7 of the appendix.)

Another aspect of party policy during this dual-union period was the setting up of 'opposition groups' within the 'reformist' needle trades unions.[17] As explained by a 1931 CPC pamphlet, it was necessary to work within the established garment unions in order to 'turn into real struggles under our leadership the fake strikes, which the company unions organize to capture the markets. An inseparable part of the activities of the [IUNTW] is the organization of our opposition work inside the reformist unions, whose duty is not to help to build these unions, but to do all in their power to convince greater and greater sections of the needle workers of the need for the industrial union [the IUNTW], and the final driving off [of] the company union[s] from the field.'[18] Clearly, then, the purpose of the party's 'opposition work inside the reformist unions' was to discredit these unions and convince the other members of these unions to secede and join the IUNTW. Hence the party's work within the 'reformist unions' was integrally related to the party's task of building a separate, 'revolutionary' needle trades union.

In 1935, however, the policy of the Communist Party of Canada abruptly underwent another significant change. In that year, the Seventh World Congress of the Communist International announced the new policy of a 'United Front against Fascism,' ordering Communists all over the world to seek broad alliances with other groups in the fight against Fascism. In terms of the Canadian labour movement, this meant that the WUL was to be dissolved and folded into the Trades and Labour Congress.[19] As a result, the IUNTW was dissolved in early 1936, and its dressmakers joined the ILGWU.[20] The dismantling of the WUL marked the end of the CPC's dual-union phase, which had been known in party circles as the 'Third Period.'[21] Nevertheless, from 1936 to the onset of the Second World War, factional fights within Toronto's needle trades unions continued. Conflicts between Communists and anti-Communists were heated in certain branches of the needle trades, as both groups vied for power within the Jewish unions.

Throughout these twists and turns of party policy, the Communists played a divisive role within the Jewish labour movement. During the early period of 'boring from within,' the intensity of the intra-union factionalism tended to weaken the needle trades unions by undermining the workers' ability to unite solidly in their fights against the employers.

This divisiveness was sharply intensified during the Third Period. At a time when solidarity was desperately needed as workers reeled from the impact of the Great Depression, the Communist party's dual-union policy was particularly destructive to the garment workers' interests. Although the Communist-oriented Workers' Unity League made some positive contributions in other industrial sectors in the Third Period by organizing workers whom no one else had yet organized, the party's dual-union policy was detrimental in the garment industry.

The following detailed analyses of the impact of party policy focus particularly, although not exclusively, on the Third Period. Constituting almost half the years from the secret founding of the Communist Party of Canada to the start of the Second World War, the Third Period was especially important in terms of the party's overall impact on the Jewish labour movement. While party policy was particularly destructive during the dual-union stage, the Third Period also left a bitter legacy. The deep antipathy between the Jewish Communists and the Jewish anti-Communists did not disappear just because the party officially changed its line in the mid 1930s.

Within Toronto's Amalgamated Clothing Workers, in particular, serious factional fighting between Communist and anti-Communist groups dated back to the early 1920s,[22] but the fighting grew more intense in the mid 1920s even before the Third Period began. At that time, Jim Blugerman, a member of the TUEL, became the centre of the controversy. The conflict over Blugerman's status illustrates the deep divisions within the ACW during the Communists' early period of 'boring from within.'

When Blugerman ran for manager of Toronto's ACW in 1925, his opponent's declaration of victory led to Communist charges that the election results had been falsified. The charges were so serious that the ACW administration was forced to hold a new election, but, this time, the Toronto Joint Board took Blugerman's name off the ballot because he owed money to several of the employers. When Blugerman again attempted to stand for election a year later, he had to appeal to the general executive board to overturn the joint board's earlier ruling that he was ineligible for office.[23]

Blugerman's appeal to the ACW's GEB led to a detailed debate over the TUEL's role within this union. Although the GEB officially disqualified Blugerman from holding union office on the grounds of his indebtedness to certain garment manufacturers, the main issue at Blugerman's hearing was his involvement in TUEL activities. A committee of anti-Communist ACW activists from Toronto appeared at this hearing to ask the GEB to rule that no TUEL member could hold union office in this city. The spokesperson for this group stated that the Communist faction in Toronto's ACW was 'working at the direction [of] an outside body' and was 'dangerous to the union.' He charged that the Communists 'initiate new members in the locals and place them in the shops at lower wages displacing other members.' President Sidney Hillman replied that 'a member of the TUEL must have d[i]vided loyalty and therefore should be prohibited from holding office in the Amalgamated.'[24]

The committee of Toronto anti-Communists also gave the GEB copies of articles from *Der Kamf* (the Yiddish newspaper of the Communist Party of Canada) that 'contained characterizations of the officers of the [ACW] as hooligans, traitors, etc.' The committee's spokesperson stated that the TUEL continually attacked the union, especially through this newspaper. At Blugerman's hearing, the GEB focused on the fact that Blugerman was both a TUEL member and president of the association that published *Der Kamf*. GEB members sought to demonstrate that Blugerman was obligated to obey all TUEL decisions and was therefore potentially disloyal to the ACW. They also argued that he had to take responsibility for critiques of the ACW that were published in *Der Kamf*. The GEB concluded that 'members who have slandered and attacked the organization cannot run for office.'[25]

Despite Blugerman's setback, the Communist faction within the Toronto ACW in the mid 1920s was powerful. Although it was not able to control the Toronto joint board, members of this faction were elected to some important positions in the union's leadership.[26] At the end of 1927, however, the Toronto Communist faction suffered a serious electoral defeat. In response, the Communists charged that the anti-Communist faction had heavily intimidated workers during this election. The anti-Communists had allegedly threatened workers with losing their jobs and had brought in gangsters to add to the intimidation.[27]

As they vied for power within Toronto's ACW in the mid 1920s, the Communists campaigned on a platform of militancy. *Der Kamf* and other CP publications continually charged that working conditions were degenerating badly because the anti-Communist ACW leaders were consistently collaborating with the bosses, whereas the Communists, they declared, stood for aggressive unionism. Blugerman, for example, criticized the local anti-Communist leaders of the ACW for allegedly refusing to take a strong stand against the contracting out of work to non-union shops. He also argued that these leaders did nothing to lead a fight against the introduction of piece work, and he called for new union leaders who would mount a real fight against the bosses. The Communists' *Canadian Labour Monthly* added the claim that the anti-Communist faction was directly responsible for the loss of a large Toronto strike in 1926. According to the Communists, the 'right wing' had been more interested in winning power in Toronto than in winning the strike.[28]

In early 1928, factional conflict reached new heights as the ACW's Communists attempted to lead a general strike against the ACW's anti-Communist leadership. The strike was precipitated by the anti-Communist faction's decision to take action against anyone involved with *Der Kamf*'s continual critiques of the ACW leadership. The Toronto joint board declared that anyone caught distributing *Der Kamf* in the shops would be severely disciplined, and the board also called upon five members of the Communist faction to account for their allegedly slanderous statements in this newspaper. When these five failed to repudiate their statements, the board decided they would be fired from their jobs. Two of the five worked at Tip Top Tailors, where they were fired after having been expelled from the ACW.[29] (The union leadership was able to exercise this kind of power over jobs because the members of the employers' association had agreed to employ only union members.)[30]

The union leadership's power did not go unchallenged. The Communist faction called upon all Tip Top workers to strike and to demand the reinstatement of these two men. Forty-eight of the many Tip Top workers pledged to strike despite the joint board's warning they would lose their jobs. When the strike took place, the ACW leadership provided Tip Top management with replacements for the strikers. In response, the Communists called on all Toronto ACW members to revolt against the ACW leadership by striking. The Communists managed to pull some people out of one other shop, but the strike did not spread any further.[31]

The anti-Communist ACW leadership was clearly in control of subsequent events. Some of the Tip Top strikers soon defected, returning to work and apologizing to the joint board for responding to the Communists' strike call. The board expelled ten of the strike leaders from the union and also decided that two men, found distributing *Der Kamf* in the shops, would be fined and banned from all union meetings for a year. The ACW leadership felt that the Communists had lost considerable support as a result of this attempted general strike.[32] For the Communists, this defeat meant that as the Third Period began, they were in a weak position within the men's fine-clothing industry in Toronto. This weakness suggests why they did not, at this point, take a strong stand for dual unionism in this branch of the needle trades.

As the fight between the Communists and the anti-Communists continued within the ACW, a particularly dramatic clash erupted at the Shiffer
& Hillman factory in 1931. A detailed examination of this clash illustrates
the pitfalls of dual unionism. The incident began when the ACW's anti-
Communist leadership attempted to have Max Tohn, a member of the
Communist faction, fired from the firm because he was selling *Der Kamf*
on the shop floor. This was an ACW shop, but the shop chairperson and
many of the workers at Shiffer & Hillman were members of the Communist faction. They moved quickly to protect Tohn's job. Informing the
manufacturer they would not allow Tohn to be thrown out of the shop,
they managed to negotiate their own independent agreement with the
boss. According to Ed Tannenbaum, a member of the Communist faction
who was involved in the dispute, the manufacturer agreed to the new
arrangement because, 'from a boss's point of view, he likes to see strife
within the union. He likes to think that this will weaken the leadership.'[33]

When the employer agreed to keep Tohn and his friends at work, the
ACW leadership called a strike against Shiffer & Hillman. Although some
of the shop's workers did strike, the majority continued to work. However, the employer apparently needed to be supplied with a full set of
workers, and the ACW leadership charged that the Communists imported
ordinary strike-breakers from Hamilton and Montreal.[34]

In reporting this turn of events, the *Worker* (the party's English-language
newspaper) championed the cause of those who continued to work. It
denounced the 'fake strike' and proclaimed that 'this is not a strike for
workers but against workers.'[35] The newspaper explained that the ACW
leadership had no right to get a worker fired for having his own political
opinions. The party press also praised the Shiffer & Hillman workers for
negotiating a new, independent agreement with the firm and for having
'literally kicked the A.C.W. parasites off their backs.'[36] In a statement that
echoed party policy of the Third Period, the *Worker* proclaimed that the
real issue here was for the 'left wing' to smash the ACW. A letter from a
tailor to the editor explained that the struggle over the Shiffer & Hillman
shop had developed into a general fight against the ACW.[37]

The Communist press claimed that the ACW leadership was terrorizing
people in an attempt to prevent the Shiffer & Hillman workers from
going in to work. Ed Tannenbaum, who worked at this shop at the time,
recalled that when he tried to persuade the ACW's picketers to stop picketing the shop, they expressed fear they would lose their jobs if they
refused to picket. Tannenbaum also stated that the ACW leadership tried

to buy him off, offering him one of the very best jobs and a lot of money if he would leave Shiffer & Hillman. He stated that he refused this bribe in the name of fighting to preserve democracy in the union.[38]

After the ACW had been picketing the Shiffer & Hillman shop for two months, however, the employer switched sides, breaking his agreement with his workers and signing up with the ACW again. The people who had been working at the shop were then locked out; in turn, they declared a strike against both the ACW and the employer. Meanwhile, the ACW provided the boss with a new set of workers for his shop. The *Worker* charged that the boss had switched sides because the ACW gave him 'thousands of dollars' to help develop his business. The party also claimed that the ACW had agreed to a 30 per cent wage cut in this shop, whereas the Shiffer & Hillman workers had been fighting against wage cuts.[39]

It is difficult to evaluate all of the charges and counter-charges in this dispute, but this much is clear: the fight between the Communists and the anti-Communists obviously provided the owner of Shiffer & Hillman with a fine opportunity to play off one group of unionists against the other. Since both groups were dependent on courting the boss's favour, he was in a good position to manipulate the situation to his own advantage.

Yet the fights between the Communists and the anti-Communists continued. A 1932 debate in the pages of the *Yiddisher Zhurnal* summarized some of the arguments being made by the two opposing sides. One of the issues was democracy, for the Communists had criticized the ACW's leadership for suppressing democracy within the union. D. Nesbit, the anti-Communist business agent of Toronto's ACW, replied it was untrue that the ACW leaders had restricted democracy by not allowing union members to criticize the leadership. Nesbit's assertion is unconvincing, however, in view of the fact that the joint board minutes provide ample evidence that union members were being disciplined for distributing copies of *Der Kamf* in the shops.

Most of the debate centred on competing claims regarding which faction was better able to uphold the workers' interests on the shop floor. Nesbit wrote that the Communists were trying to take advantage of the fact that poor economic conditions were making the workers discontented. He suggested that instead of working to improve the workers' plight, the Communists were busy playing politics for their own ends. Nesbit maintained that when the Communists had had more power within the Toronto ACW, they had driven older workers out of the trade and had filled these workers' places with young workers who would vote for the Communists' proposals. He also charged that the Communist leaders had squandered union funds.

Nesbit denounced the Communists for their role in the Shiffer & Hillman dispute and charged that they had given this firm a free hand to give out pants to non-union contractors, thereby contributing to depressing the wages of Toronto's pantsmakers. In addition, Nesbit maintained that in the previous season members of the Communist group had called on the Toronto manufacturers to sign agreements with them and to throw the ACW workers out of their shops. He claimed that, in return, these Communists had offered the manufacturers 'revolutionary' workers who would work for 25 per cent less than the ACW's wage rate. According to Nesbit's account, this Communist plan did not succeed because the manufacturers knew that most workers did not support these Communists and because they also knew that the Toronto ACW was strong enough to defeat this group. Nesbit's group also charged that in Montreal, where the WUL supported a new union that had broken away from the ACW, this union had agreed to substantial wage cuts.[40]

Nesbit's opponents replied that it was the anti-Communist ACW leadership that had been agreeing so readily to wage cuts in the industry. The Communists also continued to claim that the ACW leadership was responsible for agreeing to speed-ups and the introduction of piece work. According to this account, the ACW should have mounted a major battle against speed-ups and piece work because these changes increased unemployment in the industry.[41]

The editor of the *Yiddisher Zhurnal*'s labour page chose to end this debate with a strong warning against dual unionism. 'When it comes to a split in the union, there arises a fight between the new and the old unions, and both sides call on the bosses for help,' he declared. 'In the end, the workers lose from this ... We believe in building, not in breaking,' he added. 'We want to applaud the workers who would altogether abolish the capitalist system, but to applaud these who call for civil war, this we will not do.'[42]

In the meantime, workers who had been expelled from the ACW for their Communist activities were no longer able to work in the ACW shops and were, therefore, filling up the non-union shops in Toronto's men's clothing industry. According to Tannenbaum (whose ties to the ACW had been severed as a result of his role in the Shiffer & Hillman dispute), the ACW did not want to organize these non-union shops because this would have meant having to take the ex-members back into the union.

In the aftermath of the Shiffer & Hillman dispute, Tannenbaum and other members of the Communist faction decided to organize the non-union shops themselves. Using the office of the Workers' Unity League as their meeting place, they formed the Tailors' Council and set to work. The

Tailors' Council succeeded in organizing ten of these shops and soon had enough of a dues base to hire a Communist as business agent. The Tailors' Council was able to win wage increases, and this helped the Communist group attract non-Communist workers who also worked in these shops. Leaders of the WUL, however, advised the leaders of the Tailors' Council to try to get back into the ACW rather than to maintain the Tailors' Council as a separate union. Despite some opposition to this advice within the Communist camp itself, the leaders of the Tailors' Council began negotiating with the ACW leadership about returning to the fold.[43] In effect, although the broad outlines of CPC policy in this period supported dual unionism, the dual-union approach in Toronto's men's clothing industry was being ruled out because so many of the workers had remained inside the ACW.

Yet the Tailors' Council was unable to join the ACW in 1933 because of the ACW's unwillingness to readmit the expelled members. A year later, the ACW's joint board finally agreed to take in most members of the Tailors' Council, but with the proviso that certain leaders of the council would not be allowed to run for ACW office for at least a year. Although the members of the Tailors' Council apparently agreed to this stipulation, the ACW still refused to readmit a few of the expelled Communists. It took yet another year before all the Communists were reinstated.[44]

In the meantime, the Toronto joint board had not stopped trying to suppress Communist activity in the trade. In 1935, for example, the board declared that 'some of our members are attending meetings called by the Communist group with the object to stir up trouble in our Organization.' The board then warned that 'members attending such meetings are liable to be disciplined and in the future this decision will be strongly enforced.'[45] A few years later, however, factional conflict between the Communists and anti-Communists finally diminished within Toronto's ACW.[46]

Like the Toronto ACW, the cloakmakers' branch of the Toronto ILGWU experienced deep divisions between the Communists and the anti-Communists in the party's early period of 'boring from within' and especially in the party's Third Period. The factional fighting in the cloak trade dated back to 1923 and, in the early years, included charges of election irregularities and libel. In one incident, a Communist activist was expelled from the Toronto joint board for refusing to condemn the Yiddish Communist press for its attacks on the anti-Communist leadership of the ILGWU. Some Communists did become ILGWU officials in Toronto, and, more generally, the Communist faction seems to have achieved considerable power within this Toronto union in 1926 and 1927.[47]

As the Communists began to organize the Industrial Union of Needle

Trades Workers in 1928, they called on the cloakmakers to withdraw from the ILGWU and join the IUNTW. Although some of the Toronto cloakmakers supported this idea, the majority chose to remain loyal to the ILGWU. The resulting decrease of Communist influence within the ILGWU by the end of 1928 was reflected in the following report to the ILGWU's general executive board: 'The administration of [ILGWU] Local #14, the largest [Toronto] local ... adopted a policy [in support of the IUNTW] and the officers sabotaged the work of the [ILGWU]. The membership, acting on a rule that drops an officer absent from three consecutive meetings, elected a temporary chairman and decided on special elections ... A new chairman, joint board and executive board delegates were elected. The Communists did not have the courage to run for office.'[48]

The IUNTW continued to appeal to the Toronto cloakmakers to leave the 'reformist union' and join the IUNTW. A 1929 appeal, for example, lambasted the ILGWU in no uncertain terms. Under the headline 'A Warning in Time! To All the Cloakmakers of Toronto!' the *Worker* proclaimed that 'the corrupt officials' of the ILGWU were responsible for 'the slave conditions' in the city's cloak factories. The newspaper 'warned the workers ... not [to] allow these betrayers to confuse you.' 'The International Bureaucrats' were allegedly 'unwilling and unable to organize ... for a real fight against the sweat shop conditions' because 'all they want is to collect a few dollars from the Cloakmakers to enable them to hold their jobs and live in comfort at the expense of the Cloakmakers.' In contrast, the *Worker* described the IUNTW as the union that really fights for the workers.[49]

As the ILGWU geared up for a general strike in Toronto's cloak trade at the beginning of 1930, the *Worker*'s attacks on the 'company union' increased. In an article entitled '"International" Chief Tries Another Betrayal,' the Communists alleged that the cloakmakers had been so discontented in 1924 that the ILGWU leaders had been forced to call a 'fake strike,' during which these leaders had 'deliberately sold out the workers behind their backs.'[50] Drawing a parallel between the earlier 'fake strike' and the situation in 1930, the Communists proclaimed: 'The Needle Trades Workers know very well that if a fake strike is called by [the ILGWU's president] (in agreement with the bosses) the settlement will be made between him and the bosses BEFORE THE STRIKE IS CALLED, the only thing to come out of it being the recognition and extension of the yellow dog company union known as the I.L.G.W.U.'[51] Shortly thereafter, the *Worker*'s announcement of the beginning of the ILGWU's strike appeared under the headline, 'Fakirs, Bosses and Police United in Fake Needle Trades Strike.'[52]

A later Communist editorial on this 'fake strike' claimed that issues such as wage increases and the forty-hour week 'were bargained away by the faker negotiators for the sole right to bargain with the bosses, in which bargaining they will be able to continue selling out the workers.' According to this account, 'the workers, lured by the bait of a few of [the ILGWU's original] demands, were swindled into supporting' the 'faker officials' of the ILGWU. The Communists once again warned the workers that 'the reformist leaders haven't a thought in the world other than serving the bosses, holding on to their fat salaries – and increasing them, and [preventing] the growth of real militant unions.'[53]

In contrast, the ILGWU's leaders claimed that the strike was a success. According to this account, 1600 to 1800 workers joined the strike and, after two weeks, won a new agreement with a 10 per cent increase in piece rates, time and a half for overtime, and better observance of the forty-four hour week. One of the Toronto ILGWU leaders reported to the head office that there was 'a 100% response from the workers to the [strike] call of the Union' and that due to the effectiveness of the strike, 'the Union now controls every large shop in the city and no worker is permitted to work in the shop unless he carries a working card of the Union.'[54] Although it is not possible to ascertain the outcome of the strike reliably, the pattern of competing claims is itself significant. This pattern was to repeat itself as the Third Period unfolded.

Meanwhile, in late 1930, the IUNTW was still firm in its determination to organize all needle trades workers rather than to concentrate exclusively on the dressmakers; they could not 'leave the rest of the needle trades workers in the old, corrupt company unions that are daily betraying the working class.'[55] Nonetheless, the Toronto cloakmakers failed to flock to the Communist union. Hence, the IUNTW in Toronto became restricted almost exclusively to the dress trade despite its ambitions, and most of the pro-Communist cloakmakers had to continue to operate from within the ILGWU. During the Third Period, although there were some Communists in a few leadership positions within Toronto's ILGWU, the anti-Communist faction was clearly in control of the union.[56]

Under 'right-wing' leadership, the ILGWU mounted a series of general strikes in Toronto's cloak trade in 1933, 1934, and 1935. The *Worker*, which stridently continued to censure the non-Communist needle trades unions as 'company unions,' either ignored the ILGWU's general cloak strikes or denounced them vehemently.[57] The repetitious denunciations of the ILGWU in the pages of the *Worker* provide a vivid impression of the narrow sectarianism of the party in the Third Period. Just about any strike by the 'reformist unions' was, by definition, a 'fake strike.' In mid 1934, for example, the *Worker* condemned the ILGWU's general strike under a headline that declared, 'Cloakmakers Incensed at Sell-Out.' Proclaiming 'This Must Be the Last Betrayal,' the article announced that the ILGWU had once again 'called a stoppage in the industry and then sent the workers back to worsened conditions.'[58] In contrast, the ILGWU's leaders, supported by the anti-Communist *Yiddisher Zhurnal*, claimed they had won this strike.[59]

The Communists similarly denounced another ILGWU general cloak strike in early 1935, charging that the workers were being kept in the dark while certain employers knew ahead of time what the strike settlement would be. A prominent IUNTW leader charged that this was 'the highest expression of class collaboration' because the ILGWU was supposedly 'using the larger manufacturers, such as Superior Cloak, Durable Cloak and others who are underpaying their labour, to allegedly unionize the trade, without improving the conditions of the workers in the larger shops.' The IUNTW leader claimed that, for the past two years, the ILGWU had 'allowed the Durable and Superior firms to produce garments approximately 25 per cent. cheaper than the smaller manufacturers.' 'The compensation that the union gets from the larger manufacturers for their services,' he stated, 'is that these bosses have introduced the check-off system of dues-collecting while the union overlooks the entire situation so far as wages and hours are concerned.'[60]

Once again, the ILGWU's version of the strike was quite different. Representatives of the Toronto joint board reported to the head office that they had reached a verbal agreement with the cloak manufacturers, who then turned around and repudiated the agreement. In response, the joint board called a general strike for shorter hours, increases in minimum wage rates, more uniform costs of production, and the limitation of the subdivision of labour. According to this account, the strike, which 'tied up almost 100% of the industry,' resulted in the winning of most of the union's demands.[61]

In connection with the ILGWU's series of general cloak strikes, the Communists also charged that regardless of whether the ILGWU's strike settlements looked good on paper, the workers usually returned to work only to find that the agreements were not being enforced. The Communists blamed this failure on the anti-Communist ILGWU leaders, usually implying that these allegedly corrupt 'right wingers' never had any intention of enforcing the agreements.[62]

In Toronto's needle trades in the Third Period, the polarization between the two sides was so intense that each side had a vested interest in discrediting the other side's leadership no matter what that leadership had actually done. In the cloak trade, where the anti-Communists were in power, the Communists' deliberate campaign to disparage the ILGWU's leaders was destructive. Such criticism was demoralizing for the union members, and it served to undermine the workers' solidarity at a time when unity against the employers was essential. The fact that the Communists denounced the ILGWU's strike plans both before and during the ILGWU's 1930 general cloak strike, for example, clearly undermined the strike's chances of success from the beginning. Indeed, the party stood to gain if the ILGWU's strikes failed, for such failures would presumably have helped the party lure workers away from the ILGWU and into the IUNTW. Yet the rank-and-file workers, suffering from drastic wage cuts in the middle of the Great Depression, were those who stood to lose if the ILGWU's general strikes failed.

The Communists' claim that these were 'fake strikes' is simply not convincing. These ILGWU strikes were legitimate attempts to improve the workers' poor wages and working conditions. Even if most of these strikes failed to result in lasting gains for the workers,[63] this was not because the ILGWU's leadership deliberately betrayed the workers time and time again. It was difficult for any union to make consistent progress in a period of such severe depression. Suffering from widespread unemployment and underemployment, Toronto's cloakmakers were in a highly vulnerable position.[64] Their position was being further weakened by the continual strife between the Communists and the anti-Communists.[65]

Of course, not all the criticisms made by the Communist faction were necessarily inaccurate. But the Communists' wholesale condemnation of ILGWU leaders as deliberately selling out the workers was surely untrue, as was their description of the ILGWU as a 'company union.' The very fact that the cloakmakers themselves did not flock to the IUNTW suggests that, despite the Communists' critique, most cloakmakers felt the ILGWU was satisfactorily representing their interests. The narrow sectarianism of the party in this period meant that devoted Communists were viewing these union issues through a seriously distorted lens.[66]

In the dress trade, however, Communist influence was stronger than in the cloak trade. Although the ILGWU had formed a dressmakers' local in Toronto as early as 1914 and had continued to organize the dressmakers for another decade, this union had focused more on organizing the cloakmakers. By the time the Third Period began, the ILGWU's work among the dressmakers had lapsed for at least several years, leaving a leadership vacuum in this branch of the needle trades. The Communists moved quickly to fill this vacuum.[67]

By the end of 1928, the Communists had begun to organize the dress-makers into the Industrial Union of Needle Trades Workers (IUNTW), and, by 1930, the IUNTW and the ILGWU were fervidly competing for the allegiance of the dressmakers. The Communists, of course, denounced the ILGWU as a company union. In early 1931, the IUNTW attempted to lead the Toronto dressmakers out on a general strike, despite the fact that the ILGWU had managed to organize a large group of dressmakers by that time.[68] The Communists' critique of the 'reformist' ILGWU was embodied in the following picket-line song:

Oy, the right-wing union,
She's a no-good union.
She's a socialist union –
By the Boss!

The right-wing cloakmakers
And the socialist fakers,
They is making by us
A double-cross!
So join the Industrial Union ...[69]

This appeal was not very compelling for most of the dressmakers, how-ever, for only a few hundred of the city's three thousand dressmakers joined the IUNTW's strike. The Communist union therefore had to call off the strike a week after it had started, and the Communists blamed their defeat directly on the 'labor fakers' of the ILGWU, proclaiming: 'It is obvious to all class-conscious workers that 75 per cent. to 80 per cent. of the dressmakers could have been organized were it not for the fact that the International [Ladies' Garment Workers' Union] has openly and deliberately acted as a scab agency. The first day of the strike they suc-ceeded in mobilizing all their forces in supplying scabs as well as terroriz-ing the workers in the shops not to answer the call of the Industrial Union [of Needle Trades Workers].' The leaders of the ILGWU did indeed tell the dressmakers not to join the IUNTW's strike, and, as in other dual-union situations, this division was an important factor in the manufac-turers' victory. The Communists announced that the dressmakers were furious with the ILGWU for condoning scabbing, yet the Communist analysis failed to come to terms with the ILGWU's apparent grip on a significant number of dressmakers.[70]

In the aftermath of the IUNTW's failed strike, the ILGWU began to prepare for its own general strike in the Toronto dress trade. The Communists warned the dressmakers that:

The reformist International Ladies' Garment Workers' Union, which during the dressmakers' strike, carried through organized scabbing, now talks of a 'stoppage' in the dress trade, in order, in this manner, to try to cover up its betrayal of the dress strikers. It should be obvious to every worker that this 'stoppage,' under the leadership of the International misleaders can be only a fake. The needle trades workers must not allow themselves to fall into this new trap of the International, but must rally for genuine struggle, exposing the fake 'stoppage' (if it does take place) and converting it, under the leadership of the Industrial Union, into a real fight for better conditions.[71]

Yet, according to the *Globe*, the party vacillated in its response to the ILGWU's attempt to call a general dress strike. On the eve of the strike, the party apparently instructed the dressmakers to ignore the ILGWU's strike call, but the party turned around a day later and ordered its supporters to join the strike.[72]

Seventeen hundred dressmakers joined the ILGWU's strike. The comparison between the response to this strike call and the response to the IUNTW's own strike call indicates that the ILGWU had more clout with the dressmakers at that time. Nevertheless, the ILGWU's strike was in trouble. *Der Kamf* maintained that, during the IUNTW's strike, the ILGWU had taught the bosses how to break strikes and that the bosses, having learned that lesson, were now applying it to break the ILGWU's strike. When the ILGWU finally called off the strike after about two months, the Communist press blamed the ILGWU 'Union Fakirs' for allegedly betraying the workers by calling off the strike. The ILGWU's strike was certainly not much of a success, for the union only managed to get agreements with shops employing little more than half of the strikers.[73] The severe competition between the two unions had significantly weakened the workers' ability to stand united against the dress manufacturers. The negative impact of this competition helps explain the failures of both the IUNTW and the ILGWU to win a decisive victory against the dress manufacturers in 1931.

In the aftermath of the ILGWU's failure, the IUNTW gained strength among the dressmakers. Moe Levin, a dressmaker who actively opposed the Communists, explained that at that time the IUNTW was clearly winning its fight with the ILGWU for control of this branch of the needle trades. According to Levin, the ILGWU ceased to be a significant factor in the dress trade for several years. Like many others, Levin had to belong to the IUNTW because the Communist union had organized the shop where he worked.[74]

Levin himself was one of the leaders of the opposition group that functioned within the IUNTW. According to Levin, this group, known as the Progressive Group, was composed of Right Labour Zionists, Left Labour Zionists, members of the Arbeiter Ring, and 'plain members who were not with the Communists.'[75] Levin, a Left Labour Zionist, explained that the Progressive Group included all those who felt that the dressmakers should be in the ILGWU, even though the ILGWU was not able to play much of a role in the Toronto dress trade at that time. Levin added that some people favoured the Progressive Group but would publicly vote with the Communist group because they were afraid they would be unable to hold jobs in IUNTW shops if they did not appear to be supporting the Communists. Levin stated that he himself was kept out of a job for a while, as part of the Communists' attempt to reduce his influence among the rank and file.[76]

In commenting on the nature of the arguments between the Progressive Group and the Communist leadership of the IUNTW, Levin maintained that the members of the Progressive Group used the same tactics against the Communists that the Communists were so often using against anti-Communist union leaders in other circumstances. When the Communist IUNTW leaders would announce the terms of settlement of a strike, explained Levin, 'we said: "You should have gotten more!"' 'In a union it's very easy to criticize,' Levin declared, further stressing that he would 'tear down' whatever agreement the Communists had managed to obtain. 'I was a revolutionary!' he proclaimed.

Moreover, Levin proclaimed that 'with them, it was *easy* to criticize' because for 'their existence they had to *pay* something to the manufacturers.' The manufacturers knew that the ILGWU was waiting to regain a foothold in the dress trade, so the manufacturers would tell the IUNTW leaders that if the Communists demanded too much, the employers would turn to the ILGWU instead. 'In order to control the people, to control the union,' maintained Levin, the Communist IUNTW leaders therefore had to 'give in' to the manufacturers. He stated that the Communists 'were only out to get political, political, political [goals]. As long as they got the control, that's their main purpose.'[77]

Levin's assertion points to the potential for manufacturers to solidify their power by playing off one union against the other in situations where two unions were directly competing with each other. In emphasizing the pitfalls of dual unionism, one need not necessarily agree with Levin's

claim that the Communists' political agenda vastly outweighed the Communists' commitment to good trade unionism. The main point, here again,
is that dual unionism strengthened management's hand.

Levin repeatedly argued that the dressmakers' hand could be significantly strengthened by rallying around the ILGWU, precisely because the
ILGWU had a strong base in the United States.[78] The Communists, in
contrast, attempted to promote the IUNTW as a specifically Canadian
union. For example, one IUNTW resolution declared that 'the I.U. of
N.T.W. of Canada, is a Canadian union, completely independent of any
United States organization.' But, 'while consolidation of the capitalist
state in Canada and the increasing differentiation between conditions of
the workers['] struggle here and in the United States makes necessary the
establishment of independent industrial organizations [in Canada], [the
Canadian needle trades workers understand that the] struggle of the
working class is an international struggle [that] demands the fullest
development of international unity and co-ordination of effort.'[79] Thus,
although the Communists did emphasize that the Canadian IUNTW would
have 'the closest possible fraternal relations' with other affiliates of the
Red International of Labour Unions, they also emphasized the IUNTW's
independence from the American labour movement.[80]

Although Jewish Communists, in accordance with the party line in this
period, maintained that Canadian unions should be independent with
respect to the American labour movement, this does not seem to have
been a salient point for most Jewish immigrants in the needle trades. As
Jacob Black (an anti-Communist activist in the IFWU) has indicated,
Toronto's Jewish garment workers generally felt that the American head
offices of the needle trades unions provided valuable assistance to the
Canadian locals. Black explained part of the basis for this willingness to
work closely with American needle trades union leaders: 'Maybe there's
an affinity of feeling that it's the same people [in the needle trades in
Canada and the United States], at least up until not too long ago. The
majority were Jewish workers also in the States. There was that affinity
that we know David Dubinsky [president of the ILGWU]. He comes from
Poland, the same place that I come from. So he's got the same beliefs I
have, so we can trust him. And we can rely on him to support us.'[81]

Although the emphasis on the IUNTW as a specifically Canadian union
does not seem to have been an important part of the IUNTW's attractive-
ness, Levin's opposition group was unable to make much headway within
the Communist union. For several years, the IUNTW was able to hold the
allegiance of a large group of dressmakers despite the efforts of the

Progressive Group. Although a significant number of Toronto's dressmakers remained unorganized, the IUNTW was fairly successful when it led a series of three general strikes in the dress trade in the mid 1930s.[82]

The Communist party's subsequent policy shift to the 'United Front against Fascism,' however, was to have crucial implications for the dressmakers. In early 1936, the Communist leaders of the IUNTW, having turned right around, led the organized dressmakers into the very union they had so heatedly denounced as a company union.[83] Negotiations for unity had begun in 1935 when the Communist International had adopted the new policy. The negotiations in Toronto's needle trades were stormy, as the Communists and anti-Communists each tried to manoeuvre to gain the upper hand.

In an early phase of the negotiations, the leaders of the IUNTW declared in a letter to the ILGWU's Toronto joint board that they 'deplore[d] the internecine warfare that has characterized the relations between parallel unions in the industry' and called for 'a united trade union movement.'[84] In the name of unity, the IUNTW representatives called on the ILGWU's leaders to meet with them in order to plan joint action on behalf of the Canadian needle trades workers.[85]

During the next several months, the IUNTW repeatedly called for unity on the basis of joint action by the two unions, whereas the ILGWU called for unity on the basis of the dissolution of the IUNTW. One IUNTW leaflet, for example, condemned the ILGWU's position and proclaimed:

Our union, as well as the whole Workers' Unity League, have been, and are at present, the only champions of unity of the trade union movement in Canada. We have stated time and time again that the division in the trade union movement into five different groups (A.F. of L., A.C.C. of L., W.U.L., Catholic and Independents) is not in the interest of the workers. With all our might and in the interests of all workers, we fight against splitting tactics, against disrupting workers' organizations – we fight for real unity of all trade unions on the basis of the fullest trade union democracy and militant policies.[86]

This leaflet insisted that the dressmakers did not want to give up the IUNTW and declared that 'all talk of dual unionism about our Dressmakers' Union is just plain misrepresentation' because 'there is Only One Dressmakers' Union in Toronto.'[87]

The ILGWU's supporters maintained that real unity was only possible with all women's clothing workers united under the banner of the ILGWU. One of the leaflets issued by the Progressive Group, for example, declared that 'one cannot maintain Dual Unionism and at the same time shout for unity.'[88]

Several ILGWU leaflets scathingly depicted the irony of the Communists' sudden change of policy. Proclaiming that the 'Red Messiahs' had 'brought civil war into the ranks of the workers' for years, the writers of one ILGWU leaflet expressed amazement that the Communist IUNTW leaders were now claiming to 'deplore the civil war ... and want Unity.' The writers of this leaflet also expressed surprise that 'the International Ladies' Garment Workers' Union that was the target for slander and abuse by the disrupters for the last 15 years and was branded as an agency of the bosses, has now become respectable [in the eyes of the Communists] and worthy of conferring with.'[89] In a similar leaflet, written in Yiddish, representatives of the ILGWU wondered how the IUNTW leaders could have 'the audacity to call on those to whom only yesterday they were giving such nice names as bureaucrats, misleaders, [and] sell-outs.'[90]

The debate continued with representatives of each side claiming they were the only ones who stood for real unity. As the new party policy of the 'United Front against Fascism' became more entrenched elsewhere, however, the precariousness of the Toronto IUNTW leaders' position became apparent. Finally, a member of the Progressive Group was able to write to the ILGWU's head office that the IUNTW leaders now wanted to arrange for the dressmakers to join the ILGWU as quickly as possible. An arrangement for a joint administration was worked out, whereby the Communist and anti-Communist groups were both to have a share in the leadership of the ILGWU's dressmakers' section. Then, in early 1936, the IUNTW leaders dissolved the IUNTW and brought over a thousand dressmakers into the ILGWU.[91]

The dissolution of the IUNTW did not, however, end the fighting between the Communists and the anti-Communists in the dress trade, for both groups went on to jockey for position within the expanded ILGWU. Despite the provisions for a joint administration, the Communists, according to a key anti-Communist union leader, were soon 'practically in control' of the ILGWU's dressmakers' section.[92] The Progressive Group fought back.

In a dramatic incident in 1938, a representative of the Progressive Group used the Yiddish press to publicize charges that the Communist leaders of the ILGWU's dressmakers' section were not militant enough. He claimed that the Communists were unwilling to mount an organizing drive to reach the unorganized dressmakers and that the Communist leaders were making unwarranted concessions to the bosses in the union-ized shops without the knowledge of the workers. He also maintained that the Communist union leaders discriminated against non-Communists when distributing jobs in the shops.[93]

In response, the Communist union leaders brought formal charges against this representative of the Progressive Group for publishing 'slan-derous statements against our Union and its officers and leadership and which is a fabrication of lies and falsehoods.'[94] During the hearing, the Communists sought to suspend this man's union rights and argued that it was not in the interest of the workers to discuss the union's weaknesses 'in a newspaper which is being read by the bosses.'[95] This incident echoed the relations between Communists and anti-Communists within the ACW – with the roles reversed.

Such factional fighting undoubtedly weakened the ILGWU, as both sides must have realized. In several letters to the president of the ILGWU, for example, Communist leaders discussed the need to hammer out a new accord with the Progressive Group because they felt that a 'unified leadership' was necessary for the union to mount a strong campaign to organize the unorganized Toronto dress shops.[96] Although various efforts were made to work out such an accord, factionalism continued to be a serious problem in the ILGWU's dressmakers' section.

Among Toronto's fur workers, as among Toronto's dressmakers, dual unionism proved detrimental. Although dual unionism emerged in a different pattern in Toronto's fur industry, the eventual development of two rival fur unions led to intense interunion competition that was not in the workers' best interests.

In the mid 1920s, there was significant support for the Communists within Toronto's IFWU,[97] but this did not lead to dual unionism during the Third Period. Although dual unionism was a central feature of the fur industry in New York in the Third Period,[98] a 1929 directive in the *Worker* explained that the time was not yet right for Toronto's IFWU workers to join the IUNTW. The newspaper stated that although the Communists had many supporters among Toronto's Jewish fur workers, there was, as yet, very little Communist support in the city's two non-Jewish IFWU locals. The Communists were not against secession as a matter of principle, explained the *Worker*, but this simply was not the time for the Toronto fur workers to secede. The city's pro-Communist furriers were advised to work within the IFWU to try to develop more support so as to be able eventually to win over the union as a whole for the IUNTW.[99]

Toronto's IFWU members never were won over to the IUNTW as a group, and hence most of the city's pro-Communist fur workers remained within the IFWU during the Third Period.[100] The leadership of the Toronto IFWU, however, was captured by the anti-Communist group, headed by Max Federman.[101] The Communists then proceeded to denounce the 'right-wing' IFWU administration. These denunciations followed the same formula that the Communists were using in the ILGWU and the ACW. From the Communists' point of view, the anti-Communist leaders were 'agents of the bosses.'[102]

The denunciations of the 'bureaucratic reformist leaders and boss-controlled officials'[103] had to be modified somewhat, however, when the IFWU's 'right-wing' leadership led the Toronto collar and cuff workers in a successful general strike in 1933. The success of this strike did not lead the Communists to change their evaluation of the anti-Communist leadership. Instead, the Communist press insisted: 'Although generally substantial gains were won by the furriers, greater success could have been secured had there been more militant leadership than that given by the union officials. Settlements were made in some shops without the consent of the workers, and the officials generally advocated a policy of retreat. The great militancy of the strikers, the militant picketing and the influence of left wing furriers were responsible for the gains secured.'[104]

Although the fur collar and cuff workers remained inside the Toronto IFWU in this period, as did those who made fur coats, the Workers' Unity League did organize a group of Toronto's fur dressers and dyers. (The dressing and dyeing branch of the fur industry was totally separate from the shops where fur collars, cuffs, and coats were made from skins that had already been dressed and dyed.)[105] According to the Communist press, the IFWU had not been able to organize the fur dressers and dyers in Toronto. The Communists maintained that the major breakthrough in this branch of the needle trades occurred when the WUL led a successful strike at the large Hallman and Sable shop in 1933. This was an impressive victory, especially since the shop was composed largely of unskilled workers from over a dozen different ethnic groups. According to the *Worker*, the anti-Communist Federman tried to take over the WUL's organizing drive at this shop, but the workers remained loyal to the WUL. The Hallman and Sable workers then formed the nucleus of the WUL's Fur Dressers' and Dyers' Union.[106] When the Communist party's line changed in 1935, however, the Fur Dressers' and Dyers' Union sought affiliation with the IFWU. The general executive board of the IFWU finally agreed to grant these Toronto dressers and dyers an IFWU charter in April 1936.[107]

The 1935 change in the party's line also led to the reunification of the New York furriers. This development was to have important implications for Toronto, particularly because it led to Communist control of the IFWU's head office.[108] At the initiation of the head office, Max Federman, the main anti-Communist leader of Toronto's IFWU and one of the few remaining anti-Communist members of the IFWU's GEB, was then charged with the misappropriation of local union funds.[109] Irrespective of Federman's guilt or innocence,[110] the whole affair dramatically deepened the divisions among Toronto's fur workers. The Communists' supporters denounced Federman for allegedly being a crook, while the anti-Communists' supporters rallied to his defence and denounced the Communists for allegedly framing him.[111]

As the attack against Federman gained momentum, political factionalism intertwined with ethnic divisions. 'It was not enough for Federman to control the two Jewish locals,' the Communists charged, 'it was not enough for him and his supporters to steal thousands of dollars, but he succeeded in instigating a fight between the Jewish and Gentile workers [within Toronto's IFWU].'[112] The anti-Communists countercharged that it was the Communists who were responsible for heightening ethnic tensions within the union.[113] Yet, as Ed Hammerstein has suggested, the non-Jews were probably alienated from both the Communist Jews and the anti-Communist Jews because the non-Jews did not want to get involved in these political fights. Speaking of the non-Jewish fur workers, Hammerstein explained that 'their position was "a curse on both your houses!"'[114]

In the meantime, the IFWU's general executive board expelled Federman from the union,[115] and this led directly to dual unionism in Toronto's fur industry. After his expulsion, Federman obtained a charter from the American Federation of Labor and formed a new Toronto fur union, consisting of several hundred supporters.[116] At that time, the IFWU was an affiliate of the CIO, so the fight between the two fur unions became part of the broader fight between the AFL and the CIO.[117] Within the city's fur industry, the fight between the two unions was intense. In 1938 and 1939, the two unions were in direct competition, as members of each union tried to win particular shops over to their own side. In certain instances, the competition between the two unions led to fist fights between workers,[118] and members of both sides accused each other of using gangsters to beat up workers who opposed them.[119]

Ed Hammerstein recalled the sharp conflict between the two unions in the shop where he worked. This shop, where the pro-Communist Hammerstein served as shop chairperson, remained with the IFWU at first. Federman's group, however, had a small contingent of supporters in the shop, and, according to Hammerstein, they collaborated with the employer to try to win the shop over to Federman's AFL union. When the employer needed some new workers for his shop, Federman's group managed to bring more of their supporters into the shop. Hammerstein and his group then called a strike in order to get the new people out of the shop and keep the shop in the IFWU. When they went out on strike, however, Federman's group sent more supporters in to replace them. As a result, the shop swung to Federman's AFL union, and Hammerstein lost his job.[120]

Another fight between the two unions led to an IFWU strike at the Herman Fur Company. A representative of the Department of Labour who investigated this strike concluded that wages and working conditions were not the real issues and that the strike was the product of the struggle between the two rival fur unions. This official reported that the IFWU was picketing the Herman shop with signs proclaiming there was a strike going on, while the AFL fur union was picketing the shop with signs stating there was no strike there.[121] According to the Communist press, Federman's faction was supplying Herman's with strike-breakers. After striking for three months, however, the IFWU finally won a closed-shop contract with Herman's.[122] Unpublished IFWU records reveal that IFWU officials felt they had had to make a number of concessions to obtain this contract because Federman had been offering the firm a very poor agreement.[123]

While the Communists charged that Federman's group was making 'every effort to destroy the workers' [hard-won] conditions,'[124] representatives of Federman's union charged that the Communist leaders of the IFWU were not really interested in the shop-floor problems of the workers but were instead interested only in maintaining Communist control over the fur workers. The anti-Communists maintained that working conditions were deteriorating badly in the IFWU shops in Toronto and that the Communist leadership was doing nothing about this decline. They charged that the Communist officials were not trying to enforce their contracts with the fur employers and were even encouraging the growth of contracting in the fur industry.[125]

Given the intense competition between the two fur unions, it was hard for either union to do much to uphold the workers' interests against the employers. Indeed, the IFWU's Communist leaders privately admitted in mid 1938 that the fight with Federman meant they had had to make some concessions in the agreements with the Toronto employers.[126] In a recent interview, Lou Lipsky, an active member of Federman's AFL union, reflected on the problem of dual unionism in Toronto's needle trades in the interwar period: '[Dual unionism] wasn't very helpful in terms of getting [better] conditions for the workers because obviously this existence [of dual unions] could be utilized by the employers for their purposes, to try to get better conditions for [the employers] themselves ... And so the employers begin to side with [whichever union] they can best deal with.'[127]

The fights between the two fur unions undoubtedly weakened both unions in their fight against the bosses. In situations of such intense competition between two rival unions, the employers were in a good position to try to play off one group of unionists against the other. The claims that working conditions in the Toronto fur industry were degenerating in the late 1930s are convincing. Alongside the Depression itself, the explanation for this degeneration lies in the pitfalls of dual unionism.

In general, the fights between the Communists and the anti-Communists in Toronto's needle trades unions were often closely related to electoral struggles outside the unions. By the early 1930s, the 'right wing' of the Jewish labour movement was closely associated with the CCF, and actively opposed Communist party candidates for government office.[128] In the Jewish district, one of the most prominent Communist candidates was Joe Salsberg. Linked to the IUNTW, Salsberg frequently ran for provincial and municipal office in the 1930s.[129] In the autumn of 1937, for example, when Salsberg ran for the provincial legislature, his CCF opponent was Harry Simon, an important 'right-wing' leader of the furriers' union.[130] Similarly, when municipal elections were held one or two months later, Salsberg ran for City Council and was opposed by the CCF's H.D. Langer, another key 'right-wing' union leader, in this case from the ILGWU.[131]

This direct competition for government office heightened the factionalism within the needle trades unions.[132] During the municipal elections of late 1937, for example, bitter battles took place within the Jewish unions over whether the unions should endorse Salsberg or Langer. The conflict within the ILGWU was described by the ILGWU's Communist business agent as follows: 'The Cloakmakers['] Joint Board, after a heated debate, endorsed Langer and refused to endorse Salsberg. This action harmed the good work done by both groups to achieve a united and harmonious union. The [union's] local meetings are becoming battle-grounds, and I am certain that there will be no unanimity in any local on this question. It is brought into the shops, and becomes extremely injurious to our [union].'[133]

Much of the fighting between the Communists and anti-Communists within the needle trades unions was over political issues rather than over specific shop-floor issues. In addition to fighting over which candidates to endorse during municipal and provincial elections, there were fights within these unions concerning whether to donate money to particular 'left-wing' or 'right-wing' causes. Such fights had little to do with working conditions on the shop floor, yet this did not stop the two factions from battling it out on these kinds of political issues.

In a recent interview, Sol Abel, a pro-Communist cloakmaker, focused on these battles over political issues. Abel declared that, generally, he wished that both factions within Toronto's ILGWU had concentrated more on improving working conditions than on fighting each other. When asked to describe the factional fights, Abel, a member of the Joint Board, explained: 'When we came to a Joint Board meeting, there was a division, right and left. The left did have very few people there. And we were discussing, [for example,] a letter from the *Worker*. [The letter asked the ILGWU to donate money for a greeting from the union which would be printed in this Communist newspaper.] Now we could've wasted two and a half hours discussing that issue [at the joint board meeting]. To me, this was not union work.' Abel recalled that he and another 'left-wing' member of the joint board disagreed over how to handle this kind of situation. He described telling his ally that 'instead of wasting two and a half hours' discussing a greeting in the *Worker*, 'let's [spend] the two and a half hours *on the trade*' in order 'to better the conditions in the trade.' Abel explained, however, that he could not convince the other pro-Communist member of the joint board to accept this change in approach.[134]

Jacob Black, a 'right-wing' leader of the furriers, similarly described the kinds of issues the Communists and anti-Communists used to fight over within the IFWU: 'it was all political, nothing else, mainly political.' Black explained that support for the CCF was one of the major issues of contention within the furriers' union, and he indicated there were continual fights within the union over resolutions supporting various political causes. When asked if there were fights about specific shop-floor issues, he replied there were not. Black declared: 'Our biggest fight with the Communists was because they were trying to use the unions as political footballs for their own ends.'[135]

Yet the Communists themselves have often argued that there were important differences between them and the anti-Communists with respect to shop-floor issues, and they continually campaigned on a platform of union militancy. The Communist press opposed those union leaders who attempted to encourage union-management cooperation in order to stabilize the garment industry. Such cooperation was denounced as 'class collaboration.' Both the *Worker* and *Der Kamf* contained numerous articles which vociferously opposed piece work in the garment shops.[136] Both newspapers specifically opposed the arbitration of shop-floor grievances in the needle trades, on the grounds that the 'impartial' arbitrator was bound to favour the employers.[137] The Communist needle trades unionists continually denounced their opponents for allegedly being unwilling to lead the workers in a real fight for higher wages and better working conditions.

The Communists' militant rhetoric cannot be taken at face value. When one's own faction is out of power in a particular union, it is easy to criticize the union leadership as not being militant enough. It is easy to proclaim that a better leadership would have been able to wrest more gains from the employers. It is hard (for the historian as well as for the participants in such arguments) to prove or disprove such claims. The important point is that both the Communists and the anti-Communists made these kinds of claims in situations where they were out of power. The Communists, who were more often out of power in the Jewish unions, criticized the 'right-wing' leaders of the ACW, the ILGWU, and the IFWU in this fashion. Within the IUNTW, in contrast, anti-Communists such as Moe Levin criticized the Communist leadership in the same way. Although Communist claims that the ACW was not militant have some foundation, in view of the fact that the ACW did not mount general strikes in this period, the ACW leadership presumably felt that general strikes would not have been able to produce important gains in the midst of the Depression. In addition, while the Party's denunciation of the ACW's lack of militancy has some credibility, the party's repeated denunciation of the ILGWU's general cloak strikes as 'fake strikes' undermines the party's credibility and indicates that 'real militancy' was being defined in an intensely sectarian way.

Moreover, there is compelling evidence that the Communists' opposition to piece work was more rhetorical than real. When recently asked about the issue of piece work, Joshua Gershman, one of the key Communist leaders in the needle trades, explained that the Communists were opposed to piece work because they felt it was used to speed up the workers. He contrasted this position with the position of Sidney Hillman, president of the ACW, who supported the introduction of piece work in Toronto in order to help the employers increase production and keep their costs low.[138] However, Gershman indicated that although the Communists often stated their opposition to piece work, they did not mount a real struggle against it because that would have been unrealistic. Gershman stated that the main struggle around which the 'left wing' mobilized was to raise wages by trying to win higher piece rates. He suggested that the *Worker*'s frequent articles against piece work were misleading to the extent that they gave the impression that opposition to piece work was a big issue for the Communists in the needle trades.[139]

[On the issue of arbitration, there was a real difference between the Communists and the anti-Communists, but the difference was not as clear-cut as the Communists maintained. While the Communists were united in their opposition to arbitration, there were important divisions within the 'right wing.' The Communists' opposition to the arbitration of grievances was not just rhetorical. The IUNTW's agreements with the dress manufacturers did not have arbitration provisions even though the manufacturers had pushed for these provisions as part of the agreements.[140] In contrast, both the ACW and the ILGWU had agreed to a system of arbitration.[141] Yet, within the ILGWU's 'right wing,' there was significant opposition to the establishment of arbitration machinery.[142] Moreover, the IFWU, even when it was under anti-Communist leadership, did not agree to arbitration. 'Right-wing' IFWU leaders such as Jacob Black seem to have felt at the time that arbitration was not a good idea for their union.[143] Thus, it was not just the Communists who opposed arbitration in the needle trades unions.]

The fact that there were important divisions within the 'right wing' is also revealed in a confidential letter H.D. Langer wrote to the ILGWU's head office in 1935. Langer, who was sympathetic to Right Labour Zionism, wrote to President Dubinsky:

I take charge of cases before the Impartial Chairman, who is not being paid[,] and therefore the least one can do to retain his good will is to humor him and take him out occasionally. One must do the same with a few leading employers. It is in this manner that I have created some prestige for the local [union] leadership, so that we can now manage ourselves. But all this expense is not provided for. In fact I cannot often mention it, with Magerman [one of the other 'right-wing' leaders of Toronto's ILGWU]. A left *Poale* Zionist [Left Labour Zionist] cannot approve of such methods of class struggle, let alone provide funds.[144]

Instead of simply a clear-cut division between Communists and anti-Communists, there were important divisions within the anti-Communist camp.

The Communists were inaccurate in lumping all anti-Communists together and labelling them all as opponents of militancy. Although the ACW was notably less strike-prone than the ILGWU during the Third Period, the Communists made no real distinction between the two unions. It seems that, from the perspective of the party during the Third Period, the only 'real' strikes were the ones that were led by the Communists themselves. From this perspective, all anti-Communist needle trades activists were 'bosses' agents,' 'betrayers,' 'labor fakers,' and 'social fascists.' This perspective was part and parcel of the party's commitment to dual unionism in this period.

Although the dual unionism in the needle trades was largely the product of Communist party policy, the anti-Communists were not wholly without responsibility for the detrimental interunion rivalry that developed. Divisive tactics were used by both sides. After all, according to the ACW's own records, this union expelled members of the Communist faction for publishing criticisms of the ACW leadership in *Der Kamf,* and these expulsions paved the way for the establishment of the Communist-led Tailors' Council. Moreover, in the furriers' branch of the needle trades the process was reversed: here it was the anti-Communists who started a dual organization after some of them had been expelled from the IFWU.

Yet most of the responsibility for dual unionism lies clearly with the Communists. The shift to dual unionism in Toronto's needle trades in 1928 was part of a world-wide Communist party strategy. This strategy was designed to use the party's new 'revolutionary' unions to win over the working class and bring about the revolution. The Communists believed that the Communist party was the midwife of history, the *sine qua non* of socialist revolution. From this point of view, the interests of the party were necessarily paramount. Thus, for the Communists, the shop-floor issues in the needle trades were engulfed by larger political issues. The party's dual-union strategy was costly for the garment workers, and, in the party's own revolutionary terms, the strategy failed.

Joshua Gershman, one of the party's most important IUNTW leaders, has come to feel that the party erred in its shift to dual unionism. In an interview in the mid 1970s, he stated: 'In retrospect, I think that the decision made in those years by the Profintern, the Red International of Trade Unions, in favour of establishing separate trade union centres outside of the orbit of the official trade union movement was a mistake.' He explained:

In my opinion, in retrospect, the very fact that in 1934 and '35, we had to decide to liquidate the Workers['] Unity League and go back into the fold of the AF of L and the CIO, proved that, in my opinion, in my personal opinion, that while there were terrific achievements recorded by the Workers' Unity League, and in the unions that we helped to organize, in the needle trades and the furniture and steel and many others, from the point of view of the long range perspective, as a revolutionary party and a revolutionary movement, in my opinion, it was a mistake.[145]

The Workers' Unity League did, as Gershman suggests, make some positive contributions to the garment workers' well-being. The Communists deserve credit, for example, for their ability to organize the unskilled and ethnically diverse fur dressers and dyers of the Hallman and Sable shop. They also deserve credit for their ability, under the banner of the IUNTW, to organize a large group of dressmakers.

Yet these positive contributions must be seen within the overall context of the harmfulness of the party's policy of dual unionism. In the case of the dressmakers, for example, the rival general strikes of early 1931 point clearly to the dangers of dual unionism, for the intense fight between the two unions fundamentally undermined the dressmakers' ability to fight the manufacturers. Although it is true that the IUNTW later managed to organize a substantial number of dressmakers, the dressmakers could presumably have been organized more effectively if both the Communists and the anti-Communists had been able to work together within one union.

Other incidents such as the Shiffer & Hillman dispute show clearly that the intense conflict between the Communists and the anti-Communists enabled the bosses to play off one set of workers against another. Instead of focusing more on the main fight for better working conditions and higher wages, 'left-wing' and 'right-wing' needle trades activists spent a great deal of energy in all-out battles with each other. As garment workers suffered the ravages of the Depression, their need for solidarity was crucial. The dual unionism of this period, as well as the intense political factionalism within the unions, fundamentally undermined the garment workers in their fight against the manufacturers. Toronto's Jewish labour movement was thus torn apart by the intense fighting between Communist and anti-Communist Jews, at a time when the movement had already been experiencing serious problems in attempting to organize the non-Jews as well as the Jews and the women as well as the men.[146]

Conclusion

The Toronto cloakmakers and dressmakers who applauded eagerly and pitched their hats into the air as the bars of the 'The Internationale' filled their meeting hall in the heady days of 1919 were building one of the most advanced labour movements working people have ever created in North America. In addition to collective bargaining, the Jewish needle trades unions encompassed important social, cultural, and political dimensions. They formed a dynamic movement, born out of the vigorous reactions of a displaced people who had fled from the persecutions of the Old World to find themselves thrust out of necessity into the sweatshops of Spadina Avenue. Toronto's Jewish labour movement was fundamentally shaped by Jewish socialists who were dedicated to creating a new Garden of Eden where they would find freedom from both class domination and anti-Semitism.

Within the city's Jewish labour movement, the commitment to the class struggle was highly developed, distinguishing this movement from the more conservative unionism that characterized many Canadian and American trade unions in this period. Many Jewish workers had a strong sense of themselves as members of a working class that was in opposition to the bosses. For the leaders of the movement, as well as a significant section of the rank and file, this consciousness was augmented by the vision of an alternative socialist society. The socialists viewed strikes not only as a means to improve harsh sweatshop conditions but also as a crucial part of the larger class struggle that would eventually transform society.

-socialist's view to transform society

Toronto's Jewish unionists were rooted in a vital Jewish working-class culture that wove together the two principal strands of their identity and promoted an activist response. For the Jewish socialists especially, class consciousness and ethnic identity reinforced each other and intensified the commitment to radical social change: most had been radicalized not only in response to class oppression but also in response to the oppression they faced as Jews. Those who became Communists in the aftermath of the Russian Revolution, for example, were especially drawn to the party because they believed the Soviet Union represented an end to *both* class exploitation and anti-Semitism. The socialist currents within the immigrant Jewish community were reinforced by key themes of Yiddish literature, and some Jewish socialists also drew inspiration from Judaism's Messianic vision and the Hebrew prophets' message of social justice.

A strong Jewish working-class culture thus evolved despite the fact that a significant number of Toronto's Jewish workers were employed by Jewish garment manufacturers by the interwar years. Although family and community ties between Jewish workers and Jewish manufacturers sometimes dampened worker militancy, these ties also sometimes motivated the manufacturers themselves to make concessions to the fellow Jews who worked for them. Despite significant ties across class lines, however, bitter class conflict often erupted between Jews in Toronto's needle trades, testifying to the militancy of Jewish working-class culture and the economic pressures of competing class interests.

The Jewish labour activists, so deeply committed to both their class and ethnic identities, experienced profound difficulties in trying to incorporate their non-Jewish fellow workers into the Jewish unions. Although the Jewish and non-Jewish garment workers were sometimes able to work together within the unions, deep divisions occurred, particularly when the non-Jews failed to join Jewish strikers or when ethnic tensions led to dual unionism. In addition to the problem of communication between the Yiddish-speaking Jews and the predominantly English-speaking non-Jews, ethnocentrism and significant anti-Semitism fuelled these divisions. Ethnic divisions were also intensified by the different roles the two groups sometimes played in the labour process. Moreover, while the Jews' commitment to their unions was strengthened by the unions' response to Jewish concerns as well as to class concerns, the fundamental Jewishness of the Jewish unions probably alienated non-Jews.

Toronto's Jewish union leaders also experienced grave difficulties in trying to incorporate women garment workers, particularly non-Jewish females, into the labour movement. Although there were many cases

barriers faced by women

where women and men walked the same picket lines, the women were, on the whole, less prone to participate in union and strike activities, and there were many women workers whom the movement never succeeded in organizing. The women faced substantial barriers stemming from their particularly vulnerable position on the shop floor, from heightened employer intransigence, from heavy household responsibilities, and from the male-centred nature of the unions themselves. The Jewish unions generally did not develop special policies to appeal to the women; in fact, certain union policies, such as the common structure of wage demands, privileged the men. Moreover, the Canadian women's movement, led mainly by middle-class Anglo-Saxons and Celts, seldom helped Toronto's female garment workers.

Despite these difficulties, there were a significant number of women whose militancy contributed to the growth of the city's needle trades unions. Some of the Jewish women in particular played vigorous roles at considerable self-sacrifice. These deeply committed female Jewish activists shared the male Jewish activists' intense commitment to class and ethnic identity and acted courageously. They did not, however, develop strong feminist perspectives of their own experiences on the shop floor or within the unions. While a few women attained lower-level leadership positions, the pro-union women were basically incorporated into the Jewish labour movement on the basis of an implicit acceptance of their own subordination as women.

not feminist

The commitment to ethnic identity within the Jewish labour movement provides a counterpoint to the movement's systematic subordination of women's issues to class issues. In addition to providing a counterpoint, the intensity of ethnic concerns provides part of the explanation for the subordination of women's issues. Within Toronto's Jewish labour movement, the emphasis on both class consciousness and ethnic identity inhibited the development of feminist perspectives.

The very nature of their class analysis meant that the Jewish socialists stressed the common oppression of female and male workers; at the level of their articulated socialist ideology there was little recognition that women workers faced special constraints. While their class consciousness obstructed a strong awareness of women's oppression *as women*, it did not obstruct a forceful emphasis on anti-Semitism. From a class point of view, the critique of feminism was that an emphasis on women's rights would weaken the working class by dividing female and male workers, as the Communist party emphasized in its 1931 declaration that there was 'no room for "feminism" in our movement.'¹ Any vision of the common oppression of women, which transcended class, threatened to dilute the class struggle.

Clearly the same arguments could have been made about ethnicity. These socialists might have argued, but did not, that a focus on Jewish rights should be avoided – precisely because it would weaken the working class by dividing Jewish workers and non-Jewish workers. Yet, as we have seen, most Jewish socialists were intensely committed to Jewish rights and Jewish identity and had a profound awareness of ethnic differences within the working class. To a certain extent, Jewish socialists did fear that an emphasis on the common oppression of Jews, which transcended class, threatened to dilute the class struggle. This did not stop them, however, from being deeply committed to the fight against anti-Semitism – a fight that sometimes saw them allied with the Jewish garment manufacturers.

While the socialists' emphasis on the common oppression of all workers, regardless of gender, undermined the development of feminist perspectives, the deep ethnic concerns of the Jewish activists also undermined such a development. Because Jewish working-class women shared a common sense of oppression with many of the men in the immigrant Jewish community, not only as fellow workers but also as fellow Jews, the women were less apt to develop a clear critique of their position as women within this community. Since the family was seen as central to the perpetuation of Jewish culture, a serious feminist challenge to the traditional norms and role structures of the Jewish family would have been viewed as a dangerous cultural threat. Nevertheless, this emphasis on the welfare of the Jewish community as a whole, this perceived need for Jews to pull together in the face of serious anti-Semitism, did not prevent Jewish workers from pursuing their own class interests in opposition to the Jewish manufacturers.

Both class consciousness and ethnic identity were definitive in shaping the politics of Toronto's Jewish labour movement – despite the fact that class issues functioned divisively within the Jewish community and ethnic issues functioned divisively within the working class. By contrast, a developed commitment to feminism did not emerge, partly because of its divisive potential within both the Jewish community and the working class. Yet the Jewish labour movement was already fragmented along gender lines to a certain extent, not because women workers put forth feminist demands on the shop floor or within the unions themselves but because the movement was unable to incorporate the many women workers who remained unorganized.

One of the sharpest divisions within the Jewish labour movement developed out of an altogether different set of concerns: the movement became intensely divided along the lines of political ideology throughout much of the interwar period. The ideological differences between Communist Jews, on the one hand, and anti-Communist Jewish socialists, on the other hand, spilled over into the needle trades unions, largely because of the sectarianism of Communist party policy, and almost destroyed the Jewish labour movement from within. The party's role was harmful, particularly in its dual-union phase. Although the Communist-led Industrial Union of Needle Trades Workers made some notable gains for certain groups of workers, the main impact of party policy was to undermine the workers' struggles for better conditions by pitting worker against worker and union against union.

Meanwhile, the garment manufacturers strove to capitalize on and reinforce the fragmented nature of the labour force in this sector. Aiming to 'divide and conquer,' the employers worked to intensify divisions between Jews and non-Jews, women and men, and Communists and anti-Communists in the workforce. Moreover, the impact of economic downturns, particularly the high unemployment resulting from the Great Depression, made the workers especially vulnerable, not only to these machinations but also to other aspects of their employers' offensive.

These divisions among workers were further accentuated by the fragmented structure of the garment industry itself. Particularly in the first two decades of the twentieth century, needle trades workers were divided into home workers, workers in contractors' shops, and those in the 'inside shops.' These divisions in the labour market made it difficult for the unions to coordinate such a scattered workforce and to appeal to a strong sense of common interest. Although home work and contracting had declined somewhat by the interwar period, they were by no means eliminated. In addition, although some larger factories emerged in this sector, small shops continued to proliferate, making organizing difficult.

This structural fragmentation was a product of the highly unstable nature of this labour-intensive industry. In addition to the instability that was generated by frequent style changes and seasonal variations in demand, the low capital requirements for setting up a business meant there was fierce competition between firms in this sector and hence great instability. As a result, when union activists pressed a particular employer for better wages and improved working conditions, they had to take care not to place this employer at too serious a competitive disadvantage: a unionized firm could be driven out of business by low-wage competition if the socialist union leaders did not moderate their demands. In an industry where business mortality rates were extremely high, this was a crucial consideration. Moreover, the unionists' difficulties were severely compounded by anti-labour government policies and state repression of radicals.

As a result of a wholly different set of recent developments, Toronto's Jewish labour movement was relatively short-lived. New groups of immigrants have entered the city's needle trades since the end of the Second World War, and the proportion of Jewish garment workers has declined sharply. Although some Holocaust survivors made their way to Canada and took up work in the needle trades, the mass murder of European Jews meant that the earlier flood of Jewish immigrants from Europe to Canada was never to be resumed. In the meantime, the Canadian-born children of Toronto's immigrant Jewish garment workers did not follow their parents into the garment shops. 'Just because we had a hard life to make a living,' Bessie Kramer explained, 'we wanted our children should have it better. So no matter how poor a cloakmaker was, he wanted his son to be a doctor, a lawyer.'[2] Within Toronto's Jewish community, as within other Jewish communities in Canada and the United States, the upward mobility of the second and third generations has been dramatic. Workers who had been radicalized by appalling conditions on the shop floor have often seen their children and grandchildren prosper, especially in the professions.[3]

In the meantime, sections of the Jewish left were shocked and demoralized by the 1956 Stalin revelations, particularly because of the harsh Soviet anti-Semitism that was finally exposed. Meanwhile, in many parts of Canada, the anti-Semitism of the interwar years has yielded to an atmosphere that has become more tolerant towards Jews, and assimilation has diluted Jewish culture. As television entered the home and as the move to the suburbs took shape, the social and cultural basis of Toronto's Jewish labour movement was eroded. Assimilation and upward mobility have meant that the militant Jewish working-class culture of the immigrant activists has been left behind.

In its prime, the Jewish labour movement struggled not only to improve harsh sweatshop conditions but also to bring about a fundamental socialist transformation. Even the first of these goals was extremely difficult. Severe economic downturns, the highly unstable structure of the garment industry, sharp employer offensives, and harsh state repression made it hard for unionists to win shop-floor demands. At the same time, the movement was weakened by ethnic, gender, and ideological divisions within the workforce, divisions that were deepened by the manipulations of the employers and their allies. Although the immigrant Jewish activists were often unable to overcome these divisions, they fought courageously despite blacklists, police brutality, and the threat of deportation or incarceration. They strove for justice for working people and for Jews. The socialists among them fought for nothing less than a new Garden of Eden that proved beyond their reach.

Appendix

PART A
Statistical Information on the Jewish Population of Toronto

TABLE 1
The Growth of Toronto's Jewish Population,
1901–41

Year	Number of Jews in Toronto
1901	3,043
1911	17,713
1921	31,709
1931	45,305
1941	52,779

SOURCE: Calculations based on the *Census of Canada*, 1901, vol. I, 344–5; 1911, vol. II, 248–9; 1921, vol. I, 374–5; 1931, vol. IV, 268–71; and 1941, vol. II, 508–9.

TABLE 2
Toronto's Jewish Population in 1931,
according to Country of Birth

Place of Birth	Number of Jews in Toronto
Canada	18,612
British Isles	1,400
United States	1,216
Poland	12,933
Russia	8,717
Romania	996
Austria	726
Hungary	98
Other parts of Europe	538
Other parts of the world	69
Total	45,305

SOURCE: *Census of Canada*, 1931, vol. IV, 268–71

PART B
Statistical Information on the Garment Workers of Toronto

TABLE 3
Women and Men Employed in Toronto's Garment Industry, 1901–41[a]

Year	Total No.	No. of Women	No. of Men	Percentage of Women
1901	13,247	na	na	na
1911	13,223	7,919	5,304	60
1921	10,385	6,455	3,940	62
1931	12,605	6,917	5,688	55
1941	12,856	5,816	7,040	45

SOURCE: Calculations based on the *Census of Canada*, 1901, vol. III, 208–11; 1911, vol. VI, 264–7; 1921, vol. IV, 534–5 and 538; 1931, vol. VII, 288–9; 1941, vol. VII, 822 and 828

[a] The figures in this table should be regarded only as rough approximations. The classification scheme for this industry changed somewhat from census to census, thereby making it difficult to be precise in comparing the figures from decade to decade.

TABLE 4
Ethnicity and Gender of Toronto Clothing Workers in 1931[a]

	All Groups	Jews	E. Europeans	British	Other
Men's clothing: suits and coats					
Women	585	302	26	213	44
Men	1,351	941	76	243	91
Women and men	1,936	1,243	102	456	135
Eth w as % eth grp	30.22	24.30	25.49	46.71	32.59
Eth w as % all w	100	51.62	4.44	36.41	7.52
Eth m as % all m	100	69.65	5.63	17.99	6.74
Eth grp as % all	100	64.20	5.27	23.55	6.97
Men's furnishings: shirts, neckwear					
Women	411	126	6	246	33
Men	244	96	5	119	24
Women and men	655	222	11	365	57
Eth w as % eth grp	62.75	56.76	54.55	67.40	57.89
Eth w as % all w	100	30.66	1.46	59.85	8.03
Eth m as % all m	100	39.34	2.05	48.77	9.84
Eth grp as % all	100	33.89	1.68	55.73	8.70

TABLE 4 (*concluded*)

	All Groups	Jews	E. Europeans	British	Other
Women's and children's clothing: skirts, cloaks, waists					
Women	3,005	801	145	1,845	214
Men	2,074	1,436	65	495	78
Women and men	5,079	2,237	210	2,340	292
Eth w as % eth grp	59.17	35.81	69.05	78.85	73.29
Eth w as % all w	100	26.66	4.83	61.40	7.12
Eth m as % all m	100	69.24	3.13	23.87	3.76
Eth grp as % all	100	44.04	4.13	46.07	5.75
Hats and caps					
Women	313	162	4	136	11
Men	498	267	37	179	15
Women and men	811	429	41	315	26
Eth w as % eth grp	38.59	37.76	9.76	43.17	42.31
Eth w as % all w	100	51.76	1.28	43.45	3.51
Eth m as % all m	100	53.61	7.43	35.94	3.01
Eth grp as % all	100	52.90	5.06	38.84	3.21
Clothing not otherwise specified					
Women	1,218	280	37	800	101
Men	1,687	831	59	648	149
Women and men	2,905	1,111	96	1,448	250
Eth w as % eth grp	41.93	25.20	38.54	55.25	40.40
Eth w as % all w	100	22.99	3.04	65.68	8.29
Eth m as % all m	100	49.26	3.50	38.41	8.83
Eth grp as % all	100	38.24	3.30	49.85	8.61
Totals for all types of clothing					
Women	5,532	1,671	218	3,240	403
Men	5,854	3,571	242	1,684	357
Women and men	11,386	5,242	460	4,924	760
Eth w as % eth grp	48.59	31.88	47.39	65.80	53.03
Eth w as % all w	100	30.21	3.94	58.57	7.28
Eth m as % all m	100	61	4.13	28.77	6.10
Eth grp as % all	100	46.04	4.04	43.25	6.67

SOURCE: Calculations based on unpublished, disaggregated census data available from Statistics Canada. It was not possible to obtain further breakdowns of the various branches of the clothing industry. For example, the data does not permit one to distinguish between cloakmakers and dressmakers in particular.

[a] The figures in this table should be regarded as rough approximations since they do not correspond precisely to the available figures in the published census.

TABLE 5
Age Distribution of Female and Male Garment Workers in Toronto, 1911–41

Year	Women			Men		
	% 15–24 Yrs Old	% 16–24 Yrs Old	% Over 24 Yrs Old	% 15–24 Yrs Old	% 16–24 Yrs Old	% Over 24 Yrs Old
1911	48	na	50	30	na	69
1921	na	37	60	na	22	75
1931	na	38	62	na	24	76
1941	na	30	70	na	11	88

SOURCE: Calculations based on the *Census of Canada*, 1911, vol. VI, 264–7; 1921, vol. IV, 534-5 and 538; 1931, vol. VII, 228–9; 1941 vol. VII, 822 and 828

TABLE 6
Marital Status of Toronto's Female Garment Workers, 1924–32

Year	% of Women Who Are Married & under 50 Years Old	% of Women Who Are Married (without respect to age)
1924	15.7	na[a]
1925	15.8	na
1926	19.8	na
1927	18.9	na
1928	na	22.6
1929	na	22.8
1930	na	24.1
1931	na	25.0
1932	na	24.9

SOURCE: Annual Reports of the Ontario Minimum Wage Board, in the Ontario Legislative Assembly's *Sessional Papers*, 1925, part V, paper 64, 16; 1926, part V, paper 47, 17; 1927, part V, paper 38, 13; 1928, part V, paper 40, 13; 1929, part V, paper 40, 14; 1930, part III, paper 14, 14; 1931, part V, paper 38, 14; and 1933, part VI, paper 39, 16
[a] Comparable statistics are also unavailable for the years before and after the 1924–32 period.

PART C
The Garment Unions in Toronto

TABLE 7
Overview of the Garment Unions in Toronto

	Origins	Type of Garment Worker	'Jewish Union?'	First Formed	First Toronto Local	Period Most Active in Toronto	Additional Information
Journeymen Tailors' Union of America (JTUA)	American	Custom tailors	No	1883	1891	1910s	Merged with ACW from 1914 to 1915 (known as Tailors' Industrial Union during the merger)
United Garment Workers (UGW)	American	Makers of men's ready-made clothing	No	1891	1894	First decade and a half of the 20th century	Concentrated in men's work clothing and sports-wear in later years
Amalgamated Clothing Workers (ACW)	American	Makers of men's ready-made clothing	Yes	1914	1915	1915 through the rest of the period under consideration	Formed by secessionists from UGW (who felt UGW was conservative and anti-immigrant)
International Ladies' Garment Workers' Union (ILGWU)	American	Makers of women's ready-made clothing (especially cloakmakers)	Yes	1900	1903	1910s through the rest of the period under consideration	

TABLE 7 (*concluded*)

	Origins	Type of Garment Worker	'Jewish Union?'	First Formed	First Toronto Local	Period Most Active in Toronto	Additional Information
International Fur Workers' Union (IFWU)	American	Fur workers	Yes	1913	1913	Mid-1910s through the rest of the period under consideration	
United Cloth Hat, Cap, and Millinery Workers' International Union	American	Makers of hats and caps	Yes	1901	1905	Mid-1910s through the rest of the period under consideration	
Industrial Union of Needle Trades Workers (IUNTW)	Canadian	Dressmakers (although it originally aspired to encompass all garment workers)	Not one of the four 'Jewish unions,' but this union was led mainly by Jews	1928	1928	1928–36	Established by the Communists, during their dual-union phase, to compete directly with the other garment unions. Dismantled by the Communists when they abandoned dual unionism in 1935–6
National Clothing Workers of Canada (NCWC)	Canadian	All types, but especially makers of men's ready-made clothing	No	1934	1934	1934 through the rest of the period under consideration	Affiliated to the All-Canadian Congress of Labour (ACCL). Competed directly with the American-based garment unions and with the IUNTW. The NCWC remained small

PART D
Key Strikes in Toronto's Needle Trades

TABLE 8
Key Strikes of the Amalgamated Clothing Workers

Year	No. of Strikers	Type of Workers	Issue(s)	Outcome
1918	150	Wrkrs at Tip Top Co.	Union recognition	Wrkrs lost
1919	475	Wrkrs at Tip Top Co.	Higher wages & shorter hours	Wrkrs won
1919	75?	Vestmakers	Better conditions in all contractors' shops	Wrkrs won
1924	75	Vestmakers	Wage cuts in contractors' shops	Wrkrs won
1928	150	Wrkrs at W.R. Johnston Co.	Work being sent out to be made up out of town by non-union labour	Wrkrs won
1933	128	Wrkrs at Ont. Boys' Wear	Union recognition & higher wages	Employer settled with rival union
1934	250	Wrkrs at 18 non-union shops	Union recognition & union conditions	Wrkrs won

TABLE 9
Key Strikes of the International Ladies' Garment Workers' Union

Year	No. of Strikers	Type of Workers	Issue(s)	Outcome
1912	1,200	Garment wrkrs at Eaton's	Change in system of work (affecting pay & job security)	Wrkrs lost
1919 (May)	1,800?	Cloakmakers	Sympathy with striking Toronto metal workers	Wrkrs lost

TABLE 9 (*concluded*)

Year	No. of Strikers	Type of Workers	Issue(s)	Outcome
1919 (July)	2,000	Cloakmakers & dressmkrs	Higher wages, shorter hrs, end to piece wrk	Compromise
1920	1,800?	Cloakmakers	End to piece work	Wrkrs lost
1925	1,200	Cloakmakers	Higher wages & union recognition	Wrkrs won
1930	1,800	Cloakmakers	Higher wages, union recognition, shorter hrs	?
1931	1,700	Dressmakers	Higher wages, shorter hrs, & closed shop	half of the wrkrs. lost
1933	2,000	Cloakmakers	Higher wages & shorter hours	?
1934 (Jan.)	2,000	Cloakmakers	Higher wages & shorter hours	Compromise
1934 (July)	38	Dressmakers in 1 Eaton's department	Higher wages	Wrkrs lost
1934 (July)	250	Cloakmakers at Superior Cloak Co.	Company broke union agreement by running away to Guelph	Compromise
1934 (July)	1,800	Cloakmakers	Shorter hrs & wrk being contracted out to non-union shops	?
1935	1,800	Cloakmakers	Higher wages, shorter hrs, regulation of the use of contractors	?
1936	1,900	Cloakmakers	Employers breaking the agreement with the union	Wrkrs won
1937	1,800?	Cloakmakers	Higher wages & better regulation of the use of contractors	Wrkrs won

TABLE 10
Key Strikes of the International Fur Workers' Union

Year	No. of Strikers	Type of Workers	Issue(s)	Outcome
1923	200	Makers of fur coats	Higher wages, shorter hrs, union recognition	Wrkrs won
1930	350	Fur collar & cuff wrkrs	Higher wages & shorter hours	Wrkrs won
1932	800	All fur wrkrs	Wage cuts & union recognition	Wrkrs won
1933	375	Fur collar & cuff wrkrs	Higher wages & unemployment insurance	Wrkrs won
1934	136	Fur collar & cuff wrkrs	Higher wages & better working conditions	Wrkrs won
1936	50	Fur collar & cuff wrkrs	Shorter hours	Wrkrs won

TABLE 11
Key Strikes of the United Cloth Hat, Cap, and Millinery Workers' International Union

Year	No. of Strikers	Type of Workers	Issue(s)	Outcome
1919	150?	Capmakers	Higher wages, shorter hrs, restricted no. of apprentices, & end to piece work	Wrkrs won
1920	150?	Capmakers	Lockout: wage cuts, open shop, longer hrs	Compromise
1933	200	Capmakers	Higher wages & shorter hours	Wrkrs won
1934 (March)	400	Millinery workers	Higher wages, shorter hrs, & closed shop	Wrkrs won
1934 (Oct.)	175	Capmakers	Higher wages & shorter hours	Compromise
1935	600	Millinery workers	Higher wages & shorter hours	Compromise

TABLE 12
Key Strikes of the Industrial Union of Needle Trades Workers

Year	No. of Strikers	Type of Workers	Issue(s)	Outcome
1931	500	Dressmakers	Higher wages & shorter hours	Wrkrs lost
1934	1,500	Dressmakers	Higher wages, shorter hrs, union recognition	Wrkrs won
1935	1,500	Dressmakers	Higher wages & shorter hours	Wrkrs won
1936	1,150	Dressmakers	Higher wages & better conditions	Wrkrs won

SOURCE: More than a hundred sources were used as the basis for compiling tables 8–12 and are too numerous to list here. The most important sources are *Der Yiddisher Zhurnal*, *Der Kamf*, *Worker*, *Labour Gazette*, Strikes and Lockouts Files of the Canadian Department of Labour, *Industrial Banner*, *Toronto Star*, and *Justice*.

Notes

ABBREVIATIONS USED IN THE NOTES

AC	ACW Correspondence
AGEBM	ACW's general executive board minutes
AO	Archives of Ontario
ATJBM	ACW's Toronto joint board minutes
CLCC	Canadian Labour Congress Collection
CPCCAO	Communist Party of Canada Collection at the Archives of Ontario
CU	*Canadian Unionist*
CZP	Charles Zimmerman Papers
DDP	David Dubinsky Papers
GEB	general executive board
GW	*Garment Worker*
HW	*Headgear Worker*
IB	*Industrial Banner*
IC	IFWU Correspondence
IFWUGEBM	IFWU's general executive board minutes
IGEBM	ILGWU's general executive board minutes
J	*Justice*
JLCP	J.L. Cohen Papers
K	*Der Kamf*
LG	*Labour Gazette*
LGW	*Ladies' Garment Worker*
NA	National Archives of Canada
NC	*New Commonwealth*

PACM	Papers of the Associated Clothing Manufacturers
PTI	Papers of the Toronto ILGWU
RCPSMPE	Royal Commission on Price Spreads, *Minutes of Proceedings and Evidence*
RCPSR	Royal Commission on Price Spreads, *Report*
RDLO	Records of the Department of Labour of Ontario, Archives of Ontario
SLF	Strikes and Lockouts Files, National Archives of Canada
T	*Tailor*
TET	*Toronto Evening Telegram*
TG	Toronto *Globe*
TS	Toronto *Star*
W	*Worker*
WBCT	*Weekly Bulletin of the Clothing Trades*
YZ	*Der Yiddisher Zhurnal*

Author surnames and short titles only are used throughout the notes. Please refer to the Select Bibliography for the full citations.

INTRODUCTION

1 YZ, 23 June and 2 July; LG, Aug. 1919; interview with Isaac Shoichet
2 For a discussion of 'the quite limited cross-fertilization' between ethnic studies and working-class history in Canada and the United States see Ramirez, 'Ethnic Studies and Working-Class History,' 45–8.
3 Important contributions to this debate include Kolko, *Main Currents in Modern American History*, 67–100; Heron, *Working in Steel*, 78–87, 124, and 169; Bernstein, *The Lean Years*, 50–2 and 87–8; Brody, *Steelworkers in America*, 96–111, 119–21, 135–7, 143–5, and 259–61; Barrett, 'Unity and Fragmentation,' 229–54; Patrias, *Relief Strike*; Seager, 'Class, Ethnicity, and Politics in the Alberta Coalfields, 1905–1945,' 304–27; and Cumbler, *Working-Class Community in Industrial America*.
    The important similarities between the Canadian and American experiences should not obscure significant differences concerning immigration policy and the nature of nationalism; these distinctions are summarized briefly in Donald Avery's introduction in Harzig and Hoerder, eds., *The Press of Labor Migrants*, 284.
4 See, for example, the editor's preface in Milkman, ed., *Women, Work and Protest*, xi–xiv; Waldinger, 'Another Look at the International Ladies' Garment Workers' Union,' 87–9; Tax, *The Rising of the Women*; Tentler, *Wage-*

Earning Women; Kessler-Harris, '"Where Are the Organized Women Workers?"'; Frager, 'No Proper Deal'; Sangster, 'Canadian Working Women'; and Bradbury, 'Women's History and Working-Class History.'

5 Important historical contributions to this debate include Taylor, *Eve and the New Jerusalem*, x and xv–xvi; Newton, '"Enough of Exclusive Masculine Thinking"'; Kealey, 'Canadian Socialism and the Woman Question, 1900–1914'; Sangster, 'The Communist Party and the Woman Question, 1922–1929'; Sangster, *Dreams of Equality*; Buhle, *Women and American Socialism, 1870–1920*; and Dye, *As Equals and as Sisters*.

6 See, for example, Eliane Leslau Silverman's discussion of this approach in Silverman, 'Writing Canadian Women's History,' 523.

7 For an example of a historian who is attempting to utilize 'implicit feminism' more carefully see Kaplan's contribution to Ellen Dubois et al., 'Politics and Culture in Women's History.'

8 For example, Tentler dismisses the importance of ethnicity in *Wage-Earning Women*, and Kolko's discussion of class and ethnicity in *Main Currents in Modern American History* (67–99) largely ignores gender issues that affected the development of the labour movement.

CHAPTER 1 A Mound of Ashes in the Golden Land

1 Yezierska, 'The Miracle,' 3 and 11

2 Gordon, 'Fun An Arbayterin's Tog-Bukh,' 95. Throughout this book, the translations from the Yiddish are my own, unless otherwise specified.

3 Cahan, *The Rise of David Levinsky*, 97. Cahan was one of the leading Jewish socialists in early twentieth-century New York.

4 Interview with Jim Blugerman. On the Odessa pogrom see also Frankel, *Prophecy and Politics*, 135, 149, and 154; and Elbogen, *A Century of Jewish Life*, 394–6.

5 Howe, *World of Our Fathers*, 5–63; Vigod, *The Jews in Canada*, 4–9; Kuznets, 'Immigration of Russian Jews to the United States'; Bodnar, *The Transplanted*, 1–56; Baron, *The Russian Jew under Tsars and Soviets*, 52–75, 105, and 113–15; and the introduction to Dawidowicz, ed., *The Golden Tradition*, 29–30, 38, 46–50, 58, 62–3, and 71–6. For a discussion of why some East European Jews came to Canada instead of to the United States see Speisman, *The Jews of Toronto*, 70–1.

6 Calculations based on the *Census of Canada*, 1901, vol. I, 344–5, and 1931, vol. IV, 268–71. See also Levitt and Shaffir, *The Riot at Christie Pits*, 32 and 298.

7 See, for example, Kolko, *Main Currents in Modern American History*, 69–71;

Howe, *World of Our Fathers*, 72; and Heron, *Working in Steel*, 78–84. Women constituted 50.01 per cent of Toronto's Jewish population in 1931. This figure is derived from calculations based on the *Census of Canada*, 1931, vol. IV, 268–71.

8 Interview with Joe Salsberg

9 Speisman, *The Jews of Toronto*, 119–22, 318–23, and 332–5; and Levitt and Shaffir, *The Riot at Christie Pits*, 9–11 and 34–9

10 *Toronto Evening Telegram*, 27, 29–30 May and 5 June; YZ, 30 May and 1–2 and 10 June 1919. Note the *Telegram*'s 29 May headline in particular.

11 TET, 22 Sept. 1924, cited in Speisman, *The Jews of Toronto*, 321

12 YZ, 28 Dec. 1924 and 14 Aug. 1932; *The Worker*, 4 May 1929; Speisman, *The Jews of Toronto*, 332–5; Levitt and Shaffir, *The Riot at Christie Pits*, 152–73; and interview with Lou Lipsky

13 On traditional Jewish communities in Eastern Europe see, for example, Tobias, *The Jewish Bund in Russia*, 5–6 and 9; and Howe, *World of Our Fathers*, 7–13.

14 On the residential concentration of Jewish immigrants see Harney and Troper, *Immigrants*, 23–7; Speisman, *The Jews of Toronto*, 81–95; Hiebert, 'The Geography of Jewish Immigrants,' 144 and 295–9; and Hiebert, 'Integrating Production and Consumption in the Canadian City.'

15 On the *landsmanshaftn* see, for example, Howe, *World of Our Fathers*, 183–9; and Speisman, *The Jews of Toronto*, 110–11.

16 On the development of some of these groups in Eastern Europe see, for example, Tobias, *The Jewish Bund in Russia*, 127–8, 160–4, 172–6, 192–3, 204–15, and 259–72. Information on the development of these groups in Toronto is available, for example, in the interviews with Joe Salsberg, Molly Fineberg, Ed Tannenbaum, and Jacob Black.

17 See, for example, Speisman, *The Jews of Toronto*, 5–6, 13–16, 62–5, 81, 96–101, and 235.

18 The 5200 figure comes from calculations based on unpublished, disaggregated census data available from Statistics Canada. See table 4 in the appendix. The ratios are drawn from Louis Rosenberg, *Canada's Jews*, 176, combining 'textile goods and clothing' and 'furs and fur goods.'

19 See, for example, Antonovsky, ed., *The Early Jewish Labor Movement in the United States*, 344; and Abella's introduction to Abella, ed., 'Portrait of a Jewish Professional Revolutionary,' 185–6.

20 See, for example, Baron, *The Russian Jew under Tsars and Soviets*, 95–6 and 113–14; Antonovsky, ed., *The Early Jewish Labor Movement in the United States*, 26; Howe, *World of Our Fathers*, 59; Kuznets, 'Immigration of Russian Jews to the United States,' 109; and Liebman, *Jews and the Left*, 82.

21 See, for example, Howe, *World of Our Fathers*, 82; and Antonovsky, ed., *The Early Jewish Labor Movement in the United States*, 299–300. Additional information is available in the interview with Ida and Sol Abel. For a detailed analysis of the spatial location of both the garment industry and Jewish residential districts in Toronto see Hiebert, 'The Geography of Jewish Immigrants.'

22 Piva, *The Condition of the Working Class in Toronto*, 18–19

23 See, for example, ibid., 18; Roberts, 'Studies in the Toronto Labour Movement,' 240; *Weekly Bulletin of the Clothing Trades*, 7 Aug. 1908; and Berson, 'The Immigrant Experience,' 162–3. The interview with Joe Salsberg is also informative.

24 The interview with Max Enkin, for example, provides information on the Orthodox Jews in Toronto's needle trades.

25 The percentages for 1931 are calculated from unpublished, disaggregated census data available from Statistics Canada. See table 4 in the appendix for further statistics. The additional information has been gleaned from Belkin, *Di Poale Zion Bavegung in Kanade*, 84; J, 17 Nov. 1922; and interviews with Lou Lipsky, Moe Levin, Ed Hammerstein, Ida and Sol Abel, Bessie Kramer, and Ed Tannenbaum.

I have specifically rejected two other estimates of the proportion of Jews in this sector in 1931. Louis Rosenberg understates the proportion of Jews who worked in Toronto's clothing shops because he lumps together textile goods and clothing, despite the fact that relatively few Jews were involved in the production of textile goods. See Rosenberg, *Canada's Jews*, 386. In contrast, Dan Hiebert tends to overestimate the proportion of Jewish clothing workers because he relies on the Toronto assessment rolls, which provide details on the heads of household only. Although Hiebert's study is rich and informative in many ways, he is hampered by the fact that many garment workers (especially female workers) were not heads of households. See Hiebert, 'The Geography of Jewish Immigrants,' 323.

26 See, for example, Howe, *World of Our Fathers*, 82; Speisman, *The Jews of Toronto* 71; and Hiebert, 'The Geography of Jewish Immigrants,' 180, 270, and 324. Hiebert analyses a 25 per cent sample of Toronto garment manufacturers for 1931 and concludes that Jews owned more than half of the city's clothing firms. Further information is available in the interviews with Sam Charney, Max Enkin, Louis Posluns, Jim Blugerman, Ida and Sol Abel, and Ed Hammerstein.

27 Calculations based on the *Census of Canada*, 1911, vol. VI, 264–7

28 See, for example, ACW's Toronto Joint Board Minutes, 30 Sept. 1926, MG28 I228, reel M3705, NA; ATJBM, 7 March 1929; statement from the Toronto Joint Board to the minister of labour, box 1, file 'Strikes,' RDLO, Office of

the Minister, General Subject Files, RG7 I-1, AO; and B. Shane to J.D. Monteith, 5 Feb. 1931, box 6, file 'ILGWU, 1930–2,' RDLO, Office of the Deputy Minister, General Subject Files, 1930–49, RG7 II-1.

29 Calculations based on the *Census of Canada*, 1921, vol. IV, 534–5 and 538; and 1931, vol. VII, 228–9

30 Annual Reports of the Ontario Minimum Wage Board, in the Ontario Legislative Assembly's *Sessional Papers*, 1929, part V, paper no. 40, 14; 1930, part III, paper no. 14, 14; 1931, part V, paper no. 38, 14; and 1933, part VI, paper no. 39, 16. In comparison, a mere 10 per cent of all women who were in the paid labour force in Canada in 1931 were married. See Canada, Department of Labour, *Women at Work in Canada* (Ottawa 1965), 21.

31 *Toronto Daily Mail and Empire*, 9 Oct. 1897. See also *Labour Gazette*, Jan. and June 1901.

32 King, *Report to the Honourable the Postmaster General*, 26–7. See also *Annual Reports of the Inspectors of Factories for the Province of Ontario*, 1901 report, 12–13; 1903 report, 33; 1904 report, 32–3; 1905 report, 48; and 1914 report, 18–22. Although the shift to electricity eventually eliminated the heat and fumes from gas lights and gas irons, workers were exposed to new dangers from the electrified machinery.

33 WBCT, 7 Aug. 1908. Additional information is available in *Garment Worker*, 31 July 1914; Archives of Ontario, Committee on Child Labour, *Report*, 5; Wright, 'Report upon the Sweating System in Canada,' 8 and 33; *Western Clarion*, 20 April 1912; and interviews with Joe Salsberg and I. Cohen.

34 GW, 6 Nov. 1914

35 The quotations are from GW, 26 Nov. 1915. See also LG, Feb. and April 1901, and May, Aug., and Dec. 1914.

36 See, for example, WBCT, 7 Aug. 1908; and 1902 Factory Inspectors' Report, 25

37 Piva, *The Condition of the Working Class in Toronto*, 34, 38, and 40

38 The organizer was quoted in the *Toronto Star*, 5 Feb. 1925. See also YZ, 3 Aug. 1924; and LG, April and June 1925.

39 Royal Commission on Price Spreads, *Report*, 111

40 Interview with Ida and Sol Abel. Additional information is available in YZ, 4 Feb. 1935; Scott and Cassidy, *Labour Conditions in the Men's Clothing Industry*, 34; and the interviews with Jacob Black and Ed Hammerstein.

41 'Evidence Given by Miss Winifred Hutchison before Price Spreads Commission on Jan. 23 & 24, *Re* Conditions in Needle Trades.'

42 The statistic is from ibid. See also Scott and Cassidy, *Labour Conditions in the Men's Clothing Industry*, 9 and 40; YZ, 20 July 1932; and the following documents from RDLO, Office of Deputy Minister, General Subject Files,

1930–49, RG7 II-1: R.B. Bennett to Premier G.S. Henry, 5 Sept. 1933, and deputy minister of labour to J.D. Monteith, 12 Sept. and 6 Oct. 1933, box 9, file: 'ILGWU, 1933;' 'Evidence given by Miss Winifred Hutchison before the Price Spreads Commission on Methods of Wage Payment,' and 'Evidence given by Miss Winifred Hutchison before the Price Spreads Commission on Violations and Evasions of Minimum Wage and Factory Acts,' box 15, file 'Price Spreads Commission.'

43 Biss, 'The Dressmakers' Strike,' 368; interviews with Ed Hammerstein and Ida and Sol Abel

44 RCPSMPE, 4829; see also 4815–16

45 Ibid., 4520

46 Ibid.

47 Ibid., 4462. See also *New Commonwealth,* 4 Aug. 1934.

48 See, for example, RCPSMPE, 4829; 'The Hazards of Mercury Poisoning in the Hat Industry,' 11 Oct. 1937, vol. 10, file 2641, J.L. Cohen Papers, NA; Arbitration Proceedings, 4 Aug. 1939, box 3, file 'Arbitration, Robt. Crean, Co., 1939, To.,' RDLO, Industrial Relations Division, Conciliation ... Strike Files, RG7 V-1-b; speech of J.B. Salsberg on the Spadina area, in Ontario, *Debates of the Legislative Assembly,* 23rd Legislature, session 3, vol. 42, 4 April 1951, II-3 through II-4; and Howe, *World of Our Fathers,* 149. Skin irritations were due to the types of filling that were used in cheap fabrics.

49 See, for example, 'Evidence Given by Miss Winifred Hutchison before Price Spreads Commission on Jan. 23 & 24, *Re* Conditions in Needle Trades'; Biss, 'The Dressmakers' Strike,' 368; Annual Report of the Deputy Minister of Labour (for fiscal year 1931–2), box 8, file 'Annual Report, 1933,' RDLO, Office of Deputy Minister, General Subject Files, 1930–49; and Scott and Cassidy, *Labour Conditions in the Men's Clothing Industry,* 38–9. Additional information is available in the interviews with Alex Levinsky, Louis Guberman, Leah Stern, and Max Grafstein.

50 Interviews with Joe Salsberg and Sam Kraisman

51 *Western Clarion,* 20 April 1912

52 Biss, 'The Dressmakers' Strike,' 368

53 See, for example, Roberts, *Honest Womanhood,* 9–10; and Kraisman's address in *Souvenir Journal of the Toronto Cloakmakers' Union* (1949).

54 Interviews with Joe Macks, Abe Megerman, and Sam Kraisman

55 T, 7 July 1915; Stowell, *The Journeyman Tailors' Union of America,* 10, 51, 82–3, 86, 102–5, 112–16, 120–5, and 129–30; Forsey, *Trade Unions in Canada,* 28; interview with Lou Lipsky; and James Watt to E.J. Brais, 7 March 1915, box 55, file 14, ACW Collection no. 5619 at the Labor-Management Documentation Centre, M.P. Catherwood Library, Cornell University, Ithaca, New York

56 See, for example, Stowell, *The Journeyman Tailors' Union of America*, 86; Zaretz, *The Amalgamated Clothing Workers of America*, 77–8; Forsey, *Trade Unions in Canada*, 266–7; LG, May 1904, May 1907, Feb. 1908, April, May, July 1913; GW, 4, 11, 18, 25 April, 2, 9, 23, 30 May, 27 June 1913.

57 Zaretz, *The Amalgamated Clothing Workers of America*, 79–85, 87–90, 95–104; and Foner, *Women and the American Labor Movement*, 376–8; Josephson, *Sidney Hillman*, 47–57 and 91–110. The American Federation of Labor opposed the formation of the ACW and strongly supported Rickert's group, while refusing to investigate the reasons for the antagonism to the UGW's entrenched leadership.

58 See, for example, IB, 19 Feb. 1915; *Advance*, 21 Sept. 1917; J. Blugerman to Rabkin, 19 Feb. 1915, box 45, file 9, AC; J. Blugerman to E.J. Brais, 16 Feb. 1915, box 36, file 6, AC; J. Watt to E.J. Brais, 23 March 1915, box 55, file 14, AC; J. Blugerman to J. Schlossberg, 11 Dec. 1916, box 9, file 1, AC; H. Madanick to J. Schlossberg, 18 July 1917, box 12, file 34, AC; J. Blugerman to J. Schlossberg, 1 April 1918, box 55, file 16, AC; and H. Madanick to J. Schlossberg, 18 Aug. 1917, box 12, file 34, AC.

59 Minutes of the Associated Clothing Manufacturers, 6 and 21 Aug. 1919

60 1919 ACW agreement in the holdings of the Associated Clothing Manufacturers; and YZ, 22 Aug. 1919

61 1919 ACW agreement. If the union could not meet a request for unionized workers within forty-eight hours, the boss was then free to hire non-union labour. However, all newly hired, non-union workers had to join the union within a 'reasonable' period of time.

62 On the periodic renewal of the agreement between the association and the union see Minutes of the Associated Clothing Manufacturers. See also Scott and Cassidy, *Labour Conditions in the Men's Clothing Industry*, 4, 7, 9, 13–14, 21–2, 57–8, and 62; market adviser to R.Y. Eaton, 28 Sept. 1937, and market adviser to H.W. Maxwell, 26 Nov. 1945, box 1 (general correspondence), PACM. For a summary of the ACW's key strikes see table 8 of the appendix.

63 See, for example, Levine, *The Women's Garment Workers*, 103; Kirzner, 'Twenty-five Years of the Cloakmakers' Union,' (in Yiddish), in *Souvenir Journal of the Toronto Cloakmakers' Union* (1936); LG, May 1907 and March 1909; Logan, *Trade Unions in Canada*, 211; and Piva, *The Condition of the Working Class in Toronto*, 158–9.

64 Kirzner, 'Twenty-five Years of the Cloakmakers' Union.' See also Logan, *Trade Unions in Canada*, 211–12; Kraisman's address in *Souvenir Journal of the Toronto Cloakmakers' Union* (1949); LGW, July 1912; Levine, *The Women's Garment Workers*, 177–94.

65 For a summary of the ILGWU's key strikes in Toronto see table 9 of the

appendix. Additional information is available in Kraisman's address in *Souvenir Journal of the Toronto Cloakmakers' Union* (1949); ILGWU's General Executive Board Minutes, 3 Oct.–8 Oct. 1932, 28, ILGWU Archives, New York; Sam Kraisman, 'An Epic Strike,' 1–3, L. Kraisman Collection no. 5073, Multicultural History Society of Ontario; W, 7 March 1936; J, 1 Feb. and 15 March 1937; and 'Highlights and Activities of the Toronto ILGWU since 1937,' [fall 1939], box 74, file 3A, DDP.

66 See, for example, Logan, *Trade Unions in Canada*, 210; Forsey, *Trade Unions in Canada*, 325; Foner, *The Fur and Leather Workers' Union*, 52, 57, 59–60; 1962 souvenir book of the Fur Workers' Union of Toronto, 19; A. McCormack to A.W. Miller, 27 Jan. and 2 March 1915, and Charles De Guerre to Samuel Korman, 27 Sept. 1915, box 20, file 44, IC. For a listing of the IFWU's key strikes in Toronto see table 10 of the appendix.

67 LG, Jan. 1903, May 1907; Budish, *Geshikhte fun di Klot Het, Kep un Milineri Arbeiter*, 370 and 373; HW, Sept. 1916, Jan., Feb. and July–Aug. 1917 (the latter in Yiddish). For a summary of the key strikes in the headgear industry see table 11 in the appendix.

68 See, for example, 'Convention Souvenir ... 1st National Convention of the Industrial Union of Needle Trades Workers of Canada held May 10th, 11th, & 12th 1929,' 11–12, Communist Party of Canada Collection, AO; David Dubinsky to Bernard Shane, 24 Dec. 1935, box 80, file 7, DDP; and David Dubinsky to H.D. Langer, 23 July 1937, box 88, file 1b, DDP. For a summary of the IUNTW's key strikes see table 12 of the appendix. Although there was also a Communist-led Industrial Union of Needle Trades Workers in the United States, the party stressed that the Canadian IUNTW and the American IUNTW were separate organizations.

69 For background information on the ACCL see, for example, Abella, *Nationalism, Communism, and Canadian Labour*, 44. See also ATJBM, 20 Aug. [1931]; M. Finch to W.T. Burford, 5 Feb. 1934, and [W.T. Burford] to M. Finch, 7 Feb. 1934, and N.S. Dowd to T. MacLachlan, 15 May 1941, vol. 95, file 'Clothing Workers of Canada, National, Local 1,' CLCC.

70 Information is available in YZ, 27–28 Jan. 1920, 5 Aug. and 1 Sept. 1932, 27 Jan., 4 Feb., and 11 Feb. 1935; W, 12 April 1930, 7 April 1934; *Daily Clarion*, 16 June 1936; interviews with Jacob Black, Abraham Biderman, and Morris Biderman.

71 For a detailed discussion of the structure of the garment industry see Carpenter, *Competition and Collective Bargaining in the Needle Trades*. For the Canadian context see RCPSR, 109–10, and 365; and Hiebert, 'The Geography of Jewish Immigrants,' 258–9 and 287.

72 See, for example, Wright, 'Report upon the Sweating System in Canada,' 6,

8, 38, and 43; 1900 Factory Inspectors' Report, 21; 1902 Factory Inspectors' Report, 28–9; 1909 Factory Inspectors' Report, 61; and RCPSR, 109–11. The minutes of the Associated Clothing Manufacturers (14 March 1922) provide a graphic illustration of the proliferation of small contractors: during a six-month interval in 1921–2, thirty-five men's clothing contractors opened up in Toronto with no more than forty machines among them. See Hiebert, 'The Geography of Jewish Immigrants,' 263–6, on modifications to the contracting system by the 1930s, particularly regarding Eaton's and Simpson's practice of contracting out work to the smaller garment manufacturers in the interwar period.

73 Wright, 'Report upon the Sweating System in Canada,' 6, 8, and 24; 1909 Factory Inspectors' Report, 53; *Report of Committee on Child Labor, 1907*, 5–9; and RCPSMPE, 4818–19.

74 Information is available, for example, in the interview with Joe Salsberg.

75 See, for example, LG, Feb. 1904; *Advance*, 5 Nov. 1920; minutes of the Associated Clothing Manufacturers, 14 March 1922, 5 March 1923, 27 May 1925, 28 Feb. 1929, 17 Feb. 1931, 17 March and 27 April 1937; J, Aug. 1934, 15 Aug. 1936, 15 Feb. 1937; HW, Sept. 1917; RCPSMPE, 4808; H. Langer to D. Dubinsky, 25 Aug. 1933, and S. Kraisman to D. Dubinsky, 1 and 12 March 1934, PTI.

76 The quotation is from the interview with Joe Salsberg. Calculations based on the lists of Toronto clothing firms in *Fraser's Textile Products Directory* indicate the high rate of business mortality in this industry. Only 35 per cent of the women's cloak and suit firms listed in 1920 were still listed in 1925. For women's dress firms, men's ready-made clothing firms, and men's made-to-measure clothing firms the figures were 37, 38, and 72 per cent, respectively. Moreover, it is likely that this tabulation underestimates the mortality rate because the smaller, less stable firms were probably not listed in Fraser's directory at all.

77 The Ontario Minimum Wage Act, established to regulate women's wages in 1920, was commonly violated by garment manufacturers. See, for example, Scott and Cassidy, *Labour Conditions in the Men's Clothing Industry*, 40 and 44; and RCPSMPE, 4444, 4463, 4803, 4811–12, 4842, and 4849. Ontario's Industrial Standards Act, established in 1935, set out minimum wages for female and male workers in some (but not all) branches of the garment industry. Even if the act was well enforced (and it is doubtful that it was), the minimum wages established were significantly below the union wage scale. See, for example, J.L. Cohen's address, *Souvenir Journal of the Toronto Cloakmakers' Union*, 1936; market adviser to N. Rogers, 11 Oct. 1938, box 1 (general

correspondence), PACM; and letter from M. Enkin to T. Learie, 8 March 1938, in the Minutes of the Associated Clothing Manufacturers.

78 ILGWU, *Handbook of Trade Union Methods*, 62. Carpenter's book discusses this theme in great detail. See also Braun, *Union-Management Co-operation.*

79 See, for example, S. Kraisman to D. Dubinsky, 7 Nov. 1933, and S. Krais-man to Attorney-General Roebuck, 6 Feb. 1935, PTI; 1935 cloak agreement, vol. 2, file 2095, and 1935 cloak contractors' agreement, vol. 3, file 2134, JLCP; minutes of the Associated Clothing Manufacturers, 7 July 1921; *Proceedings of the ACW Convention*, 1924, 139. Both the ACW and the ILGWU pressed the Toronto manufacturers to use only those contractors who had been specifically approved by the unions.

80 For an example of these tensions see minutes of the Associated Clothing Manufacturers, 14 April 1925.

81 See, for example, LG, Aug. 1934; and *Proceedings of the ACW Convention*, 1924, 139.

CHAPTER 2 Pulling in One Direction

1 Kogos, *1001 Yiddish Proverbs*, 143. The translation from the Yiddish is Kogos's.

2 Interview with Joe Salsberg. Regarding missionaries, see also Speisman, *The Jews of Toronto*, 131–41.

3 YZ, 20, 22, 25 Dec. 1918

4 See, for example, YZ, 26 March and 9 April 1919, and 7 and 25 March 1921. On the 1917 boycott see Speisman, *The Jews of Toronto*, 195–6, and on two earlier boycotts see Roberts, *Honest Womanhood*, 41.

5 YZ, 22 and 30 May and 2 June 1924

6 The quotations are from the interview with Sadie Hoffman. Further information is from YZ, 28, 30, 31 March and 2 and 3 April 1933; K, 31 March and 7 April 1933; W, 1 April 1933; and interview with Bessie Kramer. For a more detailed discussion of this boycott see Frager, 'Politicized Housewives.'

7 YZ, 25 Aug. 1919

8 See, for example, YZ, 1 Sept. 1919, 6 March 1921, 30 May 1922, 28 Jan. 1935, and Speisman, *The Jews of Toronto*, 240 and 244. The *Zhurnal*'s coverage of the 1932 furriers' general strike provides a good example of the paper's tendency to omit information that might have harmed the strikers' cause. See YZ, 29 and 31 July and 1, 4, 8 Aug. 1932.

9 YZ, 28 Jan. 1935

10 Interview with Ida and Sol Abel

11 Interview with Joe Salsberg

12 For examples of liberal Jewish historians who have minimized the importance of Jewish working-class culture see Speisman's *The Jews of Toronto* and
Weinberg's *World of Our Mothers.*

13 Interviews with Ed Hammerstein and Jacob Black

14 Souvenir book, 1962, of the Fur Workers' Union of Toronto, 11

15 The quotation is from M. Kirsenbaum (director, Toronto Labour Lyceum
Association) to [president Lucchi], 7 Oct. 1936, box 15, file 24, IC. Further
information is drawn from interviews with Ed Hammerstein and Ida and
Sol Abel.

16 Interviews with Ed Hammerstein, Ida and Sol Abel, and Bessie Kramer

17 Leaflet enclosed with the letter from S. Kraisman to D. Dubinsky, 19 Nov.
1935, box 74, file 4B, DDP

18 The quotations are from the leaflet enclosed with the letter from Kraisman
to Dubinsky, 19 Nov. 1935. See also YZ, 23 April 1922, 21 Feb. 1924, 22 Jan.
1925, 22 Jan. 1935; TET, 29 April 1938; and ATJBM, 15 Nov. 1923.

19 IFWU's GEB minutes, Report of Vice-President Max Federman to the GEB, 11
May 1937, 5, box 3, file 25, IFWU Collection

20 Ibid.; ATJBM, 12 Dec. [1935] and 13 Feb. [1936]; minutes of the Toronto
Dressmakers' Joint Council, 27 May 1936, 17, box 1, ILGWU Archives; and
TET 29 April 1938

21 The quotation is from HW, July–Aug. 1918 (in Yiddish). See also HW, 10
Oct. 1919; H. Madanick to J. Schlossberg, 5 Dec. 1917, box 12, file 34, AC;
Budish, *Geshikhte fun di Klot Het,* 204; *Advance,* 9 March 1917; and YZ, 12
Feb. 1925.

22 See, for example, S. Kraisman's address, *Souvenir Journal of the Toronto Cloakmakers' Union,* 1961; A. Kirzner, 'Twenty-five Years of the Cloakmakers'
Union' (in Yiddish), and H.D. Langer, 'The Past, Present, and Future of
Our Union' (in Yiddish), *Souvenir Journal of the Toronto Cloakmakers' Union,*
1936; YZ, 11 April 1921, 29 Jan. 1924. Further evidence is available, for example, in the interviews with Sam Kraisman, Abe Megerman, Jacob Black,
Ed Hammerstein, Ed Tannenbaum, Lou Lipsky, and Joe Salsberg.

During the Communist party's dual-union phase, party activists attempted
to discredit their opponents within the Jewish labour movement by branding them as 'Right Wingers.' However, as some former Communists have
recently admitted, this was misleading because the 'Right-Wing' Jewish
labour leaders were actually socialists.

23 YZ, 18 Aug. 1932

24 Ibid.

25 Interview with Leah Stern

26 The quotation is from the interview with Leah Stern. The interview with Dave Biderman, for example, contains similar information. Neither the *Yiddisher Zhurnal* nor the various other sources indicated that there was a serious division between the Orthodox and the socialist workers with respect to Toronto's Jewish labour movement. Moreover, within Toronto's immigrant Jewish community more broadly, according to scholars Cyril H. Levitt and William Shaffir, there was not much tension between the religious Jews and the secular socialist Jews in the interwar period. See Levitt and Shaffir, *The Riot at Christie Pits*, 274–5.

27 Labour historians have often stressed that few Southern and Eastern European immigrants had become familiar with trade unionism before emigration. See, for example, Brody, *Steelworkers in America*, 136; and Kolko, *Main Currents in Modern American History*, 76–7.

28 YZ, 1 June 1919

29 The quotation is from YZ, 1 March 1921. The interview with Ed Hammerstein provides useful information as well. On the harsh conditions in Eastern Europe see, for example, Baron, *The Russian Jew under Tsars and Soviets*, 52–75, 105, and 113–15.

30 Interview with Ed Tannenbaum

31 Interview with Ida and Sol Abel

32 Interview with Bessie Kramer (who left the party after Khrushchev's report to the Twentieth Congress of the Communist party of the Soviet Union, for she became deeply concerned about the anti-Semitism in the USSR)

33 Interview with Joe Salsberg

34 On this sense of thwarted expectations see, for example, Budish, *Geshikhte fun di Klot Het*, 365.

35 Interview with Jacob Black

36 Interview with Ed Hammerstein

37 On the traditional artisanal workshops see, for example, Mendelsohn, *Class Struggle*, 10. Material on the nature of this transition and its radicalizing impact is available, for example, in the interviews with Joe Salsberg, Ed Tannenbaum, and Ida and Sol Abel. John Laslett explains the historical radicalism of shoemakers as a product of dramatic deskilling but fails to make a similar point regarding immigrant Jewish garment workers. See Laslett, *Labor and the Left*, 59–63, 88, and 98–135.

38 The interview with Joe Salsberg, for example, provides the relevant information. In general, Jewish union leaders were highly aware of the limits of trade unionism, as is apparent, for example, in an editorial in LGW, March 1914, 11–15.

39 Interview with Ed Tannenbaum

40 Interview with Joe Salsberg
41 Isaiah 1:17, *The Holy Scriptures* (Philadelphia: Jewish Publication Society of America, 1917)
42 Amos 4:1, *The Holy Scriptures*
43 Isaiah 33:15 and 58:6, *The Holy Scriptures*
44 Interview with Joe Salsberg
45 Interview with Moe Levin
46 Information is available, for example, in the interviews with Jim Blugerman, Jacob Black, Deborah Goldberg, and Isaac Shoichet.
47 The quotation is from Gutman, *Work, Culture, and Society*, 90. For an important example of the ideas of the radical wing of the Christian Social Gospel movement in Canada see Salem Bland, *The New Christianity* (Toronto 1973), originally published in 1920.
48 Mendelsohn, 'The Russian Roots of the American Jewish Labor Movement'; Antonovsky, ed., *The Early Jewish Labor Movement*, 121, 139, 299–300, and 342; and Liebman, *Jews and the Left*, 87–133 and 175–83
49 The quotations are from the interview with Molly Fineberg. The interview with Joe Salsberg is also important on this theme. Peretz's condemnation of exploitation is evident, for example, in his well-known poem 'Tsvey Brider' ('Two Brothers'), which Salsberg views as an allegory of the class struggle. See I.L. Peretz, 'Di Meisseh Fun Tsvey Brider,' in B. Vladek, ed., *Fun Der Tifenish Fun Harts: A Bukh Fun Layden Un Kampf* (New York 1917), 62–6.
50 The song appears in Rubin, *Voices of a People*, 350, and the translation is Rubin's. On the 'sweatshop poets' see Howe, *World of Our Fathers*, 420–2.
51 Nepom, *Fun Meine Teg*, 66. Nisnevitch was another Toronto Yiddish labour poet; see A. Nisnevitch, *In Loyf Fun Yoren* (Toronto 1942).
52 YZ, 1 Sept. 1919
53 See, for example, YZ, 25 April 1922. The interviews with Lou Lipsky, Ed Tannenbaum, and Jacob Black provide additional information.
54 The song is quoted from the interview with Isaac Shoichet. The interviews with Molly Fineberg, and Ida and Sol Abel, for example, provide additional information on the Arbeiter Ring's cultural activities in Toronto.
55 P. Halpern, 'The Arbeiter Ring as the "United Front" of the Jewish Workers,' in the Arbeiter Ring's 1922 convention souvenir book, 26–7 (in Yiddish)
56 YZ, 28 Jan. 1935
57 See, for example, LGW, Aug. 1912; HW, July–Aug. 1917 (in Yiddish); YZ, 10 July 1919. The interviews with Lou Lipsky and Molly Fineberg are also informative.
58 See, for example, YZ, 24, 25, and 31 Aug. 1919 and 23 July 1934; and *Sou-*

venir Book of Ten Years Labour League (1936). The interviews with Bessie Kramer, Ida and Sol Abel, and Jacob Black are also informative.

CHAPTER 3 Uncle Moses and the Slaves

1 Ash, *Onkel Moses*, 65, and 206. The translations are my own.
2 Ike Gilberg, 'What's the Matter with the Jew?' T, Jan. 1913
3 YZ, 3 Feb. 1925. On the affiliation with the Canadian Jewish Congress see, for example, ATJBM, 22 June [1938].
4 YZ, 9 Dec. 1919, and 29 and 31 March 1933; interviews with Jacob Black and Ed Hammerstein
5 Information is available, for example, in the interviews with Ida and Sol Abel, Jacob Black, and Joe Salsberg.
6 The quotations are from Hiebert, 'The Geography of Jewish Immigrants,' 300, and the interview with Ed Hammerstein. Additional information is available in the interviews with Jacob Black, Ida and Sol Abel, Alex Levinsky, Moe Levin, Bessie Kramer, and Louis Posluns.
7 Interview with Joe Salsberg
8 Ibid. The interview with Ed Hammerstein provides useful information as well.
9 Interview with Joe Salsberg
10 Interview with Max Enkin
11 Interviews with Joe Salsberg and Ed Hammerstein
12 YZ, 23 Oct. 1924
13 Ibid.
14 YZ, 30 Oct. 1924
15 Interview with Jim Blugerman
16 Interview with Jacob Black
17 Interview with Joe Salsberg
18 Minutes of the Toronto Cloakmakers' Joint Board, 23 May 1934, 42–3, box 4, ILGWU Archives
19 Minutes of the Operators', Finishers' and Drapers' Branch, Local 72, 18 May 1936, 6, box 1, ILGWU Archives
20 Interview with Joe Salsberg
21 Ibid.
22 Antonovsky, ed., *The Early Jewish Labor Movement*, 7 and 17. See also Zborowski and Herzog, *Life Is with People*, 218–20.
23 This is apparent, for example, in the interview with Sam Kraisman.
24 A. Kirzner, 'Twenty-five Years of the Cloakmakers' Union' (in Yiddish). On this particular strike see also LG, March and April 1910.

25 Speisman, *The Jews of Toronto*, 21–34, 53–4, 81, 99–100, and 197–8
26 The quotation is from an undated clipping from the *Toronto Empire* in NA, Strikes and Lockouts Files, vol. 299, file 3446. See also *Western Clarion*, 20 April 1912 and Speisman, *The Jews of Toronto*, 193–5.
27 YZ, 4, 7, 9 Sept. 1919; Speisman, *The Jews of Toronto*, 43–4, 61, and 262; and interview with Ida and Sol Abel
28 YZ, 20, 30, 31 July and 10 Aug. 1919; *Cotton's Weekly*, 17 Aug. 1911. For a brief sketch of Cohen's life see Speisman, *The Jews of Toronto*, 191, 249–50, and 322.
29 YZ, 10 Aug. 1919
30 YZ, 20 Aug. 1919
31 YZ, 20 Aug. 1919
32 YZ, 28 Jan. 1935
33 The quotation is from the interview with Sadie Hoffman. Additional information is available in the interview with Ida and Sol Abel.
34 Interview with Joe Salsberg. Further information is available in the interviews with Ed Hammerstein and Ida and Sol Abel.
35 Interview with Joe Salsberg
36 Ibid.
37 Interview with Ed Hammerstein
38 Interview with Joe Salsberg
39 Ibid.
40 Interview with Moe Levin
41 Interview with Alex Levinsky
42 Interview with Joe Salsberg
43 YZ, 20 July 1919. Related information is available in the interview with Ida and Sol Abel.
44 Interview with Joe Salsberg
45 Interview with Joe Salsberg. Ed Hammerstein, too, described socialist employers who were, in practice, very anti-union.
46 YZ, 4 Feb. 1919
47 The connection between discriminatory hiring and Jewish workers' reputation for militancy was made clear, for example, in [Charles Tovey] to J. Potofsky, 2 Oct. 1923, box 56, file 1, AC.
48 IGEBM, 11 Aug. 1919, 2
49 YZ, 27 June 1919. See also 27 Aug. 1919.
50 YZ, 27 June 1919
51 YZ, 3 July 1919
52 YZ, 5 Aug. 1919
53 [Charles Tovey] to J. Potofsky, 2 Oct. 1923, box 56, file 1, AC

54 YZ, 20 July 1924
55 TG, 3 Feb. 1925
56 TS, 4 Feb. 1925
57 Ibid.
58 TS, 5 Feb. 1925
59 TG, 3 Feb. 1925
60 The quotation is from TG, 9 Feb. 1925. See also YZ, 5 and 10 Feb. 1925.
61 The quotation is from TS, 6 Feb. 1925. See also 5 Feb. 1925.
62 J, 12 Aug. 1927
63 YZ, 12 Aug. 1932
64 Ibid. See also YZ, 21 July 1932, and TG, 8 Jan. 1931.

CHAPTER 4 'Mixing with People on Spadina'

1 Kumove, *Words like Arrows*, 141. The translation from the Yiddish is Kumove's.
2 H.D. Langer to D. Dubinsky, 12 Oct. 1936, box 74, file 4A, DDP. See also TG and TS, 9 Oct. 1936.
3 D. Dubinsky to H.D. Langer, 15 Oct. 1936, box 74, file 4A, DDP. Several right-wing populist, anti-Semitic movements arose in the United States during the 1930s. One of the most notorious and influential was headed by Charles E. Coughlin, the Canadian-born 'Radio Priest' who broadcast his sensationalist appeals from Detroit.
4 Calculations based on unpublished disaggregated census data available from Statistics Canada
5 On anti-Semitism in Eastern Europe see, for example, Baron, *The Russian Jew under Tsars and Soviets*, 52–75; and Antonovsky, ed., *The Early Jewish Labor Movement*, 18–26. The interviews with Joe Salsberg are especially useful for providing information on anti-Semitism in Toronto.
6 On Jewish life in Eastern Europe see, for example, Antonovsky, ed., *The Early Jewish Labor Movement*, 5–6, 11–18; and Baron, *The Russian Jew under Tsars and Soviets*, 81–4, 98–105, and 135–7. The tendency to lump the different types of non-Jews together was particularly apparent in the *Yiddisher Zhurnal*. For the exact proportions of non-Jews in Toronto's needle trades see table 4 in the appendix.
7 This information is available, for example, in the interview with Ed Hammerstein.
8 See, for example, YZ, 3 July 1919, and J. Watt to E.J. Brais, 23 March 1915, box 55, file 14, AC. Additional information is available in the interview with Ida and Sol Abel.

9 The interview with Ed Hammerstein, for example, provides useful information.

10 ILGWU, *Handbook of Trade Union Methods*, 30–1

11 See, for example, LGW, Aug. 1917. See also IGEBM, 25 April 1919, 29–31.

12 See, for example, Stowell, *The Journeymen Tailors' Union of America*, 86; Hardy, *The Clothing Workers*, 75, 78–84; and Foner, *Women and the American Labor Movement*, 376–8.

13 See, for example, Stowell, *The Journeymen Tailors' Union of America*, 38, 51–2, 113–30, 135; T, 15 June 1915. Useful information is also available in the interviews with Ida and Sol Abel and Ed Tannenbaum.

14 The quotations are from WBCT, 29 Nov. 1907. See also Foner, *Women and the American Labor Movement*, 376–8.

15 T, 24 Aug. 1915

16 See, for example, Belkin, *Di Poale Zion Bavegung in Kanade*, 84

17 J. Watt to E.J. Brais, 23 March 1915, box 55, file 14, AC

18 [E.J. Brais] to J. Watt, 26 March 1915, box 37, file 12, AC

19 J. Watt to E.J. Brais, 31 March 1915, box 55, file 14, AC

20 M. Sillinsky to E.J. Brais, 24 April 1915, box 37, file 6, AC

21 J. Watt to E.J. Brais, 1 May 1915, box 55, file 14, AC

22 J. Watt to E.J. Brais, 11 March 1915, box 55, file 14, AC (emphasis added)

23 On the vote see T, 7 July 1915.

24 See, for example, Foner, *Women and the American Labor Movement*, 376–8.

25 See, for example, GW, 7 Jan. and 19 May 1916.

26 See, for example, *Western Clarion*, 27 Oct. 1906; GW, 10 Jan. 1919; and J. Watt to E.J. Brais, 7 March 1915, box 55, file 14, AC.

27 H. Madanick to J. Schlossberg, 18 and 25 July, 18 Aug., and 13 Oct. 1917, box 12, file 34, AC. See also Ontario Department of Labour, *Vocational Opportunities*, 5.

28 J. Blugerman to J. Schlossberg, 4 March 1918, box 9, file 1, and 6, 15, and 16 March 1918, box 55, file 16, AC. The quotation is from 6 March.

29 The first quotation is from Charles A. Tovey to J. Schlossberg, 10 July 1920, and the second quotation is from H.D. Rosenbloom to J. Potofsky, 16 Sept. 1920, box 55, file 17, AC.

30 ATJBM, 11 June 1925

31 The quotation is from ATJBM, 10 Feb. 1927. On this incident see also 22 Feb. 1927. For other examples of friction in this union, see 22 July and 17 Aug. 1926.

32 ATJBM, 18 August [1927]

33 AGEBM, 27–29 Nov. 1930, 9, box 165, file 14

34 The quotation is from H.D. Langer to D. Dubinsky, 6 July 1937, box 88, file 1b, DDP.

35 For general information on the nationalist orientation of the ACCL see, for example, Abella, *Nationalism, Communism, and Canadian Labour,* 44.

36 LG, Dec. 1933 and April 1934; ATJBM, 9 and 22 Nov. [1933]

37 M. Finch to W.T. Burford, 5 Feb. 1934, vol. 95, file: 'Clothing Workers of Canada ...' CLCC. See also K, 9 March 1934.

38 CU, May 1935

39 M. Finch to W.T. Burford, 5 Feb. 1934, vol. 95, file: 'Clothing Workers of Canada ...' CLCC

40 M. Finch to W.T. Burford, 5 Feb. 1934, and [W.T. Burford] to M. Finch, 7 Feb. 1934, vol. 95, file: 'Clothing Workers of Canada ...' CLCC

41 On Finch's ethnocentrism see M. Finch to N.S. Dowd, 9 Dec. 1937 and 6 Dec. 1939, vol. 95, file: 'Clothing Workers of Canada ...' CLCC.

42 E. Smith to Ontario's attorney-general, 21 March 1933, box 9, file: 'ILGWU, 1933,' RDLO, Office of Deputy Minister, General Subject Files. On Smith's leading role in the ACCL's needle-trades activities in Toronto see, for example, ATJBM, 20 Aug. [1931].

43 M. Finch to N.S. Dowd, 1 April and 11 Nov. 1938, and 18 March 1939, vol. 95, file: 'Clothing Workers of Canada ...' CLCC. ACCL records also document the NCWC's deep collusion with the employer at another of the few shops this union managed to organize. The actions of the NCWC at this shop were so unethical and so compromising that the ACCL's head office had to repudiate the actions of its own affiliate in this case. See W.T. Burford to W.J. Douglas, 14 Feb. 1935, vol. 159, file: 'Toronto N.L. Council, 1935,' CLCC. See also Minutes of the National Labour Council of Toronto (ACCL), 15 March 1936, reel M2294, Labour Council of Metropolitan Toronto Collection. Interference in other garment unions' strikes seems to have been the NCWC's main form of organizing.

44 A. McCormack to A.W. Miller, 27 Jan. 1915, box 20, file 44, IC

45 A. McCormack to A.W. Miller, 2 March 1915, box 20, file 44, IC

46 Interview with Ed Hammerstein

47 IFWUGEBM, meeting of subcommittee of GEB, 12 Aug. 1931, box 3, file 15, 4. For further evidence of ethnic tensions within Toronto's IFWU, see IFWUGEBM, 25–28 Jan. 1937, box 3, file 22.

48 YZ, 21 July 1932

49 YZ, 22 and 27 July 1932

50 YZ, 29 Aug. 1932. See also YZ, 8 Aug. 1932, and W, 13 Aug. 1932.

51 YZ, 21 Aug. and 4 Sept. 1932; interview with Ed Hammerstein

52 Interview with Ed Hammerstein
53 Interview with Jacob Black
54 Interview with Ed Hammerstein
55 On the impact of key Canadian businessmen on immigration policy see, for example, Avery, '*Dangerous Foreigners,*' 16–38.
56 T, Sept. 1912
57 LGW, April 1912
58 On the union's defeat in this strike see, for example, LGW, Jan. 1913 (in Yiddish).
59 YZ, 4 Jan. 1920
60 YZ, 21 Aug. 1924
61 YZ, 22 Jan. 1925. See also 5 Feb. 1925.
62 J, 12 Aug. 1927
63 RCPSMPE, 4573
64 Ibid., 4492. See also NC, 4 Aug. 1934. For an earlier incident of the same kind, see, for example, YZ, 27 Aug. 1919.
65 The quotation is from T, June 1913. See also Dec. 1912 and June 1914.
66 The quotation is from *Cotton's Weekly*, 17 Aug. 1911. See also 20 July 1911.
67 Ibid., 14 Sept. 1911
68 Ibid., 17 Aug. 1911
69 Ibid., 20 July 1911
70 Ibid., 17 Aug. 1911
71 IB, 1 Dec. 1916
72 The quotation is from LGW, Feb. 1917. See also June 1917.
73 See, for example, Biss, 'The Dressmakers' Strike,' 367.
74 YZ, 3 Feb. 1925
75 The quotations are from Charles A. Tovey to J. Schlossberg, 10 July 1920, box 55, file 17, AC. For details on the 1919–20 agreement see the copy of the agreement in PACM.
76 ATJBM, 13 Aug. 1925
77 Ibid., 21 Oct. 1926
78 Biss, 'The Dressmakers' Strike,' 367. See also IGEBM, 10–16 Feb. 1931, 26.
79 A. Desser to Charles Zimmerman, 16 June 1935 (enclosure), box 4, file 3, CZP
80 Interview with Ida and Sol Abel
81 Fraser includes Toronto in his generalizations about the ACW, failing to notice Toronto's different ethnic composition in this sector and the different timing of Jewish immigration to Canada. Other problems with Fraser's analysis, even as it pertains to New York City, include his lack of understan-

ding of the Jewish nature of the American Jewish labour movement. See Fraser, '*Landslayt* and *Paesani.*'

CHAPTER 5 'Better Material to Exploit'

1 Interview with Bessie Kramer
2 Kealey, 'Women's Labour Militancy,' 6
3 'Labour Problems, Clothing – Women's Factory – 1925,' box 5, file: 'Misc., 1925,' RDLO, Research Branch, senior investigator, RG7 VII-1
4 YZ, 20 Nov. 1924. This assumption was also implicit in the Toronto ACW's 'Resolutions to Canadian Conference,' 25 Oct. 1920, box 55, file 17, AC.
5 GW, 14 May 1915 (reprinted from IB). See also K, 1 Jan. 1926.
6 The quotation is from YZ, 4 July 1919. See also 23 April 1919. Other evidence is available, for example, in the Toronto Joint Council, Dressmakers' Union, local 72, Grievance Committee minutes, 6 Sept. 1938, 24, box 2; and the interview with Ida and Sol Abel.
7 Interview with Joe Salsberg. The interview with Ed Tannenbaum provides further relevant evidence.
8 Interview with Bessie Kramer
9 On the 1919 general strike see TG, 5 July 1919; and form dated 4 July 1919, in SLF, vol. 316, file 254. On the general dressmakers' strike of 1931 see form dated 26 Feb. 1931, and TG, 4 Feb. 1931, in SLF, vol. 347, file 14; B Shane to J.D. Monteith, 5 Feb. 1931, box 6, file: 'ILGWU, 1930–1932,' RDLO, Office of the Deputy Minister, General Subject Files, 1930–49.
10 This conclusion has been reached by comparing information in the form filled out by the ILGWU, 20 Feb. 1933, in SLF, vol. 354, file 9, with information in the 'Statement of Cloakmakers' Union...' box 1, file: 'Strikes,' RDLO, Office of the Minister, General Subject Files.
11 It is difficult to be precise about the extent of women's militancy in Toronto's needle trades because of the highly fragmentary nature of the available evidence. (It is even difficult to ascertain the exact proportion of women workers in any given section of Toronto's needle trades in this period, particularly because the census did not distinguish well enough between the different branches of the clothing industry.) With the exception of the first decade and a half of the twentieth century, the *Labour Gazette*'s strike records seldom indicated whether strikers were male or female. Moreover, the available strike records hardly ever contained information about strike-breakers. Nor are there any reliable statistics on union membership that would allow a comparison of women's and men's union

participation rates in this sector. However, table 4 of the appendix provides some relevant statistics on the ethnicity and gender of Toronto's garment workers in 1931.

12 WBCT, 22 Dec. 1905; and TS, 12 Dec. 1905; and LG, Jan. 1906

13 TS, 11 and 12 March 1903

14 TS, 8 April 1905; LG, March 1907; TET, 8 Feb. 1907; LG, March 1910; TET, 3, 4, and 9 Feb. 1910; TS, 2, 3, and 18 Feb. and 19 March 1910; and LG, April, May, June, and Sept. 1914

15 The quotation is from K, 1 Jan. 1926. The sources that applied specifically to Toronto seldom discussed why women workers might have had difficulty organizing. The newspapers of the various garment unions infrequently contained general discussions of this issue, and these discussions were seldom astute. See, for example, HW, Sept. 1916 and March 1919.

16 For information on which jobs were held by women and for a detailed description of many of these jobs, see, for example, Levine, *The Women's Garment Workers*, 522–30, and Ontario, Department of Labour, *Vocational Opportunities in … Garment Making*. Additional information is available in the interviews with Mr and Mrs A. Bonavero, I. Cohen, Max Enkin, I. Ginsberg, and Bessie Kramer.

17 See tables 5 and 6 of the appendix. Additional information is available, for example, in the interview with M. Bochar.

18 HW, Sept. 1916

19 HW, March 1919

20 *Toronto Daily Mail and Empire*, 9 Oct. 1897 (emphasis added)

21 Interview with Joe Salsberg

22 Interviews with Bessie Kramer and Leah Stern. The amount of work necessary to make the house ready for Passover (getting rid of everything seen as contaminated with leavening) is only one example of the ways in which the demands of keeping kosher meant more work for the traditional Jewish housewife.

23 Interview with Molly Fineberg (emphasis added)

24 Interview with Sadie Hoffman. Additional information is available in the interview with Deborah Goldberg.

25 YZ, 6 July 1919

26 For brief mention of the arrests of female picketers see YZ, 10 and 18 July 1919; TG, 31 July and 6 Aug. 1919.

27 YZ, 6 May 1919 (the translation from the Yiddish is my own). Jean Juares was an outspoken French socialist.

28 HW, March–April 1918 (in Yiddish)

29 For the complaint about the washroom see ATJBM, 20 May 1926. For another complaint about lack of cleanliness see ATJBM, 18 Aug. [1927].
30 Interview with Bessie Kramer
31 Interview with Ida and Sol Abel
32 Ibid.
33 Interview with Joe Salsberg
34 Information on the lack of women's auxiliaries is available in the interview with Bessie Kramer.
35 Interview with Ed Hammerstein
36 IFWUGEBM, 23–26 June 1938, box 4, file 1, 69
37 The quotation is from Strong-Boag, 'The Girl of the New Day,' 163. See also Prentice et al., *Canadian Women*, 218–19 and 233–4; and Vipond, 'The Image of Women,' 117.
38 WBCT, 14 Oct. 1910 (emphasis added to the long quotation)
39 YZ, 13 Nov. 1922
40 Interview with Jacob Black
41 Interview with Moe Levin
42 Interview with Ida and Sol Abel
43 Interview with Joe Salsberg (emphasis added)
44 Ibid.
45 Ibid.
46 Ibid.
47 Interview with Ed Tannenbaum
48 ATJBM, 12 Feb. 1931
49 ATJBM, 10 Oct. [1933]
50 ATJBM, 27 April and 3 May [1939]. For some individualized complaints of this nature see, for example, 29 March [1933] and 5 Nov. [1936].
51 The quotation is from the interview with Moe Levin.
52 Interview with Ed Hammerstein
53 YZ, 21 July 1932

CHAPTER 6 'Just as a Worker'

1 Mary Anderson and Mary N. Winslow, *Woman at Work: The Autobiography of Mary Anderson as Told to Mary N. Winslow* (Westport, Conn. 1951, reprinted 1973), 63. Anderson was an organizer for the National Women's Trade Union League in early twentieth-century Chicago.
2 The quotations are from Joseph Schlossberg (general secretary, ACW) to joint boards, district councils, and local unions of ACW, 30 Oct. 1916, in AGEBM, box 164, file 4a.

3 Interview with Ed Hammerstein
4 The interview with Bessie Kramer is particularly informative on this issue.
5 Interview with Moe Levin. The interviews with Ed Hammerstein and Joe Salsberg also provide useful information.
6 See Scott, 'On Language, Gender, and Working-Class History,' concerning the 'masculine conception of class.' Material on the Jewish labour movement in *Der Yiddisher Zhurnal* (eg, 9 Dec. 1919) provides some typical evidence that the prototype of *the* worker was the male worker.
7 This percentage is based on weekly wage statistics listed in Piva, *The Condition of the Working Class in Toronto*, 34 and 40. For further evidence of women's particularly low wages in relation to men's wages in the needle trades see, for example, Ontario, Department of Labour, *Vocational Opportunities in ... Garment Making*, 14; Annual Report of the Ontario Bureau of Labour, 1910, 206–7; and RCPSR, 368.
8 Department of Trade and Commerce, *Weekly Earnings*, 68 and 70. This statistic applied to the city's men's and women's clothing factories.
9 Form filled out by the ILGWU, 20 Feb. 1933, in SLF, vol. 354, file 9
10 See, for example, King, *Report to the Honourable the Postmaster General*, 21.
11 Interview with Ida and Sol Abel
12 See, for example, Scott and Cassidy, *Labour Conditions in the Men's Clothing Industry*, 40; and 'Evidence Given by Miss Winifred Hutchison before Price Spreads Commission on Jan. 23 & 24, *Re* Conditions in Needle Trades,' box 15, file: 'Price Spreads Commission,' RDLO, Office of Deputy Minister, General Subject Files, 1930–49, RG7 II–1.
13 Records for 1920, box B, file: 'Assoc. Meetings,' PACM
14 For some typical examples see YZ, 17 April, 14 May, and 14 Aug. 1919; *Advance*, 25 April 1919; H.D. Rosenbloom to J. Potofsky, 20 April 1925, box 56, file 2, AC; *Toronto Labour Leader*, 6 Feb. 1931, and TS, 25 Feb. 1931, in SLF, vol. 347, file 14; LG, Aug. 1933 and July 1934; minutes of the Associated Clothing Manufacturers, 2 Aug. 1933, 19 Feb. 1935, and 27 April 1937; and form filled out by Drucker, 12 July 1938, in SLF, vol. 397, file 95.
15 There were also many cases where, although the original demands of the unions were not recorded, these unions agreed to settlements with provisions for across-the-board percentage increases. In these cases, union officials did not appear to have been at all discontented with this type of monetary formula. For some typical examples see Budish, *Geshikhte fun di Klot Het*, 370; HW, Jan. and July–Aug. 1917 (in Yiddish); K, 16 Feb. 1934; chief of the Statistics Branch to E.N. Compton, 12 Sept. 1936, in SLF, vol. 378, file 108; and forms filled out by Max Federman, 30 July 1937, in SLF, vol. 389, file 185.

16 Form filled out by the ILGWU, 20 Feb. 1933, in SLF, vol. 354, file 9
17 Interviews with Ida and Sol Abel, Moe Levin, and Joe Macks
18 The quotation is from King, *Report to the Honourable the Postmaster General*, 23. See also 9–10.
19 'Averages in the Toronto Market as in Jan. 1, 1920,' box B, file: 'Assoc. Meetings,' PACM
20 The quotation is from *Vocational Opportunities in ... Garment Making*, 10.
21 'Averages in the Toronto Market as in Jan. 1, 1920,' box B, file: 'Assoc. Meetings,' PACM. Female lining-makers were in a similar situation.
22 This is based on a search of the minutes of the Associated Clothing Manufacturers as well as other relevant documents.
23 The quotation is from ILGWU's Educational Department, *Handbook of Trade Union Methods*, 23.
24 See, for example, Lavigne and Stoddart, 'Women's Work in Montreal,' 141–2.
25 WBCT, 14 Oct. 1910. While this remark referred to the situation in America, the newspaper of the United Garment Workers of America used the term 'America' to include Canada as well.
26 'Memorandum of Agreement between the Furriers' Council and the Toronto Fur Workers' Union ... [1934],' vol. 3, file 2338, J.L. Cohen Papers
27 ATJBM, 18 April 1929
28 Ibid. Moreover, neither the ACW minutes nor the minutes of the manufacturers' association contained any further reference to this issue as the rest of the year unfolded.
29 Interviews with Ed Tannenbaum and Ed Hammerstein
30 This is based, in part, on an analysis of the benefits that are recorded in ATJBM (eg, 6 Sept. 1928). This conclusion is also based on scattered material in a wide variety of other sources.
31 See, for example, LGW, April 1918; and YZ, 31 March 1919, 27 July and 1 Aug. 1920, 6 July, 30 Oct., and 7 Nov. 1922, and 17 Oct. 1924. Sometimes the women were assessed an amount that was only slightly lower than the men's assessment. This meant that since the women's income was commonly so much less than the men's, the women were still paying too high an amount in proportion to their wages. See, for example, YZ, 19 Oct. 1919 and 27 April 1920.
32 *Western Clarion*, 20 April 1912
33 Chown, *The Stairway*, 150
34 *Toronto Daily Mail and Empire*, 9 Oct. 1897. Moreover, women workers have had to face sexual harassment not only from bosses but also from male

co-workers. In *The Rise of David Levinsky* (154–5), Abraham Cahan depicted verbal forms of sexual harassment from male workers in the garment shops.

35 On the Eaton strike see S. Kraisman's address and Max Siegerman's address, *Souvenir Journal of the Toronto Cloakmakers' Union*, 1961; and TS, 15 Feb. 1912; IB, March 1912; and LGW, April 1912. For a more detailed analysis of the strike see Frager, 'Class, Ethnicity, and Gender.'

36 A. Kirzner's and Charles Shatz's speeches (in Yiddish), *Souvenir Journal of the Toronto Cloakmakers' Union*, 1936; and LG, March 1912; *Toronto Daily News*, 15 Feb. 1912; TS, 15 and 16 Feb. 1912; and IB, March 1912.

37 Minutes of the Toronto District Labour Council, 15 Feb. 1912, vol. 3, Labour Council of Metropolitan Toronto Collection

38 Interview with Joe Salsberg

39 LGW, March 1912

40 A. Kirzner's speech (in Yiddish), *Souvenir Journal of the Toronto Cloakmakers' Union*, 1936; minutes of the Toronto District Labour Council, 7 March 1912; and WBCT, 22 and 29 March, 12 April, and 3 May 1912; IB, March and April 1912; LG, March 1912; LGW, March, April, and June 1912; and *Toronto Daily News*, 15 Feb. 1912

41 Speisman, *The Jews of Toronto*, 193–4; LGW, Aug. 1912.

42 *Lance* (Toronto), 2 March 1912

43 On the catalogues see IB, April 1912.

44 The quotation is from A. Kirzner's speech (in Yiddish), *Souvenir Journal of the Toronto Cloakmakers' Union*, 1936. See also LGW, April 1912.

45 The quotation is from W, 7 Dec. 1929. See also *Communist Party of Canada: Resolutions of the Enlarged Plenum, February 1931*, 54–5, vol. 4, file: 'CP of C: Resolutions of the Enlarged Plenum, Feb. 1931,' Tim Buck Collection, MG 32, G 3, NA.

46 See, for example, W, 25 May 1929.

47 K, 22 May 1931. For other examples see W, 28 Feb. and 1 Aug. 1931.

48 In 1931, 60 per cent of Toronto's dressmakers were women. See TG, 4 Feb. 1931.

49 W, 4 Jan. 1930

50 See, for example, K, 16 and 23 Jan. 1931 and 19 Jan. 1934; and W, 17 and 24 Jan. 1931 and 20 Jan. 1934.

51 Buller's 1951 article is reprinted in Watson, *She Never Was Afraid*, 109–13. See especially 109–10.

52 W, 28 Feb. 1931

53 Interview with Joshua Gershman

54 Ibid. Gershman was also asked about the IUNTW's structure to ascertain

whether it allowed for women to be well represented at higher union levels. Based on Gershman's reply as well as on material in *The Worker* and *Der Kamf*, it seems that the IUNTW's structure did not especially benefit women.

55 See, for example, W, 11 March 1933.
56 Interview with Joshua Gershman
57 Watson, *She Never Was Afraid*, 19, 26–30, 33–61, 64, 70, and 80; and W, 1 Aug. 1931
58 Communist Party of Canada Papers, Attorney General's Records, Archives of Ontario, 5B0293, Buller to Sam Colle, 13 Nov. 1928, cited in Betcherman, *The Little Band*, 12
59 K, 29 May 1931
60 M. Klig and J. Gershman to the Toronto joint board of the ILGWU, 25 March 1935, box 4, file 3, CZP
61 YZ, 23 June and 2 and 3 July 1919
62 LGW, Jan. 1913
63 *Cotton's Weekly*, 9 Jan. 1913
64 IGEBM, 14–20 May 1931, 12 and 25; and interview with Moe Levin
65 The quotations are from H.D. Rosenbloom to S. Hillman, 7 June 1923, and H.D. Rosenbloom to J. Potofsky, 11 July 1923, box 56, file 1, AC. Additional information is provided by *Proceedings of the ACW Convention*, 1924, 140; ATJBM, 31 May 1923; interview with Joe Salsberg; and S. Gold to J. Potofsky, 11 Oct. 1923, H.D. Rosenbloom to J. Potofsky, 2 Aug. 1923, [Charles Tovey] to J. Potofsky, 2 Oct. 1923 and J. Potofsky to S. Gold, 5 Nov. 1923, box 56, file 1, AC.
66 The quotation is from M. McNab to J. Schlossberg, 20 Nov. [1917], box 13, file 15, AC. See also McNab to Schlossberg, 17 April 1917.
67 The quotation is from M. McNab to J. Schlossberg, 5 March 1918, box 13, file 15, AC. On the salaries of the union's organizers see, for example, H. Madanick to J. Schlossberg, 25 Jan. 1918, box 12, file 35, J. Blugerman to J. Schlossberg, 16 March 1918, and S. Miller to J. Schlossberg, 12 and 17 July 1918, box 55, file 16, AC. On McNab's resignation see Schlossberg to McNab, 7 March 1918, and McNab to Schlossberg, 14 March 1918, box 13, file 15, AC.
68 The quotation is from TS, 6 Feb. 1925. See also YZ, 16 and 20 July and 20 Nov. 1924, 26 Jan. and 5 Feb. 1925, and *Women's Wear* (New York), 7 Feb. 1925.
69 YZ, 15 Sept. 1924; confidential interview
70 Interviews with Ed Hammerstein, Ida and Sol Abel, and Bessie Kramer. For further examples see the various union officials mentioned in minutes of the Toronto Dressmakers' Joint Council, and *Daily Clarion*, 17 June 1938.

71 Based on the lists of joint board members that appear in ATJBM. See, for example, July 1926.
72 Regarding the ACW's Jewish and non-Jewish business agents see, for example, ATJBM, 28 Nov. 1927; Charles Tovey to J. Schlossberg, 29 Nov. 1923, box 17, file 12, and Charles Tovey to J. Potofsky, 30 Sept. 1923, box 56, file 1, AC. Information on the Communist and anti-Communist business agents and on the scarcity of women in leadership positions is available in the interview with Moe Levin.
73 M. Finch to N.S. Dowd, 7 Jan. 1938, vol. 95, file: 'Clothing Workers of Canada ...,' CLCC. See also Minutes of the National Labour Council of Toronto (ACCL), 26 Feb. 1934 and 25 Jan. 1937, reel M2294, Labour Council of Metropolitan Toronto Collection; and Application for Charter, 7 March 1934; G.R. Hodgson to W.T. Burford, 1 March 1934; M. Finch to the editor of the ACCL's newspaper, 17 Oct. 1937; and M. Finch to N.S. Dowd, 6 Dec. 1939, vol. 95, file: 'Clothing Workers of Canada ...' CLCC.
74 The quotation is from Milkman, 'Organizing the Sexual Division of Labor,' 109. See also Frager, 'No Proper Deal,' 50–5.
75 See, for example, Milkman, 'Organizing the Sexual Division of Labor,' 98–9, 116–18, 125–8; Sangster, 'Canadian Working Women,' 67, 73; and Creese, 'The Politics of Dependency,' 127–9.
76 The quotations are from LGW, April 1912.
77 Chown, The Stairway, 151–2
78 Ibid., 153
79 The quotation is from Lance, 30 March 1912. See also the list of groups that contributed funds to the strike in LGW, Aug. 1912. For a more detailed account of this strike see Frager, 'Class, Ethnicity, and Gender.'
80 The quotation is from Valverde, The Age of Light, Soap, and Water, 120. See also Bacchi, Liberation Deferred? vii–ix and 52–5; Mitchinson, 'The WCTU.' 164–6; Pedersen, '"Keeping Our Good Girls Good,"' 20–4; 'Report of the Corresponding Secretary, Ontario Union,' in The Report of the WCTU's Annual Convention (1911); and The Canadian White Ribbon Tidings, Dec. 1924.
81 On the NWTUL's strike-support work, see Tax, The Rising of the Women, 205–40; Dye, As Equals and as Sisters, 91–4; Hyman, 'Labour Organizing,' 22–41; and Weiler, 'The Uprising in Chicago,' 114–39.
82 On this lack of sympathy see, for example, Bacchi, Liberation Deferred? 123.
83 LGW, Feb. 1917
84 HW, Feb. 1917; and Bacchi, Liberation Deferred? 122–3 and 130
85 Saul Elstein, 'Why Not a National Women's Trade Union League in Canada?' Woman's Century (Toronto), July 1918
86 Ibid.

87 WBCT, 11 March 1910, and LG, March 1910. For additional information on Denison, see Gorham, 'Flora MacDonald Denison.'
88 Biss, 'The Dressmakers' Strike,' 367
89 Ibid.
90 Ibid., 369
91 Ibid., 367–9; news clippings in SLF, vol. 347, file 14
92 On the role of the royal commission see, for example, Correspondence Scrapbook, 1934, series 9, T. Eaton Collection; and RCPSMPE, 3057.
93 RCPSMPE, 4384, 4396, 4417, 4494–5, and 4543
94 The quotation is from NC, 1 Dec. 1934. See also 4 and 11 Aug. 1934.
95 Minutes of the Toronto Local Council of Women, 3 Aug. 1934, Local Council of Women of Toronto Papers; RCPSMPE, 4796–849; and interview with Joe Salsberg
96 A.L. Hynes to A.W. Roebuck, 7 Aug. 1934, box 10, file: 'Eaton, T., Co., 1934,' RDLO, Office of Deputy Minister, General Subject Files. See also Minutes of the Toronto Local Council of Women, 3 Aug. 1934, and NC, 4 Aug. 1934.
97 Two leaflets issued by the ILGWU's dress local [July or Aug. 1934], box 10, file: 'Eaton, T., Co., 1934,' RDLO, Office of Deputy Minister, General Subject Files, 1930–49, RG7 II-1; reprinted ILGWU leaflet in W, 15 Sept. 1934
98 RCPSMPE, 4525 and 4642; LG, Nov. 1934; and NC, 4 and 11 Aug., 1 Sept., 3 and 24 Nov., and 1 Dec. 1934. For a more detailed analysis of this strike see Frager, 'Class, Ethnicity, and Gender.'
99 On the feminism of the National Women's Trade Union League in the United States see, for example, Dye, As Equals and as Sisters, 1, 3–4, and 7.
100 On Pesotta, Cohn, and Newman, see Kessler-Harris, 'Organizing the Unorganizable,' 22–3.
101 Hyman, 'Labor Organizing,' 22–41. The quotation is from page 23.
102 On the large extent to which the Canadian suffrage movement focused on middle-class (and Anglo-Celtic) concerns see, for example, Bacchi, Liberation Deferred? 3–12.
103 On the Canadian women's movement's emphasis on maternal feminism see, for example, Kealey's introduction to A Not Unreasonable Claim, especially 7–11.
104 In 1921 immigrants from continental Europe constituted less than 6 per cent of Toronto's population. (At that time, Toronto had few immigrants who had come from outside Europe and the United States.) In a number of major American cities in 1920, the proportions of immigrants from continental Europe were significantly higher than in Toronto. In that year, those who had been born in continental Europe made up 15–16

per cent of Boston's and Philadelphia's populations. In Chicago, Cleveland, and New York City, at least one-quarter of each city's total population had come from continental Europe. These statistics are drawn from the *Census of Canada*, 1921, II, 364–5, and the *Fourteenth Census of the United States Taken in the Year 1920* (Washington 1922), II, 47 and 732–6.

105 Ewen's study of immigrant Jewish and Italian women in New York City at the turn of the twentieth century, for example, lacks a deep understanding of East European Jewish culture and tends to lump the Jewish and Italian women together despite crucial cultural differences between them. See Ewen, *Immigrant Women in the Land of Dollars*.

106 Hewitt, 'Beyond the Search for Sisterhood,' 300

107 Prentice et al.'s pioneering work, *Canadian Women*, for example, is weakened somewhat by too many assumptions of strong commonalities.

CHAPTER 7 Doing Things That Men Do

1 Michael Gold, *Jews without Money* (New York 1930, reprinted 1965), 170–1

2 For a more detailed description of women's subordination within the religious sphere see, for example, Baum et al., *The Jewish Woman in America*, 4–15 and 58–61.

3 This proverb is cited in Gittleman, *From Shtetl to Suburbia*, 45. For other Yiddish proverbs attesting to the devaluation and deprecation of women see Kumove, *Words like Arrows*, 7 and 256–8.

4 See, for example, Baum et al., *The Jewish Woman in America*, 5; and Zborowski and Herzog, *Life Is with People*, 129.

5 Zborowski and Herzog, *Life Is with People*, 131. See also Baum et al., *The Jewish Woman in America*, 56; and Antonovsky, ed., *The Early Jewish Labor Movement*, 9. Although Zborowski and Herzog romanticize many aspects of *shtetl* life, they are more informative about women's roles than are most other books on Jewish life in Eastern Europe.

6 Baum et al., *The Jewish Woman in America*, 67; and Antonovsky, ed., *The Early Jewish Labor Movement*, 9

7 Smith, *Family Connections*, 30–2; Baum et al., *The Jewish Woman in America*, 56 and 67; and Zborowski and Herzog, *Life Is with People*, 131

8 The quotation is from Zborowski and Herzog, *Life Is with People*, 216. See also Baron, *The Russian Jew under Tsars and Soviets*, 119–29 and 135–7.

9 For a good description of the cult of true womanhood see Welter, 'The Cult of True Womanhood.' Welter discusses this feminine ideal for a specific time period, 1820–60, but aspects of this ideal continued to permeate North American society for years afterward. For a similar treatment of the

domestic ideology in the United States see also Kessler-Harris, *Out To Work*, 49–51.

10 On the fact that women in East European Jewish culture were not seen as fragile see Baum et al., *The Jewish Woman in America*, 12–14 and 28–9.

11 See, for example, Antonovsky, ed., *The Early Jewish Labor Movement*, 9–10.

12 On the importance of submissiveness to the ideal of the Victorian lady see for example, Welter, 'The Cult of True Womanhood,' 230–2.

13 Baum et al., *The Jewish Woman in America*, 69. The authors point out that 'women who would be considered "feminine" by Western standards could not have survived in this environment.'

14 On the traditional Jewish conception of the woman as associated with the material world see Baum et al., *The Jewish Woman in America*, 12–14. On the Victorian emphasis on the piety and purity of the ideal woman see, for example, Welter, 'The Cult of True Womanhood,' 225–9.

15 For a discussion of this type of feminism see, for example, Kealey's introduction to *A Not Unreasonable Claim*, especially 7–11.

16 This interview is cited in Karlinsky, 'The Pioneer Women's Organization,' 33. See also Glenn, *Daughters of the Shtetl*, 191.

17 For example, Kessler-Harris cited an early twentieth-century American woman worker who remarked that 'no nice girl would belong to [a union].' See Kessler-Harris, '"Where Are the Organized Women Workers?"' 102.

18 ILGWU, *Handbook of Trade Union Methods* (1937), 25

19 See Frager, 'No Proper Deal,' 48–50, for evidence that, with regard to the paid labour force more generally, women workers faced significant ideological barriers to labour activism. See also Sangster, 'The 1907 Bell Telephone Strike,' 128–9. After examining the women's columns of Ontario's anglophone labour press, Sangster argues that women workers internalized the domestic ideology and that this retarded women's unionization.

20 On this developing tendency see, for example, Smith, *Family Connections*, 30–1, 44, and 50. The terms 'work' and 'workplace' appear in quotations here because the normal use of these terms without quotations implies that women's household labour is not really work.

21 The profiles are drawn mainly from interviews with these particular women.

22 On Wedro's position on the IUNTW's GEB see K, 29 May 1931. For a detailed account of this strike see W, 9 Sept. 1933.

23 Confidential interview

24 Cited in Paris, *Jews*, 163. Some of the men in the movement considered Wedro to be abrasive, but while abrasiveness in a man was often overlooked, abrasiveness in a woman was (and still is) often considered a serious shortcoming.

25 Interviews with Joe Salsberg and Ed Tannenbaum
26 For a detailed analysis of women's roles in the Fareyn see Frager, 'Politicized Housewives.'
27 Kramer usually referred to the kosher meat boycott as a strike, thereby emphasizing that the women played an active role.
28 On traditional Jewish values which prescribed that the child's earnings belonged to the family group see, for example, Smith, *Family Connection*, 32 and 60.
29 She explained that the Social Territorialists felt that Jews should establish their own country, but not in Palestine. Some of them felt that a Jewish land could perhaps be formed out of part of Australia.
30 This refers to Jeanne Sauvé.
31 Interview with Leah Stern
32 Michael Mann's work is particularly useful in helping to differentiate the different levels of workers' consciousness. See Mann, *Consciousness and Action among the Western Working Class* (London 1973), 13.
33 On these changes see, for example, Smith, *Family Connection*, 30–1, 44, and 50; Glenn, *Daughters of the Shtetl*, 64–79; and Burman, 'The Jewish Woman as Breadwinner,' 27–39. The interviews with Molly Fineberg, Bessie Kramer, Sadie Hoffman, Leah Stern, and Ed Tannenbaum provide concrete examples of some of these issues.
34 Glenn's work, in particular, stresses that immigrant Jewish women who became labour activists were expanding women's roles beyond the economic and domestic functions women had traditionally performed in the *shtetl*. See Glenn, *Daughters of the Shtetl*, 210–12.
35 Examination of the nature of the interview process actually highlights the extent to which the women who were interviewed lacked a serious commitment to women's rights struggles. Although I tried not to bias the interviews by posing questions in ways that would reveal my own opinions, the fact of asking a lot of questions about women suggested to the interviewees that I probably supported the feminist movement. Since I usually developed considerable rapport with the interviewees, they, in turn, as part of being agreeable, probably tended to exaggerate the extent to which women's rights had mattered to them in the earlier period.
36 ATJBM, 27 March 1924
37 ATJBM, 5 June 1924
38 YZ, 19 April 1923
39 For example, the Chenstechover Aid Society, as its name suggests, was a *landsmanshaft*. On this organization see Speisman, *The Jews of Toronto*, 115–16.

40 For conclusive evidence that the Froyen Fareyn was oriented towards the Communist party, see K, 23 Jan. 1931.

41 Nisnevitch's membership card (in Yiddish) for the Yiddisher Arbeiter Froyen Fareyn, at the Multicultural History Society of Ontario (emphasis added)

42 Interview with Bessie Kramer

43 Sadie Hoffman's testimony, that the Fareyn women were mostly housewives who were not engaged in paid labour, is supported by other evidence. See W, 18 Jan. 1930.

44 W, 18 Jan. 1930, and K, 23 Jan. 1931

45 K, 23 Jan. 1931

46 For a detailed analysis of the Fareyn see Frager, 'Politicized Housewives.'

47 W, 18 Jan. 1930,

48 Ibid.

49 Sangster, *Dreams of Equality*, 39 and 58

50 In addition to the interviews with Hoffman, Kramer, and Wedro, the interviews with Deborah Goldberg and Ida Abel are also informative. All the interviews were completed before the recent ending of the Cold War and the break-up of the Soviet Union.

51 Interview with Pearl Wedro

52 The quotation is from Sangster, *Dreams of Equality*, 52. See also 26–80 and 124–64.

53 Although Becky Buhay was Jewish, she focused on other aspects of party activity and was not closely associated with the Jewish labour movement.

54 On the Finnish women's views see Lindström-Best, 'Finnish Socialist Women in Canada.'

CHAPTER 8 Pulling Apart

1 Peter Hunter, *Which Side Are You On, Boys: Canadian Life on the Left* (Toronto 1988), 19. Hunter was a Communist activist in the 1930s.

2 K, 14 Aug. 1931

3 K, 31 July 1931

4 K, 3 April 1931

5 The interviews with Jacob Black and Moe Levin provide information on the composition of the anti-Communist groups in the Toronto needle trades. The term 'Communist' is used here to refer to members of the Communist Party of Canada and their sympathizers. The term 'anti-Communist' is used to refer to all those who actively opposed the supporters of the Communist Party of Canada.

6 Although the Bundists, the Right and Left Labour Zionists, the Jewish Trotskyists, and the Jewish Anarchists became strong allies in the fight against
the Jewish Communists, these different groups represented very different
visions of the ideal socialist society as well as representing different opinions on the position of Jews. Members of the Bund, an organization founded in Vilna in 1897, believed in a decentralized form of socialism that
would allow Jews to preserve their own culture. In general, the Bund stood
for Jewish autonomy within the countries in which Jews lived, and Bundists
also believed in working to make these countries socialist. In the context of
Russian politics in the two decades before the Bolshevik Revolution, this
meant that they envisioned the creation, in the Russian empire, of a socialist society where there would be a federation such that each nationality
would have full autonomy to deal with its own concerns. The Bundists argued that Leninists were too centralist and too elitest, while Lenin, arguing
that Jews were not a nation, maintained that the Bundists were harming the
class consciousness of Jewish workers by emphasizing the Jewish identity so
much. See Tobias, *The Jewish Bund in Russia*, xv, 69, 160–1, 172, 192–3, 204,
207–15, 241, 264–6, 272, and 331.

7 Unlike the Bundists, the Labour Zionists felt that Jews would never be free
of anti-Semitism while they lived as a minority in other countries. They
therefore called for the establishment of a socialist Jewish state in Palestine.
The Labour Zionists argued that Jews needed their own homeland where
they would be able to lead their national life under a socialist order. They
felt that national autonomy must mean territorial autonomy. Since Jews had
no real territory of their own within the Russian empire and since Jewish
life had historically been centred on Palestine, emigration to Palestine
seemed to them a necessity.

The Labour Zionists, however, were split into right and left camps for a
number of years. The Right Labour Zionists argued that Hebrew should be
the daily language of the Jewish people, viewing Yiddish as the language of
oppression and degradation. The Left Labour Zionists favoured Yiddish
and, for a time, viewed the Right Labour Zionists as not revolutionary
enough in their socialism. In the immediate aftermath of the Bolshevik
Revolution, the Left Labour Zionists were sympathetic to the Bolsheviks –
except, of course, on the question of Palestine – but the Left Labour Zionists eventually moved further and further away from the Bolshevik position.
On Labour Zionism see ibid., 172–6. The interviews with Ed Tannenbaum
and Jacob Black provide further information.

There were also Jews who believed that the Jewish people needed their
own territory but who had no hope that a Jewish state in Palestine was

really possible. These people, the Social Territorialists, sought a territory for the Jews elsewhere. See Tobias, *The Jewish Bund in Russia*, 253. Further information is available in the interview with Joe Salsberg.

8 The Jewish Trotskyists' strenuous criticisms of Stalin's Soviet Union included the charge that there was much Soviet anti-Semitism in the 1930s. The Trotskyists also opposed the idea of the establishment of a Jewish state in Palestine. The interview with Lou Lipsky provides information on the Jewish Trotskyists. For further evidence of the presence of Trotskyists in Toronto's needle trades see, for example, Laible Hoffmitz to Charles Zimmerman, 25 July 1935, box 4, file 3, CZP.

The Jewish Communists felt that the Jewish question, like the question of the other nationalities in the Russian empire, was being solved with the establishment of a Communist state in the Soviet Union. Under Communism, they believed, everyone would be truly equal. Thus there was, according to this view, no need for emigration of Jews to Palestine. For quite a while, the Communists rejected the idea that Jews were in a special position, different from the other minority nationalities, because Jews had no territory of their own. Later, however, the Soviet authorities promoted the settlement of Jews in Birobidzhan, a territory in the Eastern part of the Soviet Union near Manchuria. Thus, for a time, the Jewish Communists in North America did support work for the colonization of Birobidzhan. Information is available in the interview with Ed Tannenbaum.

9 The Anarchists argued for a highly decentralized form of socialism. Information on the Jewish Anarchists in the needle trades is available in the interviews with Nick Cafiero, Julius Seltzer, and Joe Salsberg.

10 On the CPC's policy of 'boring from within' see, for example, Penner, *The Canadian Left*, 124–9, and Avakumovic, *The Communist Party in Canada*, 43.

11 On the Sixth World Congress see, for example, Cochran, *Labor and Communism*, 43. On this shift in Canadian Communist policy, see Penner, *The Canadian Left*, 133–4, and Avakumovic, *The Communist Party in Canada*, 54, 68, and 71–3. See also Angus, *Canadian Bolsheviks*, 257, and Rodney, *Soldiers of the International*, 116. As Rodney makes clear, the change in the Comintern's line had begun earlier in the year, particularly at the Profintern's Fourth Congress in March 1928. The change in policy was then emphasized at the Comintern's Sixth Congress in July and August 1928. It took a while for the CPC to carry out many of the necessary changes in Canada.

12 'Convention Souvenir ... 1st National Convention of the Industrial Union of Needle Trades Workers of Canada held May 10th, 11th, & 12th 1929,' 11–12, CPCCAO. See also W, 18 May 1929.

13 Penner, *The Canadian Left*, 133–4

14 W, 28 June 1930, cited in Angus, *Canadian Bolshiviks*, 279
15 W, 30 May 1931
16 w, 18 and 25 May 1929; and interview with Joshua Gershman
17 See, for example, W, 25 April 1931. See also *Canadian Needle Worker*, May 1931, CPCCAO.
18 *Communist Party of Canada: Resolutions of the Enlarged Plenum, February 1931*, 28, vol. 4, file: 'CP of C: Resolutions of the Enlarged Plenum ...' Tim Buck Collection. In Toronto, there were Communist 'opposition groups' within most of the 'reformist' needle trades unions. This chapter, however, focuses on the ACW, the ILGWU, and the IFWU, in particular, because the major battles took place in these three unions. On the factionalism in Toronto's headgear union see, for example, K, 12 June 1931 and 29 Jan. 1935. Information on the UGW in this period is available in the interview with Ed Tannenbaum.
19 Abella, *Nationalism, Communism, and Canadian Labour*, 3–4; Penner, *The Canadian Left*, 138; Avakumovic, *The Communist Party in Canada*, 96 and 131–2; and Cochran, *Labor and Communism*, 75–7. As Cochran points out, the change in CP policy, which was formally announced at the Seventh World Congress in July and August 1935, had actually begun more than half a year earlier.
20 D. Dubinsky to Bernard Shane, 24 Dec. 1935, box 80, file 7; and David Dubinsky to H.D. Langer, 23 July 1937, box 88, file 1b, DDP
21 On the dismantling of the WUL see, for example, Penner, *The Canadian Left*, 138.
22 YZ, 8 Dec. 1922; [H.D. Rosenbloom?] to J. Potofsky, 18 Jan. 1923, box 56; and J. Potofsky to H.D. Rosenbloom, 27 Jan. 1923, box 25, file 1, AC.
23 H.D. Rosenbloom to J. Potofsky, 3 July 1925, box 25, file 2, AC; H.D. Rosenbloom to S. Hillman, 15 July 1925, box 5, file 5, AC; ATJBM, Feb. and 15 March 1926; *Canadian Labour Monthly*, April 1928, CPCCAO; K, 22 and 29 Jan. and 5 Feb. 1926; and 'Appeal of James Blugerman...' [1927], box 45, file 10, AC. Blugerman's opponents explained that he had not been ruled ineligible for office in 1925 because the union did not find out about his debts to the employers until 1926.
24 The quotations are from AGEBM, 13–15 Oct. 1927, pp. 7 and 10, box 165, file 7. See also 'Appeal of James Blugerman...' [1927], box 45, file 10, AC.
25 The quotations are from 'Appeal of James Blugerman...' [1927], box 45, file 10, AC. See also AGEBM, 13–15 Oct. 1927, pp. 15–20, box 165, file 7.
26 See, for example, *Proceedings of the ACW Convention*, 1928, 53 and 75; K, 8 and 15 Jan. 1926; AGEBM, 13–15 Oct. 1927, pp. 2 and 9, box 165, file 7; and ATJBM July-Aug. 1927.

27 ATJBM, 28 Nov. 1927; *Proceedings of the ACW Convention*, 1928, 53 and 75; and *Canadian Labour Monthly*, April 1928, 25, CPCCAO

28 See, for example, K, 1, 8, and 15 Jan. 1926; and *Canadian Labour Monthly*, April 1928, 22–3, CPCCAO.

29 ATJBM, letter from the chair to the delegates of the Toronto Joint Board, [c. Feb.1928]; 23 Feb. and 8 March 1928; and Tovey's Report, [8 March 1928]

30 On the union's role in the hiring process see, for example, 1919 agreement, 1925 agreement, and 1931 agreement, in the files of collective agreements at the office of the Associated Clothing Manufacturers. The standard agreement between Toronto's ACW and the employers' association contained a clause on the 'preferential union shop,' which, in its details, was slightly different from the closed shop. This clause stipulated that when an employer needed additional workers, he would apply to the union. If the union was unable to supply the additional help at that time, the employer could then get new workers on his own. However, these new workers would then have to join the ACW.

31 ATJBM, Tovey's Report, [8 March 1928]

32 Ibid., See also ATJBM, 22 March and 12 April 1928. For the CPC's comments on this entire episode see, for example, *Canadian Labour Monthly*, April 1928, CPCCAO.

33 The quotation is from the interview with Ed Tannenbaum. See also W, 22 Aug. 1931.

34 W, 22 Aug. 1931; AGEBM, 25–28 Aug. 1931, 6, box 165, file 15; and ATJBM, 20 Aug. [1931]

35 W, 5 Sept. 1931. See also W, 8 and 22 Aug. 1931.

36 W, 8 Aug. 1931

37 W, 22 and 29 Aug. 1931. Several months before the Shiffer & Hillman dispute, the *Worker* had called on all men's clothing workers to repudiate the ACW and join the IUNTW. See W, 2 May 1931.

38 W, 8 and 29 Aug. 1931; and interview with Ed Tannenbaum. The *Worker* also claimed that the ACW leadership 'had the shameless gall to issue statements to the capitalist press denouncing the [Shiffer & Hillman] clothing workers as foreigners etc.'

39 W, 17 Oct. 1931. The interview with Ed Tannenbaum is also informative. Tannenbaum recalled that it was rumoured that the Shiffer & Hillman boss received a cash bribe of $25,000 from the ACW. With regard to the ACW's new agreement with Shiffer & Hillman, the joint board stated that the new agreement was similar to that which the Toronto ACW already had with the employers' association. See ATJBM, 2 Oct. [1931].

40 W, 5 Sept. 1931; and YZ, 21 July and 25 Aug. 1932

41 YZ, 28 July and 25 Aug. 1932. For similar charges against the anti-Communist leadership of the Toronto ACW see, for example, K, 2 Jan., 20 Feb., and 24 April 1931. Additional information is available in the interview with Ed Tannenbaum.

42 YZ, 25 Aug. 1932

43 Interview with Ed Tannenbaum; and W, 1 July 1933

44 ATJBM, 18 May and 15 June [1933]; 26 July, 27 Sept., and 11 Oct. [1934]; undated officer's report [c. Oct. 1934]; 13 June [1935]; 2 July 1936; and interview with Ed Tannenbaum

45 ATJBM, 13 June [1935]

46 The minutes of the ACW's Toronto joint board indicate that the factional conflict between Communists and anti-Communists died down somewhat in the late 1930s. According to Tannenbaum, a split in the anti-Communist faction occurred in this period, when one member of this faction exposed another member of the same faction as a crook. Tannenbaum indicated that, as a result of this split, the Communist faction allied with one portion of the anti-Communist faction.

47 See, for example, YZ, 1 Oct. 1923, 12 June and 20 Nov. 1924; K, 1 Jan. 1926; IGEBM, 30 Nov. 1926, 2, and 13 Feb. 1927, 5; J, 8 July 1927, 22 June, 21 Sept., and 25 Oct. 1928. See also Logan, *Trade in Unions in Canada*, 212. Logan claims that the Communists managed to seize control of the administration of Toronto's ILGWU, c. 1926–7. Although he seems to be correct that Communist power had increased at that time, it is unlikely that the Communists were actually able to control the ILGWU's administration. Information is available in the interview with Sam Kraisman.

48 The quotation is from IGEBM, 22 Oct. 1928, 2. See also 25 June 1928, 14–15; and J, 25 Oct. 1928.

49 W, 21 Dec. 1929

50 W, 25 Jan. 1930

51 Ibid.

52 W, 8 Feb. 1930

53 W, 15 Feb. 1930. See also 1 March 1930.

54 The quotation is from IGEBM, 19 March 1930, 13–14. See also J, 31 Jan. and 14 Feb. 1930; and LG, Feb. and March 1930. The *Labour Gazette*'s account of the strike was no doubt drawn from information provided by the ILGWU.

55 W, 1 Nov. 1930

56 See, for example, IGEBM, 10 April 1929, 25; and K, 16 March 1934. Further information is available in the interview with Joshua Gershman and the interview with Ida and Sol Abel.

57 The *Worker* altogether ignored the ILGWU's 1933 general cloak strike, and it

also largely ignored the ILGWU's general strike in the cloak trade in early
1934. Although neither strike resulted in a resounding victory, both of
these strikes seem to have been legitimate attempts to win better conditions
for the Toronto cloakmakers. For brief outlines of these two strikes see LG,
March 1933 and Feb. 1934.

58 W, 8 Aug. 1934
59 See, for example, A. Megerman, 'Onward to New Victories' (in Yiddish),
Souvenir Journal of the Toronto Cloakmakers' Union, 1936; and YZ, 26 July 1934.
See also YZ, 19, 20, and 24 July 1934; and LG, Aug. 1934.
60 W, 30 Jan. 1935
61 IGEBM, 27–31 May 1935, 41
62 See, for example, W, 30 Jan. 1935.
63 ILGWU officials stated that, in this period, the union's strike gains often
melted away soon after the general cloak strikes ended. See, for example,
S. Kraisman's address, *Souvenir Journal of the Toronto Cloakmakers' Union*,
1949.
64 See, for example, A. Megerman, 'Onward to New Victories,' (in Yiddish).
65 The anti-Communist leaders repeatedly stated that the union was seriously
weakened by all the factionalism. Even if one does not necessarily agree
with their wholesale condemnation of the Communists, the point that the
factionalism weakened the union is nonetheless convincing. See, for example, A. Megerman, 'Onward to New Victories' (in Yiddish); and H.D.
Langer, 'The Past, Present, and Future of Our Union,' (in Yiddish).
66 After the Communists abandoned the policies of the Third Period, there
continued to be significant factional strife within the cloakmakers' section
of Toronto's ILGWU. In 1937 one of the anti-Communist union leaders
charged that the Communists 'even went to the extent of introducing a
racial issue by agitating the members of the Gentile Local, who are 80%,
non-English speaking, that the [anti-Communist] leadership was discriminating against Gentiles and the election of a Communist as paid officer
would be a guar[an]tee that Gentiles would be given a fair deal.' See
S. Kraisman to D. Dubinsky, 5 April 1937, box 74, file 3C, DDP.
67 On the ILGWU's early work among the dressmakers see, for example, LGW,
Oct. 1914, 'Directory of Local Unions,' entry for Toronto local 70, July
1917, Feb. and April 1918; YZ, 3 Nov. 1918, 9 Feb., 2 July, and 4 Sept. 1919,
7 Nov. 1922; and J, 27 Oct. and 17 Nov. 1922.
68 See, for example, IGEBM, 22 Oct. 1928, 2, and 19 March 1930, 14; W, 4 Jan.
1930; LG, Feb. 1931; K, 16 Jan. 1931; and TG, 21 Jan. 1931.
69 Interview with Isaac Shoichet. Shoichet recalled singing this song while
helping out on the IUNTW picket lines.

70 The quotation is from W, 24 Jan. 1931. See also LG, Feb. 1931; W, 17 Jan. 1931; TG, 21 Jan. 1931; and K, 23 Jan. 1931.
71 W, 31 Jan. 1931
72 TG, 24 and 25 Feb. 1931
73 See, for example, LG, March, April, and May 1931; K, 20 March 1931; and W, 9 May 1931.
74 Interview with Moe Levin
75 Ibid.
76 Ibid. On the charge that anti-Communists within the IUNTW were discriminated against in terms of being kept out of jobs, see also Yiddish news clipping entitled 'Vi Halt Es Mit Eynigkayt Bay Di Dressmakhers?' [Toronto, July 1935], box 4, file 3, CZP.
77 Interview with Moe Levin
78 Ibid.
79 W, 1 June 1929
80 Ibid. In an interview, Joshua Gershman pointed out that, with respect to the question of independent Canadian unionism, the Profintern's line changed from time to time.
81 Interview with Jacob Black. Similarly, when Sol Abel (a pro-Communist cloakmaker) was asked if there was much discontent about the relationship between the American head offices and the Toronto union locals, he replied there was not. Abel felt that the head offices put a lot of money into helping the Toronto locals. This information is available in the interview with Ida and Sol Abel.
82 On the 1934 IUNTW general dress strike see, for example, LG, Feb. 1934; W, 20 and 27 Jan. 1934; and K, 26 Jan. 1934. On the 1935 IUNTW general dress strike see, for example, LG, Feb. 1935; and K, 25 and 29 Jan. 1935. On the 1936 IUNTW general dress strike see, for example, LG, March 1936. On the fact that there was a substantial group of unorganized dressmakers see, for example, A. Desser to Charles Zimmerman, 16 June 1935, enclosure, box 4, file 3, CZP. See also J, 1 July 1935.
83 Interview with Moe Levin; and David Dubinsky to H.D. Langer, 23 July 1937, box 88, file 1b, DDP
84 M. Klig and J. Gershman to the joint board of the Toronto ILGWU, 25 March 1935, box 4, file 3, CZP
85 Ibid.
86 IUNTW leaflet, entitled 'Who Is for Unity and Who Works Against Unity?' [Toronto, spring? 1935], box 74, file 4c, DDP
87 Ibid. See also IUNTW leaflet that begins 'To All Needle Trades Workers!' [Toronto, 8 Aug. 1935], box 74, file 4b, DDP

88 Leaflet signed by the 'Progressive Dressmakers Unity Group' and entitled 'From Words to Deeds!' [Toronto, 17 May 1935], box 74, file 4c, DDP

89 ILGWU leaflet entitled 'Union Breaking and Fake Unity' [Toronto, c. mid 1935], box 4, file 3, CZP

90 Yiddish ILGWU leaflet that begins, 'The Splitters Allegedly Want Unity!' [Toronto, c. mid 1935], box 4, file 3, CZP

91 Sam Green to Charles Zimmerman, 15 and 31 Oct. 1935 (in Yiddish), box 4, file 3, CZP; interview with Moe Levin; IGEBM, 2–7 Dec. 1935, 41–2; H. Shaul and J. Hilf [of the IUNTW], to David Dubinsky, 25 Nov. 1935, box 74, file 4b; David Dubinsky to Bernard Shane, 24 Dec. 1935, box 80, file 7; H.D. Langer to David Dubinsky, 21 Dec. 1936, box 74, file 4a; and David Dubinsky to H.D. Langer, 23 July 1937, box 88, file 1b, DDP.

92 H.D. Langer to David Dubinsky, 21 Dec. 1936, box 74, file 4a, DDP. See also Langer to Dubinsky, 31 March 1937, box 74, file 3c.

93 Toronto Joint Council, Dressmakers' Union, local 72, Grievance Committee minutes, 23 and 30 Aug. and 6 Sept. 1938, box 2. For other evidence of the fights between the Communists and the anti-Communists within the ILGWU's dressmakers' section see, for example, minutes of the Toronto Dressmakers' joint council, 23 Sept. and 18 Nov. 1936, box 1.

94 Toronto joint council, Dressmakers' Union, local 72, Grievance Committee minutes, 23 Aug. 1938, 2–3, box 2

95 Ibid., 6 Sept. 1938, 13, box 2. See also A. Richman to S. Green, 27 Oct. 1938; and H.D. Langer to David Dubinsky, 30 April 1939, enclosure, box 88, file 2b, DDP.

96 A. Richman and C.F. Foster to David Dubinsky, 16 Feb. 1938, box 88, file 1b, DDP. See also Richman and Foster to Dubinsky, 7 April 1938.

97 See, for example, Frank Currie to Morris Kaufman, 1 April 1924 and 20 Aug. 1925; and L. Liebsky and S. Shabnel to I. Wohl, 18 Feb. 1927, box 28, file: 'Locals 35, 40, 65,' IC.

98 Foner, The Fur and Leather Workers' Union, 312–13, 318–19, 331–2, and 359

99 W, 29 June 1929. For further evidence that there was significant Communist support in local 40 and that there was very little Communist support in the two non-Jewish IFWU locals in Toronto at this time see Frank Currie to Harry Begoon, 23 Jan. 1929, box 28, file: 'Locals 35, 40, 65,' IC.

100 Interview with Ed Hammerstein. Hammerstein, a pro-Communist fur worker, recalled that there was a 'lame attempt' to bring the Toronto furriers into the IUNTW but that 'it didn't take off at all.' For further evidence that most of the pro-Communist fur workers remained within the IFWU during the Third Period see, for example, IFWUGEBM, 'Report of Vice-President, Max Federman, to the GEB,' 11 May 1937, p. 2, box 3, file 25.

101 Interview with Ed Hammerstein. Hammerstein stated that the anti-Communists were able to capture the leadership of the Toronto IFWU because the failed attempt to lead the fur workers into the IUNTW had created a leadership vacuum within the IFWU.

102 See, for example, W, 25 Oct. 1930, 13 Aug. 1932; and K, 20 Feb. and 17 April 1931. For further Communist criticisms of the anti-Communist leadership of the Toronto IFWU see K, 15 May 1931, 16 Feb. 1934, and 29 Jan. 1935.

103 W, 13 Aug. 1932

104 W, 29 July 1933. See also 26 Aug. 1933.

105 Interview with Ed Hammerstein

106 W, 19 Aug. and 2 and 9 Sept. 1933. See also LG, Sept. and Oct. 1933.

107 W. Zuravinski to P. Lucchi, 30 March 1936, and Lucchi to Zuravinski, 17 April 1936, box 22, file 4, IC. On the friction between the anti-Communist leaders of the Toronto IFWU and the leaders of the WUL's Fur Dressers' and Dyers' Union see, for example, Zuravinski to Lucchi, 4 March 1936.

108 Foner, *The Fur and Leather Workers' Union*, 462, 464, and 503. The interview with Jacob Black is also informative.

109 Max Federman to J.W. Buckley, 14 March 1938, vol. 13, file 2701, JLCP. See also B. Gold and P. Lucchi to M. Federman, 29 Jan. 1938, M. Klig to B. Gold, 14 March 1938, M. Federman to B. Gold, 27 Dec. 1937, box 9, file 15, IC; Trial Committee minutes, 16 Jan. 1938; J.L. Cohen to Colonel R.H. Greer, 27 May 1938; and minutes of Special Investigation Meeting, 23 Dec. 1937, vol. 13, file 2701, JLCP.

110 See, for example, J.W. Buckley to P.M. Draper, 11 March 1938, and 'Furriers' Bulletin, issued by the Fur Workers' Union A.F. of L. Toronto, April 1938,' vol. 13, file 2701, JLCP.

111 See, for example, 'Furriers' Bulletin, issued by the Fur Workers' Union A.F. of L. Toronto, April 1938,' vol. 13, file 2701, JLCP.

112 IFWUGEBM, 23–26 June 1938, pp. 71–2, box 4, file 1. See also 7–8 and 70–1.

113 See, for example, leaflet entitled 'A Few Questions to the President of the International Fur-Workers' Union' from 'A Group of Toronto Furriers,' [late 1930s]; and *Fur Workers' Bulletin*, June 1939, issued by the Fur Workers' Union, AFL, Toronto, Collection of Fur Workers' Union Materials, Multicultural History Society of Ontario.

114 Interview with Ed Hammerstein

115 B. Gold and P. Lucchi to M. Federman, 29 Jan. 1938, box 9, file 15, IC. Charged with lesser crimes, some of Federman's supporters were also expelled from the Toronto IFWU at the same time. See H. Begoon to

J.L. Cohen, 18 April 1938; and minutes of special investigation meeting, 22 Dec. 1937, vol. 13, file 2701, JLCP.

116 On the formation of the AFL fur union see, for example, M. Federman to J.W. Buckley, 14 March 1938, vol. 13, file 2701, JLCP. Further information is available in TET, 14 March 1938, and the interview with Jacob Black.

117 IFWUGEBM, 23–26 June 1938, pp. 7–8 and 67–8, box 4, file 1; and J.W. Buckley to P.M. Draper, 11 March 1938, vol. 13, file 2701, JLCP

118 On the fist fights see, for example, TET, 14 March 1938; and TG, 12 Feb. 1938.

119 For accusations that Federman hired gangsters and then gave them union cards in an effort to make them appear legitimate see the leaflet that begins, 'Defend the Trade Union Movement,' signed by the Toronto Joint Board of the IFWU, [1938], 11–12, box 53, Joshua Gershman Papers, series F-I, AO. See also IFWUGEBM, 23–26 June 1938, p. 68, box 4, file 1. For accusations that the IFWU used gangsters see the leaflet entitled, 'An Answer to the Communist Blackmailers!' by the AFL's Fur Workers' Union, [late 1930s]; and *Fur Workers' Bulletin*, June 1939, issued by the AFL's Fur Workers' Union, Toronto, Collection of Fur Workers' Union Materials, Multicultural History Society of Ontario.

120 Interview with Ed Hammerstein

121 E.N. Compton to C.W. Bolton, 25 March 1938, in SLF, vol. 396, file 38

122 *Daily Clarion*, 17 June 1938. See also the leaflet that begins, 'Defend the Trade Union Movement,' signed by the Toronto Joint Board of the IFWU, [1938], 12, box 53, Joshua Gershman Papers, series F-I.

123 IFWUGEBM, 23–26 June 1938, p. 71, box 4, file 1

124 Ibid., pp. 7–8, box 4, file 1

125 *Fur Workers' Bulletin*, June 1939, issued by the AFL's Fur Workers' Union, Toronto. See also the leaflet entitled, 'A Few Questions to the President of the International Fur-Workers' Union,' from 'A Group of Toronto Furriers' [c. 1937], Collection of Fur Workers' Union Materials.

126 IFWUGEBM, 23–26 June 1938, p. 70, box 4, file 1

127 Interview with Lou Lipsky

128 Interviews with Molly Fineberg, Jacob Black, and Sam Kraisman

129 Interview with Joe Salsberg

130 Interview with Jacob Black; and minutes of the Toronto Dressmakers' joint council, 8 Sept. 1937, box 1, ILGWU Archives

131 H.D. Langer to D. Dubinsky, 21 Oct. 1937; D. Biderman to D. Dubinsky, 20 Nov. 1937; memo dated 26 Nov. 1937; and telegram from D. Dubinsky to H.D. Langer, 10 Dec. 1937, box 74, file 3b, DDP

132 Interviews with Ed Hammerstein and Bessie Kramer

133 Dave Biderman to D. Dubinsky, 20 Nov. 1937, box 74, file 3b, DDP
134 Interview with Ida and Sol Abel
135 Interview with Jacob Black. When Ed Hammerstein (a pro-Communist furrier) was asked about the factionalism in the IFWU, he, too, emphasized that the arguments were basically about political issues.
136 See, for example, W, 3 Jan. 1931; and K, 2 Jan. 1931.
137 See, for example, K, 11 Jan. 1935; and W, 4 April 1931. Further information is available in the interview with Joshua Gershman.
138 Interview with Joshua Gershman. As explained by Salsberg, another prominent Communist needle trades leader, Hillman's rationale was that unless the garment unions helped the employers maintain efficient production, the shops would close up. Salsberg, who later left the party as a result of the Stalin revelations, now feels that Hillman's reasoning makes sense. On the Communists' argument that the 'right-wing' clothing unions had been 'transformed into efficiency adjuncts of capitalist production,' see, for example, W, 30 May 1931.
139 Interview with Joshua Gershman
140 K, 9 Feb. 1934 and 11 Jan. 1935
141 Information is available, for example, in the interview with Jacob Black.
142 H.D. Langer to D. Dubinsky, 13 March 1935, box 74, file 4c, DDP
143 Interview with Jacob Black
144 H.D. Langer to D. Dubinsky, 5 May 1935, box 74, file 4c, DDP
145 Abella, 'Portrait of a Jewish Professional Revolutionary,' 203
146 Part of this chapter contains reworked material from Ruth A. Frager, 'The Undermining of Unity within the Jewish Labour Movement of Toronto, 1928–1935,' *Polyphony* 9, 1 (fall/winter 1987): 47–50.

CONCLUSION

1 W, 28 Feb. 1931
2 Interview with Bessie Kramer
3 On the dramatic upward mobility of Jews in North America see, for example, Stephan Thernstrom, *The Other Bostonians: Poverty and Progress in the American Metropolis, 1880–1970* (Cambridge, Mass., 1973), 250.

Select Bibliography

MANUSCRIPT COLLECTIONS

George Brown College Archives, Toronto
Papers of the Associated Clothing Manufacturers

Labor-Management Documentation Center, M.P. Catherwood Library, Cornell University, Ithaca, New York
Amalgamated Clothing Workers Collection (no. 5619)
International Fur Workers' Union Collection (no. 5676)

International Ladies' Garment Workers' Union Archives, New York
(subsequently transferred to the Labor-Management Documentation Center at Cornell, as ILGWU Collection no. 5780)
Fannia M. Cohn Collection
David Dubinsky Papers
ILGWU's general executive board minutes
Minutes of the Toronto ILGWU
Charles Zimmerman Papers

Multicultural History Society of Ontario, Toronto
Collection of Fur Workers' Union Materials
Collection of Labour League Materials
Collection of Tip Top Materials
Robert S. Kenny Pamphlet and Broadside Collection
L. Kraisman Collection

Abraham Nisnevitz Collection
Papers of the Toronto ILGWU

National Archives of Canada, Ottawa
Amalgamated Clothing Workers Collection
Tim Buck Collection
Canadian Labour Congress Collection
J.L. Cohen Papers
Communist Party of Canada Collection
Jacob Finkelman Papers
Labour Council of Metropolitan Toronto Collection
Department of Labour, Strikes and Lockouts Files

New York University
Papers of the Cloth Hat, Cap, and Millinery Workers'
    International Union
Max Zaritsky Papers

Archives of Ontario, Toronto
Communist Party of Canada Collection
Joshua Gershman Papers
Local Council of Women of Toronto Papers
Records of the Department of Labour of Ontario
T. Eaton Collection

Private Collection of the Associated Clothing Manufacturers
Minutes, arbitration decisions, and collective agreements,
    at the Association's office in Toronto

University of Toronto
Robert S. Kenny Collection

INTERVIEWS (pseudonyms have been used for many of the key interviewees)

Ida and Sol Abel, Toronto, 1983
Abraham Biderman, Toronto, 1972
Dave Biderman, Toronto, 1971 and 1972
Morris Biderman, Toronto, 1971
Jacob Black, Toronto, 1971 and 1984

Jim Blugerman, Toronto, 1971 and 1973
Mary Bochar, Toronto, 1979
Max Bomgard, Toronto, 1978
Mr and Mrs A. Bonavero, Toronto, 1978
Nick Cafiero, Toronto, 1984
Sam Charney, Toronto, 1972
I. Cohen, Toronto, 1978
Sarah Easser, Toronto, 1977
Max Enkin, Toronto, 1979
Molly Fineberg, Toronto, 1984
Sam Galinsky, Toronto, 1977
Max Geller, Toronto, 1978
Joshua Gershman, Toronto, 1984
Izzy Ginsberg, Toronto, 1978
Deborah Goldberg, Toronto, 1984
Max Grafstein, Toronto, 1972
Louis Guberman, Toronto, 1972
Ed Hammerstein, Toronto, 1977, 1983, and 1984
Sadie Hoffman, Toronto, 1978, 1984, and 1985
Jack Isacoff, Toronto, 1977
Sam Kraisman, Toronto, 1971
Bessie Kramer, Toronto, 1969 and 1984
Moe Levin, Toronto, 1984
Alex Levinsky, Toronto, 1972
Lou Lipsky, Toronto, 1978, 1984, and 1986
Nathan Litvak, Toronto, 1977
Joe Macks, Toronto, 1971
Abe Megerman, Toronto, 1971
Diana Meslin, Toronto, 1978
S. Papernick, Toronto, 1977
Louis and Irving Posluns, Toronto, 1972
Charles Posner, Toronto, 1978
M. Rotman, Toronto, 1979
Joe Salsberg, Toronto, 1978, 1979, and 1984
Julius Seltzer, Toronto, 1971
Eva and Izzy Shanoff, Toronto, 1973
Isaac Shoichet, Toronto, 1982
Leah Stern, Toronto, 1985
Ed Tannenbaum, Toronto, 1971, 1978, and 1984

U. Torrella, Toronto, 1978
Pearl Wedro, Toronto, 1971
J. Ziger, Toronto, 1977

NEWSPAPERS

Advance (New York)
Canadian Unionist (Montreal)
Cotton's Weekly (Cowansville, Quebec)
Daily Clarion (Toronto)
Garment Worker (New York)
Globe (Toronto)
Headgear Worker (New York)
Industrial Banner (London, Ontario)
Jack Canuck (Toronto)
Justice (New York)
Der Kamf (Toronto and Montreal)
Ladies' Garment Worker (New York)
Lance (Toronto)
New Commonwealth (Toronto)
Star (Toronto)
Tailor (Bloomington, Illinois)
Toronto Evening Telegram
Weekly Bulletin of the Clothing Trades (New York)
Western Clarion (Vancouver)
Women's Wear (New York)
Worker (Toronto)
Der Yiddisher Zhurnal (Toronto)

GOVERNMENT PUBLICATIONS

Canada, Department of Labour, *Labour Gazette*
Canada, Department of Trade and Commerce, *Weekly Earnings of Male and Female Wage-Earners Employed in the Manufacturing Industries of Canada, 1934–1936* (Ottawa 1940)
Canada, Dominion Bureau of Statistics, *Census*
Canada, Dominion Bureau of Statistics, *Report on the Men's Furnishing Goods Industry in Canada*
Canada, Dominion Bureau of Statistics, *Report on the Women's Factory Clothing Industry in Canada*

Canada, Royal Commission on Price Spreads, *Minutes of Proceedings and Evidence* (Ottawa 1935)

Canada, Royal Commission on Price Spreads, *Report* (Ottawa 1935)

King, W.L. Mackenzie, *Report to the Honourable the Postmaster General of the Methods Adopted in Canada in the Carrying Out of Government Clothing Contracts* (Ottawa 1900)

Ontario, Bureau of Labour, *Annual Report*

Ontario, Committee on Child Labor, *Report* (1907)

Ontario, Department of Agriculture, *Annual Reports of the Inspectors of Factories for the Province of Ontario*

Ontario, Department of Labour, *Vocational Opportunities in the Industries of Ontario: A Survey: Bulletin No. 4: Garment Making* (Toronto 1920)

Wright, Alexander Whyte, 'Report upon the Sweating System in Canada,' *Sessional Papers, 1896*

BOOKS, PAMPHLETS, ARTICLES, AND THESES

Abella, Irving Martin. *Nationalism, Communism, and Canadian Labour: The CIO, the Communist Party, and the Canadian Congress of Labour, 1935–1956.* Toronto 1973

– ed. 'Portrait of a Jewish Professional Revolutionary: The Recollections of Joshua Gershman' *Labour/Le Travailleur* 2 (1977): 185–213

Amalgamated Clothing Workers of America. *Proceedings of the Biennial Conventions of the Amalgamated Clothing Workers of America.* New York, selected years

Angus, Ian. *Canadian Bolsheviks: The Early Years of the Communist Party of Canada.* Montreal 1981

Antonovsky, Aaron, ed. *The Early Jewish Labor Movement in the United States.* New York 1961

Arbeiter Ring. *Souvenir [of the] Arbeiter Ring Convention.* Np 1922

Ash, Sholem. *Onkel Moses* [Uncle Moses]. New York 1918

Asher, Nina. 'Dorothy Jacobs Bellanca: Women Clothing Workers and the Runaway Shops,' in Joan M. Jensen and Sue Davidson, eds., *A Needle, A Bobbin, A Strike: Women Needleworkers in America.* Philadelphia 1984, 195–226

Avakumovic, Ivan. *The Communist Party in Canada: A History.* Toronto 1975

Avery, Donald. *'Dangerous Foreigners': European Immigrant Workers and Labour Radicalism in Canada, 1896–1932.* Toronto 1979

Bacchi, Carol Lee *Liberation Deferred? The Ideas of the English-Canadian Suffragists, 1877–1918.* Toronto 1983

Baron, Ava, and Susan E. Klepp. '"If I Didn't Have My Sewing Machine ...":

Women and Sewing-Machine Technology,' in Joan M. Jensen and Sue Davidson, eds., *A Needle, A Bobbin, A Strike: Women Needleworkers in America.* Philadelphia 1984, 20–59

Baron, Salo W. *The Russian Jew Under Tsars and Soviets.* New York 1964

Barrett, James R. 'Unity and Fragmentation: Class, Race, and Ethnicity on
Chicago's South Side, 1900–1922,' in Dirk Hoerder, ed., *'Struggle A Hard
Battle': Essays on Working-Class Immigrants.* DeKalb, Ill., 1986, 229–53

Baum, Charlotte, Paula Hyman, and Sonya Michel. *The Jewish Woman in
America.* New York 1976

Belkin, S. *Di Poale Zion Bavegung in Kanade, 1904–1920* [The Labour Zionist
Movement in Canada, 1904–1920]. Montreal 1956

Berman, Hyman. 'A Cursory View of the Jewish Labor Movement: An Historiographical Survey.' *American Jewish Historical Quarterly* 52, 2 (Dec. 1962): 82–94.

Bernstein, Irving. *The Lean Years: A History of the American Worker, 1920–1933.*
Boston 1972

Berson, Seemah Cathline. 'The Immigrant Experience: Personal Recollections
of Jewish Garment Workers in Canada, 1900–1930.' MA thesis, University of
British Columbia 1980

Betcherman, Lita-Rose. *The Little Band: The Clashes between the Communists and
the Political and Legal Establishment in Canada, 1928–1932.* Ottawa, nd

Biss, I.M. 'The Dressmakers' Strike.' *Canadian Forum* 11, 130 (July 1931): 367–9

Bloom, Bernard H. 'Yiddish-Speaking Socialists in America, 1892–1905,' in
Critical Studies in American Jewish History 3 (1971): 1–34

Bloor, Ella Reeve. *We Are Many.* New York 1940

Bodnar, John. *The Transplanted: A History of Immigrants in Urban America.* Bloomington, Ind., 1987

Bradbury, Bettina. 'Women's History and Working-Class History.' *Labour/Le
Travail* 19 (spring 1987): 23–43

Braun, Kurt. *Union-Management Co-operation: Experience in the Clothing Industry.*
Washington, DC, 1947

Brody, David. *Steelworkers in America: The Nonunion Era.* New York 1960

Budish, J.M. *Geshikhte fun di Klot Het, Kep un Milineri Arbeiter* [History of the
Cloth Hat, Cap and Millinery Workers]. New York 1926

Buhle, Mari Jo. *Women and American Socialism, 1870–1920.* Chicago 1983

Burman, Rickie. 'The Jewish Woman as Breadwinner: The Changing Value of
Women's Work in a Manchester Immigrant Community.' *Oral History* 10, 2
(autumn 1982): 27–39

Cahan, Abraham. *The Education of Abraham Cahan.* Philadelphia 1969 (originally
published in Yiddish in 1926)

– *The Rise of David Levinsky.* New York 1960 (originally published in 1917)

Carpenter, Jesse Thomas. *Competition and Collective Bargaining in the Needle Trades, 1910–1967*. Ithaca, NY, 1972

Chernin, Kim. *In My Mother's House: A Daughter's Story*. New York 1983

Chown, Alice A. *The Stairway*. Boston 1921

Cochran, Bert. *Labor and Communism: The Conflict that Shaped American Unions*. Princeton, NJ, 1977

Connelly, Patricia *Last Hired, First Fired: Women and the Canadian Work Force*. Toronto 1978

Creese, Gillian. 'The Politics of Dependence: Women, Work, and Unemployment in the Vancouver Labour Movement before World War II,' in Gregory S. Kealey, ed., *Class, Gender, and Region: Essays in Canadian Historical Sociology*. St. John's, Nfld, 1988, 121–42

Cumbler, John T. *Working-Class Community in Industrial America: Work, Leisure, and Struggle in Two Industrial Cities, 1880–1930*. Westport, Conn., 1979

Dawidowicz, Lucy S., ed. *The Golden Tradition: Jewish Life and Thought in Eastern Europe*. Boston 1967

Dubinsky, David, and A.H. Raskin. *David Dubinsky: A Life with Labor*. New York 1977

Dye, Nancy Schrom. *As Equals and as Sisters: Feminism, the Labor Movement, and the Women's Trade Union League of New York*. Columbia, Miss., 1980

Elbogen, Ismar. *A Century of Jewish Life*. Philadelphia 1944

Elstein, Saul. 'Why Not a National Women's Trade Union League in Canada?' *Women's Century* (July 1918): 6–7

Epstein, Melech. *Jewish Labor in the United States of America: An Industrial, Political, and Cultural History of the Jewish Labor Movement, 1882–1914*. Np 1969

– *Jewish Labor in the United States of America, 1914–1952: An Industrial, Political, and Cultural History of the Jewish Labor Movement*. Np 1969

Ewen, Elizabeth. *Immigrant Women in the Land of Dollars: Life and Culture on the Lower East Side, 1890–1925*. New York 1985

Fishman, William J. *East End Jewish Radicals, 1875–1914*. London 1975

Foner, Philip S. *The Fur and Leather Workers' Union*. Newark, NJ 1950

– *Women and the American Labor Movement: From Colonial Times to the Eve of World War I*. New York 1979

Forsey, Eugene. *Trade Unions in Canada, 1812–1902*. Toronto 1982

Frager, Ruth A. 'Class, Ethnicity, and Gender in the Eaton Strikes of 1912 and 1934,' in Franca Iacovetta and Mariana Valverde, eds., *Gender Conflicts: New Essays in Women's History*. Toronto 1992

– 'No Proper Deal: Women Workers and the Canadian Labour Movement, 1870–1940,' in L. Briskin and L. Yanz, eds., *Union Sisters: Women in the Labour Movement*. Toronto 1983, 44–64

– 'Politicized Housewives in the Jewish Communist Movement of Toronto,
   1923–1933,' in Linda Kealey and Joan Sangster, eds., *Beyond the Vote: Canadi-*
   an Women and Politics. Toronto 1989, 258–75
Frank, Dana. 'Housewives, Socialists, and the Politics of Food: The 1917 New
   York Cost-of-Living Protests.' *Feminist Studies* 11, 2 (summer 1985): 255–85
Frankel, Jonathan. *Prophecy and Politics: Socialism, Nationalism, and the Russian*
   Jews, 1862–1917. New York 1981
Fraser, Steven. '*Landslayt* and *Paesani*: Ethnic Conflict and Cooperation in the
   Amalgamated Clothing Workers of America,' in Dirk Hoerder, ed., *'Struggle*
   A Hard Battle': Essays on Working-Class Immigrants. DeKalb, Ill., 1986,
   280–303
Furio, Columba M. 'The Cultural Background of the Italian Immigrant Wom-
   an and Its Impact on Her Unionization in the New York City Garment In-
   dustry, 1880–1919,' in George E. Pozzetta, ed., *Pane E Lavoro: The Italian*
   American Working Class. Toronto 1980, 81–99
Gittleman, Sol. *From Shtetl to Suburbia: The Family in Jewish Literary Imagination*.
   Boston 1978
Glenn, Susan A. *Daughters of the Shtetl: Life and Labor in the Immigrant Generation*.
   Ithaca, NY, 1990
Gordon, J. 'Fun An Arbayterin's Tog-Bukh' [From a Female Worker's Diary],
   in B. Vladek, ed., *Fun Der Tifenish Fun Harts: A Bukh Fun Layden Un Kampf*.
   New York 1917, 94–5
Gorham, Deborah. 'Flora MacDonald Denison: Canadian Feminist,' in Linda
   Kealey, ed., *A Not Unreasonable Claim: Women and Reform in Canada,*
   1880s–1920s. Toronto 1979, 47–70
Gornick, Vivian. *The Romance of American Communism*. New York 1977
Gould, Margaret [Sarah Gold]. *I Visit the Soviets*. Toronto 1937
Greig, Gertrud Berta. *Seasonal Fluctuations in Employment in the Women's Clothing*
   Industry in New York. New York 1968
Gutman, Herbert G. *Work, Culture, and Society in Industrializing America: Essays in*
   American Working-Class and Social History. New York 1977
Hapgood, Hutchins. *The Spirit of the Ghetto*. Cambridge, Mass., 1967 (originally
   published in 1902)
Hardman, J.B.S., ed. *The Amalgamated – Today and Tomorrow*. New York 1939
Hardy, Jack. *The Clothing Workers: A Study of the Conditions and Struggles in the*
   Needle Trades. New York 1935
Harney, Robert, and Harold Troper. *Immigrants: A Portrait of the Urban Experi-*
   ence, 1890–1930. Toronto 1975
Harzig, Christiane, and Dirk Hoerder, eds. *The Press of Labor Migrants in Europe*
   and North America, 1880s to 1930s. Bremen 1985

Herberg, Will. 'The Jewish Labor Movement in the United States.' *American Jewish Yearbook* 53 (1952): 3–74

Heron, Craig. *Working in Steel: The Early Years in Canada, 1883–1935.* Toronto 1988

– 'Working-Class Hamilton, 1895–1930.' PhD thesis, Dalhousie University 1981

Hewitt, Nancy A. 'Beyond the Search for Sisterhood: American Women's History in the 1980s,' *Social History* 10, 3 (Oct. 1985): 299–321.

Hiebert, Daniel Joseph. 'The Geography of Jewish Immigrants and the Garment Industry in Toronto, 1901–1931: A Study of Ethnic and Class Relations,' PhD thesis, University of Toronto 1987

– 'Integrating Production and Consumption in the Canadian City: Industry, Class, Ethnicity and Neighbourhood,' in David F. Ley and Larry Bourne, eds., *The Social Geography of Canadian Cities*. Montreal and Kingston: McGill–Queen's University Press, forthcoming

Howe, Irving. *World of Our Fathers: The Journey of the East European Jews to America and the Life They Found and Made.* New York 1976

Howe, Irving, and Kenneth Libo, eds. *How We Lived, 1880–1930: A Documentary History of Immigrant Jews in America.* New York 1979

Hyman, Colette A. 'Labor Organizing and Female Institution-Building: The Chicago Women's Trade Union League, 1904–1924,' in Ruth Milkman, ed., *Women, Work and Protest: A Century of U.S. Women's Labor History*. Boston 1985, 22–42

Hyman, Paula E. 'Immigrant Women and Consumer Protest: The New York City Kosher Meat Boycott of 1902.' *American Jewish History* 70, 1 (Sept. 1980): 91–106

International Ladies' Garment Workers' Union. *Handbook of Trade Union Methods.* New York 1937

– *Souvenir Journal of the Toronto Cloakmakers' Union*. Toronto 1936, 1949, and 1961 editions

Jensen, Joan M. 'The Great Uprising in Rochester,' in Joan M. Jensen and Sue Davidson, eds., *A Needle, A Bobbin, A Strike: Women Needleworkers in America*. Philadelphia 1984, 94–113

– 'The Great Uprisings: 1900–1920,' in Joan M. Jensen and Sue Davidson, eds., *A Needle, A Bobbin, A Strike: Women Needleworkers in America*. Philadelphia 1984, 83–93

Josephson, Matthew. *Sidney Hillman: Statesman of American Labor.* Garden City, NY, 1952

Kaplan, Temma, contribution to Ellen Dubois et al. 'Politics and Culture in Women's History: A Symposium.' *Feminist Studies* 6, 1 (spring 1980): 43–8

Karlinsky, Janice B. 'The Pioneer Women's Organization: A Case Study of Jewish Women in Toronto.' MA thesis, University of Toronto 1979

Kealey, Gregory S. *Hogtown: Working Class Toronto at the Turn of the Century.* Toronto 1974

– *Toronto Workers Respond to Industrial Capitalism, 1867–1892.* Toronto 1980

Kealey, Linda, ed. *A Not Unreasonable Claim: Women and Reform in Canada, 1880s–1920s.* Toronto 1979

– 'Canadian Socialism and the Woman Question, 1900–1914.' *Labour/Le Travail* 13 (1984): 77–100

– 'Women's Labour Militancy in Canada, 1900–20.' Paper presented at the Annual Meeting of the Canadian Historical Association, 3–5 June 1991

Kerr, Clark, and Abraham Siegel. 'The Interindustry Propensity to Strike – An International Comparison,' in A. Kornhauser, R. Dubin, and A. Ross, eds., *Industrial Conflict.* Toronto 1954, 189–213

Kessler-Harries, Alice. *Out To Work: A History of Wage-Earning Women in the United States.* New York 1982

– 'Organizing the Unorganizable: Three Jewish Women and Their Union.' *Labor History* 17, 1 (winter 1976): 5–23

– 'Problems of Coalition-Building: Women and Trade Unions in the 1920s,' in Ruth Milkman, ed., *Women, Work and Protest: A Century of U.S. Women's Labor History.* Boston 1985, 110–39

– '"Where Are the Organized Women Workers?"' *Feminist Studies* 3, 1/2 (fall 1975): 92–110

Kogos, Fred. *1001 Yiddish Proverbs.* Secaucus, NJ, 1970

Kolko, Gabriel. *Main Currents in Modern American History.* New York 1976

Kumove, Shirley. *Words like Arrows: A Collection of Yiddish Folk Sayings.* Toronto 1984

Kuznets, Simon. 'Immigration of Russian Jews to the United States: Background and Structure.' *Perspectives in American History* 9 (1975): 35–126

Laslett, John H.M. *Labor and the Left: A Study of Socialist and Radical Influences in the American Labor Movement, 1881–1924.* New York 1970

Lavigne, Marie, and Jennifer Stoddart. 'Women's Work in Montreal at the Beginning of the Century,' in Marylee Stephenson, ed., *Women in Canada.* Don Mills, Ont. 1977

Levine, Louis. *The Women's Garment Workers: A History of the International Ladies' Garment Workers' Union.* New York 1924

Levitt, Cyril H., and William Shaffir. *The Riot at Christie Pits.* Toronto 1987

Liebman, Arthur. *Jews and the Left.* Toronto 1979

Lindström-Best, Varpu. 'Finnish Socialist Women in Canada, 1890–1930,' in

Linda Kealey and Joan Sangster, eds., *Beyond the Vote: Canadian Women and Politics*. Toronto 1989, 196–216

Lipton, Charles. *The Trade Union Movement of Canada, 1827–1959*. Toronto 1973

Livesay, Dorothy. *Right Hand Left Hand*. Erin, Ont. 1977

Logan, H.A. *Trade Unions in Canada: Their Development and Functioning*. Toronto 1948

Macleod, Catherine. 'Women in Production: The Toronto Dressmakers' Strike of 1931,' in Janice Acton, Penny Goldsmith, and Bonnie Shepard, eds., *Women at Work: Ontario, 1850–1930*. Toronto 1974, 309–331

Meltzer, Milton. *Taking Root: Jewish Immigrants in America*. New York 1976

Mendelsohn, Ezra. *Class Struggle in the Pale: The Formative Years of the Jewish Workers' Movement in Tsarist Russia*. Cambridge 1970

– 'The Russian Roots of the American Jewish Labor Movement.' *YIVO Annual of Jewish Social Science* 16 (1976): 150–177

Milkman, Ruth, ed. *Women, Work and Protest: A Century of U.S. Women's Labor History*. Boston 1985

– 'Organizing the Sexual Division of Labor: Historical Perspectives on "Women's Work" and the American Labor Movement.' *Socialist Review* 10, 49 (Jan.–Feb. 1980): 95–150

Mitchinson, Wendy. 'The WCTU: "For God, Home and Native Land": A Study in Nineteenth-Century Feminism,' in Linda Kealey, ed., *A Not Unreasonable Claim: Women and Reform in Canada, 1880s–1920s*. Toronto 1979, 151–67

Nepom, S. *Fun Meine Teg* [From My Days]. Toronto 1940

Newton, Janice. '"Enough of Exclusive Masculine Thinking": The Feminist Challenge to the Early Canadian Left, 1900–1918.' PhD thesis, York University 1987

Paris, Erna. *Jews: An Account of Their Experience in Canada*. Toronto 1980

Patrias, Carmela. *Relief Strike: Immigrant Workers and the Great Depression in Crowland, Ontario, 1930–1935*. Toronto 1990

Pedersen, Diana. '"Keeping Our Good Girls Good": The YWCA and the "Girl Problem," 1870–1930.' *Canadian Woman Studies* 7, 4 (winter 1986): 20–4

Penner, Norman. *The Canadian Left: A Critical Analysis*. Scarborough, Ont., 1977

Pesotta, Rose. *Bread upon the Waters*. New York 1944

Piva, Michael J. *The Condition of the Working Class in Toronto, 1900–1921*. Ottawa 1979

Prentice, Alison, Paula Bourne, Gail Cuthbert Brandt, Beth Light, Wendy Mitchinson, and Naomi Black. *Canadian Women: A History*. Toronto 1988

Ramirez, Bruno. 'Ethnic Studies and Working-Class History.' *Labour/Le Travail* 19 (spring 1987): 45–8

Rhinewine, Abraham. *Der Id in Kanade* [The Jew in Canada], vols. I and II. Toronto 1925 and 1927

Rideout, Walter B. '"O Workers' Revolution ... The True Messiah": The Jew as Author and Subject in the American Radical Novel,' in *Critical Studies in American Jewish History*, vol. III. New York 1971, 178–95

Rischin, Moses. *The Promised City: New York's Jews, 1870–1914*. Cambridge, Mass., 1962

– 'The Jewish Labor Movement in America: A Social Interpretation.' *Labor History* 4, 3 (fall 1963): 227–47

Roberts, Wayne. *Honest Womanhood: Feminism, Femininity and Class Consciousness among Toronto Working Women, 1893–1914*. Toronto 1976

– 'Studies in the Toronto Labour Movement, 1896–1914.' PhD thesis, University of Toronto 1978

Rodney, William. *Soldiers of the International: A History of the Communist Party of Canada, 1919–1929*. Toronto 1968

Rosenberg, Louis. *Canada's Jews: A Social and Economic Study of the Jews in Canada*. Montreal 1939

Rosenberg, Stuart E. *The Jewish Community in Canada*, vol. I. Toronto 1970

Rubin, Ruth. *Voices of a People: The Story of Yiddish Folksong*. Toronto 1973

Sack, B.G. *Canadian Jews: Early in this Century*. Montreal 1975

Sangster, Joan. *Dreams of Equality: Women on the Canadian Left, 1920–1950*. Toronto 1989

– 'The 1907 Bell Telephone Strike: Organizing Women Workers.' *Labour/Le Travailleur* 3 (1978): 109–30

– 'Canadian Working Women,' in W.J.C. Cherwinski and Gregory S. Kealey, eds., *Lectures in Canadian Labour and Working-Class History*. St John's, Nfld., 1985, 59–78

– 'The Communist Party and the Woman Question, 1922–1929.' *Labour/Le Travail* 15 (spring 1985), 25–57

Scarpaci, Jean. 'Angela Bambace and the International Ladies' Garment Workers' Union: The Search for an Elusive Activist,' in George E. Pozzetta, ed., *Pane E Lavoro: The Italian American Working Class*. Toronto 1980, 99–119

Scharf, Lois. 'The Great Uprising in Cleveland: When Sisterhood Failed,' in Joan M. Jensen and Sue Davidson, eds., *A Needle, A Bobbin, A Strike: Women Needleworkers in America*. Philadelphia 1984, 146–66

Schneiderman, Rose, and Lucy Goldthwaite. *All for One*. New York 1967

Scott, F.R., and H.M. Cassidy. *Labour Conditions in the Men's Clothing Industry*. Toronto 1935

Scott, Joan W. 'On Language, Gender, and Working-Class History.' *International Labor and Working-Class History* 31 (spring 1987): 1–13

Seager, Allen. 'Class, Ethnicity, and Politics in the Alberta Coalfields, 1905–1945,' in Dirk Hoerder, ed., *'Struggle a Hard Battle': Essays on Working-Class Immigrants.* DeKalb, Ill., 1986

Shepard, Herbert A. 'Democratic Control in a Labour Union,' in Bernard R. Blishen, Frank E. Jones, Kaspar D. Naegele, and John Porter, eds., *Canadian Society: Sociological Perspectives.* Toronto 1969, 329–37

Silverman, Eliane Leslau. 'Writing Canadian Women's History, 1970–82: An Historiographical Analysis.' *Canadian Historical Review* 63, 4 (Dec. 1982): 513–33

Smith, Judith E. *Family Connections: A History of Italian and Jewish Immigrant Lives in Providence, Rhode Island, 1900–1940.* Albany, NY, 1985

Sochen, June. *Consecrate Every Day: The Public Lives of Jewish American Women, 1880–1980.* Albany, NY, 1981

Sparks, R.P. 'The Garment and Clothing Industries: History and Organization.' *Manual of the Textile Industry of Canada,* Montreal 1930, 107–30

Speisman, Stephen A. *The Jews of Toronto: A History to 1937.* Toronto 1979

Steed, Guy P.F. 'Standardization, Scale, Incubation, and Inertia: Montreal and Toronto Clothing Industries.' *Canadian Geographer* 20, 3 (1976): 298–309

Steedman, Mercedes. 'Skill and Gender in the Canadian Clothing Industry, 1890–1940,' in Craig Heron and Robert Storey, eds., *On the Job: Confronting the Labour Process in Canada.* Kingston, Ont., 1986, 152–76

Stern, Beverly. 'The ILGWU in Toronto, 1900–1935,' unpublished paper

Stolberg, Benjamin. *Tailor's Progress: The Story of a Famous Union and the Men Who Made It.* Garden City, NY, 1944

Stowell, Charles Jacob. *The Journeymen Tailors' Union of America.* Illinois 1917

Strong-Boag, Veronica. *The Parliament of Women: The National Council of Women of Canada, 1893–1929.* Ottawa 1976

– 'The Girl of the New Day: Canadian Working Women in the 1920s.' *Labour/Le Travailleur* 4 (1979): 131–64

Tax, Meredith. *The Rising of the Women: Feminist Solidarity and Class Conflict, 1880–1917.* New York 1980

Taylor, Barbara. *Eve and the New Jerusalem: Socialism and Feminism in the Nineteenth Century.* New York 1983

Tentler, Leslie Woodcock. *Wage-Earning Women: Industrial Work and Family Life in the United States, 1900–1930.* Toronto 1979

Tobias, Henry J. *The Jewish Bund in Russia: From Its Origins to 1905.* Stanford, Calif. 1972

Tulchinsky, G. 'The Contours of Canadian Jewish History.' *Journal of Canadian Studies* 17, 4 (winter 1982–3): 46–56

– 'The Third Solitude: A.M. Klein's Jewish Montreal, 1910–1950.' *Journal of Canadian Studies* 19, 2 (summer 1984): 96–112

Valverde, Mariana. *The Age of Light, Soap, and Water: Moral Reform in English Canada, 1885–1925.* Toronto 1991

Van Kleeck, Mary. *Artificial Flower Makers.* New York 1913

Vigod, Bernard L. *The Jews in Canada.* Ottawa 1984

Vipond, Mary. 'The Image of Women in Mass Circulation Magazines in the 1920s,' in Susan Mann Trofimenkoff and Alison Prentice, eds., *The Neglected Majority: Essays in Canadian Women's History.* Toronto 1977

Waldinger, Roger. 'Another Look at the International Ladies' Garment Workers' Union: Women, Industry Structure and Collective Action,' in Ruth Milkman, ed., *Women, Work and Protest: A Century of U.S. Women's Labor History.* Boston 1985, 86–110

Watson, Louise. *She Never Was Afraid: The Biography of Annie Buller.* Toronto 1976

Weiler, N. Sue. 'The Uprising in Chicago: The Men's Garment Workers Strike, 1910–1911,' in Joan M. Jensen and Sue Davidson, eds., *A Needle, A Bobbin, A Strike: Women Needleworkers in America.* Philadelphia 1984, 114–39

Weinberg, Sydney Stahl. *World of Our Mothers: The Lives of Jewish Immigrant Women.* Chapel Hill, NC, 1988

Welter, Barbara. 'The Cult of True Womanhood: 1820–1860,' in Michael Gordon, ed., *The American Family in Social-Historical Perspective.* New York 1973, 224–251

White, Julie. *Women and Unions.* Ottawa 1980

Whiteman, Maxwell. 'Western Impact on East European Jews: A Philadelphia Fragment,' in Randall M. Miller and Thomas D. Marzik, eds., *Immigrants and Religion in Urban America.* Philadelphia 1977, 117–38

Yezierska, Anzia. 'The Miracle,' in Alice Kessler-Harris, ed., *The Open Cage: An Anzia Yezierska Collection.* New York 1979, 3–19 (originally published in 1920)

Zaretz, Charles Elbert. *The Amalgamated Clothing Workers of America: A Study in Progressive Trades-Unionism.* New York 1934

Zborowski, Mark, and Elizabeth Herzog. *Life Is with People: The Culture of the Shtetl.* New York 1965

Index

Picture Credits

Metropolitan Toronto Reference Library: needle trades sweatshop
c.1890s (T13569); designing and cutting room in Eaton's garment
factory c.1910 (T33796); Tip Top Tailors' factory building (T10066)

Labor-Management Documentation Center, Cornell University: supporting the strike 1912 (5780P, #1600)

City of Toronto Archives: cellar dwelling on Teraulay Street (RG 8-32-
251); Price's Lane (RG 8-32-320); Spadina Avenue at Queen Street
c.1926 (SC 244-7338)

Archives of Ontario: members of Arbeiter Ring (ACC 21210, 23-21, MSR
1508-10); presser 1916 (ACC 21210, 23-21, MSR 9171); Joshua Gershman (ACC 21210, 23-005, MSR 0-900-8); Labour League Camp c.1926
(ACC 21210, 23-05, MSR 0-789-2); Joe Salsberg and Max Dolgoy (ACC
21210, 23-102, MSR 8421-6); activist Jewish fur workers 1920s (ACC
21210, 23-21, MSR 1508-2); May Day demonstration early 1930s (AO
1195); making men's clothing at Tip Top 1931 (ACC 21210, 23-84,
MSR 7055-246); second convention of the IUNTW 1931 (ACC 21210, 23-
005, MSR 0-900-9); group of workers leaving headquarters of IUNTW
1932 (AO 1191); picket line during dressmakers' general strike 1933
(AO 1190); May Day parade on College Street 1935 (ACC 21210, 23-
005, MSR 0-900-31); Jewish activists relaxing at Hanlan's Point (AO
1192); Toronto joint board ILGWU 1936 (ACC 21210, 23-03, MSR 0-
785); Socialist Day at Arbeiter Ring's Camp Yungvelt 1936 (ACC
21210, 23-105, MSR 8431-49); picnic of members of cloakmakers'
branch of ILGWU (ACC 21210, 23-019, MSR 1506-6); Pearl Wedro (AO
1196); Sam Lapedes at Treblinka 1962 (AO 1193)

T. Eaton Company, *Golden Jubilee, 1869–1919* (Toronto 1919): factory
buildings of Eaton Company c.1919; employees' tribute to Sir John
C. Eaton 1919; embroidery workers c.1910s
Amalgamated Clothing Workers: Toronto joint board, 1930s